CAMBRIDGE LATIN AMERICAN STUDIES

EDITORS

MALCOLM DEAS CLIFFORD T. SMITH JOHN STREET

19

POLITICS IN ARGENTINA 1890–1930

THE RISE AND FALL OF RADICALISM

THE SERIES

1 SIMON COLLIER. *Ideas and Politics of Chilean Independence, 1808–1833*

2 MICHAEL P. COSTELOE. *Church Wealth in Mexico: A Study of the Juzgado de Capellanías in the Archbishopric of Mexico, 1800–1856*

3 PETER CALVERT. *The Mexican Revolution, 1910–1914: The Diplomacy of Anglo-American Conflict*

4 RICHARD GRAHAM. *Britain and the Onset of Modernization in Brazil, 1850–1914*

5 HERBERT S. KLEIN. *Parties and Political Change in Bolivia, 1880–1952*

6 LESLIE BETHELL. *The Abolition of the Brazilian Slave Trade: Britain, Brazil and the Slave Trade Question, 1807–1869*

7 DAVID BARKIN AND TIMOTHY KING. *Regional Economic Development: The River Basin Approach in Mexico*

8 CELSO FURTADO. *Economic Development of Latin America: A Survey from Colonial Times to the Cuban Revolution*

9 WILLIAM PAUL MCREEVEY. *An Economic History of Colombia, 1845–1930*

10 D. A. BRADING. *Miners and Merchants in Bourbon Mexico, 1763–1810*

11 JAN BAZANT. *Alienation of Church Wealth in Mexico: Social and Economic Aspects of the Liberal Revolution, 1856–1875*

12 BRIAN R. HAMNETT. *Politics and Trade in Southern Mexico, 1750–1821*

13 J. VALERIE FIFER. *Bolivia: Land, Location and Politics since 1825*

14 PETER GERHARD. *A Guide to the Historical Geography of New Spain*

15 P. J. BAKEWELL. *Silver Mining and Society in Colonial Mexico, Zacatecas 1546–1700*

16 KENNETH R. MAXWELL. *Conflicts and Conspiracies: Brazil and Portugal 1750–1808*

17 VERENA MARTINEZ-ALIER. *Marriage, Class and Colour in Nineteenth-century Cuba*

18 TULIO HALPERIN-DONGHI. *Politics, Economics and Society in Argentina in the Revolutionary Period*

19 DAVID ROCK. *Politics in Argentina 1890–1930: The Rise and Fall of Radicalism*

POLITICS IN ARGENTINA 1890–1930

THE RISE AND FALL OF RADICALISM

DAVID ROCK

CAMBRIDGE UNIVERSITY PRESS

CAMBRIDGE UNIVERSITY PRESS
Cambridge, New York, Melbourne, Madrid, Cape Town, Singapore, São Paulo, Delhi

Cambridge University Press
The Edinburgh Building, Cambridge CB2 8RU, UK

Published in the United States of America by Cambridge University Press, New York

www.cambridge.org
Information on this title: www.cambridge.org/9780521102322

First published 1975
This digitally printed version 2009

A catalogue record for this publication is available from the British Library

Library of Congress Catalogue Card Number: 74–12974

ISBN 978-0-521-20663-1 hardback
ISBN 978-0-521-10232-2 paperback

CONTENTS

PREFACE

The central theme of this book is the political inter-relationship between different social classes in Argentina during the mature phase of the primary export economy in the forty years up to 1930. I have adopted for analysis four major groups: the landed and commercial elite of the pampas region, foreign capital, as represented mainly by British interests, the urban middle class and the urban working class, both mainly in the city of Buenos Aires. Broadly I have attempted to explore the distribution of political power between them and the mechanics of their political interactions with each other. I have also tried to show why attempts to introduce a stable institutional relationship among them eventually failed.

Secondly, the study analyses the development of the Argentine Radical Party between its foundation in 1891 and the overthrow of the third Radical government in the military coup of 1930. This is an attempt to trace the development of Argentina's first major popular movement, the specific social conditions which underlay its growth, the reasons why the movement gained prominence during this period, and what it meant in terms of the benefits and advantages to specific class and regional groups. I was greatly tempted to employ the term 'populism' to describe the structure and appeal of Radicalism. It would have been useful in describing the integrative, polyclasist characters of the movement, its tendency to maintain its unity by focussing attentions onto its leader, Hipólito Yrigoyen, and its use of mass mobilisation techniques of a kind which have become increasingly familiar in Latin American politics. The difficulties with it, however, are well-known. It is easy to point to some of its characteristics, but impossible to define it with any degree of accuracy. Where the term does occur it has therefore been used in a general sense with no attempt being made to give it any technical attributes.

I have also attempted to relate each of these items to the broad course of Argentina's economic development, in terms of basic variables such as the export trade cycle. The aim here has been to explore the extent to which the features of the primary export economy overlapped and correlated in Argentina at the superstructural level of politics and institutions.

The book is also a detailed historical study, which aims to utilise a wide variety of material to create a personal picture of this period of Argentina's development. In different parts of the book I have referred to a large number of subsidiary subjects and issues and, where the occasion appeared to demand it and in the modest hope of stimulating further discussion, I have made critiques of the work of other authors in various footnotes and appendixes. In addition to the fact that it deals mainly with the city of Buenos Aires, there is one other important qualification to be made about the book. It treats much more fully the period between 1912 and 1930 than it does 1890 to 1912. Most of the material for the early sections is based on published sources, and there is here a great deal of scope for further research. These sections have been included because they are necessary for the later argument.

The structure of the work is as follows: Chapter 1 contains a brief summary of Argentina's development up to 1914 and introduces the main subjects of discussion. Chapter 2 is an account of Argentine politics before the introduction of representative government in 1912. Chapter 3 is a study of the early history of Radicalism, and Chapter 4 an assessment of working class political development before 1916. The rest of the book deals with the period between 1916 and 1930: the objectives and performance of different Radical governments, the working class problem during the First World War, and relations between the elite and the urban middle class in Buenos Aires up to the Revolution of 1930. The last chapter is an outline summary of conclusions, and an attempt to fit the study into a wider framework of Argentina's history.

I wish to record my acknowledgements to the institutions which have supported my studies. Between 1967 and 1970 I was awarded a Parry Grant for Latin American Studies by the British Department of Education and Science. This allowed me an eighteen-month period of field work in Buenos Aires in 1968 and 1969. It also took me a long way towards completing a doctoral dissertation in 1970, in which much of the material in this book appeared in a raw state. I must also acknowledge the later assistance I had from the Cambridge University Centre of Latin American Studies. Only by virtue of my appointment as research officer in the Centre, and because of the small demands it made on my time, was it possible for me to complete my work. I also had a further travel award from the Centre in 1972, which enabled me to visit Argentina for a second time to complete my data collection.

Without wishing to identify them with any of the errors I may have made, I wish, too, to record my acknowledgements to a number of friends and colleagues, who have helped me materially with my work. Among them are Mr Alan Angell, Sr Osvaldo E. Baccino, Professor Samuel L. Baily, Dr D. A. Brading, Mr Malcolm Deas, Ing. Torcuato S. Di Tella, Dr Ezequiel Gallo, Professor Paul Goodwin, Lic. Leandro Gutiérrez, Professor Tulio Halperín Donghi, Mr Paul Joannides, the late Professor D. M. Joslin, Dr Walter Little, Professor D. C. M. Platt, Dr John Street, Sr. Juan Carlos Torre and Professor Joseph S. Tulchin.

The Twenty-Seven Foundation generously provided me with funds for typing my final drafts, and Mrs Hilary Prior painstakingly typed the final manuscript.

I have also benefited immeasurably from the time I have spent in the Argentine Republic and from the many people I have had the opportunity of talking to personally.

I must, however, reserve my final and greatest acknowledgement to my wife, Rosalind, without whose support I could not have completed my work.

The translations from the Spanish and the various calculations which appear in this book are mine unless acknowledged differently.

Cambridge D. R.

CHAPTER I

The components of Argentine society 1890–1914

The hub of Argentina's economy, and Argentine society, between 1890 and 1914 was the export sector. Argentina's exports were made up of agricultural and pastoral products, of which the most important were wheat, maize, linseed, hides, wool and beef. Apart from during occasional periods of severe drought or depression, each year after 1890 Argentina exported up to 10 million tons of cereals. After 1900, following the introduction of refrigerated ships and meat-packing plants, meat exports of different types averaged out to a further total of about 350,000 tons. Between 1872 and 1915 the total cultivated area in Argentina rose from 580,000 hectares to 24 million. There was much to justify a panegyrist's claim in 1911 that 'no country in the world has ever in so short a time realised so rapid a progress, in respect of the produce of the soil'.[1] A few years earlier a former president of the republic, Carlos Pellegrini, had written:

> This Republic possesses all the requisite conditions of becoming, with the passage of time, one of the great nations of the earth. Its territory is immense and fertile, its surface being equal to that of all Europe save Russia; it is capable of supporting with care at least 100 millions of human beings; almost every climate is to be found within its limits, and, consequently, it can yield all products, from those of the tropics to those of the polar regions. Its rivers and its mountains are among the greatest of the globe. As its maritime frontier it has the Atlantic, which brings it into contact with the whole world.[2]

These grandiose claims seemed warranted by figures. By 1914 the country's population had quadrupled in a little more than a generation. Between 1880 and 1910 the value of its exports had increased sixfold. After 1860 total production had grown to an annual average of 5% per year, population by 3.4%, the crop area by 8.3%, and the railway system by 15.4%. Yet behind these impressive figures there had emerged a

[1] Alberto B. Martínez and Maurice Lewandowski, *The Argentine in the Twentieth Century* (T. Fisher and Unwin, London, 1911), p. xv.
[2] Quoted in Ibid. p. lii.

society with peculair social and political characteristics, which in many ways added up to a rather different picture from Pellegrini's. Let us look in general terms at the major constituent elements of Argentine society: its dominant social class, the role of foreign capital in Argentina, and finally the structure of urban society.

The elite

The export boom was largely a result of the expansion of the British food market and the maturing of British industry in the last quarter of the nineteenth century. In return for imports of Argentine foodstuffs, especially meat, Britain exported to Argentina a large number of industrial products. The Argentine economy was thus broadly modelled on the classic precepts of Free Trade and international specialisation.[3]

The expansion of agricultural exports took place at a time when the basic structure of landownership was already established.[4] The colonial and nineteenth-century pattern of large estates continued into the twentieth century. In Argentina, unlike in the United States and in Australia, there was no major subdivision of the land. The only important area of smallholder settlement was the central zone of the province of Santa Fe. One of the main effects of the export boom was to increase land and rental values. This, together with the increasing importance of beef after 1900, assured the survival of large units of production. The result was the consolidation of a *latifundio* structure on the land, and the emergence of a powerful elite group.

Thus the central pattern of social development in Argentina contrasted fundamentally with that of other countries similarly specialising in the production of meat and temperate foodstuffs. Argentina's elitist structure was very different from the smallholder patterns which evolved in areas originally colonised by the British. Historically the 'landed elite' had developed as an outgrowth of mercantile activities in Buenos Aires stretching back to the eighteenth century. As Argentina's overseas trade grew, at first on the basis of pastoral products, and then

[3] H. S. Ferns, *Britain and Argentina in the Nineteenth Century* (Oxford University Press, 1960).

[4] Miron P. Burgin, *The Economic Aspects of Argentine Federalism, 1820–1850* (Cambridge, Massachusetts, 1946); Roberto Cortés Conde and Ezequiel Gallo, *La formación de la Argentina moderna* (Paidós, Buenos Aires, 1967); Ricardo M. Ortiz, *Historical económica de la Argentina, 1850–1930*, 2 vols (Raigal, Buenos Aires, 1955).

towards the end of the nineteenth century on the basis of temperate agricultural crops, wealth acquired through commerce was channelled into the accumulation of land. Since initially this land was worth very little, and there were few with the means or the foresight to acquire it, it was distributed in very large segments.

A second very important feature of the situation was that the best land was nearest to the seaboard in the pampas area. This contrasted with the United States where the richest agricultural regions were in the middle of the continent. Thus the pull of the Argentine 'frontier' was much weaker. Although it existed, and progressively larger amounts of land were brought into production during the nineteenth century, the main centres of power and population remained in the east. Whoever owned land in this area was in a powerful position. He had the advantage not only of better and more productive land, but also of cheaper communications. This gave the large landowner a differential rent, which multiplied his riches at a faster rate than anyone else's. In many ways the central pattern of Argentine politics during the period of the primary export economy before 1930 was dictated by the landed elite's desire first to take advantage of this opportunity, and secondly to hold on to it.[5]

The origin of the political leadership of Argentina's landed elite is thus to be found in the manner in which an entrenched sector, composed largely, though not exclusively, of traditional creole families, took advantage of favourable external economic conditions after 1870 to become a local collaborating elite with British interests. This remains generally true although economic depressions occasionally brought changes in the composition of the elite, and although power and wealth were not distributed entirely homogeneously among its members. The most powerful group were the cattle fatteners serving the domestic and international market. The core of the elite was made up of 400 families, which were closely tied together in a number of clubs and private associations. It has been estimated that less than 2,000 persons in Argentina owned as much land as the total areas of Italy, Belgium, Holland and Denmark added together.[6]

[5] See Ernesto Laclau, 'Modos de producción, sistemas económicos y población excedente. Aproximación histórica a los casos argentino y chileno'. *Revista Latinoamericano de Sociología*. Vol. 5, No. 2 (July 1969), pp. 276–316; Carlos F. Díaz Alejandro, *Essays on the Economic History of the Argentine Republic* (Yale, 1970), p. 36.

[6] Cf. Leopoldo Allub, 'The social origins of dictatorship and democracy in Argentina' (mimeog. Ph.D. dissertation, University of North Carolina, 1973), pp. 69–71.

The wealth and influence of different members of the elite was determined largely by the proximity of their landholdings to the River Plate or, in other words, by the extent of their association with the external market. Thus the bulk of the wealth was concentrated in the cereal and beef zones of the pampas region, and within the pampas itself according to proximity to the major ports. The chief of these was Buenos Aires. Much of Argentina's troubled history in the nineteenth century was shaped by the struggle for supremacy among different regional subgroups within the elite, for access to external markets. It was only after 1880 that a relatively stable system emerged. The more powerful segments of the landed elite established control over the state and used it to create credit, taxation and monetary systems favourable to their interests. The large landowners enjoyed preferential access to the major banks, and were able to obtain an abundance of funds for capitalising their estates and expanding their holdings through speculation. State revenues were obtained not by taxing land or landed incomes but by means of excise taxes on imported goods, a system of raising revenue which fell mainly on urban consumption. During most of the nineteenth century the landed interests imposed a system of depreciating paper money, which generally ensured that internal prices, and their own costs, lagged behind the prices of the goods they exported, and for which they received payment in gold. All these factors encouraged an even greater concentration of income in the hands of the elite.[7]

Because of this fairly stable concentration of economic and political power in the hands of the elite, the years between 1880 and 1912 became known as the period of the oligarchy. By this time the major landowners had become divorced from the detailed administration of the *estancias*, and lived in Buenos Aires, and often in Paris, as *rentiers*. In Buenos Aires their interests were supervised by a number of powerful associations, the chief of which was the Argentine Rural Society (Sociedad Rural Argentina). At the same time the traditional relationship between mercantile and landed wealth persisted. Many of the largest landlords were involved in

[7] Aldo Ferrer, *La economía argentina. Las etapas de su desarrollo y problemas actuales* (Fondo de Cultura Económica, Buenos Aires, 1963), pp. 91–154; Oscar E. Cornblit, Ezequiel Gallo and Alfredo A. O'Connell, 'La generación del ochenta y su proyecto-antecedentes y consecuencias', in Torcuato S. Di Tella *et alia*, *Argentina, sociedad de masas* (Eudeba, Buenos Aires, 1965), pp. 18–59. It is worth pointing out now to prevent confusion later that Argentina's internal accounts were calculated in paper pesos, and her international accounts in gold pesos. One paper peso equalled 44 gold cents. Figures in gold pesos later in the book thus refer principally to trade and capital flow. This system applied after 1899.

various forms of commercial activity in Buenos Aires, in exporting, in banking and in land companies. In some senses the multiplicity of its activities made the elite as much an urban entity as a rural interest group.

Elite interests were also reflected in the army and to a lesser extent in the Church. Before 1900 the Argentine army was an irregular body, which combined an officer corps of volunteers, often recruited from among elite families, with a casual and haphazard array of foot soldiers. Afterwards a number of reforms were introduced, including conscription, which brought its permanent strength up to around 10,000, from whence it grew rapidly up to 25,000 in 1930[8]. Although the professionalisation of the army created a wider social differentiation within the officer corps, the basic congruence between the army and the elite was not undermined. The Church had a less important position. It was stronger in older colonial areas like Córdoba. In Buenos Aires a more secular tradition prevailed. Because of the region's late development in comparison with the rest of the Spanish Empire, the Church failed to develop the same economic and political power as elsewhere. By the late nineteenth century, certain segments of the elite had won for themselves a reputation for anti-clericalism. Even so the Church remained a factor to be reckoned with, and an important influence on elite attitudes.

Foreign capital

The second major feature of the Argentine economy over these years was its reliance on foreign capital. The great bulk of this came again from Britain. It has been estimated that in 1910 the value of British capital investment in Argentina amounted to more than £300 million.[9] Invest-

[8] Robert A. Potash, *The Army and Politics in Argentina, 1928–1945. Yrigoyen to Perón* (Stanford, California, 1969), pp. 15–30.

[9] Ferns, p. 493. The precise figure of British investment is open to some dispute. In a lecture in London in 1912 by a director of the British-owned Buenos Aires Great Southern Railway Company, the figure given was £250 million invested in companies and another £250 million in investments which were unquoted on the London Stock Market. According to these figures the British controlled 17 railways, 5 banks, 3 gas companies, 2 electricity companies, 1 tramway company, 14 land companies, 1 telephone company, and 6 shipping companies. There is also an extensive account of foreign investments in Argentina in *Review of the River Plate*, 7 June 1918. For a further summary see Pedro Skupch, 'El deterioro y fin de la hegemonía británica sobre la economía argentina, 1914–1947', in Marta Panaia, Ricardo Lesser, Pedro Skupch, *Estudios sobre los orígines del peronismo*, Vol. 2 (Siglo XXI, Buenos Aires, 1973), pp. 5–23. Skupch estimates a total British investment of £385,000,000 in 1913, and in the same year total remittances of £17,600,000 by British companies.

ment took place mainly in three forms. Before 1880 the most common was government loans. Many of the political struggles of the nineteenth century between different factions of landowners reflected the importance of the State as a source of credit and mortgage funds; control over the State meant preferential treatment from foreign bankers and considerable economic advantages. At the same time the British were also responsible for a massive wave of railway investment which lasted until 1913. At the end of it Argentina had some 20,000 miles of railway line. The development of efficient communications was the main factor making the agricultural boom possible. Finally, in the years prior to the outbreak of the First World War, as the transportation system reached completion, the British and other Europeans, particularly the Germans, began to invest in urban utilities. There were also large-scale foreign investments in banks, land companies and port works.[10]

By 1914 Britain and, to a lesser (though increasing) extent other European countries, were of prime importance to Argentina as markets, sources of imported goods, suppliers of investment funds, and finally as owners of many of the country's principal assets. Investment and ownership, rather than trade alone, gave the British preeminence. Although in the years before the First World War the Germans began to make their presence felt, especially in the import trade, thus modifying the simple pre-1900 bilateral model, the British managed to complement their advantage of having arrived first with a highly extensive system of semi-institutionalised direct linkages with the elite. They had important allies at cabinet and congressional level, and an influential voice in affairs through many of the country's leading press organs.[11] Also, long before 1914, the practice had grown up of appointing leading Argentine politicians to the local boards of British companies in Argentina. This assisted in widening their access to the government, and it created a powerful vested interest within the local elite committed to the defence of British business. The British lobby ranked with the cattlemen's association as the most powerful in the country.[12]

[10] For British banking activities in Argentina see C. A. Jones, 'British financial institutions in Argentina, 1860–1914' (mimeog. Ph.D. dissertation, Cambridge, 1973).

[11] The chief of these was *La Nación*. The other important daily newspaper in Buenos Aires, *La Prensa*, was a more independent organ of the mercantile and beef interests in Buenos Aires.

[12] '... the revolution which overthrew Spanish power produced a quite exceptional community in Argentina ... its domination by a class of poor rich, of men rich in

There was thus a close complementarity of interest between the most powerful sectors of the elite and British traders and investors. This did not mean that at times there were not differences and conflicts between them. But these involved not so much a questioning of the relationship as the distribution of its benefits. Occasionally there were disputes over matters like railway freight rates, or over the charges imposed by the power and public utility companies. Or there emerged new factions within the elite which had less direct contact with the British, and used what political power they could muster to redirect the flow of investment or credit more in their own favour.[13] Yet the landed elite did not question in principle either foreign ownership, foreign control of major sectors of the economy or the transfer of a proportion of the country's wealth abroad by foreign companies.[14] This was accepted as necessary to guarantee further investment, which was the primary and basic objective.

Industry and the distribution of population

By 1900 there was very little support among the elite for the abandonment of Free Trade in favour of protectionism and local industrial development. There were import tariffs, but these were mainly for revenue purposes. Also there was some industry – more than has traditionally been recognised – but the only large units of production were those linked to the export sector, such as the meat-packing plants. Apart

Footnote 12 (continued)
land but poor in capital. With the progress of time this class became both richer and poorer: they acquired more and more land or their holdings became smaller in size but more and more productive, but at the same time they became more and more dependent on the import of capital.' (Ferns, p. 144.)

13 The relationship is aptly expressed by Ferns as follows: 'As prosperity returned tension [between the British and the Argentines] died away. The chorus of cries for the expropriation of the Buenos Ayres Great Southern Railway continued unabated until the chairman of the Board ... visited Buenos Aires ... He went into conference with the provincial officials and emerged not with an agreement for expropriation ... but for an extension to Bahía Blanca' (p. 388). 'Whatever the differences between Argentine interests and foreign enterprise, the Argentine interests wanted to maintain the flow of capital into the country from abroad' (p. 394). The reference is to the year 1881.

14 Cf. J. Fodor and A. O'Connell, 'Argentina and the Atlantic economy in the first half of the twentieth century' (unpublished mimeog. 1971).

from this, industry only developed wherever local costs were low enough to bring prices below those of imported products. Within the industrial sector, primitive techniques and labour-intensive forms of production predominated. Also industry was generally organised on very small-scale lines. In 1914 the average industrial firm in Buenos Aires employed no more than fourteen men. Since this calculation includes the larger units controlled by foreign capital, the average number of workers in local domestic industry was very small indeed.[15]

The primacy of the export sector was reflected in the distribution of the country's population. The third national census of 1914 estimated the country's total population at 7,885,237. Almost three-quarters of this was concentrated in the pampas zone, in a rough arc between 200 and 300 miles distant from the city of Buenos Aires. The largest centre of population was the province of Buenos Aires, which was the main agricultural area. This had a population of over 2 million. It was followed by the provinces of Santa Fe with about 900,000 inhabitants, Córdoba with 700,000, and Entre Rios, to the north, with 400,000. Beyond this only Corrientes, beyond Entre Rios, and Tucumán, in the north-west, had populations exceeding 300,000. Corrientes was a marginal cattle area, while Tucumán was the centre of the country's sugar-producing region. Outside these areas only the provinces of Mendoza and San Juan, in the west, which were important for wine production, had a significant commercially orientated population. Beyond the pampas in the interior and the south, there was a mere 30% of the population, although these areas together made up over 70% of the country's territory. Many of the areas of the far north and Patagonia in the south were too underpopulated to merit recognition as provinces with their own administrations.

Also there were marked contrasts within the rural population between the pampas and the interior. On the pampas a system of commercial tenancy predominated. In the interior, plantation or subsistence forms were more common. Apart from in the sugar areas of the north-west, market conditions were often limited to satisfying the demand of local small towns, which served principally as centres of administration.

[15] For studies of early industrial development in Argentina see Eduardo F. Jorge, *Industria y concentración económica* (Siglo, XXI, Buenos Aires, 1971); Ezequiel Gallo, 'Agrarian expansion and industrial development in Argentina', in Raymond Carr (ed.), *Latin American Affairs*, St Anthony's Papers, No. 22 (Oxford, 1970), pp. 45–61; Carlos Díaz Alejandro, 'The Argentine Tariff, 1906–1940', *Oxford Economic Papers*, Vol. 14, No. 1, March 1967; Roberto Cortés Conde, 'Problemas del crecimiento industrial (1870–1914)', in Torcuato S. Di Tella *et alia*, pp. 59–81.

Finally, not only was the pampas region more highly developed than the interior, but it was also the main axis upon which political power pivoted. The interior was politically weak and was constantly engaged in a struggle to preserve and develop its economy against more powerful littoral interests.

The country's railway system reflected the same pattern. The main lines fanned out in different directions from the city of Buenos Aires, each of them serving different agricultural regions. There were fewer lines in the interior, and there had been little effort during their construction to integrate different regions. Almost all the railways on the pampas were owned by the British. Outside this area, particularly in the sugar-producing areas, the railways were owned by the State. The relatively small volume of commerce made them insufficiently profitable to attract foreign ownership.[16]

Urban society in Buenos Aires

The simplicity of the export-orientated economy was broken, however, by the high rate of urbanisation in the pampas region. The growth of urban society during these years was in many respects as dramatic and revolutionary a process as that which occurred on the land. In 1869 the urban population in towns of over 2,000 inhabitants was 28.6%. By 1895 this had grown to 37.4% and by 1914 to 52.7%. In the pampas region the proportion was much higher. It grew from 39.5% in 1869 to 48.1% in 1895, and by 1914 it had reached 62.1%. Growth was particularly marked in the larger towns. As early as 1895 almost a quarter of the population lived in cities of more than 20,000 inhabitants.[17]

Rapid urban growth was most marked in the city of Buenos Aires, which swiftly became one of the great cities of the Atlantic seaboard. By the end of the nineteenth century Buenos Aires had come to represent a central paradox in the primary export economy. While the country's actual production system was geographically extensive and decentralised, politically and structurally it was dominated by the city and its immediate hinterland in the province of Buenos Aires.

[16] The classic study of the Argentine railways is Alejandro E. Bunge, *Ferrocarriles Argentinos* (Buenos Aires, 1918).

[17] Oscar E. Cornblit, 'Inmigrantes y empresarios en la política argentina', *Desarrollo Económico*, Vol. 6, No. 24 (January–March 1967), p. 654; Zulma Recchini de Lattes, 'El proceso de urbanización en la Argentina: distribución, crecimiento, y algunas características de la población urbana', *Desarrollo Económico*, Vol. 12, No. 48 (January–March 1973), pp. 867–86.

By 1914 the city of Buenos Aires had a population of over a million and a half, something like 20% of the total throughout the country. The growth of the city was first the result of its position as the main port dealing the international trade, and as the main railway terminal. It was equally important as a centre of consumption, and stood out as a symbol of the wealth created by the growth of the primary export economy. It was also a major centre for finance capital, banking and commerce. In the city, too, was concentrated the bulk of local small-scale industry. There was also a large service sector. Finally the city's importance stemmed from its position as capital of the republic. It was the centre of federal government spending, and the main area of recruitment for administrative positions.

In the city there was a highly complex social structure with large working class and middle class sectors. The middle class was made up of industrial and commercial proprietors, white-collar workers, professional men and bureaucrats. The working class was made up of railway and port workers, the meat-packing workers in Avellaneda (just outside the capital in the province of Buenos Aires), the industrial and service workers, and finally the public utility and public administration workers.

To judge from the census of 1914, the working class made up about two-thirds of the city's employed male population, as is shown in Table 1.

Immigration

The final major feature of Argentine society in these years was immigration. Between 1857, when records were first begun, and 1916, a total of 4,758,729 immigrants entered the country. Of these 2,575,021 remained and settled. In the twenty years or so before the First World War, the proportion of immigrants to the native-born population in Argentina far exceeded that of the United States during the same period.[18] Over a million immigrants came from Italy and slightly less than a million from Spain. In 1914 there were also almost 100,000

[18] In Argentina in 1895, foreigners made up 25.4% of the population, and in 1914 29.9%. In the United States the proportion of foreigners was 13.2% in 1860, 14.0% in 1870, 13.3% in 1880. 14.7% in 1890, 13.6% in 1900, 14.7% in 1910, and 13.2% in in 1920. But of course the United States always had a much larger total number of foreigners. In 1895 there were 1.1 million foreigners in Argentina, and in 1914 2.3 million. In the United States there were 9.2 million in 1890, and 13.5 million in 1910. (Figures from Cornblit, 'Inmigrantes y empresarios', p. 644.)

TABLE 1 *The social structure of the city of Buenos Aires, 1914*[19]

	Male employed population	% of total employed*
Total male employed population	626,861	
Middle classes and above		
Rentier, bureaucratic and professional groups	97,345	15
Entrepreneurs and proprietors	53,438	8
Salaried employees in the private sector	52,443	8
Working class		
Skilled labour and artisans	202,768	32
Unskilled labour	206,028	32

Source: Third national census of 1914. See Appendix 1. Members of the elite are too small to quantify. They made up perhaps 1% of the total population of the city.

*These percentages do not add to 100% because of rounding.

Russians in the country, many of them Jews, and a similar number from the Ottoman Empire and other Balkan states. The peak years of immigration were 1889, when almost 220,000 immigrants entered the country, and the years after 1905. Then no less than 200,000 immigrants entered the country annually, and in 1912 and 1913 the figure topped 300,000.[20] Between 1869 and 1929, 60% of Argentina's population growth can be attributed to immigration.

[19] These estimates may be compared with others appearing in James R. Scobie, 'Buenos Aires as a commercial-bureaucratic city, 1880–1910 – characteristics of a city's orientations', *American Historical Review*, Vol. 77, No. 4 (October 1972), pp. 1034–75. Scobie estimates 'upper class *porteños*' to have been 7,000 in 1887, 11,000 in 1895, 16,000 in 1904, 20,000 in 1909 and 27,000 in 1914. He estimates 7,000 upper class families in 1914. However, his definition of 'upper class' includes all lawyers, doctors and students, some of whom were not members of elite families. His figures also show a decline in the percentage of persons employed in public administration: from 12.3% in 1904 to 8.6% in 1909 and 8.8% in 1914. This may be evidence for my thesis (advanced later) that pressure from 'dependent' middle class groups for administrative posts began to increase around 1905, and coincided with the expansion of the Radical Party. While the number of dependent groups grew, the proportion absorbed by government declined.

[20] For immigration statistics see *Resumen estadístico del movimiento migratorio en la República Argentina, 1857–1924* (Ministry of Agriculture, Buenos Aires, 1925).

The origin of mass immigration into Argentina is to be found in the demand for harvest labour and rural tenants. Later, as the economy became more complex, there were also opportunities for railway and port workers and for commercial and industrial entrepreneurs. Argentina offered its immigrants from Southern Europe an opportunity to enter a fully market economy, and to abandon their peasant or semi-peasant backgrounds. Clearly, wages in Argentina were significantly higher than in the countries of origin, otherwise immigration could not have occurred. Indeed there are grounds for arguing that, due mainly to the cheapness of food in Argentina, wages compared with those of Germany or France.[21] To judge from the growth of the middle classes, the amount of immigrant remittances abroad, and levels of popular savings, many of the immigrants achieved considerable social mobility. By 1914 they were in a majority among home-owners in Buenos Aires, and as owners of industrial and commercial firms.[22]

Yet other conditions point to the fact that Argentina was far from being an immigrants' paradise. Although social mobility was widespread, it still left a large number of immigrants in the ranks of the working class. There was a great deal of overt exploitation, especially in housing and rents. This quickly bred a number of tensions, and a tradition of class conflict which persisted even during periods of rapid growth. The great characteristic of the Argentine economy was its instability. It was sharply conditioned by seasonal factors and by the vagaries of the economic cycle, both of which were destabilising influences on the demand for labour and the level of real wages. Also the rate of immigration, which affected wages in Argentina, depended not only on demand for labour in Argentina, but on conditions in the countries of emigration. A characteristic of immigration to Argentina from around 1900 was its spread from areas with relatively high wage rates, like northern Italy, to areas with a much larger peasant economy, like Spain and the Balkans. Such shifts either tended to depress wages in Argentina, or prevented them from rising fast enough to maintain the rate of social mobility. As time passed it became progressively less easy to move from the working class, and the miserable and insecure position it entailed, into the middle class.

At the same time immigration was actively encouraged by the State in support of the interests of the landed elite. Immigrant recruitment

[21] Cf. Díaz Alejandro, pp. 22, 41.

[22] Cf. Cornblit, 'Inmigrantes y empresarios'.

campaigns were organised in Europe, and it was common to arrange subsidised shipping rates for third-class steerage passengers. Such measures were clearly designed to keep wages as low as possible, and to provide for an abundant and mobile labour force. Most of the immigrants went first to the city of Buenos Aires, where they worked to build up a sufficient store of capital to begin wheat growing. Much of the tension between immigrants and the elite in the city can be traced to difficulties among the former in acquiring sufficient financial backing to effect this transition from wage-worker in the city to tenant on the land. This can only be attributed to an over-immigration which saturated the urban labour market. The problem was particularly apparent during years of boom, in the late 1880s and in the years immediately before 1914.[23] By the same token the elite had some interest in keeping wages low in the cities in order to keep them under control in the rural areas. Rising wages in the city tended to reduce the availability of cheap labour on the land, even though the bulk of this labour was only required during harvest periods. Thus, although the elite had little interest in the domestic industrial sector, it was often to be found, especially after 1900, using its control over the State and the police to intervene in labour disputes against strikers. Action like this undercut the market bargaining power of the immigrants in a manner ultimately to the benefit of the elite.

The interests of the immigrants and the exporting elite, linked with the land, also crossed (at least during the nineteenth century) on the issue of monetary policy. In large part the great land booms of the latter part of the nineteenth century, which created the fortunes of the elite, were achieved by a liberal credit structure and by the use of a depreciating paper currency. Inflation pushed up domestic prices, but often wages lagged behind. A paper currency thus became an instrument of income distribution in favour of the elite and away from wage-earners, and served in effect to lower real wages.[24]

The elite's support for a distribution of income which discriminated against the wage-earner was also reinforced by the nature of its ties with foreign capital. As for the landowners, for the foreign companies, the lower the average wage, the lower were labour costs and the higher were profits. In this sense, too, the interests of both parties were complementary, and they worked hand in hand together. Foreign interests

[23] Ferns, p. 445.

[24] Ibid. pp. 440–1. This was a conspicuous feature of the late 1880s.

collaborated with the elite in, for example, reducing passenger charges over the Atlantic run to allow for more immigration; the landowners used their political power to hold back the wage bills of foreign enterprises to provide themselves with cheap services, but also to allow higher profit remittances abroad which increased the country's attractiveness as a field for further investment. Thus although wages in the pampas area of Argentina generally compared well in international terms, the growth and prosperity of the primary exporting economy, to some extent, rested on depriving the immigrants of their true market bargaining power.

For this reason immigration into Argentina was a highly fluid and unstable process. A majority of the European-born population worked on the *estancias* as agricultural tenants. Particularly after the vast inflation of land prices after the turn of the century, the rural tenant suffered from instability, and in many cases from impoverishment. Rental charges were often very high, particularly in the more profitable zones near the coast. Production techniques were primitive and linked to an extensive or rotationary type of cultivation, which prevented many of the tenants from establishing a fixed position on the land. This situation was exacerbated by a constant labour surplus, composed of more European immigrants. There were signs of this in the changing character of immigration. A common practice between the 1890s and 1914 was the so-called *golondrina*, or 'swallow' system, of harvest labour recruitment. The immigrants would come from Europe on a seasonal basis to work in the harvest and afterwards return to their home countries.[25] It proved ultimately more profitable for the immigrants to do this, although they had to incur the cost of a return journey to Buenos Aires.

However, a large number of the immigrants also settled in the city of Buenos Aires and other urban centres in the pampas area. They were attracted by the rapid expansion of urban activities in the transport, trade and industrial sectors. In Buenos Aires in 1914 almost half the total population was foreign born. Among the male population, there were 455,507 immigrants and 394,463 natives. In the other major cities in the pampas region there were comparably high foreign male populations in 1914. Of Rosario's total population of 220,000, 105,000 were foreigners.

It was the immigrants who gave the great boost to the growth of the

[25] James R. Scobie, *Revolution on the Pampas. A social history of Argentine wheat, 1860–1910* (Austin, Texas, 1964).

larger cities. In the whole urban area of the province of Buenos Aires the immigrants amounted to a little less than 40% of the population. In Santa Fe the proportion was about 31%. However, the city of Avellaneda in Buenos Aires had a foreign population of 55%, and Rosario, in Santa Fe, one of 47%. Both were considerably in excess of the respective averages for the immigrant urban population in the two provinces. Only in the backward towns of the interior were the natives preponderant. In traditional centres such as La Rioja and Catamarca they amounted to over 95%.[26]

The immigrants in Argentina were thus confronted by two basic conditions. On the one side there was the desire of the landed elite to promote immigration but to prevent wages from reaching their true level. On the other they were subject to the strong pull of urban society. Here there were relatively more opportunities for social mobility and the acquisition of skills and property than in most of the rural areas, where the land was controlled by the elite. Thus the overall results of mass immigration were the saturation of the labour market and the increasing concentration of population in the cities. However, because of the great mobility of the labour force, and the ease with which superfluous labour could be shed by the device of re-migration by the immigrants back to their countries of origin, unemployment was generally never more than a very temporary phenomenon. The great exception to this rule was during the First World War when, as a result of shipping shortages and rising passenger rates between Europe and South America, many thousands of immigrants were left indigent in Buenos Aires and elsewhere. Although

[26] Gustavo Beyhaut, Roberto Cortés Conde, Haydée Gorostegui, Susana Torrado, 'Los inmigrantes en el sistema occupacional argentino', in Torcuato S. Di Tella *et alia*, pp. 85–123. Different nationalities among the immigrants tended to be concentrated in different occupations. The British, French and Germans mainly occupied managerial positions in the sectors controlled by foreign capital. The Jews and Syrians worked in the small industrial and commercial sectors. Of the Italians and Spaniards it was said by one observer in 1918: 'It is known that the Italians predominate among the cultivators and among the skilled labour groups, (for example bricklayers, carpenters), and to some extent among the semi-skilled occupations. The Spaniards are in a majority among the small retailers, the white-collar workers, and in the less skilled occupations, as domestic servants and auxiliary workers' (Augusto Bunge, *La inferioridad económica de los argentinos nativos*, Buenos Aires, 1919, p. 38). The general pattern of immigration was for each wave of immigrants from different countries to predominate in the unskilled brackets. Thus in 1914 the Ottomans, who arrived the last of the three major national groups of immigrants, were mainly to be found in the lowest paid jobs, for example in the *frigoríficos*.

in Buenos Aires at this time there was evidence after 1900 of some disguised unemployment in the form of marginal petty commercial activities, the pampas region could be described as a full-employment economy. Yet this term ought to be used with care. It is true that in Argentina, unlike most of the other Latin American countries, there was only a very small 'marginal' or structurally superfluous labour force, and that was in the backward interior. But a capacity to sustain full employment was less an intrinsic characteristic of Argentina's system of production than a luxury provided by the mechanism of immigration. In effect, re-migration during periods of depression, or in slack periods of the year, simply shifted Argentina's potential unemployment elsewhere: Argentina's 'reserve army', and in a sense marginal labour force, was in Italy or in Spain.[27]

It is not surprising under these circumstances that political relations between the immigrants and the elite were traditionally extremely tense. The elite wanted more immigrants, but it often interfered in some way or other in the process of wage bargaining. This induced considerable unrest among the immigrants, and the elite became constantly afraid that the situation would explode and lead to an immigrant revolt. Although immigration, with foreign investment, was the main motor of economic growth, on the whole elite attitudes towards the immigrants were founded on mistrust and hostility, feelings which were often returned.[28] There was a tendency to view the immigrants as impersonal and dehumanised factors of production, to be manipulated and set against one another whenever the situation demanded it. During strikes, for example, it was common to recruit blackleg labour from other groups of immigrants. From the elite's own perspective the country was booming, and it failed to recognise that its own capacity for untrammelled self-enrichment was not always shared by the immigrants. Added to all this were the conventional prejudices of the property-owner against the worker, and increasingly vice versa.

In more general terms this points to one of the key differences between immigration in Argentina and in the United States. Unlike the urban industrial ruling class in the United States after the Civil War, the Argentine elite had no interest in supporting the economic and mobility aspirations of the immigrants as a means to expand the growth of a local

[27] Compare this with Díaz Alejandro, p. 27, and Laclau, 'Modos de producción', pp. 278, 298. Both emphasise that Argentina had full employment.

[28] Carl Solberg, *Immigration and Nationalism in Argentina and Chile, 1890–1914* (University of Texas, 1970).

consumer market. The other great contrast lies in the fact that while immigration increasingly became an urban phenomenon in Argentina, the landed elite, unlike the industrial elite in the United States, had no control over urban occupations in commerce and industry. It thus had no means of controlling the distribution of urban jobs and using this to establish political leadership over the immigrants. The result was a quite different political tradition in comparison with the United States. It was impossible for the landed elite in Argentina to develop the wide-ranging urban political machines which in the United States were the propellors of the 'melting pot', the basic instruments for the control of protest movements and for the creation of the mass political parties. Because the job nexus between the elite and the urban immigrants did not exist, Argentina's political system became biased towards restriction, repression and oligarchy. There was no means of controlling the immigrants within the political system, and it was therefore deemed advisable to keep them out of it as far as possible. The more the political role of the immigrants developed, the more likely it was that the position of the landed elite would be threatened.

This also underlay the citizenship question in Argentina. Another of the contrasts with the United States was that in Argentina the immigrants did not generally adopt Argentine citizenship. This has usually been presented as reflecting on the immigrants themselves: they had no interest in settling in the country, and wanted merely to enrich themselves in Argentina before returning to their countries of origin. In many ways such an explanation is unsatisfactory. A certain unwillingness to abandon completely countries of origin is no doubt a characteristic of every immigration process, regardless of destination. In Argentina there were special local conditions which conspired against the immigrant being willing to settle permanently: the unavailability of purchasable land, the instability of employment and the itinerant nature of many immigrants' existence. But there is also a further fundamental reason: the ruling class in Argentina could have no interest in promoting citizenship among the immigrants, because, unlike the United States, it was unable to make this the instrument of political control in such a way as to promote an acceptance and support of the established order.[29]

[29] Solberg comments: 'By 1905 the Argentine upper class found itself in a dilemma. Recent Argentine history ... indicated that continued prosperity required more immigration. But new immigrants undoubtedly ... would accelerate the social changes undermining elite power (p. 81) ... To prevent any such challenge to its political power, the oligarchy vigorously opposed movements that would encourage the masses

The relationship between the elite and the immigrants was the most pronounced conflict feature of Argentine society during the mature period of the primary export economy. Although it was often perceived and articulated in purely cultural terms, in many respects the struggle was one between social classes. There were few immigrants among the elite and upper middle class groups, although immigrants made up three quarters of the proprietors of industrial and commercial firms. However, perhaps 70% of the immigrants were concentrated in the working class in the city of Buenos Aires, and within the working class about 60% were foreign-born. Thus the lower the social scale, the greater was the proportion of immigrants. Although by 1914 the labour force contained a large and growing number of native workers, in a majority of cases to be a foreigner was to be a worker, and, one can safely presume, likely an unskilled worker.

The urban middle class in Buenos Aires

Relations between the elite and the urban middle class were more complex. One might seek signs among the urban middle class of opposition to the elite and the primary export economy along the lines of the classic European struggles between urban industrial and rural agrarian interests. As Table 1 (p. 11) shows, there were over 50,000 industrial and commercial proprietors in Buenos Aires by 1914. What worked against this was the fact that the urban class structure, in spite of the existence of an industrial sector, was rooted in the international commercial and service sectors. On the whole, industrial activities had been restricted to a narrow framework established by the leading primary sector. They were largely complementary to it rather than separate from it.[30] The local industrial sector in Argentina was dominated by large

Footnote 29 (continued)

to naturalise. Congress . . . refused to consider proposals . . . to reform the labyrinthine procedures an applicant for citizenship had to undergo' (p. 83). It is thus not surprising, as Díaz Alejandro puts it, that among the immigrants 'indifference and alienation flourished. To many the ideal was to become rich in Argentina and then return to their native land. Those who felt this way, but failed to become rich, often turned bitter towards the establishement and passed that attitude on to their children' Essays, p. 63).

[30] Jorge, Cornblit, 'Inmigrantes y empresarios', Gallo, 'Agrarian expansion and industrial development'. For a critical review of the literature see Ernesto Laclau, 'Relations between agricultural and industrial interests in Argentina, 1870–1914' (unpublished mimeograph, 1972).

units of production, like the meat-packing plants, which were integrated with the primary export structure. Smaller artisan activities developed wherever an availability of local raw materials and an advantage in transport costs reduced prices below those of the imported article. Again there was an element in these activities of complementarity to the primary export economy, rather than inherent conflict with it. Also in 1914 there was little apparent sign of anything wrong with industry. In the previous thirty years it had grown up from a very low base into a significant and sizeable proportion of total production, and there was no reason to believe that it could not continue.

Thus the urban middle class had evolved without the distinctive traits of the urban bourgeoisie elsewhere. Rather than being committed to the development of a fully industrial economy, the middle classes, and in many cases even the entrepreneurs, supported the retention of the primary export economy.

Underpinning this was their position as consumers. Although a reliance on imports for a large quantity of manufactured goods had its drawbacks, it did generally ensure, while the export sector remained secure, a painless flow of low-cost industrial goods. The Free Trade structure was supported by the urban sectors for fear that attempts at industrial diversification would produce inflationary pressures affecting the cost of living. It is interesting to note that when the industrial sector began to expand qualitatively in the 1930s, the campaign received most of its impetus not from the urban groups but from the elite. The primary aim was to correct recurrent deficits in the balance of payments by a programme of import substitution.[31] Until 1930, however, there was a broad state of consensus between both landed and urban interests. This led to considerable popular support for Argentina's quasi-colonial position, and for such traditional *caveats* of state policy as Free Trade and dependence on the British for commerce and capital investment.

What tended to undermine such consensus, however, was the inherent tendency of the primary export economy to concentrate power and wealth in the hands of the landed elite and foreign capital. This did not only affect the working class. By the beginning of the twentieth century there were signs that it was also seriously affecting the structure and composition of the urban middle class and, as a result, its political relationships with the elite. In the absence of a fully developed, mature

[31] Miguel Murmis and Juan Carlos Portantiero, 'Crecimiento industrial y alianza de clases', *Estudios sobre los orígines del peronismo* (Siglo XXI, Buenos Aires, 1971).

industrial sector, there was little scope in Argentina for the emergence of high-status entrepreneur and managerial groups.

In *per capita* income terms in the early twentieth century Argentina was among the most advanced countries in the world. However, unlike other similarly rich countries, the main mechanism for the distribution of income was not industry. This created further distortions in the urban class system. A major merchanism for the distribution of income was through the demand generated by the rich *rentier* landed interests of the coast. The demand profile of this group, in conjunction with the Free Trade structure, had certain marked features to it. The demand of the elite for investment goods and industrial products was mainly satisfied from abroad. In domestic terms its main demand was for labour and services. Of the latter, the most important were for legal, administrative and, to a lesser extent, for educational services. These were all middle class white-collar roles demanding a certain amount of intellectual expertise and a level of education and professional training. The demand for such services by the elite was a major influence in the formation of the urban middle class. The top bracket of the middle class (and perhaps junior and subordinate members of elite families, too), was heavily concentrated in these kinds of activities. Its client relationship with the elite, the great source of wealth, yielded a reasonable and relatively high level of income. In turn this group would tend to repeat the elite's demand profile, and multiply the total number of middle class groups in a similar position to itself.

The result of this was the emergence of an important stratum of the middle class in Argentina, possessed not of the aggressive entrepreneurial instincts of its capitalist counterparts in the United States, Britain or Germany, but of a clientelist, dependent – one is tempted to say mendicant – character. Social mobility in Argentina tended to occur not by virtue of a capacity to experiment or innovate – those who did this usually got no further than the street-corner store or the petty workshop – but by seeking 'friends' and 'patrons' higher up the social ladder, to use them to gain access to the wealth circulating in the train of the elite. In Argentina phenomena like 'personalism' and '*caudillismo*' have generally been regarded as unfortunate atavisms from the colonial period. But it is clear that they were also strongly reinforced by the peculiar and novel aspects of the country's pattern of growth and social system.

As Table 1 shows, the middle class in Buenos Aires was divided more or less evenly into white-collar workers and entrepreneurs on the one side, and professional men and administrative employees on the other. This second group was extremely important. It embraced a total of 100,000 men, or almost a sixth of the city's employed male population. It represented the medium and upper-level sectors of Buenos Aires middle class society, which in status terms was very similar to the technical and managerial groups of developed industrial societies.

The other important feature about this was that the majority of the urban professionals and the administrative employees were native Argentines, and not immigrants. The most common mobility pattern in the years before the First World War was from immigrant worker or entrepreneur through to the next generation of sons-of-immigrant professional or administration employee. Thus, if in general to be an immigrant was to be a worker or a small proprietor, it was even more accurate to say that to be a native was to be a member of the professions or the administration. Moreover, the rate of growth of this professional middle class had been increasing rapidly during the fifty years before 1914. It has been estimated that the middle class as a whole grew as a proportion of total urban population from 11.1% in 1869 to 25.9% in 1895 and 29.9% in 1914. Between 1869 and 1895 the industrial and commercial middle class grew from 6.2% to 17.8% of the total, and then declined in 1914 to 14.9%. The administrative and professional middle class, on the other hand, grew from 4.1% in 1869 to 6.6% in 1895 and 12.4% in 1914. This shows a much more rapid rate of growth of the administrative and professional strata after 1900.[32]

The association between citizenship, middle class status and a series of roles which may be called 'dependent' or non-productive, was the most important factor impinging upon the political role of the middle class groups and their relationship with the elite. Middle class mobility aspirations were not channelled in direct opposition to the landed elite in support of the development of the industrial sector. Rather they were governed by the question of access to professional careers and opportunities outside the industrial sector. To the extent that the landed elite opposed their access to such positions, the interests of the middle class groups clashed with it.

By the turn of the century the rapid rate of urbanisation, together

[32] Gino Germani, 'Social stratification and its historical evolution in Argentina', *Sociologia, Rivista de Studi Sociali dell' Instituto Luigi Sturzo* (1971). (I owe this reference to Allub.)

with the distorted growth of the industrial sector, had encouraged the emergence of strong cultural reinforcements to the growth of dependent middle class groups. When the new generation of sons of immigrants appeared, it tended to turn aside from the working class and entrepreneurial roles of the immigrants themselves, and to begin to compete strongly for positions in the professions. This gradually induced among the native-born middle class groups what amounted to an obsession with secondary and university education, the means through which entry into the professions could be secured.

By the same token, middle class mobility aspirations were also strongly focussed on careers in State administration. Like the professions, the bureaucracy was also regarded as the road to prestige, wealth and influence, and it became a form of unconsciously accepted substitute for a developed industrial sector. According to the national census of 1914, no less than 50,000 persons in Buenos Aires were employed by the State in different capacities, either in education or in administration. This was about a twelfth of the total employed male population and about 25% of the middle class.

Such 'career dependency' also meant dependence upon the State. This is obvious enough in the case of the bureaucracy. But the State also had considerable control over the universities. It could create new universities, expand old ones and impose criteria for entry. Thus in a broad sense it controlled the whole social-mobility mechanism for the urban middle class. Ultimately its policies and its spending practices determined the supply of dependent roles available: either it could increase spending and widen access to the middle class groups in high-status positions, or it could restrict them.

Even before the turn of the century it was apparent that segments of the ruling class recognised that this process was at work, and were far from happy at its outcome. It meant high spending by the State, a practice in conflict with notions of thrift, economy and *laissez-faire*. A minister of finance, José María Rosa, declared in 1899:

> Our budgets have constantly increased in recent years. It is notorious that the personnel of the administration is excessive, just as it is notorious that useless and expensive sinecures have been created, with the sole object of giving places to persons whose influence has been such that the State has undertaken to support them. Bureaucracy is increasing; industry and commerce, and all the spheres of free endeavour and of individual effort are abandoned by the sons of the country, who seek salaried employments or the exercise of intermediary professions which demand no effort. The number of young men who waste their time in seeking

a place, instead of devoting their energies to work, in a country which offers wealth to all who will employ a little energy, a little perseverance, is surprising. But all want an easy life, even though it be poor and without horizon, all wish to live on the budget, and in order to gain their object they exhibit all kinds of ingenuity; they go seeking recommendations and employ every means at their disposal.

This host of pertinacious beggars of place results in the creation of new employments and new services, all equally useless. The national and provincial administrations pay more than 65 million pesos in salaries and pensions. Each inhabitant contributes six golden dollars – £1 4s – towards the upkeep of an army of employees, which is an enormous sum. The public services of other countries cost per inhabitant: in Switzerland 4s 9d; in the United States 6s 4d; in England 8s 2d; in Holland 9s; in Austria 11s 2d; in Belgium 12s; in Italy 15s 9d; and in France 19s 2d. These figures show us that we have outstripped all other nations in the matter of expenditure on the bureaucracy.[33]

This was the essential nature of the political relationship between the middle class groups and the elite. The elite, in orthodox liberal fashion, was concerned to minimise State spending, and the increasingly large dependent middle class, to expand it *pari passu* with its own growth.[34] The elite also controlled the State, and the State was the main arbiter over the fortunes of the middle class groups. There were two principal areas of conflict. The elite could either try to hold back the rate of State spending and restrict the number of public servants. Or it could attempt to curtail the growth of the professional classes by restricting university intakes, reserving both the universities and the bureaucracy for its own members. Like the middle class groups, the elite had a certain vested interest in the professions and in the bureaucracy, as the number of absentee landlords and younger sons increased.

However, it is important to note that this conflict was relatively superficial in character. It was not as if the middle class groups were directly attacking the basis of the landed elite's wealth. They were not attempting to impose structural changes on the basic framework of the primary exporting economy. What the middle class was mainly interested in were the quantitative and qualitative aspects of State spending. This could only become dangerous to the elite if the middle class groups won complete control over the State. Under these circumstances they could conceivably deprive the landed elite of its access to agricultural credit. Or they could

[33] Quoted in Martínez and Lewandowski, p. 302.

[34] This did not seem to be happening after 1900. See note p. 11.

alter the country's taxation system, replacing the traditional system of taxing consumption by the excises on imports with a tax on land. One final, and more likely, possibility was that the middle class groups would spend at such a rate that they would threaten the country's credit standing abroad. This would obviously undermine the landed elite's relationship with foreign capital, since it might lead to a default on the external debt.

On the other hand, the landed elite could have few objections to a system of power-sharing with the middle class groups, which left them with ultimate control over State spending and the taxation system, but which allowed the State to meet middle class career aspirations. There was here a possibility of some sort of compromise relationship being established. It was quite different with the working class, where any form of concession immediately affected the economic interests of the elite. But how long an agreement with the middle classes could last was quite a different matter. The most crucial feature of Argentine society was that the more the primary exporting economy encouraged the growth of a complex urban society, the more likely it was that the absence of a developed industrial sector would lead to the further growth of dependent middle class groups. The question then would be up to what point could the State continue serving both agrarian and urban interests, and at what point would the linkages between them snap.

CHAPTER 2

The oligarchy and institutional reform 1880–1916

The term oligarchy refers both to the landed and commercial elite described in the last chapter and to the system of government which prevailed in Argentina up till 1912. The accuracy of the term is greater in the latter sense than in the former. It was certainly 'government by a few', though not always the same few were in power. To some extent power rotated among different factions, which represented different interests within the elite. Occasionally such differences were regionally based, at other times they were associated with specialised activities within the elite, for example, commerce, or the two main types of cattle-ranching: breeding and fattening. The term oligarchy is perhaps also misleading in that it suggests a complete homogeneity in the composition of the elite between different periods. This is more true of the period after 1900 than before.

The classic period of oligarchy as an institutional system was during the thirty years after 1880. The concern of the elite for control over the State was dictated by the role of the national government as a major source of credit and as a bridge for lucrative contacts with foreign capital. There was also great concern to maintain political stability, because, as events earlier in the nineteenth century had shown, stability was necessary for the attraction of both capital and labour into the country.[1] The result of this was that the elite itself became very highly politicised, but at the same time it strove to keep other groups out of politics in order to minimise possible destabilising influences.

Politics between 1880 and the First World War are only intelligible in terms of the elite's commitment to the preservation of stability and growth. As long as a limited oligarchical system served these ends, the system survived. Its destruction, and the advent of representative government, followed upon a period of increasing political unrest involving non-elite groups, which the old structure proved steadily incapable of

[1] The development of Argentina in the early nineteenth century is fully described by Ferns.

handling. This chapter briefly examines how 'oligarchy' worked from 1880, and then traces the transition to representative government in 1912.

Politically, the period between 1880 and the First World War divides roughly into two parts. The first, up to around 1900, and in spite of recurrent unrest in the early 1890s, was a period when the elite's dominance remained largely unchallenged. What distinguished it from the period before 1880 was its relative stability. There were still a number of important revolts and rebellions which reflected a continuing state of disunity among different regional landed interests. But the atmosphere of perennial civil war and local rebellion, which had marred the past, declined significantly. The second period after 1900 saw the emergence of a pluralist political structure under the impact of the growth of the urban sectors, and finally, in 1912, the introduction of reforms. These brought the country's institutional structure closer to a system of representative government. The main aim of the reforms was to establish a coalition between the elite and the urban middle classes. This, it was hoped, would leave the economic position of the elite intact, but restore stability to the political system. Rather than representing any revolutionary political change, the events of 1912 were thus more significant as a reflection of the elite's ability to adapt the political structure to new conditions, and to accommodate new groups in the political system.

The oligarchy

A landowning and commercial oligarchy appeared in the 1880s despite the fact that a liberal constitution, which had been introduced in 1853, was never formally abandoned. This supposedly guaranteed popular representation, the division of powers and a federal structure along the lines of the United States. What undermined this was apprehension among the landed groups that unstable regional and incipient populist currents would destroy the attractiveness of the country to its foreign backers. There was in many quarters fear of any repetition of the Rosas Government in the 1830s and 1840s, which had won for itself the reputation of a popular tyranny opposed to any further expansion of the ties between Argentina and the European industrial countries. To prevent this recurring, the elite adopted a system of disguised repression. There was an attempt to freeze political activities by a system of enforced control which would minimise the political influence of other groups. A contemporary observer defined the oligarchy in the following way:

> The governing elements are recruited from a class of citizens which, if it does not properly constitute a caste, nonetheless forms a directing class ... This class corresponds approximately to the highest social stratum formed by members of the traditional families, by the rich, and by the educated. The members of this class maintain among themselves more or less tight social and economic relations, and, as is natural, share common sentiments and opinions.[2]

The political system which appeared towards the end of the nineteenth century pivoted on organised electoral fraud. Fraud served to uphold the myth of constitutional liberties, while depriving them of any practical content. The process of institutionalised political bargaining was narrowly limited to members of the elite. As late as 1910 it was estimated that only about 20% of the native male population actually voted. This dropped to a mere 9% if the immigrants were added.[3] In any case elections were frequently rigged, or the voters bribed or intimidated. As a result, recruitment channels for elective offices remained extremely narrow. As former President Sarmiento declared in the 1880s: '[A president] does and will do what he wants, because this is a republic without citizens, without public opinion, educated by tyranny, and corrupted in recent times by a great mass of immigration'.[4]

After fraud, a second major characteristic of the political system was its use of personal rewards to construct political loyalties. The main device for this was the distribution of positions in the national government and the provinces, and sinecure posts in the bureaucracy. Either the system was exploited simply to buy off opposition or, more positively, it was used as a means to channel the benefits which came from control over the State to different groups of landowners. The main benefits at stake were credit and favours to specific regions in the authorisation of railway construction. Political loyalties and political alliances thus came to be based on government patronage and the distribution of

[2] Thomas F. McGann, *Argentina, the United States, and the Inter-American System* (Harvard University Press, Cambridge, Massachusetts, 1957), p. 53. This must not be taken to imply that the ruling class was in any sense 'feudal'. If the case is a little over-stated, the following remarks by Cortés Conde and Gallo remain broadly accurate: 'it was not a retrograde, closed group with a long tradition of landowning ... It was secular and highly dynamic. It could adapt to changing circumstances and was sufficiently flexible to avoid confrontations which endangered the system' (*La formación de la Argentina moderna*, pp. 101–2).

[3] Gino Germani, *Política y sociedad en una época de transición* (Paidós, Buenos Aires, 1966), pp. 225–6.

[4] Quoted in Roberto Cortés Conde and Ezequiel Gallo, *La república conservadora*, Vol. 5, *Historia Argentina*, ed. Tulio Halperín Donghi (Paidós, Buenos Aires, 1972) p. 71.

offices. The system also had regional and hierarchical dimensions. Subordinate local political bosses controlled elections within their spheres of influence by taking advantage of a store of patronage made available to them from above. Presidential power operated through overall control of government appointments and through alliances with provincial governors.

Since politics was largely a matter of exchanging different favours within the elite, it became a rather esoteric activity. However, the stability of the system was closely dependent upon economic expansion and upon the continuation of foreign investment. This largely provided the benefits which the State was able to distribute to the landed groups. If depression occurred, profit margins and land values sagged. The cessation of foreign investment had a severe effect on the availability of credit and upon land mortgages, which were drawn up in expectation of a continuing expansion of markets and communications. When economic depression struck, acute competition developed among the landowners for control over the State as a means of protection from the effects of contraction. This occurred in the mid-1870s and again in the early 1890s. These were both periods of rebellion and instability.[5]

In the 1880s, however, disputes of this kind declined in importance as an unprecedented wave of foreign investment, carried along by favourable conditions for exports to the British market, rapidly increased the availability of transport and credit. During this phase of uniform expansion, the oligarchy emerged in its most stable form. In 1880 General Julio A. Roca became president of the republic, and for the next generation he remained the country's most powerful political leader.

Roca's initial achievements were to push back the Indian tribes from the frontier and to defeat a major rebellion in the province of Buenos Aires. This expanded the supply of land and put paid to much of the

[5] The relationship between control of the State and access to agricultural credit is suggested by the importance of the semi-State bank, the Banco de la Nación. Senior offices in the bank were a matter of political patronage, and each government made its own appointments. It has been estimated that by 1914 50% of banking business was directly controlled by the Banco de la Nación, and another third controlled indirectly by it. Preliminary findings suggest that it is not unwarranted to define the State during this period as a major centre of finance capital in Argentina. Cf. Joseph S. Tulchin *et alia*, 'Agricultural credit and politics in Argentina, 1910–1930', *Research Previews*, Vol. 20, No. 1, April 1973 (Institute for Research in Social Science, The University of North Carolina, Chapel Hill).

military power of the provinces. Roca followed this by establishing an organised national government. For the first time the State in Argentina emerged as a unified entity with a clear monopoly of power and authority. The country was pacified, and the way left open for foreign investment on a massive scale. Political power was distributed to the members of Roca's own party, the Partido Autonomista Nacional, or the P.A.N., as it was known. Some years later a political commentator described the P.A.N. in the following way:

> It never had much faith in universal suffrage, nor in the republican form of government. In its judgement the People was not ready for the vote. Since it has been omnipotent for the past thirty years, it never occurred to it to limit the vote. It accepted all the great ideals of political liberty written in the books. It proclaimed the purity of the elections and universal suffrage, the impartiality of government, autonomy or the federalist principle, 'the free play of the institutions' and many other things, all of which it had absolutely no belief in, and indeed feared as dangerous for internal peace and material progress . . . The government has a theory, which it rarely confesses, but which is its guiding idea, and this is the theory of the tutelary function of government or of governments in relation to the People. This concept of tutelage extends to the point of defending the People lest the government fall into bad hands. The tutelary idea, which is the same as that of the Church, expounded with admirable logic in the encyclicals of Leo XIII, is incompatible with the democratic idea and with representative forms of government.[6]

Under Roca the Congress was packed with the president's supporters. Lingering opposition in the provinces was put down by a judicious mixture of bribery and force. In this fashion a system of undivided presidential authority was established.[7]

The system functioned under Roca because the process of economic expansion made it possible to broaden the basis of support for the P.A.N., and thus employ the national government as a neutral arbiter among different landed groups, rewarding them with credit and access to communications more or less uniformly. During the boom in the 1880s few of the pampas landowners failed to benefit from this in one way or another. The weaknesses of the system only became apparent

[6] Rodolfo Rivarola, 'Filosofía de la elección reciente', *Revista Argentina de Ciencias Politicas*, no. 8 (March 1914) p. 96. Quoted in Darío Cantón, *Elecciones y partidos políticos en la Argentina. Historia, interpretación y balance, 1910–1966* (Siglo XXI, Buenos Aires, 1973) p. 166.

[7] The best accounts of the 1880s are Ferns; Cornblit, Gallo and O'Connell; McGann, pp. 1–65

at the end of the decade during the administration of Roca's successor, Miguel Juárez Celman.

Juárez attempted to establish an independent power base free from Roca's influence and control. He began to place his own followers in key positions and to favour a number of different regional cliques in the channelling of funds and in the distribution of railway concessions.[8] This undermined the unity of the P.A.N. and the rough equilibrium of forces which Roca had established. The political epicentre shifted away from its main axis in the province of Buenos Aires towards Juárez's supporters in Córdoba. Juárez might have got away with this were it not for the fact that the economic boom of the 1880s collapsed suddenly and disastrously in 1889 and 1890. This deprived the political system of its basic unifying components of stability, cheap credit, the expansion of transportation and the inflation of land values. The result was a temporary return to the factional struggles of the period before 1880.[9] In 1890 the major landowners and commercial interests in the province of Buenos Aires once more organised a revolt. Although this failed, it left the president in an untenable position. In August, 1890 Juárez Celman resigned.[10]

Until some time after the turn of the century Roca reassumed his dominant position as the person best equipped to minimise tensions within the elite. The revolts of the early 1890s eventually petered out against a background of gradual economic recovery. As the old patterns

[8] I share Ferns's view that politics during this period was very closely conditioned by the expansion and contraction of the economy. For example: 'The period 1875–82 . . . may be described as one of depression and recovery or of political tension and relaxation. It is not possible . . . to make a choice between the two, for the course of economic and political development was unusually inter-connected in this part of the world at this time . . . When the pace of development slackened, tensions developed in the economic and financial sphere which projected themselves into political life . . .' p. 374). The same is true of the early 1890s. Cortés Conde and Gallo comment, referring to 1890: 'With the crisis the old parties in Buenos Aires . . . recovered their positions rapidly. Roca and Pellegrini also, who had been excluded from influence in the P.A.N. by the followers of Juárez, rapidly regained the ground they had lost' (*La república conservadora*, p. 87).

[9] The British Minister at the time described Juárez's friends as 'a collection of persons, some of whom are said to draw salaries from the Nation, and all, or nearly all, of whom have . . . within a comparatively recent period emerged from positions of obscurity and even almost of indigence to the possession of great wealth'. (Quoted in Ferns, p. 450.)

[10] The Revolution of 1890 is dealt with in more detail in chapter 3.

of growth were once more reestablished, it became easier to attract different elite factions into supporting the government. Each of the presidents who succeeded Juárez avoided his mistake of seeking to alter the distribution of power by shifting the regional flow of government benefits. By the turn of the century Buenos Aires had fully reestablished its traditional supremacy.

Between 1898 and 1904 Roca served a second term as president of the republic. His personal dominance ended only after 1906 when the death of an incumbent president led to the succession of the vice-president, José Figueroa Alcorta. Supported by Roca's opponents, Figueroa Alcorta began to intrigue against the former president's supporters in the provinces. Opposition in Congress was stifled by its temporary closure, and by other similarly authoritarian measures.[11] An impression of what part politics was perceived to play in Argentine society during these years is apparent in a commentary by Martínez and Lewandowski:

> As for home politics, they form a domain which we do not wish to enter, and on which the world of affairs bestows little enough attention, so long as they do not compromise the public peace. The Argentine, in fact, is still under a system of personal power, the Presidency of the Republic is the focus about which all the political life of the country gravitates. In default of a people conscious of its rights as of its duties, and possessed of the virtues necessary to a course of perseverance in democratic practices, it is the Government which manages the elections, and it is difficult to say whether it does so because there is no public opinion, or whether there is no public opinion because the Governments usurp the functions of the electorate. From this point of view there has been no change in the political morale of the country; the only progress to be noted is that the parties resort less often than they used to violence as a solution to their quarrels.[12]

The challenge to the oligarchy and the reform movement

However, this dominant pattern was on the point of changing. The second major division within the elite, which began at the turn of the century and which came to a head during the Figueroa Alcorta administration, was quite different from the one which occurred in the 1890s. This time it was not precipitated by an economic depression nor, in quite so direct or simple a way, by disputes among elite party factions for

[11] For an account of Figueroa Alcorta's measures see Miguel Angel Cárcano, *Sáenz Peña, La revolución por los comicios* (Buenos Aires, 1963), pp. 127–38.

[12] Martínez and Lewandowski, p. xxii.

control over the national government. Although there were still lingering signs of unrest along the traditional pattern of the 'Ins' and the 'Outs', from henceforward politics was dominated by the question of the elite's relationship with the urban sectors.

Before 1900 the only genuinely politicised sector was the elite. Then expressions of disaffection could generally be catered for by an adjustment in the receptivity of the State to different segments of the landed elite. As had happened in the early 1890s, government offices could be redistributed, and different groups allowed access to them and the economic advantages they conferred. Thus the oligarchy had a mechanism built into it through which political equilibrium could be restored, and alienated groups either won over or isolated. This was Roca's foremost ability.

After 1900 Roca's scheme was undermined by the increasing politicisation of the major urban sectors, the native middle class and the immigrant working class. The appearance of these groups on the political stage, challenging the power monopoly of the elite groups, was essentially a response to the conditions described in the previous chapter. After 1900, in spite of very rapid economic growth, political unrest among the urban sectors increased.

Pressure from the urban middle class came mainly from a new party, the Unión Cívica Radical. The important thing to note about Radicalism for the moment was that although it embraced an increasingly large sector of the native middle class, it was controlled and led by a residue of the faction which had revolted against Juárez Celman in 1890. This group of leaders was not middle class, but a segment of the elite itself, one of the 'Out' groups, which had avoided incorporation into the oligarchy. The strength of Radicalism after 1900 lay in its success in achieving popular support among the middle class groups. The threat it posed stemmed from its commitment to overthrow the oligarchy by rebellion and introduce a system of popular democracy. For many years different presidents made attempts to buy off the Radical leaders with the offer of government jobs. Before 1900 this was generally successful, and the party ceased to be much of a threat. However, as its links with the middle classes became stronger, this technique became steadily less effective. By the time of Figueroa Alcorta's administration between 1906 and 1910, it began to look simply a matter of time before the Radicals could organise a successful revolt, and triumphantly impose their ideals.

The second source of opposition to the oligarchy came from the working class. After 1900 a militant Anarchist movement established a large following among the immigrant workers in Buenos Aires. There was a series of violent general strikes, which triggered a spate of repressive measures by the government. Strikes were broken by force, and legislation was passed by Congress allowing the government to deport or imprison working class leaders.[13]

Confronted by this dual threat the elite split over how to deal with it. Roca and his followers continued to support the established system and prescribed repression. Figueroa Alcorta, and an increasing number of others, began to support the introduction of representative government. Isolated groups supporting this kind of reform had first appeared in the 1890s, although they remained in a minority until some time after the turn of the century. In 1901, however, they won a vital new recruit for their cause. This was Carlos Pellegrini, who had succeeded Juárez Celman as president in 1890, and who, with Roca, had been the main architect of economic and political recovery at that time. Pellegrini became minister of the interior in Roca's second government after 1898. In 1901 he attempted to reach an agreement with a number of European banks for a series of major loans to consolidate the national debt. He offered as collateral government revenues from the tariffs on imported goods. Responses to this measure served to illustrate the rising political weight of the urban middle class. There was a sudden storm of opposition to Pellegrini, on the grounds that he was betraying national sovereignty by handing over control of State revenues to foreign banking interests. Eventually, because of this opposition, Roca was forced to disavow the whole plan, and thus to abandon his closest political associate. The episode had a traumatic effect on Pellegrini. He was suddenly made aware of the new importance and power of public opinion. In the final five years of his life before 1906, he joined the reformers and added his voice to those calling for a readaptation of the political systems.[14]

It was Pellegrini who had most bearing on Figueroa Alcorta's decision to destroy Roca's influence, and in doing so pave the way for reform. The basis of Pellegrini's position, which the majority of reformers shared, was that the elite was mistaken in relying on a closed political structure upheld by repression. A better course would be to establish a new conservative party with mass support, thus following the example of other western countries. If it could do this,

[13] See below, chapter 4.

[14] The episode is recounted in Rodolfo Puiggrós, *El yrigoyenismo* (Jorge Alvarez, Buenos Aires, 1965) pp. 30–4.

it could buttress the conservative structure with a measure of popular consensus and mass support. It would thus be able to rule without repression, and without the fear of revolt. Pellegrini was now convinced that the old trading-of-favours system with the elite was no longer serving its objectives. It was insensitive to popular pressure, and could no longer be relied upon to maintain the unity of the elite:

> Our aim should not merely to be to seek public jobs, which are of use only to those who fill them, but to organise a disciplined political movement with a fixed objective. Our banner is today at hand: the restoration of representative government. What we ought to do is start asking and demanding from the government respect for the fundamental rights of the citizen. This will allow us to organise ourselves and fight for our interests.[15]

The Sáenz Peña Law

Besides destroying Roca's influence Figueroa Alcorta also arranged to be succeeded by one of the leaders of the reform movement, Roque Sáenz Peña. Under his auspices the reform was finally carried out in 1912. The legislation of 1912 took the form of two separate bills. The first of these authorised the preparation of a new electoral roll, free from past impurities and inaccuracies. The second measure introduced the secret ballot and established a new system of voting.

The character of the Sáenz Peña Law, as the reform became known, highlighted the concern for political stability among members of the elite who supported it. In the decision to introduce the reform the Radicals played a key role. In organising his cabinet in 1910, Sáenz Peña made a final desperate effort to buy off their opposition by the offer of a post to the Radical leader, Hipólito Yrigoyen. But Yrigoyen, as he had done on frequent occasions in the past, preferred to remain independent.[16] There seemed no other way to eliminate Radical opposition, and the danger of a Radical coup, except by making the political concessions they were demanding. Before 1912 Sáenz Peña believed that the Radicals might eventually take power through revolution, but he found it hard to believe that they could win in open elections. The introduction of the new legislation was thus initially intended by Sáenz Peña himself

[15] Quoted in Carlos Ibarguren, *La historia que he vivido* (Eudeba, Buenos Aires, 1969), p. 194.

[16] This incident is described in Ramón J. Cárcano, *Mis primeros ochenta años* (Pampa y cielo, Buenos Aires, 1965), pp. 287–94.

to act as a further barrier to the Radicals, to isolate them from popular or elite support, but in part to placate them and dissuade them from once more taking the path of revolution.[17]

Much of this was apparent in Sáenz Peña's inaugural address in 1910. It was necessary, he said, to continue the country's development along pre-established lines, but this could only be done once the political problem was solved:

> Let us not deceive ourselves; if our self-aggrandisement has begun, it is because we have been able to uphold the authority of the national government, inspiring a sense of security, peace, tranquillity and confidence. I shall not support oppression, but I condemn the revolutions which occur unless it is used or which result from it. I do not believe we can consolidate our present position except by perfecting ourselves in a climate of order.[18]

Sáenz Peña's solution was broadly the same as Pellegrini's some years before. He felt that the elite should democratise the country's institutions and organise a majoritarian popular conservative party. In this fashion the elite could legitimise its control and eliminate the more dangerous expressions of popular dissent, such as that posed by the immigrant working class. One of the president's leading supporters, Carlos Ibarguren, who soon afterwards became minister of education, wrote in 1912, during the congressional debates on the reform: 'We have nothing to fear of social struggle or democratic conflict if there are compensatory forces and the means to restrain excesses. Extremism will fail if the conservative forces, at the present discordant and apprehensive, organise a legitimate form of self-defence.'[19]

Besides the search for 'compensatory forces' to act on the elite's behalf, the government was also concerned to inculcate a tradition of democratic participation and to train the citizenry in the exercise of the vote. This was seen as a means to create an educated and moderate public opinion. The abuses and deficiencies of the old system were repeatedly mentioned in the debates: 'There are three principal ills in the country in terms of

17 Ibid. p. 303. Cárcano paraphrased Sáenz Peña's calculations in the following way: 'The Radicals may take power by assault, by means of the *coup* that they have always been trying, but this would be difficult in free elections. The National Autonomist Party (P.A.N.), which is a tradition and an historic force, rules without opposition in the whole country.'

18 Roque Sáenz Peña, *Discursos del Dr Roque Sáenz Péna al asumir la presidencia de la Nación* (Buenos Aires, 1910), p. 40.

19 Ibarguren, p. 229.

elections: the abstention of the citizenry, fraud in the elections, and the corruption which takes away the spirit of citizenship from the voter. And there is a fourth constitutional abuse which is the cause of all the others – the People does not choose . . .'[20] The reformers felt that although it was possible to use bribery to win elections with a very small electorate, such techniques for suborning loyalties would no longer play any significant part if the electorate was expanded from a few hundred to several hundred thousand.

Another key objective was the fostering of 'modern' political parties, capable of providing for the coherent articulation of different interest groups. The reformers defined this as 'organic democracy' and contrasted it with the old system of fraud, force, limited participation and 'personalist' party organisations, based on patronage and pragmatic factional alliances: 'One of the principal deficiencies of Argentine politics is the lack of parties. Parties are necessary; a democracy without parties is instability, arbitrary 'personalism', and our electoral legislation ought to . . . promote the birth and organisation of great political associations.'[21]

Fuller representation and participation, an increase in voting turnouts, and the formation of popular parties reflecting 'concrete tendencies' were all aims of the reform measures. The hope was to institutionalise political participation, and to establish the ballot box as the main arbiter of political change. Another of the leading features of the reform was its introduction of compulsory voting. Again this made apparent the concern with dissident groups. In his message to Congress proposing this form of voting, Sáenz Peña declared:

> The collectivity, which arms the citizen with the right to vote, has the right in return to demand of him not to ignore this right, because upon it depends the good or bad exercise of State administration. If we can overcome the inertia of the majority, unruly minorities, which are present in every country, will never endanger the institutional or political order, nor the foundations of social order.[22]

In this fashion it would be possible to supplant the Anarchist 'professional agitators', which had been the source of so much trouble to previous governments. A complementary feature of the legislation was its provisions for the incorporation of minorities into the parliamentary

[20] Indalecio Gómez, minister of the interior. *Diario de Sesiones*, Cámara de Diputados, Vol. 3, 1911, p. 150.
[21] Ibid. p. 177 (Lucas Ayarragaray).
[22] Presidential message to Congress. Ibid. Vol. 1, 1911, p. 807.

system. This was to be done by means of a device known as the Incomplete List. Representatives for each jurisdiction were to be divided between the party winning the majority of the popular vote and the party which ran second. The distribution of seats was to be carried out in a proportion of two to one. Thus in a province which held a total of twenty-one seats in the National Chamber of Deputies, fourteen would go to the majority party and seven to the runner-up. Likewise in the Senate the majority party would acquire two seats and the runner-up one. One of the deputies in the National Congress described the aim of this in the following way: 'The system of the Incomplete List ... has the advantage that it will tend to simplify the parties, and in making them bigger, it will both increase the size of the majorities and increase the size of the minorities.'[23]

The confidence of the elite in the new system was also buttressed by the fact that the Sáenz Peña Law was not a fully democratic measure. It enfranchised only the natives and this meant, since the foreigners made up the bulk of the working class, a form of class discrimination in the concession of the vote. In effect, the Radicals and the 'dependent' middle classes were to be given a share in government, but the immigrants and the workers were to be kept out as before. There was at this point a growing feeling that if the Radicals could be won over, the real danger to the political system would be eliminated. Sáenz Peña himself gave warm support to the following statement, which may be taken as an illustration of the reformers' attitudes towards Radicalism at this point:

> For twenty years there has existed in the country an organised, popular, party, espousing the liberty of the suffrage and openly supporting revolution as the only way to fulfil its ideals ... For a generation both government and nation have lived in a constant state of having either to suppress rebellion, or in fear that rebellion is about to break out ... A change in the electoral system is to adopt at this critical hour the only policy which the country is united upon: the policy of disarmament, to eliminate abstention from the elections and rebellion; to incorporate each active political force into the electoral process.[24]

So far as the workers went, the main aim was to allow for the limited growth of the Socialist Party in Buenos Aires, to act as an escape valve for working class demands, in such a way as to reduce the appeal of

[23] Ibid. Vol. 3, 1911, p. 122 (Juan Fonrouge).
[24] Ibid. Vol. 3, 1911, p. 160 (Ramon J. Cárcano).

Anarchism. An impression of this comes from a statement by Benito Villanueva, one of the most powerful, archetypal representatives of the old oligarchy: 'There is nothing more urgent at present than to open up an escape valve and allow two or three Socialists into the Congress, especially during these moments of working class unrest, when legislation on strikes and working regulations are about to be discussed.'[25]

But the reformers displayed no willingness at all to abandon the methods of controlling the workers, which had been employed since the turn of the century. Referring to the Law of Residence, which allowed the government to deport undesirable immigrants, Sáenz Peña declared in his inaugural speech in 1910: 'I sustain that the Law of Residence is a right of sovereignty, which is never applied against men of goodwill and only against those who threaten social order, and which should be defended actively and energetically whenever the government judges it is being attacked.'[26]

Nor did Sáenz Peña have anything radically new to deal with the working class problem. In his inaugural speech he proposed nothing beyond an end to State propaganda in Europe encouraging immigration, the encouragement of privately organised workers' housing schemes, and superficial attempts to reduce the cost of living.[27] These suggestions virtually ignored the key problems of wages and social mobility. It was easy to propose an end to State propaganda promoting immigration at a time when spontaneous factors were adding up to 200,000 persons to the labour force annually. Equally it was rather misleading to talk of ending a shortage of houses for the workers in the federal capital, when the prosperity of the agricultural sector was causing a vast boom in the urban land market and a rapid inflation of rental values. During the discussion of the reforms in Congress no parallel steps were taken to facilitate the acquisition of citizenship and political rights by the immigrants. Indeed, in the course of the debates, members of Congress supported demands to ensure stricter requirements for the granting of citizenship to immigrants convicted under criminal or anti-Anarchist legislation.[28]

Thus in spite of its emphasis on the formation of mass political parties and the incorporation of minorities, the Sáenz Peña Law did little more

[25] Ibid. Senate, Vol. 2, 1911, p. 338. The Socialist Party is discussed in chapter 4.
[26] Ibid. Senate, Vol. 2, 1911, p. 338.
[27] Sáenz Peña, p. 60.
[28] See proposals to this effect by Manuel Montes de Oca, Diputados, *Diario de Sesiones*, Vol. 1, 1911, pp. 373–6.

than open up the political system to the native-born, property-owning middle class groups and to the minority of workers who had also been born in the country. The new system was a minimum concession to restore political stability and protect the interests of the elite. It was an act of calculated retreat by the ruling class. In its desire to escape fraud, and the long-established corrupt patronage system upon which the oligarchy had operated, the reform bore all the hallmarks of progressive liberal legislation. It did not, however, modify either the position of the immigrants or of the workers.

The aftermath of reform

Sáenz Peña himself was only able for a short time to assess the effects of the reforms, for he died in August 1914. During these two years his measures did appear to be enjoying great success. The Radicals and Socialists began to take part in the elections, and the threat of rebellion diminished. After a major spate of repression in 1910, the Anarchist movement began to decline, and there were no more serious general strikes. Only in one respect did the reforms fail immediately. Because of lingering regional rivalries, and because no precise formula could be agreed on to win the support of the urban sectors, the national popular conservative party the Sáenz Peña group had aspired for failed to materialise. Instead it was Radicalism which began to flourish, to become by 1916 the most powerful political movement in the country.

Under Sáenz Peña's immediate successor, Victorino de la Plaza, there were some second thoughts about the reforms in view of the decline of the conservative parties. Plaza himself regarded the new parties as 'extreme' and declared in an ambiguously threatening fashion in a message to Congress in 1914: 'One ought to decide whether there is in the new law something antithetical to the traditional parties and whether it promotes and strengthens the advanced parties . . .'[29]

But finally the objectives which had initially prompted reform triumphed. Between 1912 and 1916 the elite's attitude towards Radicalism gradually changed. In the past it had been regarded as a Girondin party, whose success would merely leave the way open for the immigrant Anarchist Jacobins. After 1912 there emerged a fuller recognition that many of the Radicals' own leaders were themselves landowners and com-

[29] Quoted in Ibarguren, p. 267. This work also contains a detailed account of attempts by the conservatives to organise themselves into a national party.

mitted, as the oligarchy had been, to defending elite interests. Increasingly, instead of viewing Radicalism as a disruptive, insurrectionary force, important segments of the elite came to see it as the vehicle they had been searching for to unite the elite and middle class groups and to bar the way to the immigrant working class masses. Referring to rumours in 1915 that Plaza was considering abandoning the Sáenz Peña Law, a leading member of the one of the conservative factions, Carlos Rodríguez Larreta declared:

> Why is it that the conservatives are bent on preventing the Radicals from establishing control over the administration? They represent the same interests and principles as we do. We should let the People have its way, because if not we run the risk of attracting it to the really advanced parties.[30]

For the first time, presidential elections were held in 1916 under the auspices of the new legislation. The result was a victory for the Radicals. The election left the old conservatives parties with a lesser hold on the national and provincial offices they had dominated previously. They were compelled to exercise whatever direct authority they retained through Congress, and particularly through the Senate, where a nine-year tenure of office protected the majority they had won before 1912.

Yet while the elite was being forced to release its direct grip on the state, the Sáenz Peñz Law had done nothing to influence the distribution of economic power. It was this which 'conservatism' primarily represented: the rural *estanciero*, the financial and business power of Buenos Aires, the link with European markets and with British supplies of capital investment, and an exploitative and repressive attitude towards the working class. Whether the reforms would provide any permanent solution now hinged upon the extent to which the elite could afford to make further concessions. To both the middle and working classes a mere change in the institutional structure was not enough. They wanted these changes to provide the basis for a more equitable system of distribution.

[30] Quoted in Jorge A. Mitre, 'Presidencia de Victorino de la Plaza', Academia Nacional de la Historia, *Historia argentina contemporánea, 1862–1930*, Vol. 1, Section 2 (El Ateneo, Buenos Aires, 1965), p. 241. The same point is made also by Luis Alberto Romero. See L. A. Romero *et alia*, *El radicalismo* (Carlos Pérez, Buenos Aries, 1969), p. 39. The same transition can be traced in the position of the influential Buenos Aires newspaper, *La Prensa*, which by 1916 was supporting the Radicals.

CHAPTER 3

The rise of Radicalism, 1891–1916

The Unión Cívica Radical, the Radical Party, played a key role in pressuring the conservative elite into reform measures in 1912. Four years later, when the party won control of the presidency, a different era began in Argentina politics. Radicalism was the first major national political party in Argentina and among the earliest of the Latin American populist movements.[1] Its central importance stemmed from its role as an agent of political integration, pursuing the broad objectives established by the reformers of 1912. In view of its later relationship with the urban middle class, it is important to see, however, that the party began in the 1890s as a minority splinter group from within the elite. Only later, after the turn of the century, did it develop its populist features when it evolved into a coalition movement between the elite sector and important segments of the middle classes. In the twenty-five years between 1891 and 1916 there were four major stages in the party's development: 1891–6, 1896–1905, 1905–12 and 1912–16. Its growth may be traced during these different periods from a number of separate perspectives: the party's composition and the extent of its popular support, and secondly its organisational features and regional connections.

The origins of Radicalism

During the first period up to 1896, the party was led by Leandro N. Alem. This coincided with the rebellions of the 1890s when a succession of attempts were made to overthrow the national government. The party's origins are to be found in the economic depression and in the political dissent against Juárez Celman in 1890. In 1889 organised opposition to Juárez appeared in Buenos Aires in the form of the Unión Cívica de la Juventud (the Youth Civic Union), which in the following year, as it attracted wider support, became known simply as the Unión Cívica, the Civic Union. In July 1890, the Civic Union organised a rebellion against

[1] For an historiographical note on the party see Appendix 2.

Juárez in the city of Buenos Aires. This failed to capture control over the national government, but it did force Juárez's resignation. In 1891 the Unión Cívica split over its relationship with the new government led by Carlos Pellegrini, and out of the division came the Unión Cívica Radical led by Alem. For the next five years until his death, Alem tried unsuccessfully to capture control by revolution. The failure of both the Unión Cívica and the Radicals in the early 1890s was caused by the fact that once Juárez Celman had resigned, Roca's faction of the P.A.N., supported by Pellegrini, broadened its support and won over a majority of the elite. The opposition parties were unable to counteract this by achieving popular support.

The Civic Union's rebellion in 1890 has often been referred to as the first popular revolution in Argentine history. But this is a rather misleading picture. Although the rebels organised themselves into a civilian militia, their real strength derived from their support in the army. It was a sudden retraction of support by the military commander of the rebel forces, General Manuel Campos, which caused the rebellion to fail in July 1890. Also the origin of the Civic Union, out of which Radicalism grew a year later, is not to be found so much in the mobilisation of the popular sectors, but in that of segments of the elite. Their role may be traced to the resentments against Juárez among different political factions, based on the province of Buenos Aires, because of their exclusion from office and access to State patronage. This common condition of exclusion from the benefits of power, and a patrician background, was apparent in many of the Civic Union's manifestos: 'The Unión Cívica is the condensation ... of all the country's leading interests which have not been absorbed by the governing party.'[2]

The Unión Cívica, out of which Radicalism grew, was thus an expression of Juárez Celman's failure to establish a stable relationship between the politicised elite sectors. Some of these groups had also opposed Roca during his administration before 1886, but they acquired most of their support as a result of the struggle against Juárez. The first major nucleus in the coalition was made of university groups. These had organised the original Youth Civic Union of 1889. They were not members of the urban middle class, but for the main part the younger sons of patrician families, whose careers in politics and administration were placed in

[2] 'Declaration of Principles of the Unión Cívica', *El Argentino*, 1 July 1890. Reproduced in *Hipólito Yrigoyen, Pueblo y gobierno* (ed. Roberto Etchepareborda), Vol. 1 'Intransigencia' (Raigal, Buenos Aires, 1951), p. 31.

jeopardy by Juárez's sudden shift towards Córdoba in the apportionment of government favours.

A second group in the coalition was a number of personality-dominated political factions, which controlled politics in the city and over much of the province of Buenos Aires. Some of these had also opposed Roca, though again their main strength came from their opposition to Juárez. As one contemporary commentator put it, they were the 'unemployed politicians', whose main common denominator was also their exclusion from office.[3] There were two major sub-groups among them. One, representing major commercial and exporting interests in the city of Buenos Aires, was led by General Bartolome Mitre. The other was led by Leandro N. Alem. Among his followers there were a number of landowners, though Alem was a city political boss, whose fortunes had previously rested upon his ability to organise elections among the creole voters.[4] Thirdly there were a number of clerical groups, which opposed Juárez because of some recent anti-clerical legislation, the chief of which was the Civil Matrimony Law (Law 2393). Finally there was some support for the Civic Union among the 'popular sectors' of the city of Buenos Aires. These were mainly commercial retailers and petty industrial artisans.

However, in spite of evidence of the presence of this last group, the Civic Union was closely controlled by the patrician elements, with the Catholics and middle class groups subordinate to them: 'Our party has arisen as a result of a spontaneous expression of public opinion, having at its vanguard the youth and at its head the most distinguished and honourable personalities of the country.'[5]

This also found reflection in the Civic Union's position on the economic front. Although it attempted to draw political capital from the effects of the economic depression and the financial crisis on the urban sectors, its chief concern with the depression was the manner in which it exposed Juárez's monopolistic practices in the distribution of agricultural credits.[6] There was no trace of economic nationalism in its position. Its only concrete proposal for financial recovery was the negotiation of a bridging loan with

[3] 'Políticos en disponabilidad'. Quoted in Roberto Etchepareborda, *La revolución argentina del noventa* (Eudeba, Buenos Aires, 1951), p. 31.

[4] For an account of Alem's career as a city politican see Manuel Gálvez, *Vida de Hipólito Yrigoyen*, 5th edn. (Tor, Buenos Aires, 1959), pp. 30–45.

[5] Etchepareborda, *Pueblo y gobierno*, Vol. 1, p. 31.

[6] Adolfo Casablanca, 'La traición a la revolución del 90', *Todo es Historia*, Year 2, No. 17 (September 1968), p. 11.

the British financial house, Baring Brothers. Discussing the allocation of offices in the provisional government, which it was planned would take over after the July rebellion, one of the Civic Union's leaders, Aristóbalo Del Valle, declared:

> It was my opinion that we ought to trust the provisional government to Dr Vicente F. López because ... I trust that his competence and his friendship with Baring Brothers would help us save the country from bankruptcy, while the country was being constitutionally reorganised ... [and also] because I thought it convenient to offer the conservative elements of the country the guarantee of age, national respectability, and tradition.[7]

The novelty of the Civic Union lay, however, in its attempt to mobilise the urban population in its support. It accused the government of making clandestine paper money emissions, and it began to support the introduction of representative government against Juárez's 'dictatorship'. The campaign was not notably successful. The Civic Union's popular support was extremely fitful, and failed to develop on an institutional footing. Although at the height of the depression its public meetings were well attended, and there was an outburst of popular jubilation when Juárez finally resigned, there was little active popular support during the rising of July 1890. Disenchantment with the government seemed more an ephemeral expression of the effects of the depression than an autonomous demand for the institutional changes the Civic Union was offering. As one of the movement's youth leaders, Francisco Barroeteveña, put it, the popular sectors gave their support 'less to defend their rights than to protect their properties'.[8] Thus the impetus which came from the patrician groups to form a popular coalition failed against the lukewarm response of the city's population.

Also, although Alem tried to raise support for the coalition outside Buenos Aires, its influence was almost exclusively limited to the city and its environs. Outside Buenos Aires the July revolutionaries were unable to organise anything more than minor street demonstrations. Their plan was to capture the central government first and then take over the provinces.

Since the challenge offered by the Civic Union was so weak, the July 1890 revolt failed, and instead of major changes taking place, the way was left open for a solution by a simple adjustment to the distribution

[7] Etchepareborda, *La revolución del noventa*, p. 43.

[8] Etchepareborda, *La revolución del noventa*, p. 80.

of power within the elite. After the fall of Juárez the new president, Pellegrini, simply bought off the most powerful groups in the Civic Union through a different system of office allocation. Mitre, for example, was quite happy with a compromise of this sort. Pellegrini also took swift steps on the economic front which effectively defused popular discontent. These successes reflected the continuing durability of the highly elitist, bargaining mould of traditional politics.

By 1891 the process of reorganisation within the elite was virtually complete. Each faction with any real influence was drawn into contact with the government. Only the powerless groups remained excluded. At this point the Unión Cívica Radical came into being. Alem and his group found themselves excluded from Pellegrini's scheme and thus forced to continue the search for popular support and a mass base. Alem denounced the covenants (*acuerdos*) between Pellegrini and Mitre, defected from the Civic Union, and declared his commitment to 'radical' democracy.

The new party was made up largely of estranged patrician groups, disqualified for one reason or another by their previous associations from joining up either with Mitre, Pellegrini or with Roca. In regional or status terms there was very little to differentiate them from their rivals. At most they gave the impression of newer wealth and of the greater distance of their landholdings from the port of Buenos Aires.[9] In 1895 the party's branch in the province of Buenos Aires was described as being composed of '. . . energetic young men and men of fortune from our historic aristocracy'.[10]

For the next five years Alem struggled vainly for popular support and for the means to organise a successful rebellion. But popular discontent continued to subside, and his attempts to recruit the support of landed groups outside Buenos Aires ended in virtual failure. The oligarchy managed to remain united. In 1891 and 1893 the Radicals organised revolts in the provinces, but they all collapsed quickly. Only in the province of Santa Fe in 1893 was there any marked support for

[9] For an exhaustive review of the composition of the Radical Party's leadership up to 1916 see Ezequiel Gallo and Silvia Sigal, 'La formación de los partidos políticos contemporáneos – La U.C.R. (1891–1916)', in Torcuato Di Tella *et alia*, pp. 162–70.

[10] *La Prensa*, 6 February 1895. Quoted in Etchepareborda, *Pueblo y gobierno*, Vol. 1, p. 89.

them among the middle class groups. On this occasion a rising of Alem's supporters in the city of Santa Fe was accompanied by a march on the city by the Swiss colonists from the districts of Humboldt and Esperanza. Later this same area formed the backbone of Radical support in the province, and for a long time it was the only part of the country where the Radicals genuinely penetrated beyond the upper landowner groups.[11]

Thus, against all Alem's efforts, the residues of support inherited by the Radicals from the Civic Union ebbed away, leaving them by 1896 as no more than a minor splinter faction at the edge of the political spectrum. Their failure during these years can be summarised as follows:

First, it was clear that the middle class groups were at this time politically motivated only during periods of extreme economic crisis, such as in 1890. Recovery in the 1890s dissipated unrest and allowed for the restoration of the oligarchy on the basis of the *acuerdos* between the 'personalist' factions. Whatever urban support Alem had came mainly from the old creole groups rather than the new middle class based on the immigrants and their descendants.

Secondly, the national and revolutionary image the Radicals attempted to cultivate suffered from their involvement in the petty quarrels over subsidies, grants and benefits in the provinces among different landed factions. This created a rift between groups genuinely seeking to supersede the tradition of 'personalism' and jobbery, and those for whom this system was a matter of life-blood. The most significant break at this level occurred with the foundation of the *partido socialista* by Juan B. Justo in 1894.[12] Although the Radicals tried to escape the stigma of 'personalism', they were never able to do so fully. In spite of its commitment to representative democracy, Radicalism remained in many respects a traditional party struggling for control over the State in order to reward its own supporters.

Thirdly, the loss of support among the landed groups did not stop with the division of the Unión Cívica in 1891. Factions within the Radical Party were also bought off by strategically planned patronage hand-outs by successive national governments. The lesson of Juárez Celman's downfall had been fully imbibed. The ruling oligarchy increased its

[11] Cf. Solberg, *Immigration and Nationalism*, pp. 118–9. The revolts in Santa Fe in 1893 were precipitated by a fall in wheat prices and by the introduction of a provincial tax on the farm interest. For an excellent, detailed analysis see Ezequiel Gallo, 'Colonos en armas. Las revoluciones radicales en la provincia de Santa Fe, 1893' (forthcoming)

[12] See below, chapter 4.

stability by eliminating its leading Radical opponents through the distribution of government jobs. The same technique of cooperation was used with the university groups.

Finally, the strength of the party suffered as a result of the internecine rivalries between Alem and other leaders. This was apparent as early as 1893, when Alem's planned national rising failed to materialise owing to the lack of coordination among some of the provincial Radical leaders. In the province of Buenos Aires Alem was opposed by his own nephew, Hipólito Yrigoyen, and his intrigues to establish his own control were partly responsible for Alem's death by suicide in 1896.

1896–1905

During the major part of the period between Alem's death and 1905, Radicalism ceased to be important.[13] The central features of the years up to 1900 were first the emergence of Yrigoyen as Alem's successor, and secondly the reestablishment of the province of Buenos Aires as the party's main axis. This was important because, when the party did finally begin to expand, the group in Buenos Aires led by Yrigoyen maintained its overall control, progressively incorporating the provincial branches of the party into the national organisation.

In 1901, the oligarchy split once more when Pellegrini resigned from the government. From this time onwards there were signs of the growing politicisation of the urban middle class groups. At this juncture Radicalism began once more to surface.

Accompanying the unrest against Pellegrini's scheme to offer the customs revenues as collateral to the European banks in 1901 were new signs of disturbance in the universities, which led to a succession of strikes among the students. In the 1890s the student rebels belonged to the creole ruling class. Ten years later an important number of them were recruited from among the urban sons-of-immigrants group. Here the struggle was not about relations between the government and the landed elite of Buenos Aires, but about access to the urban professions.

The student strikes followed from attempts by the creole governing bodies in the universities to restrict the intake of students of immigrant descent.[14] The result was a series of campaigns for the democratisation

[13] In 1898 the Radicals again split when one of their leaders, Bernardo de Irigoyen, decided to run in the elections in the province of Buenos Aires. The leadership of Hipólito Yrigoyen began at this point.

[14] Cf. Tulio Halperín Donghi, *Historia de la Universidad de Buenos Aires* (Eudeba, Buenos Aires, 1962), pp. 110–20.

of the universities' structure and curricula. In succeeding years the student body, especially in Buenos Aires, evolved into an important urban pressure group supporting the introduction of representative government in order to change the universities.

With these more propitious signs Yrigoyen began, around 1903, to plot yet another rebellion. He revived his links with the provinces and began once again to undertake the foundation of party clubs in the city and province of Buenos Aires, in Córdoba, Santa Fe, Mendoza and Entre Rios. Dissent was still limited, however, to certain specific small groups. Besides the students, the only other important area of unrest before 1905 was among junior officers in the army, who were also struggling against the creole elite for access to more senior positions. Yrigoyen therefore turned to the organisation of a military *coup*. He won considerable support among the student groups and it was significant that he planned junior officer groups to staff the vanguard of the movement.

But the attempted Radical *coup d'état*, which finally occurred in February, 1905, was even more of a fiasco than the ones which preceded it. It made apparent that, although the Radicals had had some success in winning military support, the senior commands of the army still supported the incumbent conservative governments. Nor did the revolt prompt any answering spark in the urban population of Buenos Aires. Also it was tactically inept, and the government of the day had no difficulty in suppressing it and capturing the majority of its leaders.[15]

Yet although the *coup* failed, it had vitally important long-term effects. It served to remind the oligarchy that Radicalism was far from dead. From this time forward successive governments were haunted by the constant fear that the Radicals were engaged in clandestine intrigues to overthrow them. The other positive effect of the revolt was that it presented Radicalism to a new generation, for which the events of the 1890s had become dim and distant events. From the ignominy of total defeat the process began, which was to culminate in Yrigoyen's victory in the presidential elections of 1916.

The growth of party organisation and ideology

Between the abortive *coup* of 1905 and the Sáenz Peña Law in 1912 the Radicals made rapid strides in the recruitment of popular support. Their

[15] For accounts of the 1905 rebellion see Gálvez, pp. 110–17; Ricardo Caballero, *Yrigoyen, la conspiración civil y militar del 4 de febrero de 1905* (Raigal, Buenos Aires, 1951).

provincial and local organisations this time did not disappear, as they had done after earlier revolts. Instead they began to expand. During these years the Radicals acquired a locally based intermediate leadership composed mainly of the sons-of-immigrants groups. The bulk of the party's middle class leaders, who acquired great importance after 1916, affiliated during the years between 1906 and 1912. Most of them were urban professionals with university degrees. From henceforth, too, the party's public acts and demonstrations began to command important popular support. Around 1908 the local organisations ceased calling themselves 'clubs' and began to be known as 'committees'. Their previously cell-like and clandestine activities disappeared, as they developed into management agencies in the task of popular mobilisation.

The growth of Radicalism in the early twentieth century was closely related to the process of social stratification which concentrated high-status leader groups among the urban middle classes in tertiary occupations.[16] Besides the university groups, there were also examples of the Radicals recruiting their intermediate leaders from among former failed businessmen. This suggested a growing tendency within the urban middle class to seek, through politics, the wealthy and prestigious positions which were becoming increasingly unavailable by any other means.[17] Also by this time the educational problem had reached critical proportions, as the limitations to the growth of the industrial sector engendered cultural reinforcements to the focussing of mobility aspirations on the bureaucracy and the professions. Referring to the situation in the primary schools in 1909, President Figueroa Alcorta remarked:

> It is a fact established by the specialists that primary education is not functioning in the way it should ... [It] gets hold of the sons of the working classes like a malignant fever, who leave school disdaining common labour and aspiring to a higher level of existence, for which they are ill-equipped either by their mental resources or by their backgrounds. This deviation on the part of the popular classes from the manual arts and employments, industry and commerce, towards the teaching profession or bureaucratic positions can lead us into a real social crisis.[18]

This was the central difference between Yrigoyen's position after 1905 and Alem's fifteen years or so earlier. In the 1890s Alem had been operat-

[16] See chapter 1, pp. 26–34.

[17] For further comments on the origins of the party's intermediate leadership see David Rock, 'Machine politics in Buenos Aires and the Argentine Radical Party, 1912–1930', *Journal of Latin American Studies*, Vol. 4, Part 2 (November 1972), pp. 233–56.

[18] Quoted in Darío Cantón, *El parlamento argentino en épocas de cambio, 1890, 1916 y 1946* (Instituto Torcuato Di Tella, Buenos Aires, 1966), pp. 122–3.

ing before these conditions of strain had reached a critical point. The support he had aimed for lay among the creole groups in Buenos Aires. Yrigoyen, by contrast, tailored his appeal to the native-born sons-of-immigrants groups, employed for the main part in the tertiary sector. The new appeal of representative government lay in its relevance to these groups who blamed the creole elite for their difficulties in securing further social mobility beyond the petty industrial and retailer activities of the first generation of immigrants.

The Radicals virtually ignored the immigrants themselves, but the sons of immigrants played a leading role in their sudden rise to popularity. In internal committee elections in the city of Buenos Aires in 1918, the first year for which there is an extant list available, 46% of the office-holders bore non-hispanic surnames. Were it possible to include the descendants of Spaniards, the second largest of the immigrant communities, the proportion would be much higher.[19]

The growing links between Radicalism and the sons-of-immigrants group was noted and commented on by observers:

> If instead of looking at the leaders, we look at the masses, it is easy to see that the supporters of the conservative parties are to be found in the rural livestock areas, dependent upon the rich bourgeoisie. On the other hand the Radical Party shows most vitality in the cities and in the agricultural districts, where the arrival of foreigners has allowed for the formation of a middle class of small businessmen and farmers, whose sons offer it important and enthusiastic support.[20]

The Radicals also began after 1905 to expand the volume of their propaganda. The positive content of Radical doctrine and ideology was very limited. It was little more than an eclectic and moralistic attack on the oligarchy, to which was appended the demand for the introduction of representative government. The party operated on the basis of a number of slogans, 'Abstention' from taking part in rigged elections, and 'Revolutionary Intransigence', the determination to reject the political system and establish representative democracy by revolution. Attempts have been made to give Radical doctrines a degree of philosophical respectability by relating them to the teachings of the nineteenth-century German writer, Peter Krause. The positive side of Radical ideology was

[19] For a full list of office-holders in Buenos Aires in 1918 see *La Epoca*, 1, 2 September 1918.

[20] Leopoldo Maupas, *Revista Argentina de Ciencias Políticas*, No. 4, p. 421. (Quoted in Cantón, 'Elecciones', p. 105.)

strongly impregnated with a heavily ethical and transcendentalist flavour. Its emphasis on the organic function of the State and social solidarity conflicted markedly with the positivism and Spencerianism of the oligarchy, and was often strongly reminiscent of Krause. The importance of these ideas, which were normally expressed in an incoherent and jumbled fashion, was that they did accord with the notion of a class alliance, which Radicalism came to represent. This would have been much more difficult by adopting positivist doctrines.[21]

Nevertheless, more important than what the Radicals said was what they did not say. One of the great characteristics of Radicalism during these and subsequent years was its avoidance of any explicit political programme. There were sound strategic reasons for this. Since the party was now a coalition, its leaders were ill disposed to throw away their opportunity to advance their influence by tying themselves to specific sectional interests. The aim always was to sidestep sectional differences and to enhance the party's aggregative and coalitional character. Yrigoyen declared in a written manifesto in 1909:

> The U.C.R. is not a party in the conventional sense. It is a conjunction of forces emerging from national opinion, forged and cast in the heat of public demands. To serve and achieve these, reestablishing the country's public life to prestige and integrity, is the programme it formulated at its commencement and the one it has followed up to the present. It has been, and always will be a centre for independent spirits ...[22]

This theme continued in subsequent years:

> The U.C.R. is not refractory to any legitimate interest; on the contrary its bosom nurtures all the elements which sincerely wish to offer themselves in the service of the country's true welfare. If it does not proclaim seductive and circumstantial platforms, this is because the only preoccupation of this great party is strict compliance with the sanctity of the vote ... [This] will continue to be its enduring inspiration, to save the nation from the evils of every order that the perversion of its institutions has produced.[23]

The 'evils of every order' were never defined explicitly. It was simply contended that the corruption of the oligarchy had restricted the country's development. The freedom and expansion of the country's productive

[21] See Carlos J. Rodríguez, *Yrigoyen – su revolución política y social* (Buenos Aires, 1943); Arturo Andrés Roig, *Los krausistas argentinos* (Cajica, Puebla, Mexico, 1969).

[22] Etchepareborda, *Pueblo y gobierno*, Vol. 1, p. 313.

[23] 'Manifesto of the U.C.R. to the People of the Republic, July 1915', Ibid. pp. 404–5.

forces could only be won by means of 'democracy'. The Radicals presented this as a virtual panacea for the country's problems. Their interpretation of the role of the State was largely negative. Most of them saw it merely as the agent clearing away the obstacles from, as they put it, the nation's destined course of 'self-realisation'.

> If [material progress] had not been adversely affected by disastrous administration, and if People and Government had been brought together in the administration of the institutions, the republic would be enjoying a preeminent position in the world in terms of its moral authority; and its riches would have attained inconceivable proportions compared with those it has now . . .[24]

This also made it clear that the Radicals were not aiming for changes in the country's economy. Rather they aimed to strengthen the primary export structure by promoting a spirit of cooperation between the elite and the urban sectors, which were now challenging their monopoly of political power. This became perhaps the most vital factor which encouraged the reformers of 1912 to feel that Radical policy represented no fundamental danger to the interests of the elite, and that the danger could be eliminated by making concessions on the issue of representative government.

Where the objectives of the reformers and the Radicals did diverge was that while the former were hoping for the emergence of a rejuvenated conservative party, the Radicals were committed to superseding their predecessors and to establishing themselves as a new governing elite. They had little interest in the type of multi-party system which the Saenz Peña Law introduced. Their aim was the creation of a new single-party State. This objective became one of the central features of Radical populism: 'The U.C.R. is the nation itself ... The labour we shall perform shall be on behalf of all the Argentines, living together the life of the nation; it is destined to set fundamental and great new directions to the hitherto perverted forward march and future of the Motherland.'[25]

Hipólito Yrigoyen

The other important novelty, which further emphasised the populist character the party had acquired by 1912, was Yrigoyen's emergence as a popular leader. Hipólito Yrigoyen's opposition to the oligarchy largely stemmed from the personal frustrations he had suffered at the

[24] Ibid. pp. 312–13.
[25] 'Manifesto of the U.C.R., 30 March 1916', Ibid.

hands of Roca and his supporters. He was born in 1852, the illegitimate son of a Basque blacksmith in the city of Buenos Aires. His political career began as early as 1873, when Alem, his uncle, obtained for him the post of police superintendent in the Balvanera district of the city. However, he was dismissed soon afterwards, having been accused of taking part in election-rigging. He reappeared again in 1879 as candidate for the Chamber of Deputies in the province of Buenos Aires, and in 1880 his political services were rewarded with a senior position in the National Council for Education. At this point Roca won the presidency, and both Alem and Yrigoyen found themselves barred from more senior offices. But when his term as provincial deputy ended in 1882, Yrigoyen left politics with sufficient capital to organise a business in cattle-fattening. Later he acquired considerable extensions of land in Buenos Aires and San Luis.[26]

By the time he joined the Unión Cívica in 1890, and began to manoeuvre for control over the Radical Party later in the 1890s, Yrigoyen was well practised in the accepted techniques of election management. His later moralistic hectoring of the oligarchy for its political corruption thus contained more than a touch of hypocrisy, since he himself had for a long time juggled for promotion and pickings in and among the 'personalist' factions, exploiting his connections to acquire considerable wealth. He was thus rather typical of the early Radicals, who looked to the creation of a popular coalition to restore their political fortunes.

Yrigoyen acquired his political prestige after 1900 in a rather strange fashion. Rather than appearing, as Alem had done, as a street politician constantly in the public eye, he cultivated the reputation of a figure of mystery. The singular feature of his political career was that, except on one minor occasion in the early 1880s, he never once made a public speech. To enhance his reputation as a man of the people, he occupied at different times a number of modest houses in the poorer areas of the city of Buenos Aires. This habit, and the secluded way in which he lived, won him the sobriquet of '*el Peludo*', a hairy kind of subterranean armadillo. On the other hand, he made every attempt to give himself an air of superior status. Among his supporters in Buenos Aires he was known as 'Dr Yrigoyen', although in fact he had never completed his degree.[27]

[26] The best account of Yrigoyen's early career is still Gálvez.

[27] Gálvez contains a full account of the various quirks of personality and the charismatic imagery associated with Yrigoyen. See also Felix Luna, *Yrigoyen* (Desarrollo, Buenos Aires, 1964); Horacio B. Oyhanarte, *El hombre* (Librería Mendesky, Buenos Aires,

Yrigoyen's style was personal contact and face-to-face bargaining. This allowed him to extend his grip over the party's organisation and to establish a highly effective chain of personal loyalties. Interspersed with this were occasional providential charity gestures, which were calculated to appeal to the Roman Catholic values of middle class society. The best known example of this came on the eve of the presidential elections in 1916, when it was announced that Yrigoyen would give his salary to charity if he were elected president. His only other apparent contribution to the party was a number of rambling manifestos, which cloaked the party's slogans in a veneer of moralistic rhetoric. An example is the following quotation, in which Yrigoyen attacked the various political factions associated with the oligarchy:

> The government and the opposition factions are the same thing. The opposition consists of elements thrown out of a temporarily ruling clique, which is simply awaiting the opportunity to get back among the spoils. The whole apparatus is a pile of decaying rubbish, where nothing is ever done for the sake of any healthy ideal, but always for the cheapest motives... These men are responsible for the greatest crimes ever committed in human history... This is the Argentine Bastille, against which my energies are pitted in harmony with the soul of the nation... All we need is clean elections. This is the indispensable condition for a decorous return to the exercise of electoral rights... And once this is done, it will become apparent what a difference there is between a nation choked by competing pressures, and one breathing in the fullness of its being and spreading its vitality to the common good.[28]

The constant reiteration of this theme won for Yrigoyen a tremendous personal reputation among the middle class groups. The more seedy details of his past career were largely forgotten. He became the party's prophet, and his apparent detachment from the day-to-day political struggle came to symbolise the party's dedication to the democratic ideal and the creation of a new republic. By 1912 Yrigoyen, who by this time was already sixty years old, had become a superb political tactician. He

Footnote 27 (continued)

1916); Juan M. Cacavelos and Julio Artayeta, *Hipólito Yrigoyen, paladín de la democracia* (Santa Theresita, Buenos Aires, 1939); Felipe Cárdenas, Jr, 'Hipólito Yrigoyen – ese enigmático conductor', *Todo es Historia*, Vol. 1, No. 2 (June 1967); Gabriel Del Mazo, *El radicalismo. Ensayo sobre su historia y doctrina* (Gure, Buenos Aires, 1957). All these works have in common a tendency to accept myth for reality, although there can be no doubt that Yrigoyen was the great popular political figure of his generation.

[28] Etchepareborda, *Pueblo y gobierno*, Vol. 1, p. 110–11.

gradually pushed the oligarchy into reform with the threat of a new rebellion, while expanding his control over the party by his great abilities of personal persuasion and mass organisation.

Yrigoyen's personal style gave Radicalism much of its early moral and ethical flavour which allowed it to expand on a wave of emotional euphoria. It also became an important instrument in reconciling the diverse groups which Radicalism had come to represent. It became functional to the party's objective of reducing potential sources of division among its supporters, and maximising its support among different regional and class groups. In this fashion Radicalism developed less as a party in the strict sense than as a mass movement basing its appeal on a series of emotional attitudes. Describing the party in the turgid rhetoric for which he became famous, Yrigoyen declared: 'The majesty of the party's mission is sublime . . . Thus its labour endures and powerful is its strength; constantly it is strengthened and given vitality by the interplay of currents of opinion; it is a school and point of reference for successive generations and even forms the subject of children's dreams.'[29]

The strategy of mass mobilisation, 1912–16

By 1912, however, when the Radicals finally abandoned Abstention and began to put forward candidates for the elections, the party's organisational basis was still incomplete. There were by this time leaders and sub-leaders in most of the urban and rural areas of the pampas, and some outside this region. But the party still lacked centralised coordination and, in spite of Yrigoyen's rising prestige, a nationally recognised leadership. Some of the provincial branches of the party were still under the control of Yrigoyen's rivals from the days of Alem. Although the party committees were now established on a permanent footing, they were not yet, outside the major cities, comprehensively organised at the local level. The expansion of party organisation was thus the principal feature of the period between 1912 and 1916.

The advantage the Radicals had here was their vagueness. Their moral and heroic approach to political issues finally allowed them to present themselves to the electorate as a national party, above class and regional interests. Each one of their opponents stumbled against this obstacle. There were other popular parties, such as the Socialist Party

[29] Ibid. p. 125.

in the federal capital and the Progressive Democrat Party in Córdoba and Santa Fe. But none of them was able to transcend regional boundaries on any important scale. It was here that Yrigoyen demonstrated his political acumen. During the period after 1912 he managed to convert a provincially based confederate coalition into a coordinated national organisation. Although in the past the Radicals had emphasised their distaste for the *acuerdos* between different factions under the oligarchy, Yrigoyen now surreptitiously applied this same technique on a wide scale to win the support of the provincial landowners and their factional followings.

The great strength of Radicalism lay in its local organisation and the extensive contacts this provided between the party hierarchy and the electorate. In the major cities, especially in Buenos Aires, a system of ward bosses emerged similar to that in the United States. Although the Sáenz Peña Law ended the open purchase of votes, the Radicals quickly established a party patronage system which served equally as well to buy electoral support. In return for a biennial vote, the ward bosses, the *caudillos de barrio*, performed numerous petty services in the city and rural neighbourhoods. By establishing this close link with the *caudillos de barrio*, the original nucleus of the Radical Party, the landowners, were able gradually to escape the consequences of their lack of direct contact with the urban environment. Although the landowners had no control over urban jobs, many of the middle class sub-leaders were able to acquire sufficient influence and prestige in their local areas to overcome this weakness. They had some control over the allocation of housing, for example, through their association with the owners of the tenement blocks. Their relative affluence allowed them to provide loans for needy businessmen. Their own positions as lawyers or physicians brought them into close contact with different groups of the new electorate. They were also known for having some contact with the local police, and this allowed them to dispense immunities for all sorts of petty transgressions against the law. Along with the parish priest, the ward boss became, particularly in the city of Buenos Aires, the most powerful figure in the neighbourhood and the pivotal figure upon which the political strength and popularity of Radicalism depended.

Assisting in this task were the committees, which were organised geographically and hierarchically in different parts of the country. Thus there was a national committee, provincial committees, or in the case of the city of Buenos Aires the committee of the federal capital, precinct and ward committees, and, during election periods, a chain of subcommittees, serving smaller areas of each precinct. One of the great boasts of the Radicals was that their office-holders were elected in a free vote of party members, and this avoided the traditional 'personalist' practices of recruitment by cooptation or by ascriptive status. At least up to 1916, however, the more familiar pattern was for the national and provincial committees to be dominated by the landed groups, and the local committees by the middle classes. Recruitment to the former more often than not operated on a cooptive basis, but in the local committees open elections were held annually. These elected the president of the committee – in effect the ward boss – and a large number of subordinate officials. In each of the committees in the city of Buenos Aires there were as many as 108 committee officers elected every year. Often they remained in their posts for many years at a time, except where more than one ward boss figure was struggling for control over the party machine. In cases like this acute factional disputes were rife.

The size of the committees was exploited by the ward bosses to reward their supporters with mainly symbolic official positions, which could be used to extend loyalty and commitment to the party. The system also allowed the Radicals to extend their activities and connections over wide-ranging groups in each local neighbourhood. The party machine was thus able to acquire a great deal of penetration and flexibility. This increased its capacity to operate as a processing mechanism for the specialised demands within the electorate. By 1916 the Radicals' party organisation had evolved into an effective substitute for the lack of a precise political programme, and once more a convenient device to surmount objective conflicts of interests both between the landed and urban middle class groups, and among different groups of the electorate. A Radical pamphleteer, writing in 1915, described the role of the committees in the following way: 'this committee organisation . . . is responsible for constant propaganda, which puts the party in contact with the masses. Thus it serves to guarantee the emergence and selection of leaders of every level and maintains constant links among them.'[30]

The committee's activities reached a peak during election periods. In addition to the conventional street-corner meetings, the posting of manifestos and the distribution of party pamphlets, they were used as centres for the distribution of charity hand-outs to the voters. In Buenos Aires in 1915 and 1916, the committees founded children's cinemas, held

[30] R. Wilmart, 'El partido radical. Su ubicación', *Revista Argentina de Ciencias Políticas*, Vol. 10, pp. 367–76.

music-hall concerts, distributed Christmas gifts and supported the annual carnival celebrations. Many of the committees also founded medical clinics, legal advice centres and libraries, the cost of which was borne by active members. They also provided cheap foodstuffs, the *pan radical* and the *carne radical*, as they became known.[31] One committee in the parish of Balvanera Sur in the city of Buenos Aires reported on its activities in the year 1915. Free bread had been distributed for thirty-seven days as relief against a sudden rise in prices. The legal aid section of the committee had dealt with 172 separate cases. A thousand propaganda circulars and six thousand different political pamphlets had been issued, and the buildings of the parish disfigured with 7,400 posters.[32]

These activities emphasized some of the salient qualities the party acquired in the years after 1912. It had started in 1891 as very much an offshoot of the landowner factions; after 1905 it had penetrated the middle class groups in the cities; after 1912 it had become a fully-fledged, cross-regional popular party. But the party was still largely dominated by land-based groups. It thus maintained much of its initial character from the 1890s as a mass movement managed by upper status groups, rather than becoming a grass-roots movement operating in terms of pressures from below.

These strongly marked elements of management and manipulation from above were again partly evident in the amorphous character of the Radicals' ideology. This was pitched in such a way as to inspire commitment among the urban groups for a minimal form of redistribution, rather than for any novel constructive change: a different institutional structure, the channelling of government favours more in the direction of the urban middle classes, a greater sensitivity towards consumer interests, but the retention of the social system which had emerged from the primary exporting economy. Given the important role of landowners in the party, it is not surprising that Radicalism never became an advocate either of land reform or of industrialisation. Its conception of society was an eclectic amalgam of liberal and pluralist notions. It attacked the oligarchy on liberal grounds because, as Yrigoyen himself put it, it had failed to allow the nation 'to breathe in the fullness of its being'. But it also saw the community as a quasi-biological organism made up of functional interacting parts and reciprocal obligations. Thus

31 For detailed accounts of these activities see *El Radical*, 1915 and 1916; also Rock, 'Machine Politics'.

32 *El Radical*, 6 December 1915.

although the Radicals declaimed the liberal precept of individual competition, there was also in their position something of traditional conservative attitudes of hierarchy and social harmony.

This becomes more evident on a closer study of the party's politicisation techniques. As the activities of the committees illustrate, the Radicals relied a great deal on paternalistic measures. The main advantage of this was again that it could be used to break down divisive interest-group ties by atomising the electorate and individualising the voter. Also it reflected once more the tenuous connection between the main politicised groups, the landowners and the dependent middle classes, with productive urban employment opportunities. In many ways paternalism was a means simply to extend traditional patronage techniques at the mass level. Its further advantage was that it served to maximise the contacts between the party and the electorate, and to allow for a sharing of benefits, while minimising the actual content of the concessions which were made. Again the use of these techniques was an expression of the coalition nature of Radicalism, and of its attempt to find a common denominator among different class groups:

> Radical Bread, Radical Milk, Radical Meat, Radical Seed, and the Radical Homestead well demonstrate that the party desires a moderate form of state intervention to alleviate the rigours of economic *laissez-faire* on behalf of the poor, and for those who are unarmed in the struggle for survival; an intervention which the English fittingly term paternalism . . . It is time that a political party, organised on a national basis, should work towards these ends and carry them out efficiently.[33]

These were the guiding principles of Radical political management. They permitted the maintenance of a hierarchical structure of authority in the party, which duplicated the preexisting balance of power and structures of social status of Argentine society. They allowed for the coexistence of groups whose interests were sometimes at variance with one another. While offering certain opportunities to the urban middle classes, they maintained the hegemony of the landed interests. They won political influence for the Radicals in areas of the country dominated by quasi-feudal social relations, and yet they catalysed the aspirations of middle class idealists in the universities.

Largely because of its great ubiquity the Radical Party won the presidential elections of 1916. Of a total of 747,471 votes cast, the Radicals won 340,802, or 45.6%. Although this was not an outright

[33] R. Wilmart in Ibid. 18 August 1915.

majority, their nearest opponents, the Progressive Democrat Party, won only 99,000 votes, or 13%. For the purposes of the Electoral College, which as in the United States elected the president, the Radicals won outright in the federal capital, in Córdoba, Entre Rios, Mendoza, Santiago del Estero and Tucumán. They secured the minority representation in Buenos Aires, (where there was a strong local machine controlled by the conservative governor, Marcelino Ugarte), Catamarca, Corrientes, Jujuy, La Rioja, Salta and San Juan. The Radical vote was thus spread widely throughout the country.

Landowner–middle class relations

Nevertheless Radicalism was beset by some important problems. The chief of these was the competition among different factions of place-seekers in the party. When the Sáenz Peña Law was introduced, Yrigoyen himself at first opposed the abandonment of abstention from the elections. For some time he remained committed to rebellion, and to the freedom of action a successful rebellion would confer. However, the party itself thought differently, and eventually it was this view which prevailed.

Much of the pressure to take part in the elections came from the urban middle class groups.[34] This raised for the first time the question of the location of authority in the party, among the 'old' Radicals or among the middle class groups. It also raised the issue of where Yrigoyen himself stood, with the *estanciero* groups which had supported the Radical Party in the 1890s or with the *parvenu* groups in the party's middle leadership. For the moment the Radicals' middle class supporters were controlled by the patrician groups which had emerged through the Union Cívica in the early 1890s. Instead of founding a purely middle class party, the middle class had entered into an alliance with segments of the landed aristocracy. But no one could be sure that this arrangement would be permanent. The more the middle class grew, the more it could be expected to develop its own separate interests and be less prepared to accede to its subordinate position. Already in 1912 there were some who prophesied that this would eventually lead to the break-up of Radicalism as a coalition:

[34] For Santa Fe, see Victor Julián Passero, 'Quiera el pueblo votar. Historia de la primera elección bajo la ley Sáenz Peña', *Todo es Historia*, Year 3, No. 23 (March 1969). For disputes in the federal capital see *El Diario* 27, 28 March 1912.

> It is probable ... that the middle class will progressively begin to affirm its solidarity; but its present insufficiencies will assure for a long time the predominance of the class which has until now governed the country. Another factor which also imposes a real obstacle to the political victory of the middle class is its lack of leaders with a clear recognition of their interests. Our popular party has always affirmed its democratic creed; but the vagueness of the aspiration allows for the coexistence of incompatible interests, and I believe that any definition of the manner of achieving democracy will result in the division of the party. And I believe this because many of its leaders, by their background and temperament, have opposing interests to those of the middle class ...
>
> The victory of the Radical Party will not produce, at least immediately, a legitimate representation for the middle class; and in this sense it is predictable that as time passes, and to the extent that the voting masses of the party acquire a degree of class consciousness, they will eliminate the deputies whose parliamentary activities do not reflect their interests, or there will be a division, giving way to the emergence of a new party in which the middle class will affirm its class interests.[35]

This issue became important in March 1916, during the party's presidential convention. Here Yrigoyen's candidature was opposed by many of the former followers of Alem from the 1890s. He eventually secured his nomination by exploiting his popularity among the middle class groups. To demonstrate their support for him, he first rejected the candidature when it was offered to him, and only accepted when the convention's middle class delegates from the committees organised demonstrations outside his house. This little game was designed to reassert his leadership over the party and to put a peremptory halt to the efforts of his opponents to manoeuvre themselves into key positions.[36] The significance of this episode was that it made apparent some of the friction between the two wings of the party. It also suggested that already Yrigoyen was beginning to buttress his own position through the support of the middle class groups.

Regional aspects

Besides this problem there were also signs of conflicts of a regional character within the party. During election periods such bizarre episodes as the following were common:

[35] Leopoldo Maupas pp. 425–8. (Quoted in Cantón. 'Elecciones', p. 106.)

[36] For an account of this episode see Luis Alberto Romero *et alia*, pp. 45–9.

> On the day of the election, Colonel Pereira Rosas ... invaded the village of Villa Dolores (Córdoba) at the head of twenty men on horseback from the province of Buenos Aires. They arrived clothed in coloured *ponchos*, white headbands[37] and armed with long cane lances with filed-down points. The village people were awakened by the discharge of revolvers, shouts of support for the Radicals, and for Hipólito Yrigoyen and by slanders against ... the savage tyrants of the government. Guards were set up on the roads giving access to the village and in the proximities of the voting booths.... At first the villagers kept off the streets and away from the roads. [Our supporters] managed to supervise the installation of the voting booths, persuade the police to arrest three or four of the noisiest of the intruders, and to get the colonel out of the town-hall, where he had started acting like the village mayor. There were shouts, protests and threats, but no actual violence: the cane lances were nothing more than the symbol of an impoverished and bloody byegone age. By midday the villagers had thrown off their fears and were quietly moving in the direction of the ballot boxes ...
>
> Some days later the count took place. [We] had won in Villa Dolores, though by a far smaller margin of votes than we had anticipated. The threats, the protests, and the circus performance had had their due effect.[38]

The election 'invasion', while providing a colourful illustration of electioneering methods, also reflected the constant attempts by Yrigoyen and his Buenos Aires-based faction to control the provincial branches of the party. This posed few problems in the interior, where elections were still largely a matter of winning the support of the local *hacendado*, who could browbeat the peasants into voting whichever way he wished. But it sometimes raised difficulties in the pampas provinces, where local branches of the party had strong and independent popular followings. In these areas there were rooted historic traditions of rivalry with Buenos Aires. Thus in certain cases Yrigoyen's group came to be seen as an alien force aiming to undermine the autonomy of local interests.

The importance of this issue also became apparent, though not for the first time, in 1916. When the Electoral College was constituted, it was found that the number of Yrigoyen's electors fell slightly short of the overall majority needed. It became necessary to negotiate for the votes of a group of Radical dissidents in the province of Santa Fe, who had previously refused to support the national party ticket. The matter was only resolved after several weeks of intrigue.[39] It illustrated the

[37] These were the *boinas blancas* used by the Radicals as a party colour since the 1890s.

[38] Ramón J. Cárcano, pp. 320–1.

[39] Lisandro de la Torre, 'Una página de historia', *La Prensa*, 22 June 1919.

extent of regional tensions within the party. The underlying cause of the defection of the Santa Fe Radicals was the bias they regarded the national party as possessing towards groups in Buenos Aires. It was thus apparent in 1916 that although Radicalism was a national party, it had still not managed completely to supersede the regional rivalries of the past.

Radicalism in Argentine society: immigration and foreign capital

In 1916 Radicalism was in many respects a form of Tory democracy.[40] It combined an adherence to the economic interests of the elite with a sense of identification with the community at large. This allowed its impregnation at the ideological level with paternalistic and communitarian notions, which facilitated its ability to project itself as a cross-sectional alliance. Yrigoyen's personal position within the party also gave it a certain caesaristic and plebiscitarian air. It also had close links with established institutions of the conservative order such as the Church. Its influence was small only in the army, where the old conservatives still occupied an entrenched position.

In spite of signs of regionally based conflicts within its ranks, and although it won the support of only a minority of the landed interests, the party was a rough approximation to the alliance the conservatives had been seeking between elite group magnates and the professional middle classes, largely made up of urban groups of immigrant extraction. These two major segments were held together by an implicit *quid pro quo* arrangement. The landed interests expected conservative policies and political stability. In return they seemed ready to widen access to the professions and the bureaucracy to the middle class groups. This promised an acceleration of the changes in the universities and a more flexible and liberal response to the middle class groups in the distribution of government offices.

Although the Radicals had established these links with the 'dependent' middle class, composed largely of the sons of immigrants, they had no

[40] 'In relation to the institutional system . . . the party wants the Constitution to be be upheld . . . This means: support for the federal system and the Roman Catholic religion, the supremacy of the family and property . . . support for commerce and industry . . . [Thus] it is principally, perhaps totally, a *conservative* party.' Rodolfo Rivarola in *Revista Argentina de Ciencias Políticas*, No. 8 (March 1914), pp. 95–6. (Quoted in Cantón, 'Elecciones', pp. 164–5.)

developed contacts with the immigrants themselves, either among the urban petty industrial and commercial groups, or among the working class. This reflected in part the fact that the old Radicals from the 1890s shared in the elite's cultural prejudices against the immigrants and its acute fear and distrust of the working class. It also illustrated the manner in which the Radicals had established their popular following. Among the industrial and commercial groups there were few signs of the build-up of the economic and social pressures which had politicised the professional groups. The overall pattern of the period after 1900 suggested that the middle class groups, which were content with minor entrepreneurial roles, remained relatively satisfied. The problems emerged with the higher-status groups. Upon these the Radicals mainly latched. Finally, effective ties between the Radicals and the immigrants were also discouraged by the Sáenz Peña Law, which had excluded the immigrants from the vote, and thus placed them outside the formal political system.

In general terms relations between the Radicals and the immigrants were fairly good, because these affected in some measure the position and political loyalties of the sons-of-immigrants group. Nevertheless on occasion, in cases where they thought they could benefit from it, the Radicals were far from averse to exploiting the latent xenophobic sentiments of native society. In its final election address in 1916, *El Radical*, the party's main organ in the city of Buenos Aires at that time, defined Radicalism in part as: 'the struggle of the Argentine people against the ungrateful foreigner, unthankful to the land which embraced him.[41] A little later a member of the predominantly immigrant Retailers' Association in Buenos Aires declared: 'We believe the Radical government will be a good government if it stops being anti-foreign. They call us "ungrateful" and "newcomers" in language which implies that they are the country's original inhabitants, when in fact they are only the sons of other immigrants who arrived before we did.'[42]

Finally, Radicalism emerged as the leading political movement in the country at a moment when the primary exporting economy had already reached maturity. The institutional and political links between foreign capital and the elite had developed while the Radicals were still in opposition. They thus lacked an established structure of contact with the foreign capital lobby. However, there was no automatic reason why their attitudes towards foreign capital should have been any different

[41] *El Radical*, 2 April 1916.

[42] *Boletín Oficial del Centro de Almaceneros*, 20 April 1918.

from those of the oligarchy. They were not economic nationalists. They accepted and recognised the country's dependence on its overseas links for markets and sources of investment. Some time after 1916 a leading Radical, speaking in the National Congress, referred to Argentina's international commercial relationships with Europe in the following terms: 'If through any misfortune, those nations should suffer long years of depression . . . what would be the fate of Argentina? . . . Could we ever aspire to be rich whilst the customer for our produce remains poor?'[43]

For the Radicals the issues with foreign capital were largely the same as those which had at times led to friction under the oligarchy. Outside the inner group of direct beneficiaries of the various perquisites bestowed by foreign capital, preferential loans and positions on the local boards, there were groups within the elite which sometimes felt that they were paying more for their services and facilities than they ought to. An example of this type of conflict came in 1915, when the British railway companies unilaterally increased their freight charges for animal and food cargos. At around this time there were also a number of subsidiary conflicts of a similar kind, the main one being the question of whether the railway companies were liable to municipal rates for street cleaning and lighting services under the Mitre Law of 1907, which administered railway affairs.[44]

The Radicals played a prominent part in the subsequent campaign against the railway companies. This they justified in terms of their more general attack on the oligarchy. It was not that foreign capital was a bad thing, but the oligarchy had allowed the erection of a corrupt system of vested interests, which worked against the domestic groups. Although the following quotation is again taken from a slightly later date, it provides a convenient summary of the most dominant attitude among them:

> Among the directors [of the British railway companies] there has always existed a low estimation of the morality of South American governments. They have always been prone to see their acts as mere window-dressing . . . We remember that when present legislation regulating the railways was

43 Honorio Pueyrredón. Quoted in *Review of the River Plate*, 12 December 1919.

44 The freight rates issue came to a head in September 1915. Although the action of the railway companies was opposed by leading groups among the exporting interests, the De la Plaza administration took no action. The municipal rates issue first appeared in 1914. Both issues can be followed in detail in the *Review of the River Plate*, 1914, *passim*.

under discussion, the English directors stated in the columns of the London dailies that Argentine politicians were demanding an excessive price for their support ... Obviously the preponderant influence exercised by the railways in Argentina was paid for in large cheques. But if so, it is a thing of the past.[45]

Despite this, before 1916, the Radicals were not generally regarded by the British themselves as representing any direct threat to their interests. A British diplomatic minister, writing towards the end of 1915, was clearly more intrigued and mystified with what Radicalism was, and with the enigmatic personality of its leader, than with any possible threat it might pose to British interests. Describing the party's rise to influence and popularity, he declared:

Hipolito Irigoyen shone as a conspirator, exhibiting indisputable political skill combined with remarkable pertinacity. For the past twenty years Irigoyen has been regarded almost as a prophet by his followers. His personality is veiled in mystery, but all are agreed that he towers over the heads of all the other partisans of the Radical creed. His power lies in the fanaticism professed by the youth of his party ... He appears in public as little as possible; he has always refused any administrative or other post, many of which have been offered to him.[46]

This suggested that the British, on balance, shared the same attitudes towards the Radicals as the domestic elite groups. Radicalism was seen as a novelty not because it threatened the established order, but because its stylistic and organisational traits conflicted so completely with what had gone before. To what extent these interpretations were justified or disproved only became apparent after October 1916, when Yrigoyen took over the office of president.

[45] *La Epoca*, 20 May 1918.

[46] Sir Reginald Tower. Despatch No. 59, 17 September 1915. Quoted in Despatch No. 94, 9 April 1919, F.O. 371–3504. Yrigoyen's name was frequently spelt in this form, see below p. 99 n. 7.

CHAPTER 4

The workers and their politics in Buenos Aires, 1890–1916

The early history of the urban working class in Argentina is well documented at the level of the major events in which the workers took part, but there is very little systematic information on the development of working class social conditions. Partial or impressionistic data on wages, factory and housing conditions is readily accessible,[1] but it has never been processed sufficiently to allow for any more than generalisations on the basic questions of workers' standards of living, or the manner in which standards of living evolved in terms of such variables as the economic cycle, immigration, foreign investment and overseas trade. The general picture emerging from this period is that while working class social conditions in Buenos Aires, particularly housing, left much to be desired, average wages compared well with many parts of Western Europe, and there were relatively better opportunities in Argentina for social mobility. On the other hand towards 1910, as the frontier disappeared and land became scarce, opportunities for the immigrants declined markedly. The other major factor to be borne in mind was the high level of aspirations among the immigrants, and the great premium they placed upon social mobility. Although social mobility did occur, there were many signs that it was insufficient to satisfy aspirations fully. One final point is that many of the immigrants were previously peasants, and a part of their behaviour in Buenos Aires may be attributed to the difficulties they encountered in assimilating into an urban capitalist culture. Nevertheless to emphasise the problem of mobility and assimilation is not to deny the fact that for many immigrants conditions were unpleasant, and in some cases wretched. There were certain groups with very low wages indeed, particularly those who came from the more backward areas of Eastern Europe.

This chapter does not aim to discuss the development of the urban working class in any detail. It concentrates upon the working class's

[1] Cf. Hobart Spalding, *La clase trabajadora argentina (Documentos para su historia, 1890–1916)* (Galerna, Buenos Aires, 1970).

political role up to 1916. The most important factor affecting the development of political movements among the working class was the relationship between the workers and the ruling class, and the manner in which the State had evolved before the end of the nineteenth century into a major, though disguised, arbiter over wages and the supply of labour.[2]

The composition of the Buenos Aires working class

Of the half million or so workers in Buenos Aires by 1914, well over half were employed in the industrial sector. The major meat-packing plants, the *frigoríficos*, which were mainly outside the federal capital in Avellaneda, employed several thousand men each. But large industrial complexes of this kind were exceptional. The majority of the industrially employed labour force reflected the overall lack of concentration in the industrial sector, and consisted of workers in small factories of less than a dozen employees. There was, however, a high level of concentration of the working class in a geographical sense in the city of Buenos Aires and its environs. The workers lived at the southern end of the city, between Avellaneda and the southern side of the central Plaza de Mayo. Long before 1914, areas like the Boca, Nueva Pompeya and Barracas had become working class neighbourhoods, and centres for factory and workshop activities. Such geographical concentration assisted the formation of a working class culture and the spread of class identifications.

Other major groups of workers were those employed by the railway and tramway companies, and those in the Port of Buenos Aires or in the coastal traffic port on the Riachuelo. The size of this group as a whole lay in the region of 70,000. In the transport sector alone, the 1914 census catalogued some 30,000 workers. In the port areas there was a myriad of dockers, carters and porters, as well as a large contingent of more highly skilled workers employed either in tug and lighter activities, or by the companies dealing in coastal and river trade from Asunción and Rio de Janeiro to southern Patagonia. Another large group was employed in commercial distribution, and in service activities. Beside the multitude of shop assistants and street vendors, there were larger groups like the refuse-disposal men employed by the municipality.

Another important determinant on the political development of the working class was nationality. In 1914 more than half of the city's

[2] These aspects are discussed in chapter 1.

working class was foreign born. The great majority was Italian or Spanish by birth, or, as a result of a wave of heavy immigration immediately before 1914, from the Middle East and the Balkans. The latter were the *turcos*, so called because of their shared Ottoman Empire nationality. A less important group were the Russians, most of them Jews. Half the immigrant workers were unskilled and, among the unskilled workers as a whole, about three-quarters were of foreign birth. The few natives among them were often internal migrants from provinces beyond Buenos Aires. The number of foreigners among the skilled workers was somewhat less. Here only about half were foreigners. This reinforced the pattern noticed before with the middle classes. Argentine citizenship was associated with higher status levels.

The absence of processed data for this period on such matters as the spread of urban activities, wages and standards of living makes it difficult to relate explicitly the formation and development of the working class in Buenos Aires to the wider characteristics of the growth process. Between 1895 and 1914, however, the number of industrial firms increased, throughout Argentina, from 22,000 to 48,000.[3] Within this total, the rate of expansion in the city of Buenos Aires was probably much more than double. Expansion took the form of the great proliferation of small units of production, depending mainly on labour-intensive techniques. In some of these small firms wages may have been below average, as competing entrepreneurs struggled to reduce costs. The urban labour market was sometimes strongly affected by the demand for harvest labour. On occasion this produced labour shortages, which the seasonally recruited *golondrinas* were unable to overcome. There were cases, therefore, where urban wages would rise or fall in response to the demand for harvest labour.[4]

[3] Roberto Cortés Conde, 'Problemas del crecimiento industrial (1870–1914)', p. 78.

[4] A case like this, where urban wages rose, occurred during the harvest period of 1912 when there was a strike in the port of Buenos Aires. Against complaints by shipowners of a shortage of dock labour, the authorities claimed that the men had migrated to the harvest zones. (Cf. *Review of the River Plate*, December, 1911–January 1912.) This question of wages before 1914 deserves much more attention than it has received either here or in the past. The only real sources are various partial works by Alejandro E. Bunge, but these mainly cover the wartime period. Bunge's hypothesis for the pre-war period is that there was over-immigration after 1905, when between 150,000 and 200,000 immigrants entered the country each year. He advocated economic diversification, and especially industrial development,

The Socialist Party

In the late 1880s the first signs of working class activism appeared in the form of union, cooperative and political societies and strikes. These emerged in conjunction with the arrival of the immigrants, and the inflationary process which led to the financial crisis of 1890. But the only lasting achievement of these years was the foundation in 1887 of a railway footplateman's union, La Fraternidad. One of its founders was a North American citizen, and the union paralleled in its organisation the Railroad Brotherhoods of the United States.[5]

Neither La Fraternidad, nor the workers as a whole in any appreciable numbers, took part in the Radical Party's revolts in the early 1890s. Where their political role was at all perceptible in these years, it was quite separate from the popular alliance which Radicalism promoted. In the 1890s the number of strikes and unions increased, and the first abortive attempts were made to form inter-union federations.[6] In this rather haphazard fashion the workers began to command political significance, although their importance was still greatly overshadowed by the struggles between the oligarchy and the Radicals.

In the mid-1890s the first sustained attempt was made to exploit the political potential of the workers by the Argentine Socialist Party. This was founded in 1894, as a result of one of the splits in the Radical Party, and it had an important influence upon the working class during the next forty years. By 1912 the Socialists were gaining upwards of 30,000 votes in the elections in the city of Buenos Aires. Over the next fifteen years or so this total doubled and later trebled as they establised an important, and relatively stable position within the city electorate.

Footnote 4 (continued)

and the replacement of unskilled by more technically trained immigrants. (Cf. *La Prensa*, 24 October 1919.) There is further information on the wages/standard of living question in Adolfo Posada, *La República Argentina, Impresiones y comentarios* (Madrid, 1912). See also: Spalding, p. 185 *passim*; José Panettieri, *Los trabajadores* (Jorge Alvarez, Buenos Aires, 1968).

5 *La Fraternidad, Cincuentenario de la Fraternidad* (Buenos Aires, 1937).

6 The bibliography for the early development of unions in Argentina is copious, and has been summarised frequently enough for it not to merit any further detailed mention here. Spalding, p. 17. has a list of the major works in the field. For bibliographical sources see Carlos Rama, *Die Arbeiterbewegung in Lateinamerika, Chronologie und Bibliographie 1492–1966* (Gehlen, W. Germany, 1967); also Leandro Gutiérrez, 'Recopilación bibliográfica y fuentes para el estudio de la historia y situación actual de la clase obrera argentina', *Documento de Trabajo*, Instituto Torcuato Di Tella, Centro de Investigaciones Sociales (Buenos Aires, 1969).

The relationship between the Socialist Party and the working class is comparable in some ways with that between the Radicals and the urban middle class before 1916. In the same way as the landed groups maintained control over the middle class groups in the Radical Party, the bulk of the Socialist Party's voting strength lay in the working class, though the party itself was largely controlled by middle class groups. This feature tended to increase in the years before 1912. Comparing the class background of the party's candidates for the National Chamber of Deputies in 1898 and 1912, in the latter year there was a significantly higher proportion of representatives from the middle classes. In 1912 the proportion of working class candidates was no more than around 25%, two out of a total of eight. Also the great majority of the party's actual members were middle class. In 1920, for example, again only 20% of the members of the party were workers. The rest, with the exception of the party's leaders, who were mainly university educated urban professionals, were white-collar employees and small businessmen.[7]

The leader of the party until his death in 1928 was Juan B. Justo, who was a medical practitioner in Buenos Aires. In 1890 Justo joined the Unión Cívica and took part in the rebellion against Juárez Celman. Later he joined the Radicals, but then abandoned them when the weaknesses and contradictions of Alem's democratic populism gradually became apparent. Justo's great aspiration was the creation of a European system of parliamentary democracy. He hoped to find means of superseding the factional struggles for office, which he regarded as the main features both of Radicalism and politics in general under the oligarchy. Such 'creole politics' (*política criolla*) ought to give way to organised parties with 'principles' and 'programmes', and the rebellious factions to an educated and disciplined mass electorate.

To achieve this quality themselves, the Socialists carefully restricted the membership of their party to a small cadre of militants to maintain the homogeneity and coherence of its programme and political strategy. In 1910 party membership was no more than 1,500, and it remained less than 3,000 in the city of Buenos Aires as late as the 1920s. In the country as a whole it was no more than 10,000 during the same period.[8] This

[7] Richard J. Walter, 'Political party fragmentation in Argentina: Schisms within the Socialist Party, 1915–1930' (unpublished mimeog. Washington University, 1972). I wish to acknowledge my gratitude to Professor Walter for providing me with this unpublished data. See also Cantón, 'El parlamento argentino', pp. 52–67; *La Vanguardia*, 2 February 1920.

[8] Walter.

contrasted strongly with the structure of Radicalism which, in addition to its system of multiple office-holders, had a membership in the federal capital alone of between 20,000 and 60,000 in the years between 1916 and 1930. In similar contrast to the mass turn-outs achieved by the Radicals, in the Socialist Party's internal elections in Buenos Aires in 1920, only 1,700 party members cast their votes to choose the party's leaders. By this time the city's population was approaching 2 million.[9]

The emphasis of Justo and his party on the avoidance of rebellion and on the virtues of programmatic consistency and rational organisation suggests immediate parallels with the aims of the reformers of 1912, with their stress on 'modern' parties along European lines and what they called 'organic democracy'. The parallel becomes closer bearing in mind that the Socialists were also convinced internationalists, and made no distinction between foreign and domestic capital. What set Justo and his colleagues apart from the elite was that their support for the liberal structure – the promotion of foreign capital investment, an acceptance of the principle of the international division of labour, and opposition to protectionism – was based on the consumer interests of the urban sectors.

This may serve again to illustrate that the Socialist Party was of as much relevance to the middle class groups as it was to the workers. The Socialists were aiming not only for control over the working class, but beyond this the creation of an urban alliance, based on Buenos Aires, powerful enough to be able to reform the dominant pattern of income distribution created by the primary export economy. Thus, besides being made up largely of middle class groups, the party was equally concerned to win middle class electoral support. In this they were already relatively successful even before the new electoral law was introduced in 1912. In an election in the Boca district of Buenos Aires in 1910, of the 920 voters who supported the party, almost one-third belonged to white-collar employee groups.[10]

[9] *La Vanguardia*, 10 April 1920.

[10] Spalding, pp. 412–13. Referring to the support for the Socialists among groups of property owners, a Radical neighbourhood boss declared in 1928: 'I know the electorate well in my parish, because I have been in it since I became a doctor, in the double role of physician and politician, and I am in constant contact with the voters . . . There are in those wards various groups of small traders and businesses, and also a market, whose owners, men for the most part of independent means, vote for the Socialist Party.' (Quoted in Canton, 'Elecciones', p. 195.) A similar picture emerges from a detailed study of the election of 1904 in the Boca district of Buenos Aires, which the Socialists won. See Juan Carlos Torre, 'La primera victoria electoral socialista', *Todo es Historia*, No. 76 (1973), pp. 42–51.

There was here another important difference with the Radical Party. The Radicals had closest ties with the upper brackets of the urban middle class groups in the professions and in the bureaucracy. The Socialists by contrast appealed to the lower middle class groups in white-collar occupations in the transport, commercial and petty industrial sectors. For this reason they could afford to express their contempt for *política criolla*; the middle class which they represented was not generally involved in the struggle for patronage offices and access to professional qualifications, which was the case with the dependent middle class supporting the Radical Party. The relative freedom of the Socialists from this kind of preoccupation was perhaps the most important determinant on their political programmes and their style of operation. It allowed them to give strength and cogency to their propaganda, which few of the other parties managed to attain. Their daily newspaper, *La Vanguardia*, became staple reading among the urban working class throughout the southern cone of South America, and was also well known in Spain.

However, more than any other party in Argentina at this time, the Socialist Party was synonymous with the strict centralisation of authority and structural rigidity. While these qualities gave it the coherence Justo and his supporters wanted, they conspired against the establishment of a firm spirit of consensus within the party. For this reason the Socialist Party was always subject to debilitating internal splits. This tendency towards division became its most serious weakness.[11]

The party's socialism was of a parliamentary reformist kind, which owed a great deal to experience in Australia and New Zealand rather than Europe. Its programmes were always defined in great detail, and conventionally divided into 'maximum' and 'minimum', and 'political' and 'economic' objectives. In substance these reflected the rather tenuous theoretical links Justo had created between liberalism and social democracy.[12] If at the basis of his position was the assertion that conditions of 'capitalist exploitation' had developed in Argentina, Justo was prevented by his acceptance of foreign capital investment from adopting the commitment to nationalisation, which the Social Democratic parties in Europe developed at around this time. So far as the most vital area of

[11] The nature of these divisions is described by Walter. See also Enrique Dickman, *Recuerdos de un militante socialista* (La Vanguardia, Buenos Aires, 1949); Joaquín Coca, *El contubernio* (Coyoacán, Buenos Aires, 1961).

[12] Juan B. Justo, *Teoría y práctica de la historia* (Buenos Aires, 1910) and *Internacionalismo y patria* (La Vanguardia, Buenos Aires, 1933).

control by foreign capital, the railway system, was concerned, the Socialists largely limited their demands to improvements in working conditions. This was a characteristic of their whole approach to the working class problem. Their great rallying cry was the introduction of the eight-hour day. On the pay issue they were often much less direct, and generally gave greater prominence to measures like reducing the cost of living, which fitted in with their opposition to protection and support for Free Trade.

Support for purely working class interests was even less apparent in the Socialists' political programme. Here their aims had a more jacobinical flavour than anything else. For many years they demanded the reform of the national executive by the replacement of the president with an executive committee. This was a more radical version of the system adopted in Uruguay at the beginning of the twentieth century. They also supported the introduction of the popular initiative and popular referendum systems of election and legislation, and called for the abolition of the National Senate. The party was strongly anti-clerical and anti-militarist. It demanded the separation of Church and State, and called for the formation of popular militias to replace the professional army.[13]

Although some members of the conservative elite regarded the Socialist Party as a dangerous form of extremism, which it was imperative to combat, others recognised that the 'minimum' programme it clung to was perfectly in accord with national tradition. It was more individualistic than collectivistic, and thus conventionally liberal rather than socialist:

> The minimum programme of the Socialist Party stands inside our present juridical structure. The proof of this is there for anyone who cares to examine it and compare it with the Constitution. It has not attacked, nor opposed in any way, its individualistic declarations or the rights of man on which the Constitution bases its authority . . . Its aspirations for constitutional reform can be shared by any individualist. The separation of Church and State, for example, implies an individualist equality over matters of religious conscience. Unitary organisation with administrative decentralisation and municipal government, the most recent part of its programme, is a concept which developed anterior to Socialist doctrine.[14]

The overall aim of the Socialists was to spread out from Buenos Aires

[13] For further comments on the party's programme see Spalding, pp. 153, *passim*.

[14] Rodolfo Rivarola, *Revista Argentina de Ciencias Políticas*, pp. 95–6. (Quoted in Canton, 'Elecciones', p. 165.)

into the other urban areas of the pampas, and use their control over the region to establish national political supremacy. Justo declared:

If the foreigners with common interests join together to take part in politics together with the natives of similar common interests, no differences of language, of education, nor of traditions would be sufficient to weaken the strength of so great a movement. The result will be the organisation of organic parties, which, dominating the coastal regions, will control the Congress and national government.[15]

Of key importance in this strategy was the recruitment of the support of the immigrants on a large scale. The Socialists hoped to persuade them to take Argentine citizenship and to exploit their political weight as voters, once representative government was introduced:

The naturalisation of the foreigners, as a means of incorporating new forces into politics, we support as a necessary condition for the expansion of our party ... The class interests of the workers will be frustrated ... by the legal coercion of the bourgeoisie unless the proletariat exercises its weight within the political system. The puerile division of native and foreign workers makes no sense to us. The two, as workers, bear the same weight of exploitation by the government ... The Socialist Party, in supporting the naturalisation of the foreigners, demands that this should be done by simple inscription in the Civil Register.[16]

But this aim was completely frustrated. In 1918, when the middle class segments of the foreign communities were allowed to vote in municipal elections in the federal capital on a property franchise, only 14,000 foreigners registered. This was only a tiny proportion of the foreign population. The number of foreign workers who managed to acquire the vote always remained infinitesimal.

The most vital factor here was undoubtedly the ruling class's unwillingness to add to the strength of its opponents by simplifying citizenship procedures. The Socialists might have had greater success had they been able to offer more concrete incentives to the immigrants to naturalise. However, this would either have meant a much more radical position than they were able to adopt, or a much greater willingness to exploit whatever contacts they had with the minor entrepreneurial groups to use their control over jobs to establish an open party machine structure. But the Socialists never managed to win the support of the small entrepreneurs on a sufficient scale to do this. The further problem with this

[15] Quoted by Cornblit, 'Inmigrantes y empresarios', p. 678.
[16] *La Vanguardia*, 21 April 1912.

method of politicisation was that it also smacked too much of *política criolla*, and ran counter to the 'modern', 'organic' image they were attempting to cultivate.

As a result, in spite of the importance and popularity the Socialist Party acquired, it always tended to fall between two stools. Its commitment to social reform ran up against the problem that a large proportion of the lower middle class was composed of proprietors and entrepreneurs. At the same time its commitment to parliamentary democracy, and its antipathy to direct action and rebellion, meant ineffectiveness to promote or to force substantial change on behalf of the workers. An adherence to parliamentary action meant virtual impotence under the oligarchy. In spite of the strong support they had in the city of Buenos Aires, before 1912 the Socialists only managed to win one seat in the National Congress. Their only achievements of any importance were legislation imposing Sunday as a compulsory rest day and the regulation of female and child labour. Both of these measures were also more classically liberal than socialist in content.

The party's contradictions from a purely socialist standpoint were frequently pointed out by its critics. To the Radicals the Socialist Party was 'sectarian' and 'oligarchical', in comparison with their own open-ended system of geographical organisation and cultivated mass participation. A typical criticism was the following, which is taken from the year 1918:

> The party run by the parliamentary group is no longer a labour party, the section of the population for which it used to speak and whose rights it boasted of vindicating. The aspirations of the working man are taking a quite different path from that advocated by the old preachers. If somewhat tardily, the workers now seem to have realised that all their efforts and sacrifices have resulted in no more than the rise of a group of so-called leaders, whose ineffectual parliamentary activities have failed to yield a single class benefit or a single contribution to the physical and moral welfare of the people they pretend to represent. It is no longer possible to pretend that the Socialist oligarchy ... is still supported by the masses it has practically betrayed.[17]

An influential Italian critic, Errico Ferri, who visited Argentina before 1910, declared:

> The Argentine Socialist Party calls itself a 'Socialist Party' but in terms of its economic programme, it is no more than a worker's party (*viz.* its support for

[17] *La Epoca*, 18 February 1918.

the 8-hour day, for strikes and for higher wages). At the same time it is a Radical Party (in the French and Italian sense), in terms of its political programme (universal suffrage, abolition of clerical privileges, compulsory education). The Argentine Socialists are fulfilling the role of a fully organised (European-style) Radical Party . . . To call itself a Socialist Party, and to claim that it represents and supports socialist doctrine is an absurdity until it begins to support the socialisation of property.[18]

The result was that the major appeal of the Socialist Party was to working class groups either enjoying an aristocratic status, like the railway footplatemen in La Fraternidad, or to other very highly skilled groups, best equipped for social mobility and *embourgeoisement*. The party was particularly strong in the older areas of working class settlement in Buenos Aires, such as in the Boca. However, its ambivalence led it into one key failure, which became symptomatic of its wider failure to win the support of the immigrants. It never acquired control over the key units of working class organisation, the unions.

From 1900 onwards, when the union movement became important for the first time, the influence of the Socialists within it declined. As early as 1902, insoluble longstanding divisions between the Socialists and their opponents came to a head and led to the creation of a separate minority Socialist-dominated federation – the General Union of Workers (Unión General de Trabajadores). In subsequent years this failed to acquire any further support, and by 1907 it was virtually defunct.[19] From henceforth the Socialists had in most cases only minority support in each organisation. This reflected the underlying anomaly of their position. They were trying to win support for a class alliance among organisations which were specifically geared to conditions of class conflict. As time passed, the unions found it easier to maintain their autonomy and to attract support from groups which had formerly supported the Socialists.

Anarchism

This was facilitated further by the appearance of a competing ideology among the workers which, from the 1890s onwards, operated as an

[18] Quoted in Posada, pp. 285–6.

[19] The best accounts of the U.G.T. can be found in Jacinto Oddone, *El gremialismo proletario argentino* (Buenos Aires, 1957), and in Sebastián Marotta, *El movimiento sindical argentino: su genesis y desarrollo* (Lacio, Buenos Aires, 1960), Vol. 1, pp. 153–287.

important additional buffer against Socialist penetration of the unions. The Anarchists attacked the Socialist Party on the grounds that reformist gradualism was a betrayal of working class interests, and merely aimed to induce a sense of prostrate quietism among them. In its place they offered direct action and class revolution, as a means to achieve immediate improvements and a higher scale of benefits.

During the first decade of the twentieth century, the Anarchist movement in Argentina was among the largest and most influential in the world. In many respects it was similar to Radicalism. It was disparate and heterogeneous, and it embraced more a series of common attitudes than a developed ideological and doctrinal position. Like Radicalism too, the movement operated as a loose confederation, rather than upon the stratified, centralised structure adopted by the Socialists. Another of its strengths was that it offered both to fulfil the economic demands of the workers, and at the same time provide for the immigrants a style of action consonant with their culturally based needs, which stemmed from a feeling of rootlessness and a failure to adapt to factory production in a new environment.

The Anarchist movement in Argentina shared with the other political parties an appeal which, if often repressed or obliquely stated, was strongly geared to the demand for open avenues of social mobility. This was a particular feature of immigrant culture, which was strongly impregnated by the aspiration 'to make it in America' (*hacer la America*):

> We can say that political and economic conditions in the Argentine Republic, and the fact that it is populated by people from all over the world who have come for the purpose of enriching themselves, have facilitated the task of Anarchist propagandists, allowing them a greater success here than in other countries.[20]

The same commentator remarked how the Anarchists were able to exploit conditions of cultural isolation prevailing among the immigrants, and the polarisation between rich and poor:

> Such propaganda has also had in its favour the scarcity of public amusements, which the foreigner misses in this country, the absence of that collective happiness which is a characteristic of the European peoples, and which is the result of a common language . . . of race, and customs, all of which are apparent in a series of traditions, fulfilled in festivities and public acts, and in popular songs

[20] Eduardo G. Gilimón, *Un anarquista en Buenos Aires (1890–1910)*, La Historia Popular No. 71 (Centro Editor de América Latina, Buenos Aires, 1971), p. 36.

which speak to the soul and make life happy ... Cosmopolitanism in Argentina is an obstacle to collective existence, and the small uncomfortable houses leave no room for any welcome addition to the family. It could be said that everything leads towards everybody being unhappy, and especially those without fortune who cannot give themselves pleasures and enjoyments, whose cost makes them belong to the very rich alone, whose blinding luxury is also a powerful incentive to stimulate discontent.[21]

To some extent the Anarchist movement shared with other popular movements in Argentina a style of initial growth based upon the propaganda activities of core groups of militants. It owed much of its early development to the careful fostering of its doctrines by schooled European ideologues, mainly from Spain and Italy. The class origins of these groups were mixed, as was the content of the doctrines they espoused. The most significant single influence upon the movement's early development round about the turn of the century came from the Italian Anarchist intellectual, Pedro Gori. He was important in resolving initial differences between the Stirnerian 'individualists' and the Bakuninist 'collectivists' in favour of the latter.[22] In later years the collectivist idea remained dominant, and by comparison with other parts of the world, the Anarchist movement in Argentina was fairly moderate.

The early intellectualist tradition of the movement soon disappeared. The great majority of prominent Anarchist activists were semi-literate artisans, who crossed and recrossed the South Atlantic. In the years after the turn of the century these peripatetic and charismatic figures became familiar in all the major River Plate cities. A prominent Socialist leader, Enrique Dickman, has left a graphic account of the colour and magnetism of one Anarchist leader before 1910. Referring to a demonstration of unemployed labourers, Dickman recalled:

The symbol of synthesis of that human mass was undoubtedly old Aimami. His appearance on the scene was greeted by a trembling sensation among the onlookers. Tall, thin and starved-looking, with his pallid face and black, deep-set, luminous eyes ... he appeared to be the very Spectre of Hunger, a symbol of Man's exploitation by Man, and the incarnation of protest, of instinctive and embryonic rebellion. With him he had brought a banner, upon which was written in black against a white background, 'We demand the distribution of the surplus'. On top of his banner he had stuck a piece of bread. And although he

[21] Ibid. p. 36.

[22] For accounts of Gori's influence in early union federation meetings cf. Marotta, Vol. 1, pp. 107–14; Gilimón, p. 32.

was neither an organiser nor an orator at the demonstration, he put himself with his strange banner at the forefront of those present.[23]

The strength of the Anarchists lay more among the small industrial and service occupations than it did among large-scale concerns such as the railways or the *frigoríficos*. An exception to this was the traditional support they enjoyed among the port dockers. In a meeting of the unions' federal congress in 1902 the dockers' union claimed a membership of 3,200, which was not far short of half of the 7,600 members represented in the congress. Other important groups were the shop mechanics, the bricklayers, the bakers, the cobblers and the coach-builders.[24] Of these the bakers tended to be the most traditionally militant. They were subject to low wages, permanent nightwork and to notoriously unhygienic conditions.[25] The Anarchists also had considerable support among the unskilled groups. In this respect it is significant that their written propaganda never acquired the same level of distribution as that of the Socialists. In 1912 the Socialists claimed, probably with some exaggeration, that *La Vanguardia*'s daily circulation approached 75,000. *La Protesta* however, the principal Anarchist organ, rose only from a circulation of around 2,000–3,000 in 1905 to 15,000 in 1910. This suggested lower levels of literacy and perhaps lower wages among Anarchist supporters.

The main significance of the Anarchists lay in their role in the development of the unions. It was not until the late 1890s that efforts to establish permanent unions on a large scale were successful. During this period there was a succession of short-lived general federations, known as the Argentine Workers' Federation (Federación Obrera Argentina). These failed because support for them was weak, and as a result of the internecine disputes between the Socialists and the Anarchists.

By the turn of the century, the Anarchists had largely won control, and they were left free to consolidate their influence. Their increasing strength became apparent when the name of the Federation was changed in 1904 to the Argentine Region Workers' Federation (Federación Obrera Regional Argentina). The use of the term 'Region' emphasised the internationalist and cosmopolitan character of the Anarchist move-

[23] Dickman, pp. 71–2.

[24] Diego Abad de Santillán, *La F.O.R.A., ideología y trayectoria* (Proyección, Buenos Aires, 1971), pp. 91–2.

[25] Ibid. p. 83. See also Thomas C. Cochran and Rubén Reina, *Espíritu de empresa en la Argentina* (Emecé, Buenos Aires, 1965), p. 67.

ment. It expressed its view of the nation state as a 'fictitious being, an unnatural idea, an anti-human conception, dependent upon conventionalism and the chances of war'.[26] It also recalled Spanish practices, where the Anarchist unions were known as Regional Federations. Finally, the influence of the Anarchists was made further apparent in 1905, when the F.O.R.A.'s Fifth Congress carried a motion in favour of the goal of Anarchic Communism. In 1904 the Socialist U.G.T. claimed 7,400 affiliates, and the Anarchist F.O.A. almost 33,000.[27]

The triumph of the Anarchists in the unions at the beginning of the century coincided with a marked exacerbation of class conflict in Buenos Aires. In the 1890s strike movements had tended to be partial and uncoordinated. This allowed determined employers to recruit replacement labour from among the city's floating population. To overcome this the Anarchists began to advocate the use of the general strike. The manner in which this won acceptance among the workers illustrates the symbiotic relationship between the rise of Anarchism and the need for new tactical dimensions to the class struggle. At the moment when conflict pressures and the need for class solidarity were at their height, a conflict-solidarity ideology gained the upper hand among the unions. The great advantage of the general strike was that it could be employed to enhance solidarity, and thus restrict the availability of replacement labour during the years of heaviest European immigration into Argentina.

The period between 1902 and 1910 was thus punctuated by a series of massive general strikes, which led to the involvement of the State in campaigns of repression, and to violent confrontations between the workers and the police. The strikes expressed the extent of the division between native and immigrant society in Buenos Aires. Generally on the 1st of May each year the workers massed in the centre of the city:

> A multitude of no less than forty thousand persons left Plaza Constitución at 3 in the afternoon on its way to Plaza Lavalle. Happy and ebullient, the people made it plain with their cries how much they loved liberty, hated the tyranny and at the end of ninety days of persecution, police raids, assaults and banishment, they were still prepared to give vent to their aspirations.[28]

The demonstrators were urged on by strident Anarchist propaganda, of which the following extract from *La Protesta* in 1909 is a good example:

[26] *La Protesta*, 1 July 1916.
[27] Torre, 'La primera victoria electoral socialista', p. 44.
[28] *La Protesta*, 2 May 1905.

Let the virile protest of every good man be made today ... With a blow of sharpened hatchets fell the wall impeding the advance of our noble steps forward. Workers! Against every reasonable dictate of civilisation and progress, the sabre of the *mazorca* [the police] is raised, wielded by the parasitical, barbaric hordes brought from the pampas ... People! Let fanfares of happiness ring out to proclaim the Festival of Labour ... [for our] sufferings are common and equal ... Life or Death! Let this powerful, gigantic cry burgeon forth from each breast ... like the howl of a man facing death. Life or Death! ... Let us cast aside the ugly chains binding us ... and if at the foot of a barricade lies death, what does it matter? We shall fall, but in the moment of the blow itself, a smile of valour will appear on our lips as a last challenge to our oppressors. Workers! Men who bear the burden of a centuries' old lie, conquer your misfortunes and cast over everything trying to stifle your existence.[29]

At first, soon after 1900, the oligarchy did consider attempting to control the unions and to exclude the Anarchists by industrial relations legislation. This was the aim of the General Labour Code project presented to Congress by Joaquin V. González in 1904. But the complex systems governing picketing, and the organisation and formation of unions, were unworkable. The measure was also strongly opposed by by the workers themselves.[30] The other method attempted to control the unions was through the formation of Church working class associations. Workers' Circles (Circulos de Obreros) were founded in Buenos Aires as early as 1892 and congresses were held in 1903, 1906, 1907 and 1908.[31] But the Catholic movement had little influence in comparison with the secular associations.

As a result the authorites were forced back on a system of undisguised repression. The national government imposed a state of siege to combat the strikes on five occasions between 1901 and 1910. In 1902 and 1910 respectively, congress passed the Laws of Residence and Social Defence. These two measures come to symbolise the relationship between the oligarchy and the urban working class.

In 1916 *La Vanguardia* estimated that a total of 383 men, including 175 Spaniards and 109 Italians, were deported under the provisions of the Law of Residence.[32] This is not a massive figure, and the law was

[29] Ibid. 1 May 1909. The *mazorca* was the notorious secret police force of the Rosas era.

[30] For a description of the Ley González, as it was known, see Panettieri, pp. 148–54.

[31] The Círculos de Obreros operated on the following general principles: 'The class struggle is not only antisocial and damaging to the interests of the workers ... it is a means for the union leaders to become the bosses over the working class masses' (*Boletín del Departamento Nacional del Trabajo*, No. 46, March 1920, p. 120).

[32] *La Vanguardia*, 1 January 1916.

generally only used against those regarded as Anarchist ringleaders. However, this symptomised the oligarchy's perception of the working class problem. There was a refusal to acknowledge that the immigrants had any legitimate grievances; they were merely being manipulated by 'foreign agitators'. When the Law of Residence was applied, the normal procedure was the confiscation or destruction of *La Protesta*'s machinery, and the deportation of its contributors and editorial staff. The punishment lay not merely in deportation, since many deportees faced charges of evasion of military service once they reached their countries of origin. The Law of Social Defence added imprisonment as a further deterrent to violent strikes, and extended the scope of repression to cover native-born workers.

The rise of Syndicalism

This classic struggle had two major consequences, both of which were to prove highly significant in years to come. On the one side the challenge posed by the Anarchists was regarded as dangerous enough to help precipitate the division within the oligarchy which led to the reforms of 1912. The second stemmed from the effects of repression upon the workers themselves. Around 1906 there appeared a third movement among them, which gradually adopted a much less extreme position than that of the Anarchists. This was Syndicalism. In subsequent years the Syndicalists won a position of supremacy within the unions, and they were to take a leading part in shaping the political role of the working class during the later period of Radical government after 1916.

Although the Anarchist general strikes were for a time successful in creating a wider sense of solidarity among the immigrant working class, the response they elicited on the part of the State meant that in the end they achieved very few changes. Also the main trend of Anarchism was towards an immigrant rebellion rather than towards piecemeal economic improvements. Syndicalism differed from this in that it had much less of a political component, and that it was specifically geared to economic objectives.[33]

[33] It is also worth pointing out that the Syndicalists, like both the Socialists and the Anarchists, where strong opponents of protectionism. In 1915 the Syndicalist federations adopted the following resolution: '... although universal free trade can in certain cases injure the interests of certain groups of industrial workers, protectionism is an artificial form of fostering production, which can only be supported at the expense of the consumers, by raising the real prices of merchandises'. Quoted in Marotta, p. 188. This illustrates again the great dominance of consumer interests during this period.

At the beginning the Syndicalist movement in Argentina had a certain superficially theoretical air about it, which reflected the fact that many of its early ideas came from Europe. It began as a result of a division in the Socialist Party in 1906 over the old question of the class struggle versus democratic paternalism and parliamentary gradualism.[34] The Syndicalists supported the more positive use of the strike weapon, and demanded from the Socialists a greater commitment to immediate working class objectives. The group's doctrines were based on European Syndicalism, particularly of the Italian and French varieties, whose great exponents were Labriola and Sorel.[35] The Syndicalists were at one with the Anarchists in their acceptance of the inerradicable class basis of the modern state. They therefore regarded Socialist efforts to reform it as destined to failure. Their disenchantment with political methods, with parliamentary democracy, and with the political game in general was one of the prime features of their position:

All the political parties have programmes which in practice they do not fulfil, for the simple reason that their conduct is dictated by their own convenience, and these can be satisfied by the acquisition of power. This is the immediate objective of every group in opposition, and once power has been gained, it tries by every available means to avoid being dislodged by other groups . . .[36]

The morality of democracy is a morality of imposition and servility, since the manually employed wage labourer ought to be submissive, obedient and lacking in initiative, readily converting himself into an instrument in the hand of the capitalist. Such morality is inferior, since it creates a passive being; it is the morality of the weak . . .[37]

Oh, Politics! I hate you, because you are vulgar, unjust, scandalous and charlatan; because you are the enemy of Art and Labour; because you serve as the passport for every nullity, for every vain ambition and for every example of sloth.[38]

Like their European counterparts the ideologues among the Syndicalists regarded the trade union, or the *sindicato*, as the basic instrument to achieve the redemption of the working class. It was not only seen as an instrument of self-defence, but as the basic unit for the establishment of a new society:

[34] Dickman, p. 203; Marotta, p. 209, *passim*.

[35] For a statement of Syndicalist doctrine in Argentina see Julio Arraga, *Reflexiones y obervaciones sobre la cuestión social* (Buenos Aires, no date, *circa* 1910).

[36] Arraga, p. 18.

[37] Ibid. p. 67.

[38] *La Unión del Marino*, August 1922.

The union of the members of the *sindicato* is spontaneous and free: there is no authority, nor is this necessary; the link is established by common economic interests, and the circumstances of the struggle form the moral link among its members which give them cohesion and firmness.[39]

Behind this, however, also lay a recognition of the failure of Anarchist methods, and a determination to provide the working class with a new capacity for organisation and self-discipline:

Organisation has transformed an instinctive movement into one of consciousness and order. The old explosions of fury among the workers, who embarked on the struggle uncoordinated and unprepared – making them an easy prey to the capitalists – have been succeeded by the *sindicato*, which coordinates the workers' forces, disciplines them, and employs them at moments convenient for itself, at moments of intense economy activity, or when the enemy is at a disadvantage.[40]

This was what Syndicalism contributed to the development of the labour movement in Argentina. It appeared as something of a reaction to the Anarchists' emphasis on symbolic political challenges and mass solidarity. Given its primary concern with economic objectives, it stressed continuously the value of tactics, and the virtues of coordination, timing and planning. These were by far the most important features of Syndicalism, and they quickly overshadowed the lipservice the movement paid to the goal of class revolution.

Soon after 1906 the Syndicalists abandoned their early endeavour to provide any sophisticated ideological backing for their position and instead they began to operate on a completely pragmatic level. While middle class ideologues did something to develop strategic and tactical notions within the movement, a quickly rooted bias against middle class intellectuals prevented them from acquiring any real influence. Julio Árraga, for example, who played some part in the introduction of Syndicalist ideas from Europe, was never able to take part in any important union meetings, nor have himself elected (as Pedro Gori had done among the Anarchists) as a union delegate. The middle class Syndicalist splinter group from the Socialist Party soon lost any recognisable influence:

[39] Arraga, p. 58.

[40] *La Unión del Marino*, January 1929. In spite of the lateness of this date, attitudes like these were marked early in the movement's development.

In the *sindicato* there are no manufacturers of speeches or professional writers. And if there are those who make speeches or write, they are men who are doing no more than using these means to reflect their lives as wage-earners and their actions as combatants. The triumph of the *sindicato* is the triumph of the producers. It is not the coming of a new ruling class.[41]

In spite of its revolutionary paternity, Syndicalism represented the advent of more urbane and pacific influence within the working class. It also marked the progressive abandonment of the extreme conflict position adopted by the Anarchists in favour of a willingness to accept negotiation.

After 1906 the first success of the Syndicalists occurred when they took over the rump of the old Socialist general federation, the U.G.T. In 1908 this became known as the Confederación Obrera Regional Argentina. For some time the C.O.R.A. enjoyed only small support, and failed to make any significant headway against the Anarchist domination over the industrial workers. It began to enjoy greater influence after 1910.

For the Anarchists, 1910 was an extremely critical year. At the beginning of May 1910, labour matters in the city of Buenos Aires were described as being 'in a critical situation'.[42] The unions were strongly organised, and there were reports that a general strike was to be declared to coincide with the country's centenary celebration. The unions were demanding the release of recently imprisoned strikers, and the withdrawal of the Law of Residence. Although the now traditional day of protest, 1 May, passed off quietly, the Anarchists declared a general strike for the 18th. Figueroa Alcorta's government replied by declaring a state of siege and organising a massive dose of police repression against the Anarchists.[43] The police, assisted by an *ad hoc* civilian militia, attacked and sacked the Anarchist unions and imprisoned or deported their leaders. Both *La Protesta*'s and *La Vanguardia*'s premises were gutted by fire. At the same time legislation was sent to Congress prohibiting Anarchist associations and meetings, and imposing six-year prison sentences on 'agitators' found guilty of intimidating 'free labour' during strikes.[44] When the Anarchists replied by planting a bomb in the

[41] *La Organización Obrera*, 27 October 1917.

[42] *Review of the River Plate*, 8 May 1910.

[43] Ibid. 13 May 1910.

[44] Ibid. 3 June 1910. Other provisions of the legislation were that no flags were to be shown apart from the Argentine flag, and that restrictions were placed on press reporting on indictments under the law. There was also a death penalty introduced for persons over 18.

main theatre of Buenos Aires, the Colón, the legislation was quickly rushed through. This was the Law of Social Defence.[45]

These events proved to be a watershed in the influence of the Anarchist movement. Because of repression, and because the years after 1910 led to increasing saturation of the labour market, as the volume of immigration swelled, the unions underwent major changes. The year 1910 marked the last of the great general strikes, and afterwards the Syndicalists gradually moved into a position of dominance.

The growth of Syndicalism was thus accompanied by, and reflected, important shifts in the structure and composition of the union movement. The core of Anarchist support lay among the workers in the small-scale, and frequently marginal, industrial and craft activities. The Syndicalists, by contrast, won theirs among larger and more concentrated groups, in particular among the skilled shipping and port workers in Buenos Aires, and later among the railway workshopmen. These groups also operated in pivotal areas of the economy, linked with the export trade. This gave them, in comparison with the industrial workers, a much greater potential bargaining power. Partly because they had this advantage, and because too they now recognised the advantage of minimising the threat of State repression, these groups were much less enthusiastic about the use of the general strike. Rather they were prepared to concentrate on partial strikes and on securing concessions directly from their employers.

The rise of Syndicalism also reflected the increasing stratification of the working class according to levels of skills. Anarchism reflected conditions of relative undifferentiation among the working class, where the effects of roughly constant conditions facilitated the projection of a simple conflict ideology and the call for universal solidarity. Syndicalism, however, marked the appearance of a greater degree of heterogeneity within the working class, which tended to undercut a subjectively perceived sense of common identity and common objectives. The result was a further move away from political confrontation towards a negotiating position involving purely economic objectives.

There are also some hints that Syndicalism was associated with Argentine citizenship. This may have played some additional part in the movement's abandonment of the commitment to rebellion which distinguished Anarchism. Traditionally, the political content of Anarchism had stemmed from its relationship with frustrated mobility aspirations

[45] Ibid. 1 July 1910.

among the immigrants. With Syndicalism, however, there were signs of the appearance of a new working class composed of native Argentines, which accepted its class position, having been born directly into it, and which sought to take advantage of its higher level of skills to seek self-betterment through higher wages.

The evidence for this is first that in Buenos Aires a higher proportion of the native-born working class by 1914 was in skilled rather than in unskilled occupations. Since Syndicalism was associated with higher levels of skill, it is not unreasonable to expect a greater influence of native groups in the movement. The point can also be illustrated by comparing the backgrounds of Anarchist and Syndicalist union leaders during this period.[46]

In the 1915 the clearest variant between Anarchist and Syndicalists lay in the question of age. The latter group was composed of young men, frequently in their twenties, while many of the Anarchists were approaching middle age by this time. There was also a marked difference in nationality. The Syndicalists were mainly native-born, sons of immigrants, while the Anarchists were largely Spanish and Italian immigrants, with a large number of Catalans among them.[47] Both groups apparently had poor educational backgrounds. Both groups too were composed mainly of skilled workers. The Anarchists, however, had worked less in their trades than had the Syndicalists, and had travelled frequently between Europe and the pampas. Among the Syndicalists there were a number of creoles and naturalised immigrants, but the case of Sebastián Marotta may be said to have been the most typical. Born in Buenos Aires in 1888, the son of an unskilled Neapolitan immigrant, Marotta began

[46] Shortly before his death, I was able to hold a number of interviews with Sebastián Marotta, who was active in union circles before 1910, and who between 1917 and 1921 was secretary of the F.O.R.A. I presented Marotta with a list, about 30 in all, of union leaders active in the period between 1910 and 1920, soliciting information about their ideological affiliations, their nationalities, their occupations, their education and their ages. The following paragraph is based on the results of this questionnaire. The list of union leaders I used was that of the delegates to the Ninth Congress of the F.O.R.A. in 1915. I would, of course, recognise the dangers of making over-assertive generalisations on the basis of this data, though I believe its main points to be substantially correct. The interviews with Sr Marotta were held in 1969. I wish to record my thanks to him for providing me with this information.

[47] In later years the Anarchists frequently referred to the Syndicalists as 'creoles' and occasionally to themselves as '*gallegos*' (Spaniards). Certainly, comparing the Syndicalist *La Organización Obrera* with the Anarchist *La Protesta* during the war period, this difference of nationality is constantly apparent in style and vocabulary.

work in a semi-skilled capacity as a coach-painter. In 1904 he became secretary of a coach-workers' union. Later he moved into printing activities and he played a major role in the printers' unions before becoming the secretary of the F.O.R.A. in 1917.[48]

Further confirmatory evidence for this can be found in the development of a union which became, after 1910, the main backbone of the Syndicalist organisation. This was the Maritime Workers' Federation, the Federación Obrera Marítima. The F.O.M. was very much the creation of its secretary, Francisco García, who was Argentine-born and one of Marotta's closest collaborators. In 1919 García wrote an account of the union's early history. He recalled that the first federations, which had appeared around 1900, had been Anarchist. He himself held Anarchist sympathies, until in 1910 he joined the Syndicalist group to escape from the turmoil and confusion into which the Anarchist movement had fallen. Recalling the Anarchist period, García made apparent his own views on the development of the union movement, and the reasons why, in his opinion, Anarchism had failed. At the same time his comments exemplified some of the salient attitudes of the Syndicalists. He declared that a maritime union, founded around the beginning of the century, had prospered until, around 1905, it was 'upset by sectarian elements from the F.O.R.A. It then fell into a state of internal disorder from which there was no escape'.[49] This was the result of the influence of dogmatic groups within its midst, which led the unions answering to them in an anti-State direction, relegating to a secondary role the economic struggle.[50] García described the qualities of the early union as follows:

> As an entity it represented the qualities of the men belonging to it. It was robust, valiant, generous, loyal and honourable. A sick and useless revolutionary spirit did affect it from time to time . . . but it quickly returned to an attitude of reality and reason. Therefore, if it was not always completely impervious to the destructive influence of the sowers of hatred and useless rebellion, it was among those who resisted them most and was one of the least prejudiced by them.[51]

The F.O.M. was founded in the Boca district of Buenos Aires in April

[48] For details of Marotta's personal career see his obituary in *La Vanguardia* 21 January 1970; also Alfonso Amadeo López (ed.) *Vida, obra y trascendencia de Sebastián Marotta* (Calomino, Buenos Aires, 1971).

[49] *Boletín del Departamento Nacional del Trabajo*, No. 40.

[50] Ibid. p. 23.

[51] Ibid. p. 27.

1910. This time there was a determined effort made to prevent the Anarchists playing any part at all in the union. On its foundation a significant motion was carried, which barred all foreigners from membership of the secretariat. In 1919 García justified this step in the following way: 'The present secretary of the F.O.M. [García himself], counselled to take this step by his fellow workers, replaced the decimated ranks of the union's office-holders with Argentine citizens to make it invulnerable to the effects of the Law of Residence.'[52]

This seems to be a conclusive illustration of the association between Syndicalism and Argentine citizenship. To exclude those likely to fall within the scope of repressive legislation was to exclude the foreigners, who could be deported. It also meant the exclusion of the Anarchists, and an attempt to guide the union away from political confrontation. This was to be the F.O.M.'s main role in the future. The adoption of this motion meant the advent of native-born workers to a position of leadership in the union movement. Given the F.O.M.'s later importance, it was a highly significant step.

Until 1915 Syndicalist influence, though rising rapidly, was still restricted to the smaller of the two federations in Buenos Aires, the C.O.R.A. In 1914, however, the C.O.R.A. was disbanded, and the decision was taken to join up with the Anarchist F.O.R.A. In April 1915 the F.O.R.A. held its ninth congress. By an adroit piece of backstage manoeuvering the Syndicalists managed to acquire a majority among the delegates present. They gained control of the chairmanship, and before the Anarchist old guard could mobilise its supporters, the resolution was carried abolishing the commitment to Anarchic Communism accepted in 1905[53] Only after the Congress did the Anarchist rump fully realise what had occurred. In the columns of *La Protesta* they organised a campaign of vilification against the Syndicalists. This finally resulted in the creation of a breakaway Anarchist federation. It kept the name F.O.R.A., but added to it 'del Quinto Congreso' as a sign of adherence to the congress of 1905 which had accepted Anarchic Communism. However, only the bakers, some of the dockers, the street carters and a number of the smaller industrial and artisan unions re-joined them.[54]

52 Ibid. p. 29.

53 Marotta, Vol. 2, pp. 182–98.

54 According to *La Protesta*, 3 April 1915, the only groups which opposed the Syndicalists' attempt to abolish the commitment to Anarchic Communism were the carters, the carpenters, the bricklayers, the painters, the cigarette and shoe workers

The Syndicalists were left in control of the F.O.R.A. proper, and they gained an important new recruit with the affiliation of García's F.O.M.

The year 1915 marked a second important stage in the demise of Anarchism as a mass working class movement in Argentina. Its main significance had been twofold. It had prevented the unions from being absorbed by the Socialist Party, and it had helped to crystallise and establish the tradition of repression in relations between the State and the urban working class.

Although the Syndicalists won this important victory in 1915, their control of the union movement did not mean that at this point they led a movement with massive support within the working class. Membership figures for the unions are difficult to estimate with any degree of accuracy. It was later claimed that in the seven months between the 1915 congress and the end of the year a total of 21,332 members, from fifty affiliated unions, had paid monthly subscriptions. The figure was an aggregate for the seven months, and taking a simple average, it would appear that total membership ranged around 3,000.[55] It was only a tiny proportion of the working class of Buenos Aires. Nevertheless, the influence of this small nucleus kept alive the tradition of competing loyalties within the working class, and prevented the Socialists from achieving their long standing goal of harnessing the unions to their own cause.

The workers and the State, 1912–16

The relationship between the workers and the State underwent no overt change in 1912 after the introduction of the Sáenz Peña Law. This was illustrated by the government's handling of a major strike of railway footplatemen in 1912. While the new electoral law was still being debated in 1911, the drivers' and firemen's union, La Fraternidad, presented the foreign-owned railway companies with a comprehensive list of demands, covering wage scales and working conditions. The minister of public works, Ezequiel Ramos Mexía, who dealt with railway questions, immediately determined to break the strike. He publicly called

Footnote 54 (continued)
and a number of small bakers' unions. The carters and bakery workers continued to be the most important in later years.

[55] Figures taken from the F.O.R.A.'s press organ, *La Organización Obrera*, 7 December 1918.

the strikers 'pirates', and took steps to help the companies find replacements. In February 1912, some two months after it had begun, the strike began to collapse. Those suspected of union activities were dismissed. Sáenz Peña, in spite of a number of promises to the men, did nothing practical in their favour.[56]

The government's unconditional support for the railway companies during the 1912 railway strike again clearly expressed the limitations of Sáenz Peña's reformist objectives. It reflected the inflexibility of the elite's position and, in spite of its efforts to promote a new atmosphere of stability, its adherence to the attitudes which had been manifest during the Anarchist period from 1900 onwards. Thus while the reforms led eventually to an acceptance of Radicalism, they failed to result in any significant change in attitudes towards the workers.

However, the Sáenz Peña Law did have some relevance towards the working class in one key aspect. It enfranchised the native-born workers, who were mainly concentrated in skilled occupations, and who were now, through the Syndicalist movement, beginning to move into a position of control over the unions.

In spite of the inflexibility of the government's position towards the railway workers, the new importance of the working class vote became evident as soon as the electoral reforms were implemented. During the railway strike there were occasional voices raised in Congress in token support of the men's position.[57] Also, during the strike, La Fraternidad made a first attempt to exploit the new electoral law in its own favour. In a circular to its local branches in February 1912, the union leaders issued the following orders: 'We know that commerce is protesting on account of the lack of transport services – Cargoes are not being moved – IT IS IMPERATIVE THAT THESE PROTESTS ARE SENT DIRECTLY TO THE CHAMBER OF DEPUTIES AND NOT TO THE MINISTRY OF THE INTERIOR.'[58]

[56] The course of the strike may be followed in the *Review of the River Plate*, 1 December 1911, *passim*, and in La Fraternidad's internal files, see *Documento Huelga*, 1912. Ramos Mexía was among the most noted of the 'railway ministers' during this period. He was often referred to directly as 'the Paladin of the private railways' owing to his great confidence in the developmental possibilities of the railway system. For many years he made frequent contributions to the *Review of the River Plate*. His presence in Sáenz Peña's cabinet again illustrates the highly conservative character of this administration.

[57] For a facsimile of the congressional debates on the railway strike see Fraternidad, pp. 256–320.

[58] La Fraternidad internal files: *Huelga, 1912*, Circular of 8 February 1912.

If this heralded a potential change as a result of the new legislation, it had little effect on the outcome of the strike, although major congressional elections were due the following month. Any early efforts to attract the working class vote suffered from improvisation, and from the patently opportunistic impulses underlying them. None of the parties appeared, in principle, refractory to some measure of social reform. But it was easy to introduce legislation; the problem lay in forcing it through the committee stage in Congress, which frequently lasted up to five years.[59] Delays like this made it evident enough that the reformers' hearts were rarely in their work, and that they were generally motivated merely by a desire to embarrass the Socialists.

Legislation which was accepted was extremely limited in scope. The more common practice was to leave the matter to private initiative. In 1912, for example, a number of Catholic humanitarians announced the creation of a workers' housing scheme. But the committee's capital was no more than 3 million pesos, sufficient for no more than 3,000 houses in twenty years.[60] It was a scheme of derisory proportions, considering that the city's tenement population amounted to 150,000. In 1913 it was estimated that 80% of the working class population of the city of Buenos Aires lived as families in single room tenements, in 'a rotting heap of nationalities and languages', as one observer described them.[61]

Interest in the working class problem was still largely dominated by fears of the 'professional agitators' and the Socialist Party. Referring to the proposals for social legislation, a speaker in Congress in 1912 declared:

> I see these laws of social improvement not as socialist laws, but as laws of civilisation and progress... I would rather call them anti-socialist laws, because they are designed to put an end to class differences, to unite the capitalist with the worker, the powerful classes with the working classes. These laws will close the furrows opened by sectarianism and by the prejudices which divide society.[62]

Thus in 1916 the overall position can be summarised as follows. First there were signs that the Sáenz Peña Law did imply certain marginal changes in the position of the working class. On the other hand, the traditional fears and resentments on the part of the elite against the immi-

[59] This was the fate of a proposal for the regulation of domestic labour introduced in the Senate in 1913. The legislation was not passed until 1918.

[60] Alejandro E. Bunge, *La Prensa*, 24 June 1919.

[61] Panettieri, p. 181.

[62] *Diario de Sesiones*, Camera de Diputados, Vol. 2, 1912, p. 129. The speaker, incidentally, was a Radical, Rogelio Araya.

grants and the 'agitators' had not declined. Third was the rise of Syndicalism and the changes it implied for the unions and in the tactics chosen for the pursuit of the class struggle. Fourth was Radicalism, a movement seeking to add to its mass following in order to supplant the oligarchy as a ruling elite. The convergence of these conditions was to prove the most dramatic of the immediate short-term effects of the political changes occurring after 1912.

CHAPTER 5

The first Radical government, 1916–22

The general course of Argentine politics after 1916 was shaped by the relationship between successive Radical governments and the conservative elite groups which they replaced. The election victory won by the Radicals in 1916 appeared initially a reflection of the capacity of the traditional ruling class for retrenchment and self-preservation. Although the original objective of creating a majoritarian conservative party along the lines laid down by Pellegrini and Sáenz Peña had failed, and direct control over the administration had passed into new hands, there was no reason to believe that the real power of the elite had disappeared or diminished in any significant way. The army and navy had the same commanders as before 1916. The major lobby associations representing the elite's interests, such as the Sociedad Rural, were still intact. Also, powerful members of the elite still retained their positions of close contact with the foreign business groups.

The Radical government in 1916

In many respects the oligarchy appeared to have merely changed its form. In Yrigoyen's first cabinet in 1916, five out of the eight ministers were either cattle-owning landowners in the province of Buenos Aires or closely connected with the export sector. The minister of finance was Domingo E. Salaberry, who was involved in exporting, banking and real estate.[1] The minister of agriculture, who later became minister of foreign affairs, was Honorio Pueyrredón, a major landowner and patrician from the province of Buenos Aires. The minister of marine was Federico Alvarez de Toledo, who also possessed large areas of land in Buenos Aires and in the province of Mendoza. Pablo Torello, the minister of public works was, like Pueyrredón, a major landowner. Yrigoyen's first minister of foreign affairs, Carlos Becú, was a person

[1] In 1923 Salaberry committed suicide after having been impeached by Congress for the corrupt distribution of licences to export sugar in 1920.

with similar background. He and Pueyrredón had until comparatively recently belonged to parties opposed to the Radicals. Becú was a political protégé of Estanislao Zeballos, who was Roca's foreign minister in his second term. Pueyrredón had remained a member of General Mitre's Party, the Unión Cívica, until after 1912. The other ministers, Ramón Gómez, the minister of the interior, Elpidio González, the minister of war and José P. Salinas, the minister of education, came from more humble backgrounds. They owed their rise to their control of the Radical party machine in different key provinces, Gómez in Santiago del Estero, González in Córdoba and Salinas in Jujuy.[2] The vice-president, Pelagio Luna, who died in 1919, was also chosen because of his provincial connections in Salta.

Under these circumstances the influential groups within the elite, which had finally become resigned to a change of government, were encouraged to believe that they had simply delegated their former direct power to the new government. The Radicals seemed in many respects to have the same general objectives as themselves, and to be worthy of carrying on where Sáenz Peña had left off.

Radicalism still largely retained its more conservative features. For example, many of the leaders of the new administration, most particularly Yrigoyen himself, were more markedly clerical than most of their predecessors, many of whom were Freemasons. In 1918, *La Vanguardia* declared: 'Never has the influence of the Church been greater than at present ... the government is pursuing a Christian Democrat policy with the help of the Church, a paternalistic protective attitude towards the workers, so long as they remain submissive and resigned.'[3]

Also Yrigoyen had failed to win control by force. He had obtained the presidency as much by courtesy of Sáenz Peña and his successor, De la Plaza, as by his own efforts. In 1916 the Radicals won little more than the office of the presidency. They were still in opposition in most of the provinces, and they were also still a minority in the National Con-

[2] Gómez, the minister of the interior, was a constant butt for the ridicule of the opposition parties. In April 1917, he travelled to Córdoba on a party mission apparently disguised as a chauffeur, where he was arrested by the local police on the grounds of suspicious behaviour. (Cf. *La Vanguardia*, 9 April 1917.) Salinas's foremost ability was to conduct conversations in Latin. Elpidio González was generally regarded as the epitome of the parvenu elements promoted by Yrigoyen. He was often sneeringly referred to as a person who, before his political career began, 'tocaba la guitarra' (used to play the guitar), in his native province of Córdoba.

[3] *La Vanguardia*, 14 April 1918.

gress. There the government only managed to win a majority in the popularly elected Chamber of Deputies in 1918. In the Senate, whose members enjoyed the lengthy term of nine years and were normally elected by the provincial legislatures, the conservatives continued to hold a majority until 1922 and beyond. In addition to their other prerogatives, the conservatives therefore kept control over government legislation.

In 1916 Yrigoyen's position was thus still relatively weak, and his policies were sharply conditioned by his relationship with the elite. His mandate was the achievement of two general objectives. First he was bound by the need to uphold the economic interests of the landed groups. Secondly he had to establish a new relationship with the urban sectors, which had been the main source of political instability since the turn of the century. In many respects these two objectives seemed contradictory and incompatible. The principal reason why the conservative groups themselves had failed to organise a mass party was because they had been unable to adapt their position as producer interests to the need to offer something concrete to the urban groups. Only the Radicals had been apparently able to surmount this difficulty. They had become 'inorganic'. They had avoided drawing up a specific programme. They had cloaked their objectives in a veil of moralistic rhetoric, and their real commitments with a deceptively generous effluence of paternalism. Upon this had been superimposed continual hints at wider access for the middle class groups to government offices.

This principle of mediating between elite and urban interests shaped the character of political conflict after 1916. It was not so much that the new government was impelled consciously into attacking the elite's economic interests directly. Like their predecessors, the Radicals evaluated their own successes in terms of their ability to expand and consolidate the primary export economy, rather than attempt to change it. At the end of Yrigoyen's term in 1922, it is difficult to point to any significant change in the deeper texture of Argentine society. In 1922 the export sector still dominated the country's economy as it had done before 1916. The currency, taxation, tariff and land systems also remained the same, and the connections with the British were still as strong as they had been before. The net achievements of the Radical government were very few indeed, and these either complemented what had gone before, or were mere tamperings which could easily be reversed.

The Radicals were unable to develop any wider commitment to more substantial change at this point because they themselves, as a coalition of landowners and non-industrial middle class groups, were immediate beneficiaries of the primary export economy as producers and consumers. Their objectives were redistributive, rather than structural in implication. What they were primarily aiming for was to democratise *estanciero* society by rationalising and improving the system of social and political relations which had emerged from it. These objectives are aptly captured in the following statements, which are taken from the year 1920:

> [The country's 'social constitution'] will be unobtainable until governments appreciate their inescapable duty to provide the means for justice to extend its benefits to every social rank ... Democracy does not simply consist in the guarantee of personal liberty: it also involves the opportunity of everyone to enjoy a minimum level of welfare.[4]

> In assiduous and direct contact with the People and with the progressive activities of the nation, President Yrigoyen, the true democrat, has managed to win something which the Presidents of Class were never able to win – the love and confidence of the citizenry.[5]

The dual emphasis on 'welfare' and 'contact' also indicates that the Radicals were aiming to achieve political integration and a state of class harmony. They intended to maintain the existing socio-economic framework, but promote institutionalised political participation outside the traditional ruling class. These objectives involved the government with two key groups, the 'dependent' professional middle class, which already before 1916 had become an important component of Radicalism, and secondly with the urban working class. The government's contacts with these two groups shaped its relationship with the elite and beyond it with foreign capital. The final quadruple relationship which emerged came to occupy a dominant place in Argentine politics up to 1930.

The central problem stemmed from tendencies on the part of the Radical goverment to move too closely into line with the interests of the urban groups. This triggered dangerous expressions of political conflict, when it began to threaten the elite's relationship with foreign capital, and overseas markets. Each of the major crises of the Radical government, in 1919 and in 1930, were directly related to a process of this sort.

[4] Message to the National Congress, 30 September 1920. Quoted in Puiggrós, pp. 53–4.

[5] *La Epoca*, 11 January 1920.

At the same time the inclination towards the urban sectors underlay the survival of conservatism during these years, and the eventual failure of the elite to delegate the supervision of its interests to the Radicals.

The techniques of popular leadership

In one respect the advent of the Radical government marked a revolutionary change in the style of Argentine politics. The staid, closeted atmosphere of the oligarchy was swiftly swept away in a wave of popular euphoria. When Yrigoyen was sworn in as president, his coach was dragged through the streets by his supporters from the party committees in the federal capital.[6] Yrigoyen himself, through his dependence on novel methods of leadership, and through his control over a mass party with ramifications throughout the country, came to occupy a very different position from that of his predecessors. Although with Roca, Juárez Celman, Figueroa Alcorta, and at an earlier date with Rosas, there had been a tendency to personalise policies and issues, with Yrigoyen this became one of the central stylistic elements of Argentine politics. It became the accepted convention for the Radicals to prefix their actions and statements with lengthy panegyrics to their leader. Equally the opposition reserved its most biting attacks for the president himself. In Buenos Aires there was one newspaper, *La Mañana* (which became known as *La Fronda* in 1919), which discussed nothing else but the alleged failures and shortcomings of the *peludo*, as Yrigoyen now universally became known:

> Sr Irigoyen[7] is a simple boss, wise and supple in the manoeuvres of the committee. The great orator, writer and thinker! He is nothing more than a legend

[6] Events like this marked the introduction of mass psychology techniques to Argentine politics. The day after the inauguration, *La Epoca*, the government's press organ, published references to the ceremony which it attributed to a foreign diplomatic observer. This makes a good example of the type of mass appeal the Radicals were aiming for: 'I do not remember – and this is not meant as gratuitous flattery – anything comparable to this magistral scene where the Ruler surrenders himself into the arms of his People, and is led, amidst an electrified multitude, to the highest seat of the leadership of his country... I was quite entranced by the spectacle... I felt impelled... to run forward myself, mingle with the gathered throngs, cry out with them, close to the leader to cheer, to applaud, to acclaim him' (*La Epoca*, 7 October 1916).

[7] The 'Señor' was a constant derisive reminder of the fraudulent claim Yrigoyen had made to hold a doctoral degree. Until 1918 his name was always spelt with an I. The change to 'Y' was probably a personal conceit which he used to distinguish between himself and contemporaries bearing the same name.

of mystification, who after thirty years of obscurity, has suddenly exploded into the government, as the exponent of ignorance, regression and brigandry.[8]

At the same time there was always a great deal of fascination with Yrigoyen's personality. In spite of their distaste for his methods, and their jealousy of his political acumen, many members of the opposition betrayed more than a touch of incredulity at the manner in which the new president defended and manipulated his position. A leader of the conservative opposition, Rodolfo Moreno, declared in 1918:

A man incapable of facing public debate, because he lacked the necessary gifts to do so. A man who relied for his prestige on surrounding himself with a veil of mystery. What popular fantasy could have created a statesman out of a man who has never delivered a speech, written a book, traced out a programme, obtained a university degree and has never taken part in conventional social intercourse ... and who, in a word, possesses none of the qualities which stand out in a democracy, an ability to discuss matters, and subject himself to free examination?[9]

Yrigoyen was indeed something of a strange novelty in Argentine politics. Even when he became president he still refused to make public speeches. During his period of office the practice of delivering the presidential address at the beginning of the congressional sessions in person was abandoned, much to the chagrin of the staid elements of the conservative opposition. Instead Yrigoyen would write a rambling preamble to the message, most of it unintelligible to the average politician (often intentionally so), which the vice-president or his deputy would read. He appears to have spent much of his time in confabulation with his party collaborators, not in the presidential palace, the Casa Rosada, but in his modest and run-down home near the Plaza Constitución. His public appearances were still very limited, and often the only time he would be seen was while attending the funeral of some apparently minor party dignitary. The opposition parties called this necrophilia, though it can be explained in terms of the high premium placed by Yrigoyen on loyalty to his political friends, and his emphasis on personal relationships in administering and supervising the party.

The president was also known as something of a sexual adept. Although he never married, he produced at least a dozen children by a succession of mistresses. Later in life – in the late 1920s during his

[8] *La Fronda*, 14 November 1919.

[9] Quoted in *La Mañana*, 14 January 1918.

second presidency – cabinet ministers would complain of being kept waiting for days at a time, while Yrigoyen entertained bevies of young widows, who had come as claimants for State pensions. Until he became president in 1916 photographs of him were extremely rare. On the occasion of his brother's funeral in April 1916, press photographs of the event unmistakeably revealed his tall frame, although his face was intentionally covered by a hat. He was said to object to photographs because of his Kraussian principles, which forbade the reproduction of his 'soul'. More likely this was all a little ploy to exploit the curiosity of the population. When he discovered the importance of the mass media for election purposes these petty idiosyncracies swiftly disappeared. By 1919 his portrait was plastered from one end of the country to the other. A union organiser from the period recalled a journey he had made around 1920 to the *yerba mate* plantations in the northern territories of Chaco and Misiones in search of recruits for his union. His efforts met with very little success. The Indian labourers proclaimed that their sole loyalties were to the 'Father of the Poor', Hipólito Yrigoyen, whose effigy they treasured on small alloy brooches given to them by Radical agents.[10]

The mystery and adulation surrounding Yrigoyen can be further illustrated by anecdotes and reportage. An example, given currency by an opponent in 1919, comes from the province of Mendoza. It refers to Yrigoyen and to the Radical leader of the province, José Néstor Lencinas. It seems that notions like this were sometimes put about, and the semi-hispanicised population of areas like Mendoza were encouraged to see their national leader, and explain the vagaries of his policies, in its anarchically apocalyptic terms:

> About three years ago, the present governor of the province of Mendoza, Dr José Néstor Lencinas, whose friendship with the president of the republic is well-known and appreciated throughout the country, suddenly began to express dissent with several aspects of his policy. But in reply to my protests against the iniquities of the national government, the governor made known to me a personal revelation.
>
> He said to me, 'I also used to stand in protest against Yrigoyen, but four nights ago, as I lay asleep, there spoke in my ear the voice of a dearly loved soul – that of my brother Santiago – which said to me in an ethereal, magnetic tone: "President Yrigoyen is not Hipólito Yrigoyen. Our teacher, friend and apostle is at present tending a flock of sheep in the Guaminí district. On 12

[10] My interview with José Otero of the Federación Obrera Marítima.

October 1916, he completed the mission set for him by his party and his Motherland. On that same day, transmuting himself into Yrigoyen's human form, there arrived from India, Joaquín Chrisnamurty, also known as Alcione, a young man of twenty-eight years old, and a veritable fountain of scientific knowledge, which he had set down in a book in eight days at the age of fourteen in the University of Oxford – a feat which would have demanded three thousand years of labour from any other person. This Chrisnamurty is a second God. You can believe me', added Dr Lencinas, 'that whatever he may do from the presidency will be for the happiness of each one of us. He may destroy the country, but surely will rebuild it better. It is possible that the present generation may not comprehend his labours, but when in two thousand years time, humanity studies the history of Argentina, it will possess a true insight into this miraculous leader.'[11]

Such bizarre extravagances were rare, although it was not infrequent even in Buenos Aires to find party stalwarts in public meetings frenetically crying 'Yrigoyen es un dios' (Yrigoyen is a god). This purely symbolic appeal may have played some part in mobilising support for the Radicals in the more backward zones of the country, but generally in the cities the attempt to recruit allegiances was based on something more concrete and material than this. An example is the following, again given currency by a person hostile to the Radicals, but which does not have to be taken literally for the point to be made:

Sr Irigoyen was an assiduous visitor to the baths in Calle Suipacha, 'The Arabian Palace'... Each of the junior employees of the house cherished a kind of adoration for their client, who treated them with friendliness, delicacy and courtesy, never forgetting to ask about their families, their affairs and their needs. It was a unanimously held opinion, among those who talked with him, that he knew how to use to advantage his innate gift of friendly conversation, and also a quality of suggestiveness which escaped few of his hearers.

While he was president on the first occasion, he ceased attendance, assuredly absorbed in giving attention to his duties... A number of his friends continued their attendance as clients of the house. Among them was Sr Crovetto, who was later governor of the province of Buenos Aires and president of the National Mortgage Bank...

In the establishment there worked as a chiropodist a young man named Guarino, who was no less expressive than the others in his regard for the president. As he was attending Sr Crovetto one day he lamented that he came no longer... 'Just now when I need him', he added, 'and surely he would have attended to the request I wish to make to him'. 'If there is anything I can convey on

[11] Raúl Villanueva, a Radical dissident, in *La Fronda*, 14 November 1919.

your behalf . . . ?', the client courteously offered. Guarino, emboldened by this, launched off into an explanation. A sister of his had passed out as a trainee teacher, but had tried without success to acquire the necessary authorization to allow her to seek a stable position . . .

Two days later the influential Crovetto arrived in haste at the baths, and finding Guarino, said to him, 'Get your apron off at once, put your jacket and hat on and come with me' . . . A moment later, Guarino, who did not know what was happening, was sprawled out on the seat of a luxury car at the side of his patron and on the way to Government House. Arriving there, they proceeded immediately to the presidency, entering by a special door, without having to pass through the throngs of jobbers, functionaries and legislators who sometimes had to wait months to be received.

The president was waiting for them and, seeing them enter, went quickly towards Guarino to embrace him. Patting him on the back he said. 'My dear friend, you have no idea how pleased I am to see you here, above all knowing what Crovetto had told me of your needs and how I can help you with the request you have come to make of me.'

In the meantime, Guarino, overcome with emotion at such a reception from no less a person than the most excellent president of the republic, wept like the Magdalene and was unable to say a single word. When finally he managed to control himself a little, he managed to stammer out the details of what he wanted.

At the call of the first magistrate appeared a secretary who was bidden to summon the president of the National Council of Education. He was brought in from the mass outside, where he had been ordered to remain until required. In the presence of his chief he was presented to 'My good friend Guarino', for whom there were words of eulogy, extolling his fidelity and good qualities. Immediately the president issued an order, 'Return to your office with this gentleman to whom you will hand over an authorisation for the appointment of the head of School No . . . for his sister.'

Guarino's face turned to him. He thought he was dreaming of a story from the *Thousand and One Nights*, and still more when his powerful friend added on dismissing him, 'Send to me with Crovetto a list of your relatives who require positions, and the corresponding details of their occupations.'

He was not slow to send on the necessary information and, from then on, he and his privileged relatives increased the number of those who would have been prepared to die in the defence of their idol.[12]

The new popular style of politics was also accompanied by a much greater political involvement on the part of the urban groups, which had been relegated to only an occasional or indirect role before. The Radicals viewed this as symptomatic of a new spirit of democracy. The opposition

[12] Angel Carrasco, *Lo que yo vi desde el '80* (Procmo, Buenos Aires, 1947), pp. 246–8.

groups, on the other hand, including the Socialists, frequently described it as mob rule. They referred to the Radicals' supporters in the committees as the *chusma*, the rabble, whose distinguishing traits were an inordinate venality, and an insatiable appetite for corruption.

Nevertheless, the presence of these groups served to accelerate the slow transformation which had been taking place among the political parties since the 1890s. At every level of politics it injected new patterns and styles of contact between the politicians and the electorate. Electioneering, apart from in the remote subsistence areas of the interior, ceased to be a matter of simple bribery, and evolved fully into a problem of mass organisation. There was a parallel revolution in the art of political propaganda, and a new style of popular journalism appeared. Finally, as a reflection of the much greater range of articulated demands within the political system, the process of government decision-making, and the span of government activities, began to acquire new complex dimensions.

Radicalism itself remained a hybrid conglomeration. The regional and class disparities it enshrined, but had failed to conquer, prevented it further from acquiring the 'organic' forms the reformers of 1912 had aspired for. In many ways it remained an offshoot of the 'personalist' parties of the past, with many of the same authoritarian features as the governments of the oligarchy. The heterogeneous environment in which it operated, and the conflicting demands to which it was subject, preserved an impression of improvisation and confusion in the party. In 1919 one of the leading opposition conservative newspapers, *La Nación*, declared:

> The Radical Party lacks any concrete concepts of government. It would be unable to define a fully integrated and precise strategy. Its ideals are nebulous and its aspirations only reveal themselves in the vague claim of unlimited self-virtue. Its sense of common identity is no more than a torrential impulse of the memory of its days of opposition, which are negative by self-definition. The only thing it has . . . which is positive, is the person of its chief, Señor Irigoyen. He is the exclusive past and present point of reference.[13]

The Argentine economy during the First World War

Before beginning to explore the relationship between the government and the urban groups in more detail, it is important to review in brief economic developments during the war and immediately post-war

[13] *La Nación*, 24 November 1919.

periods. When Yrigoyen took over in 1916, the country was in the throes of a serious depression. This began in 1913 with the sudden interruption of foreign investment, which was related to the financial crisis in Europe triggered by wars in the Balkans.[14] The same year the harvest failed and the volume of foreign trade declined. With the outbreak of war in August 1914, the depression deepened. Foreign investment ceased completely, land values declined and a serious shipping shortage developed. The balance of payments was only maintained by a serious contraction in imports. The shortage of imported goods persisted throughout the whole war and post-war period, as Britain and other European countries shifted their resources to war production. Only after 1917 did Argentina's export trade recover, as demand for foodstuffs for the Allied troops in Europe increased.

The war and post-war period, on the economic front, thus divides into two major phases. The first, between 1913 and 1917, was a period of depression. The second, between 1918 and the beginning of the post-war depression in 1921, was a period of boom, which was created primarily by rising external demand for Argentine exports. During the first period there was considerable unemployment, which mainly affected the urban working class in areas of the economy linked with the export sector. This found reflection in the fact that between 1914 and 1916 over 170,000 former immigrants left the country.

The main effect of the war, which was most marked in the second period, was rapid inflation. Rising prices affected both imported and domestically produced goods. The price of imports rose as the war rapidly raised production costs in Europe, and as a result of the rapid increase in international shipping rates. By 1918 the volume of imports had declined to 50% of the 1910 level, while during the same period prices increased by 300%.[15] The prices of domestically produced goods were affected to the extent that they depended on imported raw materials.

[14] Guido Di Tella and Manuel Zymelman, *Las etapas del desarrollo económico argentino* (EUDEBA, Buenos Aires, 1967), pp. 291–3. There are also accounts of this period in Vernon L. Phelps, *The International Economic Position of Argentina* (University of Pennsylvania, Philadelphia, 1937); Joseph S. Tulchin, 'The Argentine economy during the First World War', *Review of the River Plate* (19 June, 30 June, 10 July, 1970); E. Tornquist and Co. Ltd, *Business Conditions in Argentina* (Buenos Aires, 1914, *passim*, quarterly). There is a long discussion of the effect of the crisis in 1913 and 1914 on Argentina in A. G. Ford, *The Gold Standard, 1880–1914. Britain and Argentina* (Oxford, 1962), pp. 170–88.

[15] Tornquist, (summary for 1919).

The most vital commodity affected was imported coal. In 1913 over 4 million tons of coal were imported. By 1913 this had dropped to little over 700,000 tons. After 1917 further inflationary pressures were generated by rising foreign demand for Argentine agricultural products. Since supply remained relatively inelastic, external demand had a growing effect on local consumer prices. By 1918 these had increased by 75% in comparison with 1910.[16]

Table 3 summarises these developments in index form, employing the year 1914 as a base. This shows the increase in the volume of exports after 1914 (except in 1917 when the harvest failed), and the parallel decline in imports, until the post-war boom in 1920. It also portrays the manner in which prices rose, particularly those of imported goods: while the volume of imports dropped, their total value rose considerably.

TABLE 2 *Indices of foreign trade, 1914–22*

	Volume of exports	Volume of imports	Value of exports	Value of imports
1914	100	100	100	100
1915	127	84	116	114
1916	112	81	129	142
1917	79	70	171	176
1918	113	62	174	256
1919	135	86	190	244
1920	133	111	200	276
1921	116	103	138	228
1922	153	112	109	188

Source: Based on Di Tella and Zymelman, pp. 320, 352.

Inflation was one of the most important factors governing the relationship between the landed elite and the urban sectors during the first Radical government. Its effect was to redistribute income from the urban sectors to the rural and exporting groups. While the landowners and the exporting interests profited from inflation through the higher prices they received for their goods, between 1914 and 1918 the urban cost of living rose by about 65%. The average cost of food went up by 40%, rents by about 15%, and specific consumer items like clothing, which was

[16] Ibid.

either imported or whose production depended on imports of European raw materials, by almost 300%.[17]

The government's political strategy

In 1916 the effects of inflation on the urban consumers put the Radical government in a rather difficult position. It was committed to ending political tension between the elite and the urban sectors and consolidating its own position with the electorate at a moment when, as a result of inflation, the interests of the two groups were diverging sharply. The government could not afford to prevent the landed interests from profiting from the wartime boom in primary food products. On the other hand, unless it attempted at least to mitigate the effects of inflation it ran the risk of forfeiting its links with the urban groups. This would leave the way open for its competitors like the Socialist Party, which was more explicitly linked with urban interests. It was thus necessary to find some way of appeasing the urban groups without simultaneously alienating the elite.

So far as the urban middle class groups were concerned, the only practicable way of doing this, it was found, was by increasing the supply of bureaucratic and professional positions. The readoption of the traditional mechanisms of political patronage, and its long-term effect on patterns of State spending, eventually became the central feature of relations between the urban middle class and the conservative elite, and the basic condition governing the Radicals' ability to maintain their middle class support. Of course the use of such expedients did not mean that the whole of the voting native middle class obtained a job in the bureaucracy. Offices were used primarily to establish and maintain the nexus between the government and the party committees, and in turn the committees operated as the main device for the mobilisation of the electorate, often using more conventional techniques.[18]

[17] Tornquist. There is a large amount of material relating to the urban cost of living during the war period in Alejandro E. Bunge, *Los problemas económicos del presente* (Buenos Aires, 1919).

[18] Radicals who denied that patronage played an important part in mobilising popular support neglected to mention the manner in which the system operated: 'With 4,000 offices to share out, you cannot win an election in the capital. Let's suppose that 10,000 have been handed out. What importance can this have for a party so colossal that it wins 400,000 votes ... Is it really fair to say that the 64,000 votes we won in the last election for deputies ... were obtained through prebends and public posts ...?' Andres Ferreyra, 1922. (Quoted in Cantón 'Elecciones', p. 183.)

However, the patronage system did not develop immediately. The main short-term problem in 1916 was that any increase in State spending to expand the bureaucracy would require an increase in taxation. In the absence of reforms to the country's taxation system, this could only be achieved at the cost of the urban sectors themselves. The bulk of State revenues came from tariffs on imported goods, and was thus levied on consumption. To change this, the only conceivable major modification to the taxation system would be a tax on land. Such a tax was difficult to envisage. It would be a direct attack on the landed elite and, apart from anything else, it would endanger the coalition character of Radicalism itself. But it was equally very difficult to increase tariffs when already the prices of imported goods were so high.[19]

Before 1919, when imports and revenues began to pick up, the government proved unwilling to increase public spending by any dramatic amount. It was able to justify this up to a point by invoking some of its principles from its years in opposition. Although few, least of all the urban middle classes, had taken them seriously, the Radicals had claimed before 1916 that once in power they would end the traditional Spoils System, as part of the programme of 'moral regeneration' they had taken on themselves. Consequently the patronage system was rather slow in developing. Most of the appointees of previous administrations, at least in the national government, were allowed to keep their positions.[20]

Instead in its first two years of office the government attempted to promote a number of mild reform schemes in Congress which were aimed mainly at the rural tenant groups. There was a proposal for the creation of an agricultural bank to help with colonisation schemes. Also an attempt was made to impose a temporary tax on agricultural exports to relieve destitute farmers, and to promote a public works scheme to help cope with the urban unemployment problem. Another piece of

[19] There was a slight increase in tariff values at the end of June 1920. It is significant that at this moment the government began to attempt action to reduce the cost of living. See below, chapter 9. For a study of the tariff question see Carl Solberg, 'Tariffs and politics in Argentina, 1916–1930', *Hispanic American Historical Review*, Vol. 53, No. 2 (May 1973), pp. 260–84. This provides additional interesting data, though its conclusion – that the Sociedad Rural Argentina dictated tariff policy – is a little disappointing in its simplicity. There is no doubt that there were wider issues at stake than this.

[20] With some exceptions, which are dealt with in the next chapter.

projected legislation aimed for the purchase of shipping, which could be used to reduce freight charges on the Atlantic run.

These measures are best interpreted as an attempt by the government to consolidate its grip over the rural sectors in the pampas area, and to win control over the provincial administrations of Buenos Aires, Córdoba and Entre Rios. This was also plainly the reason why the conservative opposition refused to consider such legislation. One of Yrigoyen's later most prominent opponents, Federico Pinedo, described the measures in the following terms:

> When Yrigoyen became president in the style of a Messiah, and his redemptory legislation was being awaited after its twenty years of preparation and gestation, he produced a grotesque balloon of nonsense in the shape of four bills. The only outstanding quality of these was their laughable childishness. In one of his messages he announced his intention of reforming the agrarian sector by means of a State-controlled colonisation scheme. This, it was said, was necessary to correct the evils of private enterprise. In fact the proposal consisted of an authorisation to the executive to employ the ridiculously high sum of 30 million pesos in loans to farmers for such different things as buying private or public land, housing construction or the purchase of livestock. The allocation of all this money was to be decided exclusively by government officials, without the law saying anything about the recipients or the conditions of the loans. Everything was left to the government's whim.[21]

The opposition groups in Congress refused to accept these tax changes because of their apprehensions that the revenues from them would be employed for openly partisan purposes. Without being unfair to the government, there is no reason to believe that the opposition was wrong. The Radicals were in a weak position in the Congress and in many of the provinces in 1916, and were seeking means to consolidate their position.

Another of the government's proposals was that it should be authorised to negotiate a loan with a number of New York banks to consolidate the public debt. This again illustrated its financial orthodoxy at this point, its unwillingness to increase public spending and its initial search for alternatives to a patronage system based simply on increased State spending. Similar legislation had been attempted in the past. The only real novelty was a proposed income tax scheme introduced in 1918. How-

[21] Federico Pinedo, 'Testimonio', *Revista de Historia: La crisis de 1930* (Buenos Aires, 1958), p. 116. In 1916 Pinedo was only a youth, but his later prominence in the 1920s makes him an authoritative commentator.

ever, none of these projects prospered except, some time later during the export boom, the temporary tax on agricultural exports.[22]

The export tax was finally passed by Congress on 18 January 1918, soon after a major grain deal at guaranteed prices had been negotiated with the Allies. Its acceptance by Congress at this point reflected the opinion that the burden of the tax would either fall on the Allies or the exporters, and not on the producers. The income tax scheme was extremely mild, and can hardly be instanced as more than a token measure to reverse the effects of inflation on the distribution of income. Working class and middle class incomes between 2,500 and 10,000 pesos per year were to be taxed at $\frac{3}{4}\%$ per year, with the rate progressively increasing to 7% for incomes over 150,000 pesos. The estimated revenue from the tax was 30 million pesos, a sum which would not have solved the revenue problem. Nevertheless this measure was more than the conservatives had attempted.[23]

The development of the patronage system

In spite of not unwarranted conservative fears that any change in the tax system would be used by the Radicals as subsidies for their election campaigns, the failure of this legislation illustrated the extreme unwillingness of the conservative majority in Congress to back the reforms they had made in 1912 with further tangible concessions. Under these circumstances of political *impasse*, in 1918 and 1919, the government's resort to cruder patronage techniques became marked. By 1919, as imports picked up again after the war, the revenue position also improved. Also by 1919, as will be seen later, there were signs that middle class support for the government in the city of Buenos Aires was beginning to crumble.

Between 1919 and 1922 the use of government offices for political purposes developed into the principal nexus linking the government with the middle class groups. Yrigoyen made administrative posts available to the party's local bosses in the committees, and they applied them to establish firm bridgeheads of support among the native-born electorate. During these years Yrigoyen's personal position as leader of the government and the party came to rest almost exclusively on his ability to mani-

[22] For a fuller description of the scope of the legislation see Roberto Etchepareborda, *Yrigoyen y el congreso* (Raigal, Buenos Aires, 1956).

[23] For a description of the income tax scheme see Tornquist (August–December 1918).

pulate State patronage. The following remarks by *La Vanguardia* in 1922 are a bitter, though substantially accurate, comment on the importance the system had acquired by this time:

Affiliation to the Radical Party is becoming a kind of passport or safe-conduct for all kinds of posts. This system owes its origin to the need to reward the nepotistical hordes of the 'Cause' with public offices. It has converted each of the national and municipal administrative departments into asylums for degenerates.[24]

The major recipients of these benefits were the urban 'dependent' middle class groups of immigrant extraction in Buenos Aires, and to a lesser extent in the other important cities near the Atlantic coast. These were the core groups of the Radical Party's committee organisation, who had joined the party in increasing numbers after 1900. On the other hand, the system discriminated against the immigrants, who had no vote to be won. Equally it did not benefit the working class, and the entrepreneurial groups, both of which were largely beyond the lure of jobs in the administration. Not surprisingly, the system was strongly opposed by the Socialist Party. It gave their main followers very little.

The main result of the growth of the patronage system was the great expansion of the links between Yrigoyen himself and the middle class *caudillos de barrio* in the party committees. As the system became more established, these representatives of the urban middle class groups began to appear among the upper reaches of the bureaucracy, and to compete with members of the party's traditional leadership for candidatures for elective offices.

Another of the leading features of Yrigoyen's government was thus a struggle for control over the party between the middle class groups and the elite wing, which had supported Radicalism since the early 1890s. This division had been foreshadowed in the disputes over Yrigoyen's candidature in 1916. Afterwards it put increasing strain on the cross-class character of the party. Opposition to Yrigoyen on the part of the party's aristocratic wing crystallised in the form of an attack on presidential 'personalism' and in a demand for the separation of the party and the government. The aim of this was to check Yrigoyen's power by rupturing the direct link between him and the middle class groups. At

[24] *La Vanguardia*, 18 January 1922. Before 1916 the Radicals had often described their movement as 'the Cause', as a means to contrast it with the oligarchy, which they called 'the Regime'.

the end of 1918 the elite wing, which was still a majority in the official, but increasingly powerless, organs of the party such as the National Committee and the Committee of the Federal Capital, issued an important manifesto. It provides a convenient summary of the dissident's objectives, and illustrates their growing disenchantment with Yrigoyen:

> Public opinion has no reason to see in our party any more than what it is today: a movement with no further programme beyond that of supporting the government... Let us proclaim therefore the need to react against the spineless instinct of unconditional support, against 'personalism', the lack of ideas, the predominance of mediocrity... Radicalism ought to continue to be an independent association of the citizenry, resolving to direct its actions by its own deliberations and by its own will. All interference or outside influence, especially of the 'personalist' kind, contradicts the definition of democracy... The party ought to define its position on the most urgent and important political problems... On indicating the need for such a programme, we do not mean to invest the party with an encyclopaedic collection of abstract principles. The Radical ideal, which most interests the electorate, is to assure good public administration. This ideal depends for its realisation upon the qualities of the individual, upon known competence, intellectual capacities and upon the behaviour of both functionaries and governors. Radicalism will fulfil its mission if it criticises those who do not fulfil these conditions... It is necessary to make a just assessment of the values of individuals to put the party into the hands of the most competent and capable.[25]

In 1918 and 1919 the party was brought very near to a major split on this issue. Yet in spite of the pressure of the 'Blue Group', as it became known, attempts to control or reverse the trend of Yrigoyen's increasing involvement with the middle class groups and with the precinct party bosses were unsuccessful. The elite group failed to obtain control of the party because it lacked access to the sources of party patronage, and consequently the means to construct a popular following. Its members depended themselves upon Yrigoyen for their political careers. Ultimately they were forced either to accept his leadership or a position of irredeemable political isolation. When in 1919 the opposition movement finally collapsed, the relationship between Yrigoyen, as the source of patronage, and the party committees, as the source of electoral support, became the party's dominating feature.

Thus the importance of the committees cannot be overstressed. They were the central link between the government and the electorate, and the most vital factor allowing Yrigoyen to consolidate his personal popularity.

[25] A facsimile of this document appears in the *Revista Argentina de Ciencias Políticas*, Vol. 17 (1919), pp. 484–7.

Equal in importance were the presidents of the committees, the precinct bosses or *caudillos de barrio*. From 1916 their influence began to increase markedly when they were appointed to serve in a legislative capacity in the Buenos Aires municipal council.[26] This gave them access to vital new sources of patronage. One of the perennial features of politics in Buenos Aires during these years was the tremendous rivalry for control over the committees between different aspirant ward bosses. In the annual party elections it was not unusual for two evenly balanced factions to emerge in each city *barrio*. Because control over the committees meant so much in terms of wealth and social standing, the elections were fought with keen intensity and with a total absence of scruple. It was far from unusual for bombs to be planted and gun-fights to break out among rival groups. Similarly to some extent organised crime and local politics evolved hand in hand.[27]

In certain cases the *caudillo de barrio* operated by linking up with local city interest groups.[28] But the more common characteristic of boss politics was a close personal tie with a specific neighbourhood. In 1918 *La Vanguardia*, arguing against the system, commented about the Radicals' choice of candidates for the municipal elections in Buenos Aires:

> The candidates are men with extensive contacts with the neighbourhoods in which they live. They can pretend that they are fully acquainted with local needs and offer a guarantee that they will make their contributions to them . . . But all this makes the council an arena for petty issues, where the general and permanent interests of the population become completely lost from view. Every preference is given to the play of local interests and minor rivalries.[29]

[26] In 1918 a system of proportional representation was introduced for the city council of Buenos Aires.

[27] The most notable example was the prolonged struggle in the 8th Ward of Buenos Aires, Balvanera Norte, between Benjamín Bonifacio and his opponents from 1921 onwards. At various junctures there were bombings, stabbings and gun-battles. Bonifacio eventually won, but made the mistake of joining the anti-Yrigoyen Antipersonalist group in 1924.

[28] An example was the relationship between the Radical boss José Amuchástegui and the Retailers' Association, the Centro de Almaceneros. At a banquet given in his honour in 1922 Amuchástegui recalled how his association had begun: 'In the city council there was an attempt to impose a new tax on you, and there were some there, in complete ignorance of your high vocation, who slandered your honour with indecorous allegations. I got up indignantly and protested with all my strength against these false imputations . . . From this moment my links with you began' (*Boletín Oficial del Centro de Almaceneros*, 5 June 1922).

[29] *La Vanguardia*, 29 August 1918.

By 1922 the Radical Party, made up of its local committees, became the largest single association in the country, with a membership in the federal capital alone of no less than 50,000.[30] This issue of control over the committees continued to be of fundamental importance during the 1920s, and it came eventually to dominate the relationship between the professional middle class and the elite groups up to 1930.

Regional issues

Yrigoyen's conflict with the party's elite wing was also significant in terms of the regional distribution of power within the party and the government's relationship with different regional groups. After 1916 Yrigoyen's following was strongest in the city and province of Buenos Aires and also in the province of Córdoba. In the province of Buenos Aires there was the largest concentration of the electorate, and this was also the most important export-based region. The other provinces came a poor second in terms of central government responsiveness to their interests and their influence within the national Radical Party.

Consequently the interregional tensions within the party, which had been apparent before 1916, particularly in Santa Fe and Entre Rios, intensified afterwards. Several of the leaders of the elite dissident faction, who emerged as the opponents of 'personalism' in 1918 and 1919, had direct links with these two provinces.[31] After 1919 the conflict deepened when the dependent middle class groups in Buenos Aires established a stranglehold over national government spending. This privilege generated antagonisms among some of the middle class groups in other provinces, where there was also an important dependent urban population.

A comparable situation developed in terms of the Radical government's relations with most of the non-pampas provinces in the interior. Their traditional position of economic and political subordination did not diminish with the advent of the Radicals to power. Particularly after 1919, the old practice of federal intervention, through which the national government assumed direct control over the provinces to correct local abuses of power, was resorted to on an increasing scale. The immediate aim was to create local carpet-bagger regimes subservient to the president,

[30] See Rock, 'Machine politics', pp. 249–53. This figure is an estimate based on the numbers voting in the annual committee elections.

[31] Examples are Leopoldo Melo and Miguel Laurencena. However, this point needs further investigation.

which would be in a position to control elections to the National Senate.[32] But the long-term effect of this system of indirect unitary control by the national government was an acceleration of the process of centralisation of power and wealth in the province and city of Buenos Aires.

To a certain extent this was a consequence of the widening of the franchise in 1912. The reforms gave the government the incentive to orientate its policies towards the more populous areas, where there was a higher concentration of the electorate. But the problem had other, more complex, angles to it. It reflected the difficulty of reconciling the interests of the urban consumers with those of the exporting interests, and it also emphasised the regional distribution of political influence within the landed elite.

To support the urban consumer interests during a period of inflation without injuring the stock-breeding and cereal interests in the province of Buenos Aires, Yrigoyen attempted to transfer the burden of making concessions to the urban groups to the politically weaker areas of the interior. Among the many examples of this was the sugar expropriation measure of 1920. This was a blatant attempt at discrimination against the producer interests of the interior to support the urban consumers while avoiding action against the pampas interests. In response to measures like this, and to the parallel use of federal interventions to impose corrupt client regimes on the interior provinces, a strong tradition of anti-*yrigoyenismo* had emerged before 1922 in some of the more influential provinces of the interior like San Juan, Mendoza and Tucumán. Similar regional conflicts were also to play a vital role in later events during the 1920s.

[32] The most notorious of these local administrations was that of Governor Amable Jones in the province of San Juan between 1919 and 1921. Jones was eventually assassinated. The result was the state of tension between Yrigoyen and the major landed groups in San Juan, which had an important bearing on events in the 1920s. During these years the Radicals were not averse to rigging the elections in many of the interior provinces. They took over the postal system, and prevented the opposition parties issuing their propaganda. It was also common for their opponents to be held in gaol during election periods. In an election in the province of Catamarca in 1919 a number of supporters of an opposition party, who had apparently been working in the neighbouring province of La Rioja, were prevented from reentering the province with the argument that they had contracted bubonic plague. Of course, all this made nonsense of the Radicals' claims to have 'purified' the political system. Where they had the opportunity, they were in many respects as corrupt as their predecessors under the oligarchy. For a statement of the constitutional issues involved

The main expressions of the growing linkage between the Radical government and the urban middle class groups were thus fivefold: the creation of a patronage system of party control, the inflation of public spending after 1919, a tendency to discriminate against the urban sectors not in a position to benefit from the growth of the bureaucracy, signs of tension within the elite wing of the Radical Party, and finally an increase in the tributary relationship between the provinces of the interior and Buenos Aires.

The university reform of 1918

The achievements of the Radical government on behalf of the middle class groups have been best remembered in terms of the university reform of 1918.[33] Although later this had a great impact on university movements throughout Latin America, it had its origin in the prosaic conflicts at the beginning of the century between the creole elite and the new middle class groups over the question of access to the universities and beyond them to the urban professions. It was thus closely related to the general phenomenon of social strain among the middle class groups which stemmed from the restriction upon the growth of the industrial sector in the primary export economy.

In 1918, first in the University of Córdoba, and subsequently in other universities, there was a succession of student strikes, some of which reached violent proportions. They had as their object changes in curricula and an end to traditional scholastic and clerical influence in higher education. The reformers presented their ideas in terms of a philosophy of education and society which was markedly different from that of the past. For the first time they popularised notions of educational democracy and student participation in the government of the universities.

Footnote 32 (continued)

in federal interventions, and for a critical account of Yrigoyen's use of them, see Rodolfo Moreno, *Intervenciones federales en las provincias* (Buenos Aires, 1924). There were precedents for Yrigoyen's most common practice of imposing interventions by decree, but there were few for the openly partisan fashion in which he used them. Many of the interventions after 1919 were made necessary by splits among the Radicals in each province, as different factions attempted to monopolise the available patronage.

33 Joseph S. Tulchin, 'La Reforma universitaria-Córdoba, 1918', *Criterio*, No. 1599 (9 June, 1970), and No. 1600 (23 June, 1970).

Although the Radical government found itself rather hopelessly confused when it tried to cater for some of the more metaphysical of the students' objectives, it did act positively in response to their more concrete demands. After protracted negotiations between members of the government and student leaders, criteria for entry into the universities were simplified and curricula underwent a major reform. But the real significant step came later when the government founded new universities. This amplified the availability of higher education to the middle class groups.

By 1922 the middle class groups had thus come to occupy a quite different political position in comparison with the period of the oligarchy. They were now fully and directly involved in the activities of the State and had become one of its chief beneficiaries. Apart from dramatic episodes such as the university reform, the change came about gradually without any serious shocks to the stability of the new political system. To a large extent what occurred was a predictable result of the widening of the franchise in 1912. By allowing this the elite had conceded its willingness to tolerate a widening political role for the middle class groups as a means to win their acceptance for its own position. The problems which finally emerged from the new system only did so at the end of Yrigoyen's government during the post-war depression, which began in 1921. Until then the landed interests profited from the export boom, and material concessions to the middle class groups generally came at the expense of other social sectors.

Radicalism and the working class

The main source of friction between the Radical government and the elite before 1922 came from another quarter. The most dramatic of the Radical government's innovations was its attempt to go beyond the middle class groups, and to include in its project of political integration a new relationship between the State and the urban working class. Its experience in this field provides the best illustration of the character and the overall results of the political changes introduced in 1912. It also expresses some of the central characteristics of Radical populism, and highlights the precise nature of the relations between the elite and the urban sectors.

Before 1916 the Radicals paid scant heed to the working class problem. Their few references to it were made in a *pro forma* fashion simply as a means of adding to their more general complaints against the oligarchy.

Also when they did so, their complaints were phrased very much in terms of orthodox liberal conceptions. There was very little in their position which could be described as a reformist orientation. One charge against the oligarchy, for example, was that its authoritarian control had led to the growth of class sentiments. The implication was that these should be avoided at all costs: 'The vices and complications of the old [European] societies have been reproduced here. The working classes, finding even their just petitions ignored, consequently represent an element of economic disruption and are creating grave problems which the government ought to foresee and resolve more opportunely.'[34]

An antipathy towards the notion of class was one of the salient features of the party's doctrines and ideology, which continued beyond 1916. In 1919 Francisco Beiró, one of Yrigoyen's close collaborators in the National Chamber of Deputies, declared:

> Nor do we accept class differences, or that there should be any classes in the Argentine Republic ... We do not fail to see that there are conflicts between capital and labour, but we do not accept that there is a proletarian or a capitalist class, even if 95% of the Argentines were to fall into what in Europe is called the proletariat. Nor is it right to bring into our new America, here where new ideals of human solidarity are being formed, such sentiments of hate on account of differences of race, religion or class.[35]

Similarly, before 1916, the Radicals condemned the repressive legislation used by the oligarchy against the Anarchists, not because it was an instrument of oppression, but simply because it violated liberal notions of the due process of law: 'The workers have seen their claims ignored, or they have been met with armed violence and with a body of repressive legislation which grants the police the extraordinary faculty of banishing abroad, as a dangerous criminal, anyone who protests against them. This being done without any clear reason being given and without due process of law.'[36]

Another of the leading features of Radicalism at this time was its reactionary, almost paranoid, attitude to anything that might seem like 'socialism'. Its antipathies to Justo's Socialist Party were in many ways even more marked than those of the oligarchy:

[34] Etchepareborda, *Pueblo y gobierno*, 'Abstención', p. 302.

[35] Francisco Beiró, *Diario de Sesiones*, Cámara de Diputados, Vol. 5 (1918–19), p. 293. Beiró became vice-president elect in 1928, but died before his inauguration.

[36] Etchepareborda, *Pueblo y gobierno*, Vol. 1, 'Intrasigencia', p. 104.

But how can the maximum or the minimum programmes [of the Socialist Party] be accepted and at the same time the principle of private or public property be maintained intact? . . . Socialism implies the denial of many, if not all, of the inherent faculties of property. And since Proudhon, its originator, uttered the celebrated phrase, 'Property is robbery', each one of the claims to which the party subscribes in its programmes is a menace to the very foundations of property.[37]

Accompanying this was an exaggerated and dogmatic assertion of the opportunities there were in Argentine society for social mobility. The following quotation is taken from the year 1920:

Here all that is required to win through is health and strength of will: to go from labourer to employer from employer to tycoon . . . Because the air we breathe here is that of democracy. There have never existed in this country titles of nobility, nor privileges, nor classes, nor any kind of aristocracy . . . What does exist is nobility of sentiment, generosity, the liberty of healthy ideas and reasonable human fraternity. This is the meaning of true democracy, so far superior to what is called 'socialism'.[38]

To judge from this, and in spite of the Radical Party's cross-class aggregative character, there was no reason why the Radical government should have displayed the interest in the working class which it did. What primarily forced it to do so were electoral considerations and its struggle after 1916 for congressional supremacy. The vote of the native-born workers, who had been enfranchised by the Sáenz Peña Law, was, despite their being a minority in terms of the working class as a whole, one of the major keys to the political control of the city of Buenos Aires.

The search for political control over the working class was one of the most significant effects of the widening of the franchise from 1912 onwards. Yrigoyen was not alone, nor the first, to be propelled in this direction. There are a number of interesting parallels elsewhere. An important precedent were the policies of President José Batlle y Ondoñez in Uruguay. This may have been a model for Yrigoyen. It would be interesting to compare Batlle and Yrigoyen at more length, and to show why reformism had so much more success in Uruguay than in Argentina. Batlle was always in a much stronger position than Yrigoyen after his defeat of the conservative National Party in 1904. Yrigoyen's revolt of

[37] Ibid. 'Abstención', p. 323.

[38] Enrique C. Ruiz, 'El obrero en la democracia argentina' (pamphlet serialised in *La Epoca*, 30 September 1920, *passim*).

1905 failed, and eventually he came to power with the position of the conservatives still largely intact. The scope of Batlle's measures in Uruguay, which included advanced welfare legislation and went much further than the Argentine Radicals ever proposed, possibly reflected Uruguay's need to compete with Argentina for immigrants. In the early twentieth century the Uruguayan landed interests around Montevideo, which Batlle's Colorado Party represented, were attempting to diversify from pastoral production into agriculture, but found this difficult because of labour shortages. Batlle's reforms may have been partly inspired by the need to attract more immigrants. In other respects there were close parallels between him and Yrigoyen. Both aimed to eliminate the threat of Anarchism, and both sought ties with the working class through the trade unions.

There were also precedents for Yrigoyen's policies in the province of Santa Fe. In 1912 after the first election held under the Sáenz Peña Law, a Radical administration was elected, led by Manuel Menchaca. Here a determined attempt began to exploit control over the administration to win support among the workers. The main example came during a strike of tramwaymen in Rosario in 1913, when the provincial authorities intervened in the dispute to help the men. Later this led to accusations against the Radicals in Santa Fe that they had bribed local union leaders to support them.[39] In Santa Fe, as later in Buenos Aires, electoral considerations were uppermost in prompting attempts to create this relationship.

In Buenos Aires the search for working class support was also a means to halt the growth of the Socialist Party and to prevent it from expanding outside the federal capital into the other major cities of the pampas region. In the federal capital in the congressional elections of 1912, 1913 and 1914 the Socialists won a succession of victories. At that moment it seemed that they were about to become a serious threat. They were united and were obviously also winning middle class support in the federal capital. They were helped by Figueroa Alcorta's purge of the Anarchists in 1910. This removed the main obstacle to their expansion.

[39] The evidence for this is considerable. In a speech in April 1918, Juan B. Justo recalled that in 1913 he and his colleagues had gone to Rosario during the strike. When they met the city's intendant, who was a Radical, he told them 'You Socialists are not going to have any luck here in Rosario, because the Anarchists are with us. I've got the Workers' Federation in my pocket.' Justo alleged that the same relationship had continued until 1918. This throws further interesting light on the railway

In 1915, however, the Socialists lost one of their most influential leaders, Alfredo L. Palacios, in a party split. For the next few years he led a separate party, the Argentine Socialist Party, in the elections.[40] In 1916, in the presidential elections, the Radicals for the first time made the winning of the working vote one of their principal objectives. Their campaign was organised along the conventional lines of ward boss paternalism and committee charity activities. Such 'services' to the community were contrasted with the 'false promises' of their opponents. The following newspaper precis of a street-corner speech during the election campaign amusingly captures the flavour of the propaganda techniques they invoked:

> in the 7th ward alone ... there had been sold at reduced prices and on a daily average 855 kilos of bread, 298 litres of milk and 3,200 kilos of meat, which represented a daily economy of 900,400 pesos. This figure multiplied by the number of wards in the city yields an average daily saving of 18,000 pesos, or 6,588,000 annually, equivalent over fifteen years to 98,820,000 pesos. Over the same period, the Socialists, making the same rigorous calculations, would have gushed forth 117,992,000 words, from which the working classes have obtained not the least benefit.[41]

The Socialists replied in kind. When it was announced just before the elections in March 1916 that Yrigoyen intended donating his emoluments to charity in the event of being elected, *La Vanguardia* declared: 'Do not let Sr Irigoyen think that he is going to conquer the will of the

Footnote 39 (continued)

strike of 1918, which will be analysed in the next chapter. (For Justo's speech see *La Vanguardia*, 15 April 1918.) The other interesting feature about this is that the Radicals in Santa Fe established their relationship with the Anarchists, and not, as in Buenos Aires, with the Syndicalists. It suggests that the Anarchists were sometimes less than the intransigent revolutionaries they purported to be. In 1969 I interviewed Manuel Menchaca a few weeks before his death. He confirmed that a relationship had existed between the provincial authorities and the Anarchists. I also talked to Diego Abad de Santillán, who was a noted member of the Anarchist movement at that time. He also confirmed that close ties had developed with the Santa Fe authorities. On a number of occasions after 1912 Anarchist fugitives from the federal capital had been given refuge in Santa Fe. Santillán also declared that until some years previously he had occasionally visited Menchaca to reminisce over their old associations. Again I must acknowledge the great kindness shown to me by these people in allowing me to interview them.

40 For details of this split see Walter. Like the European Social Democratic parties, the Socialist Party in Buenos Aires was thrown into confusion first by the war and then by the Russian Revolution.

41 *El Radical*, 30 August 1915.

electorate by laying bare a Christian and charitable soul, offering it the protection of asylums and hospitals, in order to deceive it, as the Roman emperors used to do, with bread and circuses.'[42]

This was the measure of the acute rivalry which developed between the two parties in years to come. For the first time in 1916 the Radicals won an election in the city of Buenos Aires. Their share of the vote increased from 33% in 1914 to over 40%. But this was still a minority vote, and in spite of all their efforts, the Radicals failed to make any decisive headway in capturing the working class vote. Although they increased their support in working class areas of the city, they were still a long way behind the Socialists. What gave them victory in 1916 was the disappearance of their conservative rivals from previous years. In 1914 two conservative parties, the Unión Cívica, (the vestige of General Mitre's following from 1890), and the clerical Constitutional Party, had taken part in the election, and had together won almost a third of the votes. The Radicals had won another third. The other third in 1914, a slight majority, had gone to the Socialists. In 1916 the Union Cívica made way for the Progressive Democrat Party, which had expanded into Buenos Aires from the province of Santa Fe. The church party affiliated with the Radicals. In 1916 the Progressive Democrats won a mere 8% of the total vote. The two Socialist parties, led by Justo and Palacios, however, won 50% of the vote, a proportion considerably higher than in 1914. The evidence was thus clear enough that the Radicals gained only at the expense of the conservative groups, and that it was only because the Socialists were split that they managed to win the elections.[43]

The election of 1916 suggested an imperviousness on the part of the working class electorate to the committee–charity style of electioneering adopted by the Radicals. It showed that the committees were best suited to the middle class groups, among which there was a higher degree of social atomisation, a relatively low degree of class identification and a prevalence of individualised aspirations for social mobility.[44] If the Radicals were to be successful in their efforts to capture the working

[42] *La Vanguardia*, 27 March 1916.

[43] For election data see Darío Cantón, *Materiales para el estudio de la sociología política en la Argentina* (Instituto Torcuato Di Tella, 1968), Vol. 2, p. 7, *passim*, also Appendix 4.

[44] There is possibly also a more precise point that the Radical *caudillos de barrio* were themselves rack-renting landlords, controlling some of the tenement blocks.

class vote, they would have to approach the problem in a different fashion. During a period of acute inflation, which affected the working class more than other groups, it was necessary to offer something in the way of benefits more durable and substantial than charity.

It was thus that the Radical government embarked on its attempt to win working class support by establishing close ties with the trade-union movement. In 1916 the unions were an obvious target for the new government. They were the only remaining bulwark against the influence of the Socialist Party among the working class. Secondly as class institutions, they had a certain standing and legitimacy in the eyes of the workers themselves. Benefits which came through them had a much better chance of being accepted than anything which came from the committees. They were in principle an ideal substitute nexus through which contacts with the workers could be established. Thirdly, and most important of all, the union movement itself was changing significantly. There would have been little hope of the Radicals winning working class support had the Anarchists still been in a position of dominance. Soon after Yrigoyen became president, *La Protesta* asked:

> Can a government, or a president, however democratic he may be, stand frankly and decidedly on the side of the workers? . . . The democratic ideals of modern rulers, the ideal made manifest through the 'altruism', the 'simplicity' of a president, which has become incarnate in the figure . . . of a misanthrope like Hipólito Yrigoyen, is only a temporary form of government in tune with the present moment of historical time . . . The struggle, comrades, should be decidedly revolutionary, without admitting the influence of anyone, nor asking favours of the government.[45]

But the Anarchists were now in decline, and their influence was being rapidly superseded by the Syndicalists. With them gradually declined the extreme anti-State stance adopted by the unions. The new role of the Syndicalists meant that the unions had come under the control of a more moderate current, interested less in confrontation with the State than in improving the economic position of the workers.

During the election campaign in 1916 there were already signs that

[45] *La Protesta*, 10 December 1916. When the new government took over *La Protesta* greeted it with the following comment: 'People: The new government will be like those of the past and those of the future. It will fulfil the true and only mission corresponding to such an entity. It will oppress and enslave the people . . .' (Ibid. 15 October 1916).

the Radicals were beginning to appreciate the importance of the unions. In August 1915, the committees organised a workers' propaganda group, which they called the Federación Obrera Radical 'Alberdi'. This title was chosen because its initials, F.O.R.A., were the same as those of the major federations. The aim was to lure as many as possible unsuspecting union affiliates into contact with Radical propaganda.[46] There were several other petty schemes like it.

Yet while the Radicals now had a strategy with which to approach the working class problem, they were still confronted by the question of the scale of benefits they would be able to provide. The Syndicalists were interested in wages and were unlikely to be attracted by merely token gestures. Also the Radicals were strongly committed in principle to *laissez-faire*. But here too there was a certain coincidence of approach. Neither they nor the unions were particularly interested in legislation, and they were both committed to preserving free market conditions for labour. The Syndicalists saw legislation as either an attempt to institutionalise the subordination of the workers, as had been apparent with the abortive Labour Code introduced some years earlier by Joaquín González, or as capable, like the Socialist measures, of providing only marginal benefits, which avoided the basic question of wages. Almost by virtue of their adherence to *laissez-faire*, the Radicals escaped the difficulty of the Socialists, who could be portrayed as trying to convince the workers to accept measures they did not particularly want.

The central problem with the question of benefits for the unions and the workers stemmed from its potential effects on the position of the conservative elite. In part the reforms of 1912 had been carried out to bring the workers sufficiently into the political system to undercut the position of the unions and the 'foreign agitators'. However, the railway strike of 1912 had shown that the elite still remained strongly opposed to an attempt to buttress working class political participation by any material concessions. It was unable to do this because of its own vested interest in maintaining a supply of cheap labour and because of its links with foreign capital. In attempting to make changes, the Radicals therefore ran up against the opposition of the elite. More than any other factor, this complex conflict of interests and objectives between the government and the elite shaped the character and the fate of the first Radical government.

[46] For comments on the F.O.R.A. see *El Radical*, 16 August 1915, 27 December 1915; *La Vanguardia*, 2 January 1916.

CHAPTER 6

The strikes, 1916–18

This chapter is a detailed examination of the Radical government's labour policies. It analyses the main points of contact between the administration and different groups of workers, attempting to develop an interpretative scheme illustrating the main factors and calculations underlying the relationship. It shows that the government did not indiscriminately take the side of the workers, but only tended to do so when such action promised political pay-offs, usually in voting terms. The aim also is to show how the relationship was challenged and modified by different employer groups, and the way they sought to develop contacts with powerful lobby groups to mobilise political support in their favour. This also raises the question of the political influence of major foreign companies in Argentina during this period. The general trend of events is that after a few early successes in 1917, the government found its policies triggering increasing opposition among the employer and lobby groups, the outcome of which was a formal alliance between domestic and foreign business interests. This presaged the major political crises of 1919.

Because both the Radicals themselves and many of the workers had no interest in legislation, and because the government did not control Congress, contact between government and the workers occurred almost exclusively during strikes.[1] The government's actions on the strike front

[1] At the very beginning of Yrigoyen's administration in November 1916, there was talk of a public works scheme to relieve unemployment (cf. *Review of the River Plate*, 17 November 1916). This suggested initially that the attempt would be made to win working class support by modifying the flow of government spending. What undermined the scheme was the government's parallel commitment to financial stringency. While it was announcing the need for economies and attempting to curb the demands of its middle class supporters for patronage positions, it was hardly in a position to start assisting the workers. So far as legislation is concerned, there were a large number of paper projects introduced by the government. Most of them were concerned with institutionalising the position of the unions. But the remarkable feature about them is that they always appeared immediately after the government's attempts to support the unions in strikes had failed. This occurred in May 1918 after the railway strikes, in June 1919 and again in June 1921. This timing suggests that while legislation was eventually seen as the only means to control class conflict, it was introduced as a sop to the workers after the failure of other policies.

serve to illustrate the general objectives and the strategic details of its working class policy. Equally they serve to express the manner in which its conflicts with the conservative elite developed.

The strikes themselves were mainly the consequence of the effects of inflation during the war and immediately post-war period on real wages. Before the war a number of studies were made of the cost of living for working class families. These were based on an assumed monthly income of between 100 and 120 pesos per family, and they may be taken as standard subsistence levels before the war. Taking wartime inflation into account, money wages ought to have risen to around 160 pesos by 1918.[2] However, for the majority of the workers who took strike action between 1916 and 1919 money wages were in the region of between 50 and 100 pesos. This may illustrate the extent to which the war had the effect of redistributing income away from the working class, and the pressures which encouraged strike outbreaks. The other major characteristic of the strikes was that they mainly affected the sectors of the economy controlled by foreign capital, especially in areas which were dependent upon irregular and expensive supplies of imported raw materials and fuel.

The strikes between 1917 and 1919 also compared, in number and in terms of the workers involved, with the height of the Anarchist period in the previous decade. The highpoint of the previous decade was in 1907 when almost 170,000 workers struck in the city of Buenos Aires. This included a major general strike for that year. In 1917 the figure was 136,000, in 1918 133,000 and in 1919 309,000. In 1907 some 231 strikes were recorded in the city, in 1917 138, in 1918 196 and in the first half of 1919 alone 259. However, there was one great difference between the two periods. In 1907 the strikes overwhelmingly affected the small-scale industrial sector. In 1917, by contrast, some 70% of the strikers were involved in transport activities. Although by 1919 the number of transport workers involved in strikes was much smaller than this, it still exceeded the figure for 1907 by a considerable amount. The respective figures of striking transport workers for 1907 and 1919 were 13,000 and

[2] For the standard of living question see Alejandro E. Bunge, *Los problemas económicos del presente.* (Buenos Aires, 1919). Bunge himself, who was director of the National Statistics Department during the war, recommended to the government as early as October 1917 that wages for State employees should be raised to a minimum of 2,000 pesos per year, or 166 pesos monthly. He based this on an estimated rise in the cost of living of 35% since 1913.

31,000.[3] This also marked an important aspect of the transition from Anarchist to Syndicalist control over the trade unions.

The government's involvement in the strikes stemmed from its ability to use its police powers to favour one side or the other. By withholding the police it gave the strikers the means to picket effectively, and in some cases to resort to sabotage. This was an important change. It contrasted with past practice in the sense that strikers could now use their bargaining power effectively, and not be prevented by state action from winning benefits when conditions were generally favourable to them. In many respects the Radical government's labour policy can be reduced to this single specific decision – whether to use the police, (or troops), for or against the strikers.

The other important element of the policy was the question of access and communication to the central agents of government decision-making. The government often favoured the unions by granting them preferential access either to Yrigoyen or to other ministers to plead their case. The Radicals themselves claimed that in doing this they achieved a levelling out of class privileges and a state of 'class harmony'. The State, they claimed further, played a major role in this transformation. It became the arbiter of class conflict and an instrument linking the workers with the rest of society. The claim was stated in the following way:

> Only when President Yrigoyen took over the government did the objectives of a forward-looking, modern administration appear. Excessive capitalist privileges disappeared ... Working class organisations ceased to be regarded by the State as dark and menacing hives of anti-social outcasts ... They were converted into a living part of Argentine society, worthy of being listened to and attended to.[4]

Besides aspiring for this change in the status of the unions, Yrigoyen himself saw an open system of communications between the workers and the State as being capable of achieving 'distributive justice' and the political assimilation and integration of the workers. This meant the end of their traditional isolation and the disappearance of nationality as a divisive issue. Yrigoyen himself wrote after 1930: 'When we attained control over the government there was nothing to be heard but the echo of protests and nothing to be seen but different coloured flags. This

[3] For strike figures see 'Anuario Estadístico', *Boletín Oficial del Departamento Nacional del Trabajo*, No. 42, 1919; *Review of the River Plate*, 15 August, 19 September 1919.

[4] *La Epoca*, 27 June 1918.

all turned into great demonstrations linking together everyone under the Argentine flag. Also the strikes disappeared, which before had weighed so heavily upon the nation.'[5]

Finally there was the aim of bringing the unions into the Radical Party, thus allowing it develop its character as a class alliance even further. The following quotation is a newspaper precis of a speech by one of the party's leaders in the city of Buenos Aires in 1918:

> Dr Tamborini said . . . that organisations particularly concerned with combating social injustice will affiliate with the Radical Civic Union, these being the intentions lying behind actions of the executive. He cited the recent strikes which had occurred since Dr Yrigoyen took charge of the government. He has shown respect for the unions and has made it evident that for the Radical government, justice is the fundamental question in conflicts between capital and labour.[6]

Mostly, however, all the workers got from this was encouragement and moral support. There are only rare examples of the government going beyond this narrow framework. In certain cases it used its influence to reinstate dismissed strikers. In others it had one of its own nominees appointed to arbitrate over specific disputes, and used this power to favour the men further in the final settlement.

At the same time government support for the workers in the strikes was far from automatic. It was narrowly conditioned by voting calculations. Except during the railway strikes, it only supported the workers in the federal capital. This made apparent that its main object was to combat the Socialist Party. Secondly the government only dealt with the Syndicalists. They proved to be the only group receptive to its intervention. One of the salient features of the period up to 1919 was the swift growth of Syndicalism and its further emergence to a position of

[5] Testimonies to the Supreme Court. Etchepareborda, *Pueblo y gobierno*, Vol. 2 Appendix 1, p. 328.

[6] *La Epoca*, 8 February 1918. Very occasionally the Radicals can be found actively supporting unionisation in what was an anticipation of Perón's methods a generation later. This was particularly so in their dealings with groups like the Tucumán sugar workers. In 1920 a Radical deputy from Tucumán declared, referring to his own province: 'The present administration believed, without being the enemy of capital . . . that it ought, in fulfilment of the mandate for which it had been elected, to raise the standards of living of the classes which had contributed to its winning power. It recognised that, more important than detailed legislation, it was necessary to bring the workers together, and . . . it favoured the unionisation of the workers; the workers now have their unions, and in this way they achieved wage increases and some other improvements in their standards of living.' (Quoted in Cantón, 'Elecciones', p. 177.)

dominance within the union movement. The Anarchists, who became steadily less important, were disqualified from receiving State support either by the fact that they operated among the non-voting immigrant groups, or by their open support for embarrassing direct action tactics. There was also an inclination on the government's part only to support the workers in strikes which affected the sectors dominated by foreign capital. This was in part because it was only here that the workers were concentrated in any numbers. But the aim too was to avoid alienating the domestic interests by making the foreign companies pay for concessions. However, even this only happened, as the frigorifico strikes showed, when supporting the workers added up to specific pay-offs in electoral terms. Finally, whenever the government, or a subsidiary administration controlled by it, was directly involved in the strikes as an employer, the workers again received no support. Either the government saw itself as threatened by the strike, or it was unable to afford wage concessions, or it felt that in doing so it had something to lose in prestige terms with other groups.

Given the modesty of the objectives, and the numerous subsidiary constraints upon them, it is hardly feasible to evaluate the Radical government's labour policy by the criterion of how it affected the distribution of income. In this respect the most it did was to allow a minute proportion of the working class to keep pace with inflation. When real wages eventually began to rise after the war, they did so as a result of the market demand for labour rather than as the result of any action taken by the government. The policy can only be evaluated in the terms the Radicals conceived it, as a means to secure the political integration of the workers, to halt the growth of the Socialist Party and to establish a new role for the unions.

The maritime strikes, 1916 and 1917

Even so, there was no doubt that in 1916 the new government saw its dealings with the working class as one of its main priorities. Within two months of taking office it was already embroiled in the strikes. On 30 November 1916, there was a sudden outbreak of strike action among the personnel of the coastal shipping companies, which operated from the River Riachuelo in the Boca district of Buenos Aires. The men involved were affiliated to the Maritime Workers' Federation, the F.O.M., the most powerful of the Syndicalist federations. The men were made up of deckhands, boilermen, coxswains, steersmen, waiters and cooks. They also worked the lighters and tugs in the main overseas port of Buenos Aires. The strike thus affected overseas shipping as well as the coastal shipping companies.

This strike was the first of its kind organised by the F.O.M., and the first in the port since 1912. By November 1916, the union had won the affiliation of about a quarter of the skilled work force in the port zone, some two thousand out of eight or nine thousand men. The strike had as its aim improvements in pay to compensate for the rising cost of living and also for the fact that since 1914 wages had been forced down as a result of a rate war between the two leading coastal shipping companies, the Mihanovich line, or as the British called it, the Argentine Navigation Company, and the German-owned Hamburg–South America line. At the beginning of the strike the F.O.M. pointed out that since 1914, money wages alone had declined by 25%, from an average of 120 pesos per month to 90 pesos.[7]

The strike was also carefully timed by the union. Its outbreak occurred during the first week of the harvest shipments. The aim of this was to deprive the transatlantic shippers of access to tug and lighter services, and to force them to put pressure on the coastal shippers to make a speedy settlement.

Before the conflict had reached this stage, the government suddenly intervened, in a manner which was to become familiar over the next two years. First the minister of the interior, Ramón Gómez, issued a press statement, in which he took the men's side and condemned the companies for refusing to negotiate.[8] The next day, 5 December, Francisco García led other members of the F.O.M. and the Syndicalist F.O.R.A. to an

[7] Interview with Francisco García, *La Prensa*, 8 December 1916. The rate war is an example of the manner in which the British government used its control over coal supplies during the war to assist British commercial interests. The Mihanovich Company was partly owned by a British consortium but was suspect to the British because of the Dalmatian (and thus Austro-Hungarian), origin of the Mihanovich family, and because at the beginning of the war it had arranged a pool with the German company. It was given the option of ending this and renewing competition (to the benefit of the British, who used its lighters and tugs), or being placed on the British Statutory List (the Black List) and losing its coal supplies. One of the secondary effects of the use of the coal embargo was that it increased pressures to force down local wages in sectors like Argentine coastal shipping. There is a long discussion of the matter in British Foreign Office papers. See Despatches No. 51, 14 August 1914, F.O. 368–928, Nos. 161, 12 June 1915 and 330, 7 November 1915, F.O. 368–1203, No. 7, 8 January 1916, F.O. 368–1479. Also Confidential Report for 1915, F.O. 368–1203.

[8] *La Prensa*, 5 December 1916.

interview with the president of the republic.[9] From Yrigoyen the F.O.M. obtained the important concession that the port police would not be used, as they had been in previous similar disputes, to recruit and protect blacklegs. The government could thus pose as a neutral party to the dispute in the best tradition of *laissez-faire*, but give the strikers the means to picket effectively. This step led eventually, in the last week of December, to the men's victory. Each side agreed to await the results of an arbitration enquiry conducted by the chief of police. When this appeared it gave the men the main concessions on pay they had been seeking.[10]

This succession of incidents is the best example of the essential pattern of government policy. Yrigoyen had established personal contact with the leaders of the main Syndicalist union and had used this to demonstrate his support for the workers.[11] The same happened a few months later during a second strike on the Riachuelo in April 1917. Once more the F.O.M.'s leaders had no difficulty in gaining access to Yrigoyen, who this time promised to plead their case before Mihanovich. Again the port police were kept out of the affair as much as possible, in spite of a succession of violent incidents. Once more the union was finally victorious. The employers abandoned their attempt to destroy the F.O.M. by forming their own union, and they agreed that the ships' crews would be selected by negotiation with it.[12]

The municipal workers' strike

However, the other side of the coin soon became apparent. Although the government remained on extremely good terms with the Syndicalists, and especially with the F.O.M., its conduct towards other groups was often quite different. The reason for the F.O.M.'s privileged position was twofold. First the union operated in the Boca, which was a major centre of support for the Socialist Party in the federal capital. By enhancing the position of the union the government obviously thought that it was

[9] This was not the first ever meeting between a president and the leaders of the unions. In 1912, during the railway strike, Sáenz Peña had met the leaders of La Fraternidad. But this time the outcome of the meeting was quite different.

[10] *Boletín Oficial del Departamento Nacional del Trabajo*, No. 40, (February 1919).

[11] There was also no opposition to the government here beyond the coastal shipping companies. The British were still suspicious of Mihanovich's possible connections with the Central Powers.

[12] *Review of the River Plate*, 27 April 1917.

weakening the position of the Socialists.[13] Secondly the government feared that the conservative governor of Buenos Aires province, Marcelino Ugarte, was himself manoeuvring to win support in this area.[14]

The negative side of the government's policy was revealed in March 1917 during a strike of the refuse collectors employed by the municipal government in Buenos Aires. This dispute also rose from a pay question. During the war, the municipal authorities, like the national government, found themselves seriously short of funds. Between 1913 and 1916 their revenues declined from 51 million paper pesos to just over 40 million.[15] Attempts to make economies led in 1916 to wage cuts among the refuse collectors. There was no doubt that the refuse men were badly paid. Even before the wage cuts, their monthly wages were no more than 60 pesos, a mere two-thirds of the average 90 pesos which drove the maritime workers to strike action in December 1916.

The wage cuts had been implemented before the Radical government took over, and before 1917 there had already been a number of minor stoppages in the department. The refuse collectors' cause was taken up by the Socialists. In 1916 they made complaints in Congress about the way the men were being treated and began the attempt to organise them into a union.[16] When there was a further outbreak of strike action in 1917, the Radicals immediately concluded that the Socialists had organised it. It was said of the strike by the government newspaper, *La Epoca*: 'Socialism is responsible for the ferment of agitation among the municipal workers. This is a group, as the Socialists well know, which is malleable and easily influenced by their intrigues. It is not a conflict in which the unions are involved, only the Socialists, two quite different considerations.'[17]

[13] In 1916 the Socialists had a majority of over a thousand in the Boca. The district had a large electorate of over 12,000. Support for the union was also a way of winning the sympathies of the local retailers and shopkeepers, who supported the men's demands for higher pay. Higher wages for the men enriched the whole community.

[14] See British consul-general's report. Enclosure in Despatch No. 361, 15 December 1916, F.O. 368–1689. This point was also made to me by Sebastián Marotta, who was a member of the delegations meeting Yrigoyen. Ugarte was deposed by federal intervention in April 1917.

[15] For the effects of the war on municipal finances see Tornquist, 1915 and 1916.

[16] Cf. *Review of the River Plate*, 28 July 1916.

[17] *La Epoca*, 16 March 1917. The Socialists made their role in the strike apparent by including demands for an 8-hour day and the observance of the Sunday Rest Law among the strike demands presented to the authorities.

This gave the cue to the municipal authorities to attack the strike with a heavy hand. The men were all dismissed, and the police were used liberally to prevent them from organising picketing. It was significant that many of the strikers were Spaniards, and that senior municipal officials talked in terms of 'getting rid of the *gringos*' (foreigners).[18] Their treatment by the police was so bad that the Spanish Ambassador finally intervened.[19] The Socialists also produced documented evidence that the municipal authorities were replacing the strikers by men recruited by the Radical Party committees.[20]

Thus although the government had not yet begun to weed out its opponents in the administration in any systematic fashion, it was not averse to doing so in a case like this. The same occurred during a strike of postal workers in September 1918. On this occasion the skilled employees who were reinstated after the strike were closely vetted for their party affiliations.[21]

The other aspect of the municipal workers' strike in 1917 was the Radicals' concern to avoid involving the Syndicalists. In *La Epoca* a number of tortuous attempts were made to draw distinctions between the municipal workers' strike and the second of the strikes in the port:

> Superficially the position of the river workers is the same as that of the refuse collectors. It appears that both are seeking improvements in their conditions and in their pay. But a more careful examination shows that this similarity is more apparent than real. It is important to recognise that the juridical position of a State employee is not equal to that of an employee in a private company. A State functionary – regardless of seniority – acquires a special identity by submitting himself to certain conditions which he accepts from the start. He makes an agreement which he cannot violate. In exchange for advantages he alienates aspects of his private interest, subordinating his personal situation to the supreme law of public welfare, which he is committed to serve.[22]

18 Cf. *La Vanguardia*, 21 March 1917. '"Gringos" the Radicals call the workers. And among these "gringos" are the poorest and most humble. Sr Quartino [a municipal official] declares, "We'll have to get rid of these gringos once and for all". Here you have an expressive synthesis of the Radical mentality.'

19 *La Nación*, 27 March 1917. Police actions against the strikers were reported to have included herding them together in open compounds, severe beatings and simulated executions.

20 *La Vanguardia*, 21 March 1917.

21 The course of this strike can be followed in *Review of the Plate*, 10 September 1918, *passim*.

22 *La Epoca*, 21 March 1917. The precedent invoked was Georges Clemenceau's handling of a strike of public employees in France before the war.

The Syndicalists were initially rather reluctant to get involved in the strike, since they also recognised the hand of the Socialists in it.[23] But when the reports of police brutality became known, they felt obliged to complain to the government. On 28 March, the leaders of the F.O.R.A. informed Yrigoyen that unless a settlement was reached with the strikers, a general strike would be declared. Once more Yrigoyen deferred to their wishes. The strikers whose jobs had not been filled were reinstated. The rest were given the option of a fortnight's wages or the promise of employment on the government's mooted public works scheme.[24] In this fashion the strike was solved.

The municipal workers' strike had four interesting features. First, the government was much less favourable to the strikers during disputes which affected public services and to which it was itself a party. Secondly, it demonstrated the extreme hostility between the Radicals and the Socialists. Thirdly, the strike made it apparent that members of the ruling party were, if not prepared at that point to find jobs for their supporters by increasing public spending, quite happy to make room for them by discriminating against the immigrants. Finally, the strike showed that if these considerations were important, Yrigoyen was not prepared to defend them at the cost of his relationship with the Syndicalists.

The railway strikes, 1917–18

The port and public employees' strikes served to demonstrate the basic outlines of the government's policies. But the more significant movements before 1919 were the railway and frigorifico strikes between June 1917 and May 1918. By the beginning of the First World War the Argentine railway system was among the largest in the world outside Europe and North America. In 1914 there was over 22,000 miles of track, of which some 14,000 miles, or 65%, was British owned. From their beginnings in the 1850s the railways had absorbed around a third of total foreign investment. The British stake was in the region of £200 million.[25]

The origins of the railway strikes in 1917 and 1918, like the other labour disputes, are to be found in the economic effects of the war. Between 1900 and 1913 the track length of the Argentine railways had

[23] The F.O.R.A. later described its intervention as stemming from a 'duty of sentimental solidarity' (*La Organización Obrera*, 1 May 1917).

[24] *Review of the River Plate*, 6 April 1917.

[25] Cortés Conde, 'Problemas del crecimiento industrial'.

doubled. But with the onset of financial crisis in Europe in 1913, foreign investment ceased, and new construction was quickly brought to a halt. This was followed by the depression in 1914 and the sharp contraction of Argentina's exports. Immediately the railway companies began to feel the effects. Gross revenues declined from a total of 140 million gold pesos in 1913 to 118 million in 1917, a year in which the grain harvest was very poor. Total tonnages transported declined from 42 million tons in 1913 to a mere 31 million tons in 1917.[26] The railway companies were also faced by rapidly rising costs which resulted mainly from the precipitate rise in the price of imported coal fuel. In 1913 the cost of a long ton of coal was 9 gold pesos. By 1918 this had risen to 30 gold pesos, a rise of 244%.

This led to attempts at saving. New acquisitions of rolling stock ceased, and there was a progressive run-down in track improvements and maintenance. In spite of this, between 1913 and 1917 total costs on the railways increased by about 60%.[27] The result was the contraction of profit margins. According to the railway companies' figures, net receipts declined by almost half between 1913 and 1917.

TABLE 3 *Railway traffic and receipts, 1913–17*

	Passengers carried	Tonnage of goods transported (long tons)	Total Product (gold pesos)	Working Expenses (gold pesos)	Net Receipts (gold pesos)
1913	82,322,800	42,033,300	135,619,800	83,735,200	51,884,600
1914	75,103,800	33,506,800	111,861,500	72,923,000	35,938,500
1915	67,401,100	35,655,700	121,029,000	76,623,900	44,395,100
1916	64,829,900	36,630,600	125,568,800	81,404,900	44,163,900
1917	57,595,700	31,562,000	118,502,000	89,118,200	29,877,300

Source: Compiled from Tornquist, quarterly reports.

The effects of this were reflected in falling dividends and in the falling quotations of Argentine railway stock on the London Stock Exchange. Until 1913 the largest of the railway companies, in terms of capital investment, the Buenos Aires Great Southern Railway, generally paid a

[26] Tornquist, quarterly reports.

[27] For a detailed and highly informative study of the railways during the War see Alejandro E. Bunge, *Ferrocarriles argentinos*.

dividend of about 7% on its ordinary shares. By 1918 this had declined to 1%. In the second largest company, the Central Argentine, the decline was from 6% to 1%. In 1913 the Great Southern's stock was quoted at an average of 120 in London, 20 above par. The 1918 average was 72. The Central Argentine Railway's stock declined over the same period from 105 to 60.[28]

The most important of the companies' economies during the war was the pruning of their labour force. Table 4, is again taken from the companies' own figures.

TABLE 4 *Railway labour force, 1913–18*

	Management	Track labour	Traffic operatives	Station personnel and workshop employees	Total
1913	5053	55,881	35,202	35,856	132,810
1914	5844	47,497	32,754	32,844	118,939
1915	5151	45,688	32,330	33,897	117,066
1916	3982	39,485	34,001	34,707	112,175
1917	5009	30,361	32,504	34,745	102,619
1918	5942	28,844	39,161	38,292	112,239

Source: *La Nación*, 9 March 1921.

These figures suggest that the bulk of the layoffs came in the track labour branch, the section which had been formerly engaged in new construction. They are probably not accurate, since other partial data suggest that staff pruning went further than this, and affected the other branches also. Even so, as they stand, the figures still amounted to a reduction of about 15% in the railway labour force over the period.

Similar reductions took place in the companies' total wage bill, though again the precise figures are open to suspicion. According to the companies' figures, the total wage bill declined from 44,121,675 gold pesos in 1913 to 41,143,039 in 1918.[29] This is a decline of 9%, some 6% less

[28] *Review of the River Plate*, 13 October 1922. It should also be pointed out that the railway companies had also been guilty of 'watering' their capital before 1914. This made it less easy for them to sustain depression years and maintain dividends on ordinary shares.

[29] Alejandro E. Bunge, *Ferrocarriles argentinos*, p. 178.

than the decline in the labour force. It may be accounted for by the fact that lay-offs were made among the lowest-paid, unskilled workers. It is, however, again contradicted by other partial data, which suggest that all sections of the labour force suffered a reduction in money wages. But even taking the figures as they stand, even a possible rise in money wages was too small to have compensated for inflation. During the war this ran at an average of between 6% and 7% annually. From 1914 onwards, therefore, the railway workers, like other groups of workers, were confronted by the dual threat of lay-offs and falling real wages.

Labour relations on the railways had been in a poor way ever since La Fraternidad's abortive strike in 1912. The footplatemen still wanted the wage increases they had tried to win in 1912, as well as an eight-hour day, a workable pensions scheme and the reinstatement of those dismissed in the strike. There was some progress with pensions. One of the few items of social legislation accepted by the National Congress was the railwaymen's pensions law passed in 1915.[30] But two years after this the scheme was still not being implemented. The railway companies failed to provide an adequate census of their employees, and delayed the measure further by a series of legal wrangles over the proportion of their own contribution to the scheme.[31] Disputes of this sort, coupled with unrest over redundancies and pay, constantly served to keep alive the possibility of a new resort to strike action.

One of the major failures of the strike of 1912 had been the lack of support for it among the workshop and station personnel. In subsequent years La Fraternidad's most important objective was to encourage the unionisation of these groups. It was no easy task. The companies were alive to the danger, and took every precaution they could to guard against it. Also there were great problems of organisation and coordination in the face of the men's dispersal.

During the strike of 1912 the Syndicalists had founded a railwaymen's union in Buenos Aires. This was the Railwaymen's Federation, the Federación Obrera Ferroviaria (or Ferrocarrilera), which became known as the F.O.F. The organisation of this union was part of a wider strategy being developed by the Syndicalists. They already had some influence in the port through the F.O.M., and this they wished to complement by

[30] For commentaries on La Fraternidad's complaints, see *Review of the River Plate*, 11 March 1913, 30 January 1914, 8 May 1915; *Buenos Aires Standard*, 21 January 1914. For the pension law see *Review of the River Plate*, 18 June 1915, *passim*.

[31] *Review of the River Plate*, 14 April 1916, *passim*.

establishing a bridgehead among the railway workers. In this way they could develop control over the nerve-centre of the country's economic system: its links with its international markets.

From the start the F.O.F. had enthusiastic, if rather patronising, support from La Fraternidad. While the footplatemen welcomed the possibility of a national union of workshopmen, they were jealous of their own independence, and regarded themselves as the senior partners in any alliance which might emerge. For a long time the F.O.F. stagnated in semi-clandestinity, unable to establish any firm base of support outside the city of Buenos Aires. It was only in 1916 that the first signs of progress appeared when La Fraternidad offered the F.O.F. the use of its union rooms, and proposed the establishment of a joint strike committee.[32]

La Fraternidad's preparations for a showdown with the companies increased after the change of government in October 1916. As it had shown during the 1912 strike, when it attempted to raise support for the strikers in Congress, the union fully recognised the potential change implied by the new electoral system. Such hopes were encouraged when the Radical government intervened in the men's favour in the first port strike. In their annual report for 1916, which appeared soon after the port strike, La Fraternidad's leaders declared: 'We have high hopes that this government, with its eminently popular origins, will listen to our demands and resolve them with justice.'[33]

Soon after, in January 1917, La Fraternidad's leaders obtained an interview with Pablo Torello, the new minister of public works. The aim of the visit was to present a petition of complaint against the railway companies for having blocked the pension scheme. Significantly, their reception from Torello was very similar to the one the F.O.M. had received from Yrigoyen barely a month before. It was also notable that Torello's attitudes towards the railway companies were, if not exactly hostile, much less pliant and obliging than those of his predecessors under Sáenz Peña and De la Plaza:

> The minister received us with every mark of respect and invited us to describe fully and frankly the reason for our visit ... He listened with great interest ... asking us to explain and clarify aspects of the men's work and other questions

[32] For accounts of the early history of the F.O.F. see *La Vanguardia*, 6 December 1918; Martín S. Casaretto, *Historia del movimiento obrero argentino* (Buenos Aires, 1947), pp. 143–50.

[33] La Fraternidad, 'Memoria', 1916 (unpublished internal file).

which particularly interested him. Speaking of pensions, the minister stated categorically that the companies ought to comply with the law ... and ... he added that the government is ready to take them to the courts if necessary. We received an excellent impression of him. He is a simple and attentive man who, although not deeply familiar with railway questions, is interested to learn about them to improve the effectiveness of his own actions. One clear advantage stands in our favour: he has no prejudices against the workers, and on the contrary he has expressed extremely complimentary opinions about them. If he shows any prejudices at all, they are against the companies on the grounds of their unlawful action.[34]

La Fraternidad was greatly encouraged by this reception from Torello. After discussions with the F.O.F., it was decided to organise a general strike for the end of 1917. Then the railway companies, it was hoped, would be likely to seek a swift settlement to prevent delays in the transportation of the harvest to the ports.

The Central Argentine Railway strikes

But these plans were suddenly undermined by a succession of spontaneous strikes in different parts of the country between June and September 1917. The most important were in and around Rosario in the workshops of the British-owned Central Argentine Railway. They were the direct result of efforts by the company to reduce wages and prune its labour force. It was later reported that the men's real wages had dropped to one third of the 1914 level; low-paid apprentices had been brought in as cheap labour; men working with mechanical tools had their wages cut even further on the grounds of the lesser physical effort involved in their work. The men's plight was so bad, it was said, that many of them had accumulated rent arrears of up to fourteen months in the primitive housing the company provided for them.[35]

[34] Ibid. Circular No. 3 (17 January 1917).

[35] This was the conclusion of a special report commissioned by Torello. See *La Nación*, 15, 16 August 1917. The British consul-general reported that his enquiries revealed that railway labourers in Rosario were being paid between 1.50 and 2 pesos a day. This brought their monthly earnings to around 50 pesos, about half the recognised subsistence level, and a long way below the wages of the Buenos Aires municipal workers. (British consul-general's report. Enclosure in Despatch No. 439, 10 October 1917, F.O. 368–1693.) There is also confirmatory evidence for the men's allegations of staff-pruning. The British chief engineer of the Central Argentine Railway in Rosario reported to the British minister in Buenos Aires: 'At the outbreak of the War, I began to weed out ... the Germans in our department. However, at the end of July, last year [1916], our financial situation assumed such an unfavourable aspect

There was first of all a minor strike in the Pérez workshops near Rosario in June. It quickly collapsed but, when the men returned to work, two of their fellows were dismissed in reprisal. There was then a state of semi-strike until the company imposed a lockout. This united the men in the demand for the reinstatement of the two dismissed men. Soon after the strikes spread to other workshops in Rosario itself. By the end of July 1917, some five thousand men in all were affected.[36]

The great keynote of this strike was its extreme violence. Attempts to keep the trains running on the Central Argentine line around Rosario goaded the strikers into a state of open rebellion. There was widespread sabotage of company installations, mob attacks on British employees, who continued working, and several occasions where coaches were burnt.[37] To some extent the violence reflected a low degree of organisation among the strikers. At the time of the first strike in Pérez, the F.O.F. sent a delegate to the scene with instructions to urge the men to return to work pending the completion of arrangements for the general strike. At first he had some success, but later he was completely ignored. What little control there was over the men was exercised by a group of local anarchists, who did all they could to exclude the Syndicalists.[38]

Footnote 35 (continued)
that I considered it necessary to make a material reduction in the number of men employed in the workshops . . . Towards the end of 1916, I had to put all my remaining men on short-time.' (Mr. J. P. Crouch to British Consul in Rosario. Enclosure in Despatch No. 326, F.O. 368–1693.)

[36] *Review of the River Plate*, 27 July 1917; *La Vanguardia*, 10–21 July 1917.

[37] Impressions of the strike appear in the statutory affidavits enclosed in Despatch No. 69, F.O. 368–1877.

[38] In this they were strongly supported by *La Protesta* in Buenos Aires. One of the Anarchists in Rosario was Pedro Casás, who had taken part in the Ninth Congress of the F.O.R.A. in 1915. The British chief engineer, Crouch, described his role as follows:

'Early in August, last year [1916], there was an attempt at a movement, and on August 15th, I called a deputation of some fifteen discharged men to my Office, and I explained to them that the Railway Company was in an unfortunate position, owing to the War . . . of having to make this material reduction in its staff . . . A man named Pedro Casás was at the back of this movement, but I succeeded in suppressing his activities. This man Casás is well known amongst working men in Rosario, and he has tried on several occasions, to stir up trouble amongst my workmen: he is not a Railwayman, and it is not clear how he obtains his living. The police know him well: he is said to have committed two murders, one here and the other in Montevideo, and also to be useful to the Rosario authorities politically. Towards the end of 1916 street meetings were held, Casás taking a prominent part.' (Enclosure in Despatch No. 326.)

Suspicions of Casás's role were also linked in the minds of British observers with

The problem of control, and the fact that the strike spread rapidly outside Rosario soon forced the unions to abandon their attempts to impose restraint and give the strike their support. Finally a general strike developed on the Central Argentine Railway. At the beginning of August, the two unions, La Fraternidad and the F.O.F., issued a joint manifesto summarising their long-standing grievances against the foreign companies. This contained some novel and interesting arguments. Instead of simply justifying the strike on pay grounds, the unions made every effort to attract wider support. The companies, they claimed, by maintaining high freight rates and reducing the wages of their employees, were forcing the country to finance the British war-effort, since the bulk of railway profits were being paid to the British government in tax.[39]

The manifesto was carefully calculated to appeal to the Radical government, and the unions' hopes of support from this quarter were quickly justified. It was not long before close contacts were established with Torello and with Yrigoyen. Yrigoyen helped the unions by holding back the despatch of troops to Rosario, while Torello offered to mediate personally in the Rosario dispute. Eventually, after a month of extreme conflict, Torello brought the dispute to an end by threatening to levy

Footnote 38 (continued)
the role of the chief of police in Rosario during the strike. The British consul in Rosario reported in the same enclosure that he was in league with the union leaders and that he had received orders from Yrigoyen to treat them as gently as possible:

'I would again draw attention to the attitude of Señor Nestor Noriega, the Jefe Politico. Until recently he was very friendly towards the English. He was still markedly so when the present disturbance first broke out. Mr Crouch informs me that he then spoke strongly on the subject of maintaining discipline. Shortly afterwards he visited the Federal Capital, when he conferred with some of the ministers and, I believe, with the President himself. When he returned to Rosario, his attitude had changed completely. He has since then courted popularity with the strikers, the railway authorities have been helpless, and I have it on fairly good authority that he has in forcible terms said that he will do nothing for the English. He has certainly acted in this spirit. Our people are openly attacked in the streets and the police look on and refuse to help them'. (Ibid.)

This ties in with what was said earlier about the relations between the Radicals and the Anarchists in Rosario. In this case it seemed that Yrigoyen was attempting to compete with the provincial administration in Santa Fe, with which he was on bad terms, for working class support.

39 Cf. *La Vanguardia*, 6 August 1917. The specific terms used in the manifesto were 'a war-tax on behalf of British interests'. The same expression had been used in Congress in 1915 during debates on freight rate increases introduced by the companies. This attempt to appeal to nationalist instincts is again an illustration of how much the union movement had changed with the decline of Anarchism and the emergence of a native-born leadership.

fines against the company unless it reinstated the two dismissed men.[40] Throughout the strike the government consistently took the men's side against the company. It managed to withhold sending troops to Rosario until the situation got completely out of hand. When the troops were finally sent in August, they were given strict orders to take no action against the strikers.[41]

The government thus dealt with the railway strike in the same fashion as it had dealt with the first port strike some eight months earlier. It used its police powers to force concessions for the workers. The difference with the port strike was, however, that this time there was a barrage of bitter criticism against the government in British circles. The *Review of the River Plate* declared:

> The strikers have triumphed. Foreign capital has been humiliated. The government is now acclaimed as the protector of the poor. [There were] ... several unmistakable indications of its desire, if not actually to propitiate, then at least not to offend the proletariat, when conflicts between capital and labour have occurred ... It seems to us, to put the matter quite plainly, to be the not unnatural result of the policy of a government which has come into power on a popular vote of unprecedented magnitude, and which is anxious not to alienate the working class vote by any manifestation of antagonism.[42]

The government was confronted by a very different situation in the railway strikes from what it had faced when it only had to deal with the weaker coastal shipping companies. From this time forward the railway companies, led by their local directors, began a determined attempt to win outside support.[43] Signs of this came in the commentaries of *La Nación*, one of the two leading newspapers of the conservative elite groups in Buenos Aires. There was for the first time talk of the 'confidence of foreign investors'. *La Nación* also made as much as it could of rumblings of discontent among the troops, which had been sent to Rosario, over the passive role they had been compelled to adopt:

> The conduct of the government in the recent strike ... was characterised by absolute weakness ... As a symbol of all this, it is quite enough to recall the occasion when troops of our armed forces were made to descend from trains and were tied up by the strikers. Whatever feelings of tenderness the government

40 *Review of the River Plate*, 24 August 1917.

41 Cf. the statutory affidavits, Despatch No. 69.

42 *Review of the River Plate*, 24 August 1917.

43 The role of the local directors was crucial in later events. They acted as the main intermediaries between the foreign companies and the domestic business elite.

cherishes towards the working classes, it never becomes admissible for it to forget its essential police function, as the agent of common order.[44]

For the moment these attacks failed to attract any important wider support. There was still considerable resentment against the railway companies for the arbitrary manner in which they had increased their freight rates in 1915. *La Prensa*, the leading organ of the major domestic business groups, for example, criticised the:

imperfect knowledge of this country possessed by European directors, resulting in the general conduct and administration of the businesses being left to two or three officials, often only to a general secretary. These frequently have no adequate conception of their relations with the State and their activities are confined to increasing the dividend.[45]

Referring to relations between the government and the railway companies, *La Prensa* further declared:

The executive power and Congress ought to adopt a uniform policy in their relations with the great public utility companies exploited by foreign capital in the republic. It ought to be a policy of conciliation and one of protection for those enterprises, without involving, however, the sacrifice of any of the aims of national progress, which inspired their organisation, nor any of the benefits deriving from them to which the country has a right.[46]

The general railway strike, September–October, 1917

After the Central Argentine Railway strike, the government would probably have been happy to let the matter rest there. But the wage issue had not yet been resolved. At the beginning of September 1917 there was another spate of spontaneous strikes, again centring on the province of Santa Fe. Once more the strikers took to sabotage, and the companies were forced to make swift concessions. At this point it became evident that there was a growing division between the F.O.F. and La Fraternidad. La Fraternidad was still hoping to defer any major action till the end of the year. But the F.O.F. was continually being pushed into supporting the strikes by Anarchist-influenced rank and file pressure.[47] This made the problem of coordination even greater.

[44] *La Nación*, 26 August 1917.
[45] *La Prensa*. Quoted in *Review of the River Plate*, 10 August 1917.
[46] Ibid.
[47] *Review of the River Plate*, 7–21 September 1917.

What further encouraged the F.O.F. to act alone was that it suddenly, if ephemerally, won tremendous popularity among the railwaymen in different parts of the country. Within a month, in September it found itself with self-elected representatives in all the major branches of the national railway system. This was an endorsement for direct action and for an immediate general strike.

On 22 September a general railway strike was finally declared, which lasted for over three weeks. Although the strike eventually won for the men a number of concessions on wages, and on La Fraternidad's demands for the introduction of a scheme of working regulations,[48] it destroyed any further chance of cooperation between the two unions. Eventually it also destroyed the F.O.F. too. Unlike La Fraternidad, which was composed of a relatively homogeneous group of workers–the footplatemen–the F.O.F. had wide local variations in wages and working conditions to deal with. These prevented it from developing a consistent negotiating position acceptable to the footplatemen. Also the two unions had different objectives. The F.O.F. was basically concerned with the wage question, La Fraternidad more with questions of status and fringe benefits. Because it was unable to control its members and because, also, it was unable to obtain radical improvements on the pay question, already before the end of the general strike the F.O.F. was showing signs of disintegration and atomisation.[49] In this fashion its sudden rise to power and influence was followed within a few weeks by an equally precipitate collapse.

The further importance of the general strike lies in the light it throws on the government's position. While Yrigoyen and Torello maintained their contacts with the union leaders, and did what they could to offer them moral support, this time they did little positive on their behalf. The lines were well policed, and the government press studiously avoided taking sides in the dispute. The reason was that, in contrast with the Central Argentine strike, this time the railway companies began to receive massive public support.

The sudden change of attitude, both towards the unions and towards the government, was one of the most critical events stemming from the strikes. It exposed at once the real structure of political forces in Argen-

[48] *La Vanguardia*, 17 October 1917.

[49] After the general strike La Fraternidad refused to support the F.O.F. any further and did not take part in the later strikes. Although afterwards the F.O.F. declared general strikes on several occasions, the movements were of a purely local character. In December 1917, there were attempts to patch up the quarrel between the unions but these failed (cf. *La Vanguardia*, 16–20 December 1917).

tine society and the objective obstacles to the government's project of 'class harmony'. It made apparent that the more the Radical government attempted to spread the net of its appeal among the workers, the less able it was to sustain its position in other key areas. The general strike demonstrated that if the domestic business groups were disgruntled with the railway companies on the freight tariff question, they were not prepared to carry their hostilities to the point of throwing over their traditional dependence on them, and entering into an alliance with the working class.

The main effect of the general strike on the railways in 1917 was thus that it crystallised the real nature of the relationship between foreign capital and the elite. The strike on the Central Argentine Railway had been tolerated. It caused only partial interruptions to freights and traffic, and it was skilfully exploited by some of the elite groups to make clear to the British railways that they ought not to ride roughshod over the interests of local producers. But the general strike suddenly paralysed the country's export trade. There was immediately widespread talk, as *La Nación* and others put it, of 'killing the goose that lays the golden egg'.[50]

The general strike revealed, as in 1912, that the unions had a hopeless case when they tried to mobilise domestic support with their arguments about the 'war-tax to British interests'. Not only did the domestic producers turn rapidly against them, but they also began to turn against the government when it was seen to be taking the workers' side against the railway companies. The first signs of growing impatience with the government among the domestic business groups came when the president of the Sociedad Rural, Joaquín S. de Anchorena, offered his services to the government as a mediator in the strike.[51] When this failed to have any effect, there was a flood of angry petitions to the government demanding immediate action to end the dispute. Finally, in the second week of October, meetings of important business leaders were held in Buenos

[50] In the National Senate Benito Villanueva, one of the leaders of the conservative politicians, and a leading supporter of the British, declared: 'I do not speak out of a spirit of opposition to the workmen's aims... and I wish they could be given everything they want. I am in favour of the Pension Law for instance... but with one condition: that it is possible to apply it without killing the goose that lays the golden egg, and that it can be demonstrated that under the present circumstances the companies can bear these additional costs.' *Diario de Sesiones*, Senadores, Vol. 2, 1917, p. 1131 (29 September 1917).

[51] *La Prensa*, 2 October 1917.

Aires under Anchorena's chairmanship. There was discussion of a general lockout, and although the final decision was taken merely to send a delegation to Yrigoyen, there was no doubt that the domestic business groups were now united in opposition to the strikes, and in complete loyalty to the companies. Soon after the strike, the railway companies announced a further 22% increase in freight charges. This time, in contrast to 1915, it was not the companies who were blamed, but the government and the unions.[52]

What further facilitated this sudden change of attitudes was that in the second week of September an international scandal broke in Buenos Aires. The American State Department in Washington forwarded to Buenos Aires copies of telegrams to Berlin, which had been intercepted from the German Minister in Buenos Aires, Count Luxburg. They contained derogatory remarks about leading members of the Argentine government.[53] This action by the Americans was aimed to bring pressure on Yrigoyen to abandon neutrality, which had been declared by De la Plaza in 1914, and to enter the war on the side of the Allies. It led to a motion in the National Senate in favour of breaking diplomatic relations with the German Empire.

It also gave the railway companies a powerful instrument with which to deal with the government. They began to blame the strikes on the activities of German agents and to accuse the government of favouring German interests. From this it was only a small step to the traditional conservative conspiracy theory of working class unrest – that the strikes were caused not by legitimate grievances among the workers, but by 'agitators'. The first point of attack was the manner in which the F.O.F. had been able to expand its membership in the weeks before the general strike. The British Consul-General reported a meeting between Torello and the local directors of the railway companies in Buenos Aires in the following terms:

> One of the railway representatives pointed out that he has absolute information that at least 50% of the men on the Western Railway, who had joined the Federation, had done so within the last fourteen days, a very large proportion

[52] *Review of the River Plate*, 2 November 1917.

[53] The telegrams were reproduced in the *Review of the River Plate*, 14 September 1917. They mainly referred to Honorio Pueyrredón, who at that point was acting minister for foreign affairs. It seems possible that the British government may have had some part in releasing the telegrams at such a propitious moment for the railway companies, although I have not found any direct evidence of this.

of them under threat and intimidation. He went on to say that he had put the figure at 50% so as to be quite certain, but that he believed they numbered 70–80%, which is a concrete proof that the organisation of the societies was not caused by their treatment but was a result of the events of the last months.[54]

As time passed, attempts by the companies' representatives to exploit the alleged conspiracy element in the strikes grew. A little later *La Prensa* paraphrased the words of one of the leading local directors, Manuel Montes de Oca, in the following way:

Dr Montes de Oca continued with further points of view over the social problem which is at present disturbing the republic. The agitators were seeking not only improvements in detail for the workers – this is only a pretext... They were seeking the means to introduce their own social policies, which meant the elimination of all order and discipline and the suppression of the fundamental principles which until now have ruled the country's social and political organisation.[55]

As well as coming under fire for helping the 'agitators', the government did not help itself. It attempted to defend itself from the charge that it was helping the Germans by insisting that its support for the unions simply responded to electoral objectives. This immediately antagonised the local directors who, as appointees of previous administrations, were leading members of the conservative opposition. Reporting on a meeting between a delegation from the railway companies and Torello on 25 September, the British Consul-General reported:

one of the Railway representatives said that any acceptance of the terms submitted would mean that the Railway would be ruled by the Society. The Minister

[54] British consul-general's Strike Report, 10 October 1917, F.O. 368–1693.

[55] *La Prensa*, 22 November 1917. There is one other element in the situation which deserves mention. In early December Pueyrredón, the minister for foreign affairs, received a warning from the Argentine consul in Carmelo, Uruguay, of plots to organise an 'armed revolution' against the government (cf. Pueyrredón to Gómez, the minister of the interior, *Ministerio del Interior*, Vol. 1, 1918, File No. 121). The consul reported visits to Carmelo by 'Argentine politicians' who were seeking arms and who were using the deserted islands in the Paraná delta near the city of Buenos Aires as training camps. What this meant it is difficult to say. The most likely explanation for it was that it was part of preparations for a rising in the province of Buenos Aires to wrest control from the Radicals who had taken over the province by federal intervention in April. But it may also be interpreted as an anticipation of the events of 1919, and it showed that even at this early juncture the Radical government was fast losing support among the conservative elite groups. The 'revolution' in the province of Buenos Aires, incidentally, never materialised.

replied (and this information is given in confidence), that these societies consisted of more than 120,000 members, and that their votes enabled them to practically rule the country. He further stated that they had grievances that warranted their being so powerful.[56]

In spite of these protestations, the government nevertheless fell foul of the charge that it was 'pro-German', which contributed further to a weakening of its grip on the situation. During the railway stoppage there was a strike in a German-owned electricity company in Buenos Aires. In what seemed in stark contrast to its behaviour during the railway strike, the government sent in marines to operate the plant, and in a short time the strike collapsed. This created something of a furore.[57]

The general strike on the railways had thus brought several important developments. First it united the domestic business groups behind British capital. Secondly it reduced the standing of the Radical government among both these groups. It was both suspected of being pro-German, and regarded as tolerating the activities of the 'agitators'. In November there was strong criticism of the government in London when the railway companies held their annual general meetings. Sir Alfred Bowen, chairman of the largest company, the Buenos Aires Great Southern, declared:

The Government appears to have forgotten or to ignore that the prosperity of the country has been created to a large extent by the 15,000 miles of railway

[56] Strike Report, F.O. 368–1693. The figures are bogus and exaggerated, but they do show how importantly the Radicals viewed the union movement at this point.

[57] In fact this strike ought to be seen as a parallel to the municipal workers' strike. In areas which affected the consumer electorate in Buenos Aires the government always gave short shrift to the strikes. There is no evidence at all of German influence in the railway strikes, or that the Radical government was pro-German. British observers could not understand how the railway strikers could last out so long when they were crippled by such extremes of poverty. The main explanation for this is that throughout the country they were given credits for the duration of the strikes by local shopkeepers. This was one of the central features of all the strikes, that they were supported by sectors of the petty commercial middle class. Also the belief in British circles (see, for example, the consul-general's Strike Report) that Spanish Anarchists had arrived in Argentina in 1916, equipped with German money, 'to organise strikes' is pure fantasy, which has its parallel in the false notion of the 'Russian agents' in 1919. Sir Reginald Tower, the British minister, made enquiries about the presence of a German espionage network in Argentina, and turned up no concrete evidence whatever. The only information he could find to substantiate his belief that leading Radicals were in collusion with the Germans was that members of the government were heavily in debt to the German Bank in Buenos Aires, the

lines built by railway capital ... The Government appears to have imagined that the railway companies are a species of fortunate being who ought to pay the cost of all [its] experiments.[58]

The government immediately replied to this through *La Epoca*. Its statement was revealing. Although it attempted to deny that it had taken the side of the unions during the strikes, it did make clear that it was not mounting an attack on foreign capital. Its aim was merely to end its privileged status, and to bring it within the control of the State:

Without being over-severe with railway capital, it is to blame for the poor conditions of its staff ... Its duty lies in the elimination of these conditions so as to fulfill honourably its contracted obligations ... We hasten to add that nothing could be more erroneous than to interpret these opinions as antipathy

Footnote 57 (continued)

Banco Alemán Transatlántico. But there is no reason to regard this as anything more than a simple credit operation which all landowners of every political hue might have resort to. Among the customers of the Banco Alemán Transatlántico were Joaquín S. de Anchorena, the president of the Sociedad Rural, and Marcelo T. de Alvear, Argentina's diplomatic representative in Paris. They were both strong public supporters of the Allies from 1916 onwards. The best explanation for Yrigoyen's continuing support for neutrality comes from a report of a conversation he held with the president of Uruguay, Balthasar Brum, early in 1919. Brum reported to the British minister in Montevideo afterwards: 'As regards Irigoyen's attitude towards the Allies ... he felt that they were trying to drive him into a particular line of conduct, and he did not like to be driven. At the same time Irigoyen confessed that he had no confidence in the United States and regarded Wilson as an Imperialist who aspired to exert authority throughout the Americas. Of England he has a holy horror ... He regarded England as a Power sunk in materialism and which, having grabbed half the world and being sated, could now put on a hypocritical mask of generosity' (Mitchell-Jones to Foreign Office, 8 April 1919, F.O. 371–3504). This ties neutrality in with the general subject of the Radicals' attempt to reform the status of British companies in Argentina. As regards the Americans it is an early expression of the fears which contributed towards the campaign against the oil companies in the 1920s. In spite of the Luxburg telegrams the government had no difficulty in maintaining neutrality until towards the end of 1918. There were many groups within the Radical Party and among the conservative elite which were prepared to prevaricate until it became clear which side would win the war. During the German spring offensive of 1918, elections were held in Argentina which were regarded as a test of the government's policy. These the Radicals won. Pressure on it to join the Allies only became intense when Germany began to collapse in October 1918. This followed upon widespread fears of Allied commercial reprisals after the war. The issues of neutrality from a British angle are discussed in full in Despatch No. 94, 9 April 1919, F.O. 371–3504.

[58] Quoted in *Review of the River Plate*, 9 November 1917.

on our part towards railway capital. We stand impartial on the issues between it and its employees . . . A policy adverse to the interests of capital would be a crime against the national economy, which is ever in demand of labour and capital. The government is not likely to fall into an error of this sort. It has scrupulously respected the concession laws in all its relations with the companies. Railway capital, like other capital invested in the country, is under the protection of the law and counts with the friendship of both people and government. On the other hand, it cannot demand . . . a privileged status . . . But now we see that the railway companies regard as hostility what is essentially justice. Accustomed as they have been to preferential treatment, they have seen with surprise and displeasure that the present government does not intervene as a partisan in the question which have arisen between them and their employees. For the first time they have seen that the government does not consider strikes to be subversive acts which must be suppressed by violence.[59]

The crucial question now was how far was the government capable of carrying out its principles. Between November 1917 and the end of April 1918, there were other outbreaks of unrest on the railways, again mainly prompted by pay questions. Their effect, however, was to unite the opposition even further and gradually undermine the government's ability to pursue an independent line of action.

The end of the railway strikes

The most revealing incident came in February 1918. At this point the government was especially keen to appear to be doing something for the workers, because interim congressional elections were due in March. It was also struggling for control over the province of Buenos Aires in gubernatorial elections. Here it had something to feel confident about because in January 1918 negotiations had begun with the Allied governments for the purchase of the whole of the grain harvest for the troops on the Western Front.[60] The agreement was regarded by the government as its leading achievement on the economic front, and likely to pay big electoral dividends in the province of Buenos Aires. But in early February there was a sudden new spate of railway strikes. The British Minister, Sir Reginald Tower, peremptorily informed the government that, unless the strikes ceased, the cereals agreement would be abandoned, and further that the British government would impose a shipping boycott on Argentine ports.[61]

[59] *La Epoca*, 9 November 1917.

[60] For details of the negotiations see Despatch No. 7, 4 January 1918. F.O. 371–3130.

This confronted the government with a crucial decision. It was compelled to choose between its support for the agricultural interests, or its support for the unions. Although for some time there were attempts to temporise the issue, eventually Torello was forced to issue a decree virtually banning any further railway strikes.[62] In an interview with the French-language newspaper in Buenos Aires he described the measures he had taken:

The real effect of this decree is that of a heavy roller ... Now neither the Railway Companies, nor their workmen are in a position to justify any stoppage of service ... In the case of this disposition being disregarded by any party, the Government has the means to make itself obeyed and respected ... The Minister of Public Works, before deciding on these measures ... consulted neither the delegates of the strikers nor the representatives of the Railway Companies ... The Government never had the need to ask the opinion or the consent of the strike delegates on the matter, nor has it waited for their assent.[63]

When at the end of February there was yet another short spate of strikes, Torello's strictures against the men grew more bitter. He described one strike as:

a veritable act of treachery ... We have had enough of it and now we are at the end of our patience ... The Government will not hesitate to adopt any rigorous procedure to repress these manifestations of bad faith. [Troops are being sent] ... with orders to act without due scruples ... The authors of these excesses will be arrested without delay and handed over to justice.[64]

[61] Telegram No. 103, 11 February 1918, *ibid.* Tower had been seeking a pretext of this sort to put pressure on the government for some time. During the general strike in October 1917, he threatened a shipping boycott (cf. Despatch No. 80, 24 October 1917, F.O. 371–3150 and Despatch No. 471, 22 November 1917, F.O. 368–1693). In February 1918 his threat to abandon the cereal agreement was an empty one, as the Foreign Office informed him that there were already 120 ships on their way to Argentine ports.

[62] Before this the government attempted to placate the British with a number of secret petty gestures. The main one was a favourable arbitration award to the British-owned Primitiva Gas Company in Buenos Aires, which was in dispute with the municipality over its charges. The award was announced to Tower before being made public, and a promise was made that more positive action would follow once the 'present anomalous political situation has disappeared'. The reference was to the March elections. This was an example of the increasingly erratic character of the government's behaviour (cf. Despatch No. 7, 4 January 1918, F.O. 371–3130).

[63] *Le Courrier de la Plata*. English facsimile in *Review of the River Plate*, 15 February 1918.

[64] Ibid. 1 March 1918.

From this time forward both police and troops were used liberally to cope with further unrest. When the strikes eventually died away, the companies were able to reassert their old authority. They avoided any further concessions on wages, and they managed to dismiss a majority of the men who had served as union delegates. In this quarter the government had obviously failed in its efforts to modify the position of the workers or to extend State control over foreign capital. By the middle of 1918, although La Fraternidad had managed to survive, the F.O.F. had collapsed completely. It was not until 1922, with the foundation of the Unión Ferroviaria, that a new attempt was made to unionise the railway workshopmen.

The frigorifico strikes, 1917–18

There is one other sequence of strikes which also throws interesting light on the government's labour policy and the precise calculations weighing upon its decisions. At the end of 1917 there was a series of stoppages in the American-owned frigorificos in the province of Buenos Aires – in Berisso, a suburb of La Plata, the provincial capital, and in Avellaneda. Here the government's response was markedly different from what it had been during the railway strikes.

At the beginning of the strike in Berisso at the end of November 1917, marines were immediately sent to guard the companies' installations. The same happened in Avellaneda in December. Their presence was exploited by the frigorifico managers, both in Berisso and in Avellaneda, to recruit blackleg labour. As a result of this the strikes eventually collapsed.

The sending of marines to the frigorificos has been used as evidence for the conclusion that it is false to attribute to the Radical government any real desire to support the working class. It has also been said that this decision was the result of the pressure of the Sociedad Rural Argentina, and proof of the government's subservience to the major cattle interests.[65] It is important to resolve this question, because it impinges directly upon the relationship between the government and the conservative elite groups and foreign capital.

The maritime and railway strikes had shown that the government did

[65] Peter H. Smith, 'Los radicales argentinos y la defensa de los intereses ganaderos', *Desarrollo Económico*, Vol. 7, No. 25 (April–June, 1967), pp. 795–829. Smith's position and my objections to it are discussed in detail in Appendix 3.

support at least some working class groups, and that it was prepared to do so, to a point, even to the detriment of its relations with foreign capital, and with domestic business groups like the Sociedad Rural. The frigorifico workers differed from the railwaymen in terms of their political importance. They were concentrated in small areas in two cities, in a province where the electorate was dominated by the exporting interests. In the province of Buenos Aires the working class vote, except among major groups like the railwaymen, was unimportant. Also the Socialist Party had only negligible influence in the province. Finally, a large number of the frigorifico workers were Balkan immigrants with no political rights and with little influence among the major Syndicalist federations.[66] In this respect the government's action during the frigorifico strikes was nothing more than an example of its ability to tailor its actions according to the composition of the electorate with which it was dealing at any one time.

The second point, that the government deferred to pressure from the Sociedad Rural during the frigorifico strikes, is also mistaken. A detailed examination of the precise course of events shows that the government used marines because the frigorifico managers threatened to transfer their contracts to Uruguay unless they received full protection. Later attempts by the Sociedad Rural to press the government into using even more troops were simply ignored.[67] This, and other similar events during the strikes, suggests an important general conclusion about the Radical government. Its support for the exporting interests was not conceived as a means to protect the elite groups alone; it emerged out of consideration for wider groups in the electorate. There was thus no automatic inter-identification of interest between the government and elite pressure groups like the Sociedad Rural.

Unless this is recognised it is impossible to understand the nature of the conflict between Radicalism and the conservative elite which emerged from the strikes. While the government attempted to support the unions and to impose a measure of State control over the foreign companies, eventually the Sociedad Rural – and the whole conservative elite – took the side of foreign capital indiscriminately. This is the major

[66] A large number of police detainees during the strikes were described as *turcos*. This is an illustration of an earlier point of the manner in which the incorporation of the immigrants took place in Argentina. Immigrants from the Ottoman Empire were the last of the major groups to arrive in the country before 1914, and they were concentrated in poorly paid jobs, such as in the frigorificos.

[67] These details are analysed in Appendix 3.

trend from October 1917 onwards. The strike threat ended the divisions which had appeared between the domestic and foreign groups during the railway freight rate controversy in 1915. It emphasised that this division was relatively superficial, and that there was an underlying interdependence and solidarity between the two groups.

The growing impatience of the major business groups with the government and the unions first became evident during the general railway strike in the discussions of a general lockout. In November 1917, *La Prensa*, which had completely abandoned its earlier talk of State supervision over the foreign companies, ominously declared:

Criminal acts ought not to meet with any tolerance, and the government has the obligation to ascertain who are its authors and hand them over to justice. More still, its credit and respect as a public power will be compromised until they are found. If the nation will not protect the property of the companies and of individuals, then individuals and companies will have to protect themselves at all costs and by any means, with the resulting perilous disturbance of public order . . . Also it is necessary to eliminate from the country the propensity to anarchy which all social movements have revealed in recent times.[68]

This resulted in the foundation of an employers' association, which became known as the National Labour Association, the Asociación Nacional del Trabajo. On the 20 May 1918, under Anchorena's chairmanship, a meeting was held in the Buenos Aires Stock Exchange attended by representatives of the frigorifico and railway companies, the shipping companies, the exporters and importers, the Industrial Union (Unión Industrial Argentina), the Rural Society, and a number of other less important groups. The meeting was declared to have as its aim: 'the adoption of measures of defence against the prospects of a general strike . . . which is about to occur once more to upset the different branches of our activities.'[69] There was widespread condemnation of the

[68] *La Prensa*, 10 November 1917.

[69] *Versión taquigráfica de lo deliberado por la Asamblea General en la Bolsa de Comercio el día 20 de mayo de 1918* (Buenos Aires, 1918) p. 1. The original organisations and companies which joined the Labour Association were the Rural Society, the Central Argentine Railway, the frigorifico La Blanca, the Industrial Union, the Cereal Exporters' Association, the Centre for Transatlantic Navigation, the Central Fruit Market, the Grain Exchange, the Centre for Coastal Shipping, the Port Carting Association, the Coal Importers, the Anglo-Argentine Tramway Company, the Italian Electricity Company, the Wool Exporters, the Chamber of Commerce and the Consignees Association. The railway and tramway representatives also served

unions. The Association also denounced its determination to protect 'free labour', and organise the defence of: 'the rights and interests of commerce and industry insofar as they may be affected by illegal and abusive procedures on the part of employees or workmen.'[70] It was decided to finance the Association by means of contributions of 1% of the total wage bill of each member organisation.

The immediate background to the formation of the Labour Association were rumours of a general strike, which followed the dismissal of a number of men from the Great Southern Railway in a final spate of railway unrest in April and May 1918. But during the meeting there were strong complaints voiced over the position the government had taken during the strikes. This made it evident that the Association had emerged not only as a means to combat the unions but also the government, which was held responsible both for the strikes and the growth of the unions.

By the end of 1918 the government's labour policy was already showing signs of having failed to achieve even its limited aim of compensating small groups of workers from the effects of inflation. The government's only success was that it had managed to increase the Radical vote in the federal capital in the election of March 1918. Even here, however, it again had benefited more from the division of the Socialist Party than from its intervention in the strikes. The only reasonably stable contact with the unions which had emerged was with the F.O.M. This reflected the inability of the coastal shipping companies to mobilise wider support.

The reverse was the case with the railway companies. Although they had initially been forced into concessions, Yrigoyen's commitments to the electorate in the province of Buenos Aires had eventually allowed them to win back the ground they had lost. The government's hopes of controlling the railwaymen through La Fraternidad and the F.O.F. had failed completely. The frigorifico workers, like the municipal workers in the city of Buenos Aires, had not been worth supporting.

On the other hand, the government's policy had succeeded in reuniting the domestic elite groups and foreign capital against its attempts to

Footnote 69 (continued)

for other companies. Several of the representatives were British-born, Macadam of the Importers, Boxwell of the Transatlantic Shippers, Ford of the Cereal Exporters and Lloyd Davies of the Coal Importers. Pedro Christophersen of the Industrial Union was later elected president of the institution and Lloyd Davies its treasurer. (Cf. press reports 21 May 1918, *passim.*)

[70] *Versión taquigráfica*, pp. 8–9.

win the support of the unions and in a crusade against the foreign agitators. There was now widespread talk of plots and conspiracies. By May 1918, *La Nación* was recalling the railway strikes in the following terms:

If one remembers the development of the railway strikes, one may perceive the presence of a coolly matured plan of action with preestablished tactics. Sabotage, assaults on the industry and its faithful personnel, organised pressure against the agents of order, each developed with rhythmical regularity without one being able to notice in them the spontaneous or unduly violent character which is the mark of the collective explosions that in any given moment may burst the dykes of discipline and social solidarity. The work of destruction and violence at carefully selected moments, at vital points, and executed with scientific precision are all signs of the existence of a planning unit possessing abundant economic resources and the means with which to act. And it has all been assisted by the most deplorable lack of foresight on the part of the authorities.
The existence of the professional agitator element is therefore undeniable... It is not yet a revolutionary organisation against the key industries, but an imported plague. The Argentine working classes ... have always presented their claims and have been successful without ever forgetting the bonds of solidarity with their own country ... They have never, even in extreme cases, behaved like criminals or arsonists ... All this goes to show the foreign origin of the leaders of the recent strike movements.[71]

It was now becoming apparent how little things had changed since the introduction of the Sáenz Peña Law. In the following year, 1919, the situation was to become even clearer as the power struggle between the government and the conservative elite acquired even more dangerous proportions.

[71] *La Nación*, 7 May 1918. For similar comments see Adolfo S. Carranza, *Trabajos sociales* (Buenos Aires, 1918), p. 16.

CHAPTER 7

The Semana Trágica

During the first half of 1919 the tensions between the government and the conservative elite over the strike question produced a number of complex situations in which two major political crises can be discerned. These called into question the whole scheme of representative government introduced by the Sáenz Peña Law in 1912. They brought to a head the issue of the real location of political power, and in doing so they further exposed the weak objective supports for the changes Yrigoyen had tried to implement. For the first time the armed forces were brought directly into politics as arbiters over the fate of a civil administration. Also 1919 saw the emergence of a new popular alliance, the Argentine Patriotic League. This, if not directly or openly antagonistic to Radicalism, was controlled by the conservative elite groups, and in a position to exercise decisive leverage over the government.

On several occasions in 1919 the Radical government was forced to struggle desperately for survival. It finally managed to do so, though it was compelled to abandon the genuinely progressive aspects of its policies. Increasingly, on a whole series of fronts, and most notably in its relations with foreign capital, it was coerced into returning to the established moulds of the past. By the end of the year its attempt to change the position of the unions had almost entirely collapsed. Finally, the government was compelled to make a number of major readjustments to its techniques for dealing with the mass electorate. Instead of promoting new policies, it was forced back on a patronage system of control, which relied essentially on an increase in State spending, and upon a largely symbolic style of popular leadership. To a large extent the appearance of these two features became a measure of its weakness rather than its strength. Whereas between 1916 and 1919 the government's relations with the conservative elite were largely determined by the working class problem, afterwards the more important issue became the Radicals' relationship with the urban middle class.

Thus 1919 has a whole series of elements to it. Besides vividly portraying the pressures to which liberal reformism in Argentina gave rise, it was also an important year for the Argentine working class. It shows quite graphically both the manner in which the workers acquired an important political role at this stage of Argentina's history, but also their great weaknesses against other power groups within the political system. The first major crisis in which the workers were involved came in January 1919, in the episode subsequently known as La Semana Trágica, the Tragic Week. It began with a general strike, the first of its kind for almost ten years. It ended in a bloody pogrom against the immigrant communities. Out of this counter-insurrectionary movement, the militant Right was born. In view of its symbolic importance to the working class movement in Argentina, it is worth trying to unravel this complex episode in some detail.[1]

Wages and unionisation trends

The broad background to the role of the workers in the Semana Trágica is again the rising cost of living which stemmed from the war. While the prices of imported goods continued to rise, by 1918 Argentina was caught up in the boom demand for primary foodstuffs abroad. This brought new prosperity for producers and exporters, but it increased the pressures on the urban consumers. The only compensation for the workers was that the unemployment problem began to diminish after 1917. By 1918 total domestic industrial production had reattained its pre-war levels, and had begun to diversify into new fields as a result of import substitution. Employment was also stimulated by the expansion of the export sector. But this had little effect on the downward trend of real wages. General developments are summarised in Table 5.

The initial effect of this combination of conditions – falling wages and rising employment – was to spur the growth of the Syndicalist union movement. By 1918 the Anarchist movement was rapidly losing significance. In most of the strikes in 1917 and 1918 the Anarchists had played only a minor role. In July 1918 they attempted to trigger a general strike in the city, using as a pretext the dismissal of a number

[1] The Semana Trágica is also very interesting from the point of view of comparative class political action. See David Rock, 'Lucha civil en la Argentina, La Semana Trágica de enero de 1919', *Desarrollo Económico*, Vol. 11, No. 42 (March 1972), pp. 165–215. For a further, more polemical, commentary see by the same author, 'La Semana Trágica y los usos de la historia', *Desarrollo Económico*, Vol. 12, No. 45 (June 1972), pp. 185–92.

TABLE 5 *Employment, incomes and industrial production 1914–22*

	Unemployed as % of labour force (winter levels)	General cost of living (1910 = 100)	Real wages (1929 = 100)	Volume of industrial production (1950 = 100)
1914	13.4	108	–	20.3
1915	14.5	117	61	18.2
1916	17.7	125	57	18.7
1917	19.4	146	49	18.5
1918	12.0	173	42	22.1
1919	7.9	186	57	23.0
1920	7.2	171	59	23.8
1921	–	153	73	25.1
1922	–	150	84	27.9

Source: Di Tella and Zymelman, pp. 309, 317, 339, 343.

of railwaymen by the Great Southern Company. But the strike was a total failure and the only significant group which supported it were the port carters.[2]

The Syndicalists, by contrast, gained from the victories won by the F.O.M. in 1916 and 1917, and from their determined efforts during the initial stages of the railway strikes. By and large, where the strikes had been successful, the Syndicalists had led them. Table 6 summarises the growth of the Syndicalist F.O.R.A. from 1915 until the advent of the post-war depression in 1921. It is no more than an estimate of the number of the workers subscribing monthly to the federation in any one year, and not an exact indication of total membership. However, it does show well enough the main features of the federation's growth.

In 1917 and 1918 both the number of affiliated unions and the total number of dues-payers rose sharply. In 1919 the rise was more marked in terms of the number of affiliated unions. This mainly reflected the manner in which by 1919 the unionisation process began to affect small-scale industrial and service activities in Buenos Aires. A large number of small unions affiliated, but there would appear to have been some hesitancy among the workers about joining them, and paying their dues, until 1920. That year the monthly average of dues-paying members was

[2] For reports on the Anarchist general strike see *La Vanguardia*, 14 July 1918, *passim.*

TABLE 6 *The Syndicalist F.O.R.A., 1915–21*

	Number of affiliated unions	Total dues-paying members	Monthly average of dues-paying members
1915	50	21,332 (8 months)	2,666
1916	70	41,124 (12 months)	3,427
1917	199	158,796 (12 months)	13,233
1918	232	428,713 (12 months)	35,726
1919	530	476,203 (12 months)	39,683
1920	734	749,518 (11 months)	68,138
1921	–	240,101 (9 months)	26,678

Source: J. Rodríguez Tarditti, 'Sindicatos y afiliados', *Revista de Ciencias Económicas*, No. 29 (1927), p. 973; *La Organización Obrera*, 1 May 1918, 1 May 1920, 24 January 1921; *El Diario*, 10 December 1918. *Boletín Oficial del Departamento del Trabajo*, No. 41 (April 1919); Alfredo L. Palacios, *El Nuevo Derecho* (Claridad, Buenos Aires, 1934), pp. 190–1.

almost double what it had been a year before. Finally, with the advent of the post-war depression in 1921, the F.O.R.A. underwent a sharp decline.

In 1918, however, this expansion of its influence made the F.O.R.A. extremely cautious. At the end of the railway strikes there was some talk of following the Anarchists and declaring a general strike. But instead it was finally decided to concentrate on growth in the hope of out-manoeuvring the new employers' federation, the National Labour Association. At the end of 1918 these objectives were formally accepted when the F.O.R.A. held its tenth Congress. It was decided to support only limited strikes, and the strategy for 1919 was to be based on the port, where the F.O.M. was about to present a list of demands to the ship-owners.[3]

Meanwhile, the Anarchists continued to campaign for a general strike, though, it is important to note, with very little success. A further indication of their weakness came at the end of November 1918. This followed the escape from imprisonment in the penal colonies of Tierra del Fuego of Simón Radowitsky, one of the great Anarchist heroes from the previous decade. In 1909 Radowitsky had assassinated the city's chief of police, and after barely escaping the death sentence had been condemned to life imprisonment. His escape in 1918 was short-lived. He reached the Chilean

[3] For reports on the Congress see *La Organización Obrera*, 29 December 1918.

side of the island, but there he was recaptured and immediately handed back to the Argentine police.

The episode led to an Anarchist demonstration in Buenos Aires and to a plan for a mass march on the Chilean Embassy. Given Radowitsky's fame and reputation, this ought to have provided the rallying cry the Anarchists were hoping for. Instead it attracted very little support, and although there was a running gun-battle in the streets, the marchers were easily dispersed by the police.[4]

By the end of 1918 there were thus few hints that the new year was to bring such traumatic events. The unions were controlled by moderates, and the traditional extremists were rapidly losing support. One tradition has it that the general strike, which began the Semana Trágica, can only be understood with reference to events in Europe.[5] Certainly the war, the Russian Revolution and the Armistice did have an effect on the left-wing intelligentsia in Argentina.[6] But there was little evidence to show that the masses, too, were politicised and radicalised to any extent by external events. The Syndicalists, who were best equipped to discern any changes of this sort, saw evidence only of factionalism and atomisation during the period before the general strike:

In spite of the notable and positive progress achieved by the F.O.R.A., it cannot yet be said to have attained sufficient strength for it to be able to lead the Revolution. The dead weight of ignorance is too strong, and a general lack of

[4] *La Prensa*, 30 November 1918.

[5] Carlos Ibarguren writing in the 1950s declared: 'The Semana Trágica in Buenos Aires was undoubtedly caused by Russian agitators, the revolutionary agents of the Soviet, who provoked the rising by taking advantage of the atmosphere of unrest prevailing among the working class' (*La historia que he vivido*, pp. 324–5).

[6] The Syndicalists declared soon after the November Revolution in Russia: 'This war is opening up vast horizons for us. It seems to have prepared the conditions which have made possible the destruction of the czars. This was inevitable enough, but the war hastened its coming . . . Things are happening quickly in these times, and especially for the proletariat' (*La Organización Obrera*, 2 February 1918). In a post-Armistice speech, Enrique Del Valle Iberlucea, the Socialist Party senator for the federal capital, declared: 'The unproductive struggles of people against people, in which men have killed each other without knowing why, or to serve the ambitions of the powerful, have finally ceased. Now are beginning the social wars of the peoples against their tyrants and exploiters. The face of the whole world is an immense furnace, where men can discern for the first time as a tangible and immediate possibility a new era for humanity in which we all may feel ourselves brothers in labour and justice' (*La Prensa*, 18 November 1918).

consciousness is one of its chief obstacles. There are too many disorientated groups around still with a fixed idea of some mystical revolution to come about with the arrival of some new holy prophet. Others believe that words alone are sufficient to carry the proletariat forward to reaching the decision to create a new world.[7]

The real source of the general strike lies in the combination of two circumstances. The first was inflation and the cost of living, and the effect this had in stimulating an atmosphere of militancy. The second was that although the unions were growing rapidly, at the end of 1918 only about a quarter of the workers were unionised. At that point the F.O.R.A. claimed a membership of 80,000, but there were well over 300,000 male workers in Buenos Aires.[8] Most of the participants in the general strike were made up of these non-unionised groups, and the strike itself marked a major stage in their efforts in organisation.

This is of some importance in understanding the type of action the strike led to. To a large extent it explains its marked lack of structure and organisation. Also the strike showed that the Radical government's hopes of using the Syndicalists as a medium to extend its influence among the working class were destined to failure. The Syndicalists had neither the support, nor the strength, to be able to exercise this role. While they controlled the mainstream of the union movement, they were not in a position to control the forces which were leading towards spontaneous mass actions. The general strike of 1919 illustrated an underlying solidarity impulse among the working class of Buenos Aires, but it exposed the absence of the institutional structures able to channel it in constructive directions. The result was little more than a chaotic outburst of mass emotion.

The Vasena strike

In December 1918 there was a strike action in the large metallurgical factory, Pedro Vasena e hijos Ltda, which was situated in Nueva Pompeya, close to the heart of the working class areas of Buenos Aires.[9] The metal-

[7] *La Organización Obrera*, 7 December 1918.

[8] Palacios, pp. 190–1.

[9] Nueva Pompeya was an area of new settlement in Buenos Aires and populated by the last wave of immigrants between 1910 and 1914. The Vasena Company was owned by a British syndicate, which had bought out the Vasenas, though it continued to employ them as local managers. For details of the company's financial history see *Review of the River Plate*, 14 November 1919.

lurgical industry in Buenos Aires was badly affected by the war. It was completely dependent on not always reliable supplies of high-priced raw materials and coal fuel. In an effort to reduce its costs, the firm became a large employer of the most destitute members of the immigrant communities – Spaniards, Ottomans, and even Japanese[10] – which it supplemented with large contingents of women and children.[11] During the war there had already been several strikes, some of them over the question of union recognition after attempts had been made to organise a city-wide metallurgical workers' federation. During one such movement in October 1917 there was considerable violence, when attempts at picketing resulted in conflicts with strike-breakers.[12] By December 1918, the firm was notorious for its starvation wages and the police measures it frequently took against its employees to guard against further strikes. It was a situation not unlike that in the frigorificos. According to an official report, average wage rates in the factory had declined in nominal terms from 104 pesos to a mere 52 pesos by the end of 1918.[13]

Again like the frigorifico workers, the metallurgical workers had been for some time the object of attempts by the federations to organise unions among them.[14] In November 1918 a union was established in the Vasena factory, and this led quickly to the outbreak of a strike in the first week in December.[15] Police measures against the strikers were at first brusque

[10] *La Vanguardia*, 5 October 1917; *Ministerio del Interior*, Vol. 3, 1919, File Nos. 155 and 4711. These contain petitions and signatures from the Vasena workers.

[11] *Review of the River Plate*, 14 November 1919.

[12] *La Vanguardia*, 5 October 1917. Requests that the police be brought in to curb 'endemic agitation' were made as early as April 1918 (*Ministerio del Interior*, Vol. 14, 1918, File 3212).

[13] *Boletín Oficial del Departamento Nacional del Trabajo*, No. 42, February 1919. This was about the same rate as the men in the railway workshops in Rosario and Pérez were being paid in June 1917. The difference was eighteen months of further heavy inflation. On the factory shop-floor there was an organised espionage system. Beatings were frequent and the workmen were subjected to summary fines covering a whole range of minor transgressions against discipline. (Cf. *La Vanguardia*, 3 December 1918.)

[14] The *Third National Census* (Vol. 7, p. 317) catalogued a total of 1,600 metallurgical workers in the city of Buenos Aires in 1914. This made them an important target for the union federations to organise.

[15] *La Vanguardia*, 20 January 1919. The Vasena men at first joined the Anarchist federation, though the links between them did not develop to any extent. The Anarchists took little notice of the Vasena strike as their attentions were still focussed on the sequel to the Radowitsky episode. The Anarchists did not initially see in the Vasena strike the means to precipitate a general strike. (Cf. *La Protesta*, 1–10 December 1918.)

in the extreme. Some impression of what they involved may be gained from the following extract from a letter to *La Vanguardia*:

> Conditions are impossible near the Vasena factory for those who have the misfortune to occupy the same house as one of the strikers. We are harassed continually, and cannot even stand at the doors of our homes without the police attacking us. On December 5 at 5 p.m., a brother of mine, fifteen years old, was arrested after, out of mere curiosity, he had gone over to join a group on the street corner. He was held in the police compound till midnight, although he is ill and off work on doctor's orders.[16] On the 13th at 4.30 p.m. he was standing at the door of the house. He was ordered to move by a police officer. When he asked where he was supposed to go when he was already in his own house, the officer began to push him inside with his horse. These barbarities are being inflicted upon all the households near the scene of the strike, and especially upon those who do not carry a membership card of the Radical Party. It is necessary to give currency to these brutalities because, given the frame of mind of those barbarians, one of these days they are going to do something really bloody for which they will have to count the cost.[17]

Suddenly towards the end of the month, although the strike still continued, the police, apart from a token patrol force, were all withdrawn. This encouraged the strikers to press on with their attempts to halt production in the factory completely. On 4 January, the company's manager, Alfredo Vasena, petitioned the ministry of the interior for police reinforcements. He complained of a state of 'open revolt' among the strikers. They had cut the telephone lines and interrupted the water supply. Their pickets launched daily attacks on the carts which brought the firm's materials into the factory from an outside depot.[18]

In the days that followed the violence increased. On 5 January there was an armed clash between the police patrol and the strikers, and a young officer was killed.[19] In retaliation the police organised an ambush two days later outside the factory. When the strikers massed to stop the carts, the police fired on them. There were four deaths as a result.[20]

[16] The illness could have been influenza, which was sweeping the western hemisphere at that moment. That it was so common suggests that many workers were without any means of support at that moment, a factor which may have been important in the build-up to the general strike.

[17] *La Vanguardia*, 20 December 1918.

[18] *Ministerio del Interior*, Vol. 3, 1919, File No. 296.

[19] *La Prensa*, 6 January 1919. At his funeral there was mention of the 'new theories' infecting the workers. This was an example of the way in which the fear of revolutionary plot gained ground among the police.

[20] *La Nación*, 8 January 1919. All the victims were non-strikers who lived in the zinc and wooden huts surrounding the factory.

The process of mobilisation

The general strike, which marked the beginning of the Semana Trágica, was largely a response to this single event during the Vasena strike on 7 January. However, it is important to point out a subsidiary process, which occurred over the two days between the affray at the Vasena factory on the 7th and the outbreak of the general strike on the 9th. Once the news of the clash became known, the unions immediately began to show signs of a major split. A few of them declared strike action for the 9th as a show of homage to the victims of the police. Others simply issued notes of protest, and decided to send delegations to the funeral cortege, which was planned for the 9th. Among the latter group were the most powerful of the unions, the F.O.R.A. and the F.O.M. This meant that those supporting a strike were largely bereft of leadership by the unions. The Anarchists, as before, proved incapable of taking over the role the Syndicalists had spurned.[21]

[21] Although the Anarchists seized on the events of 7 January as the opportunity they had been waiting for to avenge Radowitsky and force a general strike, they were again ignored. *La Protesta*'s leading articles on 9 January make this clear, as they berated the workers for their failure to act, as the Anarchists had demanded, the day before: 'The people of Buenos Aires are still quiet. The horror has escaped through to the sky and from the people there is not even a gesture of indignation, not a hint of protest. Where have the superior, worthy, valiant men been buried? Why is there no solidarity after the monstrous murder of bourgeois Vasena's strikers? Tell us that we may go and dig them and raise up their manly strength against the colossal crimes of the Radical government' (*La Protesta*, 9 January 1919). Nor did they have any influence on events during the strike. The F.O.R.A. del Quinto Congreso sent a small delegation to accompany the funeral procession. Afterwards the Anarchists disappeared from the scene. If Anarchist sympathisers may have taken part in some of the acts of violence which occurred, their numbers were too small to have had any important or leading role. My own view of this is at variance with that presented by Julio Godio in his work, *La Semana Trágica de enero de 1919* (Gránica, Buenos Aires, 1972). After the *Semana Trágica* the decline of Anarchism continued. The Anarchists had a very peripheral role in the events of mid-1919 and were unable to take much advantage of the further spread of trade unionism up to the end of 1920. On 14 March 1920, the F.O.R.A. del Quinto Congreso attempted to promote a general strike after the police discovered a group manufacturing bombs in the Liniers district of Buenos Aires. As before, this was a complete failure. From henceforth the movement largely subsisted as groups of individuals with only slight influence among groups like the dockers in Buenos Aires and Rosario. The only major incident in which Anarchists were involved after 1919 was the assassination in 1923 of Colonel Héctor Varela, the commander of the military expedition to Patagonia in 1921 and 1922. Later in the 1920s there were a number of bomb outrages.

Nevertheless, although the unions did not support a general strike, the mass of the workers did. The main pattern of events during the general strike was as follows. January 8 was taken up with preparations for the funeral on the next day.[22] On the 9th, according to an official police report, at around 7.0 a.m. hundreds of workers began to converge on Nueva Pompeya. They were told that the funeral would be held at 2.0 p.m. They then split up into small groups to look for further support for the strike in other parts of the city.[23] There followed a total stoppage of activities among the industrial workers in the neighbourhoods surrounding Nueva Pompeya. There were also major stoppages on the tramway system. In Nueva Pompeya itself the Vasena men were still active. In the morning they launched an assault on the company's offices, where there was a directors' meeting taking place. This finally developed into a gun battle which lasted until the evening when police and troops arrived.[24]

During the funeral procession there were more incidents, which were mainly the work of a group at the head of the column, which had set out from the Vasena men's union rooms. Cars were overturned and set alight, a passing attack was made on a tramway station, a church orphanage was ransacked, and there were attempts to loot guns.[25] When the procession, which by this time had grown to several thousand strong, reached the municipal cemetery, the police were waiting. In the ensuing battle at least a score of workers were killed.[26]

The general strike thus developed spontaneously out of the Vasena affray. The mobilisation process which occurred was governed by three general parameters. First, violence among the strikers depended to some extent upon the degree of proximity to the Vasena plant. It was particularly marked among the neighbourhood residents of Nueva Pompeya, who had suffered at the hands of the police over previous weeks. There was little support for the strike, for example, across the

[22] José R. Romariz, *La Semana Trágica. Relato de los hechos sangrientes del año 1919* (Hemisferio, Buenos Aires, 1952), pp. 87–90.

[23] Ibid. pp. 110–11.

[24] *La Nación*, 10 January 1919. *La Vanguardia* alleged later that there were 30 victims of the police, and that their bodies were immediately taken away and buried (*La Vanguardia*, 16 February 1919).

[25] *La Nación*, 10 January 1919.

[26] This figure is derived from the personal testimony of Andrés Cabona, with whom I talked in 1969. The morning after the funeral, on his way home, he had passed through the cemetery where the corpses were still lying.

Riachuelo in Avellaneda. Secondly, the mass of the strikers were industrial workers. Support for the strike among the more concentrated groups like the railwaymen and the port workers was much less marked. The railwaymen were still disorganised after their defeat in the previous year, while the port workers were more concerned with their own separate movement led by the F.O.M. As a result, and thirdly, apart from the funeral procession, the great characteristic of the action was that it occurred mainly among small groups with little coordination between them. Because of this, the strike swiftly collapsed once troops arrived in the city. Much of the violence attributed to the strikers was in fact the work of gangs of youths, among whom class perceptions were very low.[27]

This pattern was to an extent broken by one group, a section of the city's tramwaymen. In their case it is less easy to establish any association between action and proximity to the Vasena factory. Also the tramwaymen proved themselves more coordinated and more capable of planned action than the majority of the other groups. A witness described one of their actions as follows:

> I could see that a group of rioters had stopped a bus and were obliging its numerous passengers to get off. They did so quickly and without protest. Immediately the driver and conductor were made to do the same, which they did with manifest unwillingness. I saw how the rioters sprinkled the inside of the vehicle with liquid from some bottles, which for sure they had not found lying in the street. Suddenly everything was consumed in flames. I was beside myself with indignation not so much because of the act of arson, but because of the hysterical madness, the dancing, the leaps of savage delight and the cries of unbridled passion among the authors of the deed.[28]

It is significant that one authority dates the foundation of the tramwaymen's union as 10 January 1919.[29] Elements of coordination

[27] The *Manchester Guardian's* correspondent in Buenos Aires, for example, asserted that 'holidaying school children' were responsible for much of the street violence (*Manchester Guardian*, 16 January 1919). To *La Prensa* the strike was the work of 'revolutionaries' aided by 'thousands of delinquents and a multitude of vagabonds, composed of adults and adolescents ...' (*La Prensa*, 14 January 1919). A national senator declared: 'And the most serious thing is the part being played by youths and boys between ten and twenty years old. They have been at the forefront, the ones throwing the first stone and lighting the first matches' (Pedro A. Echagüe. *Diario de Sesiones*, Senadores, Vol. 2, 1918–19, p. 39).

[28] Carrasco, p. 195.

[29] Alfredo Fernández, *El movimiento obrero en la Argentina* (Plus *Ultra*, Buenos Aires, 1935), Nos. 7–8, pp. 6–7.

and strategic planning, which sabotage suggests, implied a certain affinity between the tramwaymen and groups like the Rosario railway workers in 1917 and the frigorifico workers in Berisso and Avellaneda. Each of these groups was undergoing a process of incipient unionisation, and violent action among them reflected efforts to impose solidarity.

Apart from exceptional cases like the tramwaymen, who used the Vasena affray as a pretext to press forward with their own claims, the action of the majority of participants in the general strike is largely explicable in terms of the trigger effects of the events outside the Vasena factory on 7 January. But this does not make the strike a casual or accidental event. It was sharply conditioned by the economic deprivations of groups like the Vasena, tramway and industrial workers. The role played by the Vasena affray was that it determined the spontaneity of the strike, and its emotional and aimless character.

In spite of the action of the tramwaymen, there was nothing in the strike to suggest either an attack on the State or an assault on the capitalist system. It is thus going much too far to conclude that the general strike was a prototype for working class revolution or the 'armed struggle'. Also the strike was extremely ephemeral. The tramwaymen were active on 10 January, and over the weekend of the 11th and 12th. Elsewhere there were isolated attacks on exposed motor vehicles or carriages. But there were no more mass demonstrations. Once the troops took over the city and began to organise patrols in the working class neighbourhoods, what remained of the strike swiftly disappeared. The latter half of the seven day span from 9 January was taken up with minor food riots, as shortages became marked. In broad terms the general strike of 1919 was more a series of unarticulated riots than a genuine working class rebellion. The movement was largely limited to certain geographical areas of the city, and it attracted the support of some groups much more than others. The division between the unions and the rank and file workers was also one of its salient characteristics.

The process of countermobilisation

The rapid collapse of the strike did not mean the end of the *Semana Trágica.* Its real tragic phase had yet to begin. From the moment that troops appeared in the city, a civilian para-military movement emerged, composed of members of the upper and middle classes. This was the first of the most significant events in 1919. On 10 January there were mass meetings in the centre of Buenos Aires to demand action against the strike. Armed private citizens organised patrols and began to accompany the police and troops. In this fashion a counteractive movement of the Right made its appearance on the scene.

The peculiar thing about this was that it was not directed against the strikers. Nor did it concentrate upon the original centre of the disturbances around Nueva Pompeya. It was directed mainly against the Russian-Jewish community, which lived for the main part in a more central zone of the city, in an area known as Villa Crespo. This reflected the belief that the strike formed part of a revolutionary conspiracy led by Russian-Jewish communists. In subsequent days scenes like the following became frequent:

> In the middle of the street I could see piles of books burning and heaps of old furniture... People were fighting inside and outside the buildings. The case was that of a Jewish shopkeeper who was said to be a Communist propagandist. The same punishment was being meted out to other Jewish families in the vicinity. The sound of furniture being violently thrown into the street mingled with cries of 'Death to the Jews. Death to the maximalists.'[30]

Incidents of this kind increased after 12 January, when the police issued the sensational notice that they had uncovered a Bolshevik cell amongst the Russian immigrants. The press interviewed three battered and semi-conscious prisoners, but it was soon evident enough that they were completely innocent. The 'President of the Socialist Republic' turned out to be a contributor to a Zionist journal, and his 'Minister

[30] Juan E. Carulla, *Al filo del medio siglo* (Paraná, 1945), p. 159, quoted in Godio, p. 183. It was not only the Russian Jews who suffered. Among the suspects were also the Catalans, who had traditionally played a leading role in the Anarchist movement. The distinction between Anarchists and 'Maximalists' was quickly lost, and in the latter stages of the week anyone who resisted arrest was likely to meet with a summary fate: 'I went once more to that sad, mournful household. I asked what had happened, and a boy led me to a place where there stood a beaker for drinking milk. I picked it up. It was covered in blood and punctured by a hole. I asked what it was and the boy told me that it had been in the hands of a 13-year-old girl, Paulina Viviani, the moment the police entered and opened fire. Terror-stricken, she was hiding behind the door of the kitchen when a bullet came through the door and hit the beaker. Not satisfied with this a police agent went into the kitchen and bayoneted her. She fell dead instantly... The young man then showed me into another room where there was a chair also with a bullet hole through it. Here, he told me, his 21-year-old brother had died. When they had finished off the girl they had come in here. His brother took up a piece of wood to defend himself. At that moment they had fired and he fell mortally wounded' (*La Vanguardia*, 14 January 1919).

of the Interior' a petty Jewish factory-owner. For the moment, however, the whole city gullibly accepted the existence of a revolutionary conspiracy:

> Symptoms like these suggest the carefully prepared work of a vigorous organisation, lurking in the rear of the strike disturbances to exploit them to its own advantage. And the police have discovered one of the agitators' centres, organised in the form of a soviet by foreign subjects, who have come to this republic with the express aim of taking over its government, and of sowing the seeds of anarchy on the model of the country in which it originated.[31]

Such fears, it must be said, were complete nonsense. There were no Russian agents in the city, nor was there any kind of revolutionary conspiracy. Later enquiries revealed that between the Armistice and the general strike only two Russians had arrived in Buenos Aires to promote support for the Bolshevik regime in Moscow. Having made little headway in Argentina, they had quickly left for Chile.[32]

The *Semana Trágica* was significant for the class neuroses it revealed among the upper and middle class groups, and the automatic association they immediately made between strikes and political conspiracies. This habit of mind originated in the previous generation. After remaining relatively dormant after 1910, it had once more been revived during the railway strikes. In 1918 the gathering state of hysteria among the upper and middle classes in Buenos Aires can be clearly traced. It was on them rather than the working class that the Russian Revolution and events in Central Europe immediately after the Armistice had their greatest impact. Commenting upon the use of forceful picketing measures during a strike in Rosario in October 1918, *El Diario*, a conservative afternoon newspaper in Buenos Aires, asked: 'What is the difference between this and the terrorist scandals in Europe? This is a criminal act of an organised and determined soviet, which is behaving just like the soviets of Muscovite maximalism.'[33]

Such fears gained ground after the Armistice as the international telegraphs reported the immediate effects of peace in Europe. They were fanned by the popular parades celebrating the Armistice, when the Socialist Party brought out the Red Flag. Soon afterwards the Socialists were forced to deny a rumour, which came from the police,

[31] *La Nación*, 13 January 1919.
[32] Ibid. Based on interviews with arrested Russian Jews.
[33] *El Diario*, 9 October 1918.

that they were plotting revolution.[34] This was followed by the Anarchist demonstration at the end of the month. On the following day in the central Avenida de Mayo, where the demonstration had been broken up by the police, crowds scattered after false reports that bombs had been planted.[35] On 8 December there was a strike among the police in Rosario. Although it was obvious enough that the main cause of this strike was that the police had pay arrears stretching over a period up to nine months, immediately talk of communist infiltration became rife. The *Review of the River Plate*, for example, thought it perceived in the strike 'at least the germ of a soviet'.[36] There were also rumours that Russian agents were daily landing in the country. On 10 December, the British minister made a formal complaint about this to the government.[37] Finally at the end of the year came the news of the strike the F.O.M. had scheduled for 1 January.

In some cases, as with the 'Russian agents', these fears were based on complete fictions. In others, false connections were made between entirely dissociated events. At the end of November, José Ingenieros, a prominent left-wing sociologist, delivered a lecture on the subject of maximalism. This, and the controversy it aroused, was another factor which encouraged the climate of unfounded rumour. In noting the public reaction to his lecture, Ingenieros echoed the state of alarm which was developing:

> Just look at the bourgeois newspapers. On the next day [after the lecture] the bishop of Córdoba issued a manifesto condemning maximalism... Two days afterwards the Anarchists held a meeting which ended with fatalities on the Avenida de Mayo... Eight days later the police and the firemen went on strike with the workers: clashes, deaths and woundings. Now, so I am told, a great revolutionary strike is being organised for harvest time by the railway and port workers. Meanwhile manifestos are being distributed among the army and the police... and in every public place in the Republic pamphlets are appearing linking my name with maximalist propaganda.[38]

From this the impulse towards counter-action developed, as the following extract from a speech by a conservative member in the Chamber of Deputies on 8 January makes apparent:

[34] *La Nación*, 19 November 1918.
[35] Ibid. 2 December 1918.
[36] *Review of the River Plate*, 13 December 1918.
[37] Despatch No. 362, 14 December 1918, F.O. 371–3503.
[38] Quoted in Delia Kamia, *Entre Yrigoyen e Ingenieros* (Meridión, Buenos Aires, 1957), p. 122.

A short time ago, standing on my balcony, I watched a demonstration pass by.[39] It was one of a type clearly prohibited by the Law of Social Defence... When the mob came across an Argentine flag ... there were howls of 'Down with the Argentine flag!' And the police were standing there impassively in the face of slogans subversive of the values of patriotism... There is throughout the length and breadth of the country a large number of professional agitators, whose position is far ahead of our Socialist gentlemen ... The agitators are offering the mob the maximum programme... and this recommends the use of any kind of violence to achieve its aims... We are today entirely without defence. Let us rise to the situation and request the government, without any ill-will, to find the remedy to bring to an end the evil which is undermining the solid cement of Argentine society.[40]

Finally, as the general strike occurred, the impulse towards counter-mobilisation was fuelled by the rumours crossing the city. Confused and embellished reports of the day's events began to circulate:

The news is grave: the strikers are armed to the teeth; they have put up barricades in all the neighbourhoods of the city; they have burnt four churches and two orphanages and are preparing to attack the railway stations. In Plaza Once they have been fighting since three o'clock in the afternoon... I decided to walk towards Plaza Once... Absolute silence. Only from time to time did the ringing of an ambulance bell pierce the silence of that summer's night.[41]

The important feature of this 'patriot' movement, as it styled itself, was that its appeal cut right across party lines, and it united extremely diverse groups within the Argentine bourgeoisie. It was supported by both Radical and conservative opposition members in the Congress, and they helped to fan it into action on 10 January when the mass meetings were held in the central Plaza Congreso. In the different districts of the city it was supported by members of the rural-based gentry, as well as by politicians, members of the Radical Party's local committees, priests, military officers and businessmen. Within a short time 'defence committees' had appeared in the different districts, using local police stations to organise patrols and distribute arms. Sons of the gentry borrowed family cars and used them to make incursions into the immigrant areas of the city.

[39] The speaker was referring to the Radowitsky demonstration.

[40] Luis Agote, *Diario de Sesiones*, Cámara de Diputados, Vol. 5 1918–19 (8 January 1919), pp. 70–2.

[41] Arturo Cancela, 'Una semana de holgorio', in *Tres relatos porteños* (Anaconda, Buenos Aires, 1933), pp. 116–17.

Within a short time the movement acquired a high level of organisation, leadership and a chain of command. Its leaders were a group of senior members of the armed forces, who met each day in the Naval Club. Here orders were issued to attack the Jews, and preparations were made to train civilians in the use of arms in nearby military garrisons. All this was in complete contrast to the structural characteristics acquired by the strike. Finally a notable feature of the patriot movement was that it maintained pre-existing status roles. Members of 'high society' led the action, while the bulk of the rank and file groups came from members of the urban middle classes.

The appearance of the patriot movement also reflected a widespread belief that the Radical government, as in the railway strikes of 1917, would be nothing to control the strike, and that it would thus leave the way open for a revolutionary movement among the immigrant working class. In this fashion the fears and prejudices which had been apparent during the period of mass immigration a decade before, suddenly revived.

Government responses

The emergence of this para-military organisation radically changed the balance and distribution of political power. The anti-strike groups, whose unity had become apparent through the foundation of the National Labour Association in May 1918, now had two vital allies. The activities of the group in the Naval Centre showed that they enjoyed considerable military support. They had also acquired important popular middle class support, even from within the Radical Party itself. From this time forward the key question was what sort of response would come from the government.

When the Red scare began in November, the government at first greeted events coolly. *La Epoca* declared: 'The sort of maximalism which can be called Argentine is no more than literary. It is a pose among a few unemployed boys who pass their time imagining adventures.'[42] There were signs of apprehension, however, after the Anarchist demonstration at the end of November: 'there is no room in this republic for the "maximalists" who have acted as lightning conductors for the revenge of the atrophied soul of the *mujik*.'[43]

By the time of the police strike in Rosario the government was begin-

[42] *La Epoca*, 25 November 1919.
[43] Ibid. 30 November 1918.

ning to panic. *La Epoca* blamed the Anarchists for the strike, and declared that Bolshevik propaganda had been found in the city.[44] After this, pathetic, but increasingly threatening, appeals were made to the workers to avoid strikes:

> This is not the time for inflamed agitation ... It is the time for silent hard work. This is the time for everyone to join in together to reestablish the nation's prosperity ... Of President Yrigoyen, of his patriotism and his sympathies for the dispossessed classes, the workers can have no doubt. They have seen him readjusting the directions of Argentine society, making it more humane and just, separating the interests of the State from the conveniences of capitalism, and mediating impartially in every dispute arising between workers and employers. It would be judicious on their part to put their confidence in him and to avoid embarrassing the State, which has as many problems as they have at the present time. If they do not do so this they are making a preposterous mistake, whose consequences they will be the first to lament.[45]

This made it apparent that the government no longer felt itself able to adhere to the officially neutral position it had adopted in the past. Its growing weakness at this point was not only due to the strikes. In the final weeks of the war it had been under constant pressure to join the Allies. When in November 1918 the first municipal elections were held in Buenos Aires under a new local government suffrage law, the Radicals were soundly defeated by the Socialists. The Socialists had become strong supporters of the Allies, and this defeat, the first of its kind since 1914, was widely regarded as a condemnation of Yrigoyen's neutralist position.[46]

In addition to this there was also inceasingly militant opposition against the government within the conservative elite. In October 1918 a Youth Committee, the Comité de la Juventud, was founded by members of the conservative opposition. This began in a belligerent fashion to draw parallels with the 1890 rebellion, when Juárez Celman had been forced into resignation.[47]

[44] Ibid. 11 December 1918.

[45] Ibid. 19 December 1918.

[46] During the Armistice parades, gangs of supporters of the government attacked the marchers with firearms, on one occasion from the doors of the building housing *La Epoca*. (Cf. *El Diario* 14 November 1918.)

[47] For a discussion of the Youth Committee see Nicolas Babini, 'La Semana Trágica', *Todo es Historia*, Year I, No. 5 (September 1967). The foundation of the committee was reported in *El Diario*, 21 October 1918.

Also the government had a critical problem at this point with the rebellious Blue Group in its own party. Members of the cabinet were involved in the intrigues and each, it seemed, brought the party closer to disintegration.[48] Finally the government was itself receiving warnings about Bolshevik activities in Buenos Aires. The Argentine consul in Rio de Janeiro warned of the discovery of a Bolshevik plot in Brazil and of plans to extend it to the River Plate area.[49] In Buenos Aires the United States ambassador made a request to the government for a precautionary investigation after Washington had reported that a plot was being hatched in Argentina to assassinate President Woodrow Wilson.[50]

At the beginning of the strike in the Vasena plant early in December, *La Epoca*, with uncharacteristic haste, denounced it as the work of 'foreign agitators', and laid emphasis on the fact that the police guard was being sent.[51] This may simply have reflected the government's apprehensions after the Anarchist demonstration, but there is a more convincing explanation for it. At the side of *La Epoca*'s report on the strike there was an article vigorously denying rumours of imminent changes in the cabinet. The person linked with these rumours was Leopoldo Melo who, it was said, was about to be appointed minister of the interior. Melo was one of the most prominent supporters of the

48 See *El Diario*, November–December 1918. The general role of the Blue Group is discussed in chapter 5, pp. 99–100.

49 *Ministerio del Interior*, Vol. 1, 1918, File No. 162.

50 Ibid. File No. 166. On 15 January 1919, the Argentine consul at the Hague warned of the embarkation of a large number of Russians for Buenos Aires. In a personally written note to Gómez (the minister of the interior), Pueyrredón, the minister of foreign affairs, suggested that this was linked with the general strike. (Ibid. Vol. 8, 1919, File No. 180.) It is worth noting that the ministry files corresponding to the second week in January 1919, have disappeared. They ought to have been deposited in 1928, the year of Yrigoyen's reelection to the presidency. Ultra-opposition groups like *La Mañana* accused Yrigoyen of fomenting the Red Scare to distract attention away from his own problems. On 30 November 1918, *La Mañana* declared: 'The *peludo*, taking note of his lack of public prestige . . . has seen in maximalism his salvation. He is thus magnifying the importance of the maximalist movement in the country and presenting a pathetic picture of the dangers it represents to public order.' But this is hardly a fair picture. The evidence is that the government panicked like everyone else, although it can be blamed in part for the violent *denouement* to the Vasena strikers' picketing.

51 *La Epoca*, 6 December 1918.

Allies, and a leader of the dissident Blue Group.[52] But more important still, he was also a director and legal adviser to the Vasena company.

It would seem, therefore, that the government's initial use of the police during the Vasena episode was an attempt to win over Melo. This interpretation is supported by the fact that when Melo later finally announced that he still opposed Yrigoyen, the police were immediately withdrawn from the factory, and matters allowed to run their course until 7 January.[53]

On 7 January, the government officially took the side of the police, and blamed the strikers. But it also reestablished contact with the F.O.R.A., and tried to bring the strike under arbitration.[54] The outcome of this was an agreement between the government and the F.O.R.A. that the police would be kept in their quarters to avoid further incidents during the funeral procession.[55] The undertaking was faithfully carried out, and it partly explains why the police only appeared so late in the day on 9 January. In broad terms, therefore, before the general strike, while the government was still unwilling to break its contacts with the unions, its overall position was marked by stress and increasing weakness.

[52] The advantage of having Melo in the cabinet was that it would encourage hopes of changes in foreign policy, it would win the support of the alienated river provinces, Entre Rios and Santa Fe, for the government and, finally, it would heal the party breach. The negative side was that it would mean a much harder line on the working class issue. The government's action on the Vasena strike thus shows that it was more concerned with party unity than with its reputation among the workers.

[53] On Christmas Day Melo published an open letter criticising presidential policies in the province of Mendoza. This was taken to mean his rejection of a post in the cabinet. One can only speculate how different the course of the Radical government would have been had he accepted it.

[54] This was clearly the message of a speech made in the Chamber of Deputies on 8 January by Horacio Oyhanarte, one of Yrigoyen's leading supporters. At the same time his words represent perhaps the most bitterly ironic commentary on the government's role during the episode: 'Since 12 October 1916, the Argentine working classes have been aware that a new era has dawned in this country and that none of their rights will be undermined, nor any of their legitimate claims betrayed. This the working classes have fully understood, because they have nominated the president of the republic their arbitrator in past disputes . . . Today our workers know that the spectacle to which we had grown accustomed under the old regimes have now happily passed . . . They know that the arms of our conscript soldiers will never again be pointed at their breasts' (*Diario de Sesiones*, Cámara de Diputados, Vol. 5, 1918–19, p. 68).

[55] *La Epoca*, 9 January 1919.

There is only one extant account of what the government was doing on 9 January, which comes from the British minister, Sir Reginald Tower. When the directors of the Vasena company found themselves imprisoned by the strikers in the firm's offices, they immediately contacted Tower by telephone. He spent several hours trying to contact the minister of foreign affairs, Honorio Pueyrredón. A delegation of employers then arrived to see him, led by the leader of the Sociedad Rural, Joaquín Anchorena. Together they went to Government House in the hope of seeing Pueyrredón. He, it transpired, was absent. At that moment his name was linked to reports of impending changes in the cabinet.

After a long delay the delegation was met by Acting Minister Diego Luis Molinari, and then by Gómez, the minister of the interior who, according to Tower, 'treated our representations with less attention than we would have wished'. Finally the Chief of Police, Elpidio González, who had been appointed only that morning, appeared from the cabinet meeting. He announced his intention of visiting the scene of the disturbance. It was a long time before González returned, because the strikers burned his car. Only then was the decision taken to use the police.[56]

Thus in spite of its obvious disorientation, the government did not take the decision to use its police powers lightly. It was still concerned to avoid blame for what might occur. Also, *La Epoca*'s commentaries show that it still wished to protect its relationship with the Syndicalists. Discussing the strike, it denied that it was a movement in which the workers were taking part. Instead it laid blame on the traditional scapegoats, the Anarchists:

> This is an absurd adventure provoked and directed by Anarchists, who are alien to all social discipline, and who are also estranged from the real labour

[56] Despatch No. 7, 10 January 1919, F.O. 371–3503. This also throws further light on the position of the Sociedad Rural, and may be seen as further confirmatory evidence for the thesis which appears in Appendix 3. Anchorena's reaction to the strike was to seek the assistance of none other than the delegated representative of His Majesty's Government in Argentina. Again this makes apparent how little influence the Sociedad Rural felt it had. Tower also reported that Anchorena became so frustrated with Yrigoyen at this point that he threatened to go to the Vasena offices himself, even, as he put it, at the risk of his life. When action finally came from the government, it was not based on any desire to conform to the wishes either of Tower or of the business groups.

organisations. This is not a workers' movement: those who say so are lying... They are only joining in the strike because they have been forced to do so by a minority of madmen and by the fear of reprisals. And even the workers who appear to have been involved ... have been mere instruments in the hands of agitators.[57]

Eventually on 11 January an agreement was reached between the government and the Syndicalists. In return for the release of police prisoners and wage increases of between 20 and 40% for the Vasena men, the F.O.R.A. declared its willingness to announce the end of the strike.[58]

But by this time the government had almost lost all control over events. Another of the central dramatic events of the Semana Trágica occurred on the afternoon of 9 January. The commander of the military garrison outside the federal capital in the Campo de Mayo, General Luis F. Dellepiane, arrived unexpectedly at Government House. He brought with him a troop battalion equipped with light artillery and machine-guns. There is an unsubstantiated tradition that Yrigoyen, on being confronted by Dellepiane, offered his resignation in the belief that a *coup d'état* was being staged.[59] Certainly, had he wished to do so, Dellepiane could under these circumstances have taken over the government. There were also firm grounds for Yrigoyen's fears. Dellepiane himself afterwards revealed that before entering the capital he had been approached by a group of 'retired militarv men' with a view to staging a military revolt.[60]

[57] *La Epoca*, 10 January 1919.

[58] *La Organización Obrera*, 23 January 1919. The F.O.R.A.'s other condition was that the government should not interfere with the port strike led by the F.O.M. It was still clearly more concerned about this than with the Vasena strike.

[59] Babini, p. 22.

[60] Dellepiane admitted this in a conversation two months afterwards with the British military attaché. (Cf. enclosure in Despatch No. 65, 15 March 1919, F.O. 371–3503). Dellepiane had been chief of police in the federal capital between 1909 and 1912 and had taken a leading part in the purge of the Anarchists in 1910. In his letter to the British military attaché in 1919 he described the background to his action as follows: 'Lately I could not hide from myself that my previous work [in 1910] had been destroyed little by little ... Among other things the excessive indulgences allowed by the government – for instance all those bad characters which I had deported as undesirables during my term of office had been allowed, in violation of the law, to return to the country.' The strange thing about this account was that the dates were all wrong. Although he was only writing in March, Dellepiane thought that the Semana Trágica had

The military revolt did not materialise because Dellepiane himself was an old sympathiser of the Radical cause from the 1890s. However, his continuing support, without which the government would have become completely isolated and a prey to the supporters of a *coup d'état*, was contingent on firm steps being taken to put down the general strike. Because of this the Radical government underwent a major *volte face* on 9 January. Instead of adhering to its original conciliatory position, it was forced to join in the witch-hunt. From henceforth its voice was as loud as anyone else's in denouncing the strike as a revolutionary conspiracy. It encouraged party members to join the vigilante bands. Also it began to exploit for its own purposes the exposed position of the immigrants, and the traditional prejudices against them. In a dark reference to the Russian community on 19 January, *La Epoca* declared: 'the true authors of recent events only represent 1.18% of the population of the country and 1.79% of the population of the federal capital.'[61] A week later *El Diario* recorded that a number of Radicals from the parish committees had resigned on the grounds that other committee members had been boasting that they had dispatched forty-eight Jews in a single day during the crisis.[62]

Yet while the government, and many of its supporters, must share the moral responsibility for the events of the Semana Trágica, the real point was that it had been caught in a political vice. The speed with which the patriot movement appeared showed that the government's labour policy had no backing in either conservative or middle class opinion. The intervention of a vital new power factor, the army, meant that it had to join the campaign to repress the strike, and seek out scapegoats for the alleged conspiracy, or be overthrown. From henceforth its apprehensions over the threat of a military revolt became the most fundamental conditioning factor on its policies.

Footnote 60 (continued)

taken place in February. The events of 9 January he described as 6 February. Sir Reginald Tower commented on his report: 'General Dellepiane's account shows the manner in which this country is being governed. That a General commanding what is equivalent to Aldershot could elect to descend on the Capital with his forces, entirely on his own initiative, and to proceed to dragoon the city, is perhaps typical of the Argentine' (ibid.).

[61] *La Epoca*, 19 January 1919. The figures are from the national census of 1914.

[62] *El Diario*, 24 January 1919.

CHAPTER 8

1919

In the events of January 1919 the Radical government was not a very long way from being destroyed in a military *coup d'état*. For much of the rest of 1919 it was engaged in a struggle to salvage the wreck of its labour policies, and to hold at bay its military-backed opposition. The most important short-term result of the Semana Trágica was the swift growth and institutionalisation of the conservative-led vigilante organisation, which had emerged during the general strike. On 19 January a meeting was held in the Naval Club, presided over by Rear-Admiral Domecq García. It was attended by representatives of all the leading aristocratic clubs in Buenos Aires, including a number of important military associations. Among them were delegates from the Jockey Club, the Círculo de Armas, the Círculo Militar, the Yacht Club, the Association of Patrician Ladies, and members of the ecclesiastical hierarchy. This was almost the whole of the conservative elite. A resolution was carried to continue the war against 'foreign ideologies' and the 'foreign agitator' as well as:

> above all to stimulate the sentiment of Argentine patriotism, and the spirit of citizenry, regardless of religious beliefs, political opinions, age or fortune, and the memory of the heroism and generous sacrifice of our forefathers who made us a nation ... To inspire the people with love for the army and the navy, that to serve in their ranks is a duty and an honour ...[1]

[1] Quoted in *La Epoca*, 20 January 1919. Four days earlier on January a group had met which styled itself the Committee for the Defence of Order (Comisión pro-defensa de orden). Among its sixty-seven members were Samuel Hale Pearson, Santiago O'Farrell and Manuel Montes de Oca, local directors of the British railway companies, Rear-Admirals Juan P. Sáenz Valiente and Manuel Barraza, Radical Party politicians Arturo Goyeneche and Delfor Del Valle, conservative politicians Enrique Santamarina, Ernesto Bosch, Benito Villanueva and Julio A. Roca, Jr, and the prominent banker, Carlos Alfredo Tornquist. The group cut right across party lines. (Cf. *La Epoca*, 16 January 1919.) Later it evolved into a provisional committee of the Patriotic League. Serving on this were Joaquín de Anchorena, Manuel Carlés, the Radical dissidents Vicente C. Gallo and Leopoldo Melo, former ministers from past conservative governments Estanislao Zeballos and Carlos Murature, and the most prominent member of the conservative ecclesiastical group, who was later important in the Great National Collect, Miguel de Andrea. (Cf. *La Epoca*, 8 February 1919.)

Out of this came the Argentine Patriotic League (Liga Patriótica Argentina), which remained over the next three years the most powerful political association in the country.

The roots of the League lay in the period after the turn of the century during the period of mass immigration. It was in many respects a continuation of the nativist movements which had appeared at different times among the traditional elite groups as a reaction to the immigrants and to Anarchism. This paternity dictated the markedly chauvinistic features of its doctrines, its tendency to glorify and mythologise the country's early history, before the impact of mass immigration had made itself felt. It was also apparent in its structure, which was strongly biassed towards elitism and established social hierarchy. The difference between the League and similar organisations in the past lay first in its sophisticated para-military organisation. Also, whereas other nativist associations had often been directed against the immigrants *en masse*, the distinctive feature of the League was that class largely replaced nationality as the determinant criterion underlying its objectives. By 1919 nativism and 'patriotism' had become class ideologies. They had ceased to be restricted to small enclaves of the creole landowning groups, but had won considerable acceptance among the sons-of-immigrants sectors, which occupied a leading position within the urban middle class. The League was supported as much by them as it was by the conservative elite.

From the start the League was a loose and heterogeneous coalition. It incorporated the traditional conservatism of the clerical groups, as well as the neo-conservatism of the Freemasons and the liberals. Its broadly defined aims allowed it to recruit support from many different quarters, and thus maintain and extend the alliance which had emerged in January:

> Disgraced politicians, parish *caudillos* . . . powerful industrialists, rich ranchers, an occasional battling priest at the side of well-known clericalists, a good number of military chiefs, who dream of leading the 'White Guards' to victory, excellent citizens who are afraid their patriotism may be doubted, and former government ministers awaiting whatever pickings might come their way. All these are present, including Radicals and conservatives.[2]

In this respect the League possessed an affinity with Radicalism. The internal coherence of both movements was maintained by means of a simplistic, and largely vacuous ideology, which owed a great deal to historical myth or to a primitive irredentist morality. For Radicalism it

[2] *La Vanguardia*, 1 April 1919.

was the 'restoration of the Constitution', and for the Patriotic League the destruction of Bolshevism and Anarchism. The League thrived on romantic rhetoric and groundless fears, rather than upon any close or sophisticated complementarity of economic or social interests. It always found the formulation of constructive programmes for action extremely difficult. It was also, like Radicalism, prone to division, usually between obscurantist advocates of *laissez-faire* and the more imaginative proto-fascist groups, whose support for reform on occasion went as far as demands for workers' profit-sharing in industry.[3] There was also a strong petty bourgeois strain in the League, which reflected the extent of its strong middle class support:

> Organised capital and organised labour mean the same thing; each acts in its own interest with no consideration for the rest of humanity. In their egotistical covetousness for power, they are fighting a violent battle which is socially destructive. The middle class, which really represents three-quarters of the People, is entirely unprotected between these two forces, undergoing attack from both. However the conflict is solved, the organisations always win, and never lose: only the middle class staggers under the burden and suffers the losses.[4]

The League was financed officially by individual subscriptions, although it received strong financial support from the aristocratic clubs. It was also supported by the major foreign companies. In June 1921 the identity of its treasury committee became known. Serving on the committee were Samuel Hale Pearson and Santiago O'Farrell, who were local directors of the Central Argentine and Pacific Railways respectively, a member of the Mihanovich shipping family, and members of the Lacroze and Chevalier Boutell families, which between them controlled the tramway companies in Buenos Aires.[5] This made it clear that the foreign business groups had a very direct say in the League's affairs.

However, the power of the League, and another feature setting it apart from similar associations in the past, lay in its military support. It came to symbolise the alliance between big business and the army to extirpate the 'agitators' and keep the workers in their places. The struc-

[3] Cf. *Primer Congreso de Trabajadores de la Liga Patriótica Argentina* (Buenos Aires, 1920).

[4] Ibid. p. 95.

[5] *La Vanguardia*, 26 June 1921. In 1923 the maritime workers' newspaper, *La Unión del Marino*, published a facsimile of a receipt acknowledging payment of a subscription to the League by the Rosario–Puerto Belgrano Railway. (Cf. ibid. January 1923.)

ture of the alliance is evident from the League's major office-holders in 1919. The League's first and second vice-presidents were Luis S. Zuberbühler, a pro-British former president of the Commercial Exchange (Bolsa de Comercio), and a former director of the National Bank (Banco de la Nación), and General Eduardo Munilla, a former president of the Military Club (Club Militar).

The League's president was Manuel Carlés, who was a foremost ideologue of the romantic, nostalgic brand of patriotism which the movement exemplified. He had close contacts both with the country's political leaders and with the army. Before 1912 he had served several terms, on behalf of different conservative factions, in the Chamber of Deputies. His army contacts stemmed from long periods of service in the select professorial bodies of the Escuela Nacional de Guerra and the Colegio Militar de la Nación.[6] Carlés' career thus made it apparent that 'patriotism' in 1919 was very far from signifying economic nationalism. Like every other major political movement at this time, the Patriotic League based itself upon an acceptance of the primary export economy. Thus the foreign business groups could attach themselves to it without their presence being regarded as in any way anomalous.

Relations between the government and the Patriotic League were ambiguous from the outset. Carlés himself, in spite of his conservative party background, was not known for any deep-rooted hostility towards the Radicals. For the main part of 1918 he served as Yrigoyen's federal interventor in the province of Salta. The critical problem was Yrigoyen's relationship with the workers. If they struck *en masse* once more, and the government attempted to protect them, then it was more than probable that the League would turn against the government. Between support and hostility there was thus a thin dividing line. Whenever *La Epoca* mentioned the League, it did so with an effusive show of respect. In March 1919, Gómez, who had survived as minister of the interior, personally authorised the League to display its propaganda in the post offices.[7] It was not until August that the government summoned up the courage to ban its local meetings from being held in the police stations.[8]

[6] For an outline of Carlés' career see Pedro Maglione Jaimes, 'Una figure señera', *La Nación*, 12 January 1969. He was also legal representative for many years to the city Retailers' Association, the Centro de Almaceneros, which was composed, ironically enough, mainly of foreigners.

[7] *Ministerio del Interior*, Vol. 8, 1919, File No. 2011.

[8] *La Epoca*, 10 August 1919.

The maritime dispute of 1919

In spite of the League's ominous presence, after the Semana Trágica the government did what it could in the short term to retrieve its position among the working class. It was encouraged to do this by the prospect of a vital senatorial election due to be held in Buenos Aires in March 1919. To prevent the Socialists capitalising further upon recent events, it again turned to the unions and to the strikers. Its first opportunity came during the maritime stoppage, which dragged on over the first four months of the year.

By 1919, in contrast to the incipient state of unionisation among other groups within the working class, the maritime workers were strongly and comprehensively organised. The men had the advantage of relative job stability, high-level skills and geographical concentration in the port area. Also, the F.O.M. had been successful during the two strikes in 1916 and 1917. Eighteen months after the second strike in 1917 the union had a total membership of over 9,000 among the coastal shipping sailors and the tug and lighter operatives in the port of Buenos Aires. This was about 95% of the total personnel employed, an achievement which had few parallels in the development of the Argentine union movement up till that time.[9]

The F.O.M. was also financially in a very strong position. In 1916 and 1917 it had needed subsidies from the F.O.R.A. and from 'popular committees' supporting it in the Boca. At the beginning of 1918 its savings stood at 15,000 pesos, even after sizeable sums had been granted to the F.O.R.A. for propaganda purposes and financial assistance given to to F.O.F. during the railway strikes.[10] It was now the lynchpin of the F.O.R.A.'s general strategy to establish a national union movement. At the end of 1918 the F.O.M. was beginning to spread its influence among the maritime workers in the other coastal cities of Argentina and to establish links with its Uruguayan counterpart in Montevideo. Its strength lay in its stable leadership and in its high standard of discipline. This had allowed it to establish a stranglehold over the port area and to impose boycotts at will, most notably during the frigorifico strike in Avellaneda at the beginning of 1918.

By September 1918 the union felt itself strong enough to demand

[9] See the report on the F.O.M. in *Boletín Oficial del Departamento Nacional del Trabajo*, No. 40 (February 1919), pp. 105–7.

[10] Ibid. p. 72.

consultation by the coastal shipping companies whenever job vacancies appeared. This demand, plus others for wage increases and the improvement of working conditions, led it to present a general ultimatum to the Coastal Shipping Centre (Centro de Cabotaje), in December. After an attempt at negotiation, the coastal shippers imposed a general lockout at the beginning of January.[11]

The F.O.M.'s organisation during the lockout was impressive. Each afternoon the men met in a Boca football stadium and union officials reported on the state of negotiations. Plans were set afoot for the distribution of free food, and a refectory was established with seating capacity for over 700. As in 1916 and 1917, the men had strong local support in the Boca. Tons of food and numerous private donations flowed into the union's headquarters.[12]

There is no need to follow in any detail the tortuous negotiations to which the dispute gave rise. Its first main feature was that it presented the government with an opportunity to favour the men without being plagued by the problem of recurrent violence. For example, on 24 January an agreement had been worked out in principle. The shipowners offered to increase wages in return for the F.O.M. abandoning the boycott weapon. However, at this point the minister of marine, Alvarez de Toledo, intervened to insist that the clause restricting the use of boycotts be kept secret.[13] The aim was, it seemed, to associate the government with a union victory which would appear to the electorate much greater than it really was. It failed because the proposal was put down in writing, and once the shipowners had rejected it, they found themselves in possession of a piece of incriminating evidence which they used to good advantage to force the government to retract its demands. In the later stages of the dispute the government repeatedly attempted to impose a solution by making the Customs Authority responsible for the running of the port in order to prevent daily confrontations between the union and the shipowners over such matters as boycotts and the selection of

[11] Unlike during the wartime strikes, this time the coastal shippers had the support of the transatlantic shippers. Soon after the Armistice the two had got together and decided upon a common plan of action. By imposing a total lockout, they hoped to turn the port dockers against the F.O.M., but although the affair dragged on into April, the dockers proved too disunited to have any serious effect on the dispute. (Cf. Dispatch No. 18, 18 January 1919, F.O. 371–3503.)

[12] *La Vanguardia*, 7 February 1919, 17 February 1919; *La Organización Obera* and *La Union del Marino*, January–April, 1919.

[13] Despatch No. 29, 28 January 1919, F.O. 371–3503.

crews. For a long time during this phase the great stumbling block was the men's claim for lockout pay. This the government finally resolved by introducing a supplementary port levy on the shipowners which was then used to indemnify the men.[14]

This unusual step illustrated the extent of the government's commitment to the men. Gestures like this were made possible by the inability of the Labour Association, which conducted most of the negotiations on behalf of the shipowners, to project the dispute beyond its limited context in the port area into the sort of issue which would invite the attention of the Patriotic League. In spite of the virtual closure of the port of Buenos Aires, there was little effect on overseas trade. The bulk of trade was simply transferred to other ports. Also, the absence of violence made it difficult to mobilise outside support by invoking fears of the 'professional agitators'.

However, the Labour Association did all it could to prevent the government reaping any political benefits from the dispute. On the eve of the election, in the middle of March, it issued a press manifesto which, among other things, made as much as possible of the letter containing Alvarez de Toledo's proposal that the boycott agreement be kept secret.[15] Simultaneously there were attempts by conservative members of Congress sympathetic towards the Association to discredit the government with the middle class voters. Referring to the manifesto, a leading conservative deputy, Matías Sánchez Sorondo, who had been one of the government's foremost critics during the Semana Trágica, declared: 'This [manifesto] deals with the sad, shameful case of the port strike. In it there is evidence of culpable inaction and even complicity on the part of the executive with the labour agitators; it is shown to be plotting against the most fundamental interest of society.'[16]

Not only the conservatives attempted to exploit the dispute. It was also seized upon by some of the dissident Radicals for the same purpose. At one point during the lockout the coastal shippers seemed about to capitulate to the government's demand that the men be compensated with lockout pay. What prevented this was rather spurious opposition from the shipowners' lawyers, the chief of whom was Ricardo Aldao. He was Radical deputy for the province of Santa Fe, a member of both the

[14] *Review of the River Plate*, 4 April 1919.

[15] Press reports, 18 March 1919.

[16] *Diario de Sesiones*, Cámara de Diputados, Vol. 6, 1918–19 (18 March, 1919), p. 474.

Labour Association and the Patriotic League, and a prominent figure among the Radicals opposing Yrigoyen.[17]

In this fashion the shipping dispute became bound up with more general political rivalries between Yrigoyen and his opponents. *La Epoca* responded to these manoeuvres in kind. As had happened during the railway strikes, there were frequent complaints made against the local representatives of the foreign companies. Commenting on an article in the London *Times* which criticised the Argentine government's conduct towards foreign capital, *La Epoca* declared: 'There is no harassment of British capital. What is happening is that the British companies – with certain honourable exceptions – are being run by their local directorates, whose members are playing about with politics, getting themselves mixed up in affairs beyond their sphere of action.'[18]

What gave these complaints further colour was that the company lawyers, in league with the Labour Association and the shipowners, also lent their support to the old idea of a shipping boycott. This was first mooted, as in 1918, by Sir Reginald Tower, whose relations with both the shipowners and the Labour Association were extremely close. Tower's extreme dislike for the government had grown rather than receded since the Armistice, largely because he had failed to drag it into the war. His first step in February was to seek to involve the French, Italians and Americans in the port dispute. However, the French and Italians were unwilling to risk cutting off their supplies of Argentine foodstuffs, while the Americans declared their unwillingness to become embroiled in a local political issue whose outcome, if successful, could only help the British. It seemed that their attitude was that any embarrassment to the British was to their advantage.[19] By this time the British shipping companies, urged on by their representatives in Buenos Aires, were supporting the idea of a boycott. The problem was, as in 1918, that the British were also in vital need of food supplies. When in April the companies acted unilaterally to organise a boycott, the Foreign Office, on the advice

[17] Despatch No. 79, 15 March 1919, F.O. 371–3503.

[18] *La Epoca*, 4 April 1919. This was always the government's let-out from criticism that it was attacking foreign capital. Earlier, in March, *La Epoca* welcomed the forthcoming visit to Argentina of the chairmen of the British Railway Companies since it would restore a 'measure of supervision' over the local directors, which had 'lapsed' during the war.

[19] Telegrams, Nos. 81, 86, 2 and 6 March 1919, F.O. 371–3503.

of the British ministry of shipping, requested Tower to use his influence to have it called off.[20]

The boycott issue was important, not least because it was an early example of the growing rivalry between the British and the Americans in Argentina after the First World War. It also showed that the British had no direct means to exercise leverage against the government. The only real way they could make their influence felt was to work within the framework of local politics by manipulating the various pressure groups which had emerged.

In the election campaign the Radicals did all they could to exploit their favours to the men in the shipping dispute. A street-corner election speech was reported by *La Epoca* as follows:

> He [the party speaker] emphasised the impartiality of the Radical government in the struggles between capital and labour ... He referred to the maritime strike, praising the discipline the workers had maintained ... saying that they had shown themselves more conciliatory than the shipowners ... Afterwards he praised the intelligent and efficient Syndicalist organisation, and compared it with the Socialists who seduced the workers merely for electoral profit.[21]

In spite of this there was no sign that the government's handling of the maritime dispute affected voting patterns in the election to any significant degree. The Radicals did manage to win, but only by 3,000 votes from a total vote of 99,000. This was an improvement on the municipal elections the previous November, but it was considerably behind their performances in March 1916 and March 1918. Apart from the fact that the Socialists were showing signs of recovery after their disastrous splits during the war, the most significant thing about this election was the fact that the Progressive Democrats won over 36,000 votes. This suggested a strong swing away from the Radicals on the part of the middle class groups. The results were in great part a vote of censure against the government for its conduct during the strikes.

[20] Telegram No. 115 (and Foreign Office comments), 28 March 1919, and ministry of shipping to Foreign Office, 11 April 1919, ibid.

[21] *La Epoca*, 24 February 1919. The Radicals' candidate for this election was one of the leading dissidents, Vicente C. Gallo. This prompted the following remark by *La Vanguardia* on 12 March: 'The government proposes to play a two-faced card in this election campaign ... It proposes to flatter the popular and working class mass with deceitful and hypocritical pretensions of social reformism, and at the same time to give absolute securities to the conservatives of this country by granting them candidates who are the flower and pollen of Argentine ultraconservatism.' This was an accurate observation.

Also the Radicals' attempts to win over voters from among the Syndicalist unions appeared to have been unsuccessful. When the results were announced in one ward where the members of the unions were thought to be strongly concentrated, a local Radical politician was reported by the Socialists as saying: 'Our defeat here alarms me more than anything else, because we had hopes of picking up the votes of Syndicalist voters in this ward. We were counting on their votes. The president has treated them so well. Now it looks like we have been deceived.'[22]

This possibly suggests split loyalties among the working class – a tendency to support the Syndicalists in the unions and the Socialists in the elections, in spite of the often extreme hostility between them. Certainly there was nothing to show that the Radicals had made any headway at all in their efforts to capture the working class vote.

The surprising thing about this was that it made very little impact upon the central aspect of Yrigoyen's strategy, which was to seek support from the Syndicalist unions. Although from this time forward, because of the Patriotic League, he found it difficult to intervene in the strikes, he did not, as a result of the elections, relinquish his support for the F.O.M. in the port. In a conversation with Tower, which was concerned with the maritime workers' claim for lockout pay, Yrigoyen compared himself with Lloyd George, and his reformist policies with those of the Liberal Party in Britain before 1914. Business, he said, had made spectacular fortunes out of the war, largely at the expense of the workers, and he would continue to support their 'legitimate claims'. He declared that the deadlock in the port was due to a conspiracy among his political opponents, whose aim was to provoke another general strike 'to embarrass the government'.[23] Some time later Tower reported a personal argument between the president and Leopoldo Melo. When Melo complained about the strikes and demanded action to curb them, Yrigoyen retorted 'You forget I am President of the Poor.'[24]

This, apart from its apparently genuine idealistic aspects, expressed the nature and the calculations underlying Yrigoyen's position. To organise the workers behind the Syndicalists would favour his general aim of at least preventing the Socialists from extending their influence among the unions. Over the short term it would help to establish firmer barriers against another mass, spontaneous general strike, and prevent

22 *La Vanguardia*, 29 March 1919.

23 Despatch No. 79, 15 March 1919, F.O. 371–3503.

24 Despatch No. 161, 22 June 1919, F.O. 371–3504.

the reactivation of the 'patriots'. It also expressed the degree of opportunistic intrigue there was among the conservative opposition to place the government in the sort of situation which could well invite a military coup.

The strikes of mid-1919

The second critical phase of 1919 occurred in the middle of the year. According to a report later published by the National Labour Department, over the first half of 1919, and excluding the general strike in January, there were 259 strikes in Buenos Aires, which involved over 100,000 workers.[25] These strikes were again closely related to inflation and to the rapid increase in the number and influence of the unions. The process can be illustrated by the figures in Table 8 which represent the total affiliates of the Syndicalist F.O.R.A. over the twenty-four-month period from January 1918.

Since the total number of workers in Buenos Aires at this time was around half a million, the number of the F.O.R.A.'s affiliates grew from about 12% of the working class at the beginning of 1918 to around 24%

TABLE 7 *Union membership, 1918–19*

Month	Number of affiliates 1918	1919
January	58,400	83,000
February	60,100	85,100
March	63,000	87,000
April	66,900	90,200
May	68,000	94,100
June	69,000	98,000
July	70,500	100,100
August	74,200	107,000
September	74,200	107,000
October	75,000	110,000
November	78,500	113,300
December	79,800	118,200

Source: Alfredo L. Palacios, *El Nuevo Derecho*, pp. 190–1.

[25] See *Review of the River Plate*, 15 August 1919.

at the end of 1919. During the Semana Trágica the proportion was about 16%, less than a fifth of the total number of workers. But what these figures show is the great expansion in the rate of unionisation which took place in 1919.[26] During 1918 the monthly average rate of affiliation to the F.O.R.A. was about 1,600. This increased to 3,000 in 1919. The largest rise came in April (3,900), and in July (6,900). During the five months between March and August 1919, affiliations increased at the average rate of 4,000 per month.

The strikes emerged directly from this process. Either they reflected an attempt by employers to curb the sudden accelerated spread of the unions, or they marked attempts by recently formed, but established, unions to struggle for higher wages to compensate for the rise in the cost of living since 1914.[27] After a telephone workers' strike in March, the textile industry was seriously affected in April. The most serious and protracted dispute, which involved some 6,000 workers, was a strike which developed in the British-owned wholesale and retail concern, Gath and Chaves. At the same time there was a strike among the clerks of the Bank of Spain. During May the strikes acquired epidemic proportions as large numbers of industrial and service workers all came out on strike. There were also strikes in the metallurgical industry, including the Vasena factory, and they spread once again to a section of the tramwaymen, as well as barbers, newspaper reporters, waiters, electricians, telegraphists and even funeral undertakers. On 9 May, *La Vanguardia* reported that a total of 25,000 workers were out on strike.[28]

The prime feature of many of these movements was that they involved groups which had never before taken strike action. On the other hand, they did not generally affect the more traditional areas of unrest.[29]

26 The rate of unionisation may have been greater because not all unions affiliated with the F.O.R.A. This was especially true of a number of white-collar unions which appeared for the first time.

27 In many cases employers quickly surrendered. *La Vanguardia* commented: 'All the lists of conditions being presented to employers have as their principal demands an increase in wages and a reduction in the hours of labour. A large number of capitalists have already acceded to these demands, showing more resistance towards those which refer to the recognition of the unions and of the representative functions of their delegates' (*La Vanguardia*, 19 May 1919).

29 The figures were taken from the National Labour Department's statistics.

29 *La Vanguardia* commented on 10 May: 'A notable fact about the present situation is that the long-established historic unions are playing little part in the present strikes . . . The pressure stems from that enormous mass of workers which for one reason or another has held itself aloof from organisation and action.'

There was also an important contingent of lower middle class groups taking part, among which the bank employees were the most notable. Partly because of this, and because the strikes mainly affected the smaller industrial plants and the geographically disparate service industries, there were no traumatic, polarising events like that which brought the Vasena dispute to its tragic denouement in January. Also, this time the F.O.R.A. played a much more active leadership role than it had done at the end of 1918.

Under these circumstances the *Review of the River Plate*, for example, was happy to record a decline in what it called the 'malignant growth of maximalism'.[30] It seemed that Yrigoyen's support for the Syndicalist unions was finally beginning to pay dividends. As *La Epoca* frequently declared, there was 'nothing suspicious' about the strikes, since they were merely a reflection of the effects of wartime inflation: 'All these strikes suggest is a desire for welfare, which is quite distinct from any doctrinaire political objective. The purely economic character of the strikes is the reason for the sympathies they have evoked and for the rapid acceptance of the claims the strikers are making by employers.'[31]

Nevertheless the strikes brought with them an atmosphere of acute crisis, which had important effects on the government's position. Their first result was to galvanise the Labour Association into action. Over the three months between April and July, the Association managed to double its membership.[32] It rejected any attempt to negotiate with the unions, and instead organised a system of strike-breakers and a network of armed guards to protect them.[33] There was also another attempt to organise a general lockout in Buenos Aires.[34]

30 *Review of the River Plate*, 9 May 1919.

31 *La Epoca*, 4 May 1919.

32 *La Vanguardia*, 30 July 1919.

33 Ibid. 14, 15, 16 May 1919.

34 This failed as in October 1917, but the help of the Labour Association was often decisive in a number of important victories won by employers (ibid. 16 May 1919). At the end of May the Gath and Chaves strike collapsed after a duration of two months. Later the same happened with a number of taxi and tramway workers' strikes. Later figures published by the National Labour Department showed that 55% of the strikers over the first half of 1919 failed to secure anything from them. Among the strikes principally concerned with wage questions, only 27,000 men out of a total of 62,000 were successful. (An abstract of the report appeared in the *Review of the River Plate*, 15 August 1919.) It is also important to note that the Labour Association was strongly attacked by the government for this. There were further rows reported

The source of the political crisis in mid-1919 was, however, the fear the strikes evoked of a new general strike and in revolutionary conspiracy. The growing consolidation and unity of the unions and the employers was accompanied by a third major process – the sudden tremendous growth of the Patriotic League. Before April the League was still mainly limited to the aristocratic and military clubs. But afterwards, in conjunction with the strikes, it became a mass movement, with a membership ranging from the *haute bourgeoisie* to white-collar employees and street-corner retailers. It also rapidly acquired further influence in military circles. In July the extent of its military support became known. Among its declared members were 6 generals, 18 colonels, 32 lieutenant-colonels, 50 majors, 212 captains, 300 lieutenants, and over 400 sub-lieutenants.[35]

As soon as the strikes took hold, the League issued a manifesto declaring its intention to 'adopt the necessary measures so that its members can organise themselves in neighbourhood associations, which can then cooperate in any police action against movements of an anarchist character'.[36]

A multitude of neighbourhood brigades were established in Buenos Aires on the basis of the defence committees which had appeared during the Semana Trágica. These were often led by army officers. Lectures and

Footnote 34 (continued)

between Yrigoyen and Anchorena, with Yrigoyen threatening to dissolve the institution. This is yet another example of the government's lack of deference towards the business groups; it was afraid not of them but of the Patriotic League. (Cf. *La Epoca*, 11, 12 May and 16 June 1919; *La Vanguardia*, 6 June 1919.) What detracted from the Association's capacity to win support from the government at this point was the fact that arbitration was supported by the Patriotic League, its concern being not so much the strikes, but the 'agitators' allegedly taking advantage of them. Also at different times there were reports of disagreements within the Association. Although temporarily it attracted the support of a large number of the smaller domestic business groups, these never blended together with the large foreign enterprises. There were soon rifts between them, as the smaller employers began to object to their client status. One final suggestive commentary on the strikes was that police reports for the federal capital in 1919 showed an appreciable reduction in crime figures. There were some 7,000 offences against property in 1919, about 25% down on the previous year. (Cf. *Review of the River Plate*, 27 August 1920.)

35 *Review of the River Plate*, 25 July 1919. Later in September Carlés, who seemed unaware of the irony, petitioned Congress for the revision of the army's pay. (Cf. *La Vanguardia*, 28 September 1919.)

36 *La Vanguardia*, 1 April 1919.

propaganda classes were organised for the League's members, and it again became a common practice to instruct new recruits in the use of firearms.

Government responses

Eventually the government's apprehensions pushed it into adopting openly the repressive measures it had previously avoided. The critical moment came at the end of April with rumours that a general strike would occur in May, thus reviving the Anarchist tradition of ten years before. The rumours were swiftly denied by the Syndicalists, but from *La Epoca* there began to appear touchy assertions of the government's authority. These made apparent the efforts being made to prevent any unilateral action developing on the part of the Patriotic League:

> The executive is completely sure of itself. It knows that it has the material and moral authority to guarantee everyone's free exercise of their rights... Such awareness of the government's strength had had a beneficial effect on the situation. It has strengthened the panickers, and convinced every social class that nothing out of the ordinary will be tolerated. Thus public confidence has revived.[37]

Soon afterwards the government acted. On May 5 a police edict was issued ordering the Laws of Residence and Social Defence to be applied against all known Anarchists. A brutal spate of mass arrests and deportations followed.[38] The other interesting feature of this was that it was also calculated to win the support of the British. On 24 April, Tower recorded a visit from the chief of police, Elpidio González, whom he reported as saying: 'the Argentine government must perforce take immediate action in the sense of repressive measures against individuals who were disseminating pernicious doctrines among the half-educated people here, largely of foreign origin or descent, but who were only too prone to fall under the influence of the malcontent agitators.'[39]

[37] *La Epoca*, 1 May 1919.

[38] The measure again affected the immigrant communities most of all. It was not long before complaints of wrongful arrest were reaching the minister of the interior. (Cf. *Ministerio del Interior*, Vol. 8, 1919, File No. 2011.)

[39] Despatch No. 122, 24 April 1919, F.O. 371–3504. González also granted an extensive interview to the *Buenos Aires Herald* to explain the scope of the measures. (Cf. 11 May 1919.) Also when Tower met Federico Alvarez de Toledo, who was now Argentine minister-designate to London, Alvarez expressed his 'embarrassment', as Tower put it, over the effects of the government's 'previous' labour policy on foreign capital. He declared that Yrigoyen now shared his opinion, and had for this reason decided to take action. (Despatch No. 139, 9 May 1919, F.O. 371–3504.)

Thus although the government felt that it could more or less ignore the National Labour Association, it was much more deferential towards the British government, which it obviously saw as capable of priming the Patriotic League into action.[40] From henceforth the Radical government gave the British no further serious trouble. The effort made to court the British in May 1919 continued afterwards, and it gradually led to much better relations. Early in May several of the chairmen of the railway companies arrived in Buenos Aires. No effort was spared by the government to allay their suspicions and win their goodwill. Early in April 1919, *La Epoca* had been accusing the railway companies, probably correctly, of financing the election campaigns of opposition parties. But later in 1919 when the railway chairmen left the country, they declared that their impression of Yrigoyen as 'a revolutionary Socialist' was due to 'a misunderstanding'.[41]

The government's difficulties stemmed not only from the opposition to it in sections of the army and among the foreign companies. By this time the Patriotic League was showing signs of having won over the great bulk of the government's former popular support. At this moment, it is interesting to note, the Patriotic League closely approximated to what Pellegrini and Sáenz Peña had been searching for in the previous decade, a mass movement dominated by the traditional conservative elite. The more the League grew, the more the government's authority and legitimacy crumbled. An impression of how desperate the situation was becoming comes from a description of the National Day parades on 25 May:

Yesterday there were two patriotic demonstrations. One was led by Sr Irigoyen and made up of administration employees and a few military chiefs who had been ordered to attend ... The other was headed by Dr Carlés, president of the

[40] It does need emphasising, however, that the influence of the British was still indirect. There is no hint in Tower's correspondence of support for a *coup d'état*. At the end of April the government had made an astute move by appointing General José F. Uriburu to head the military garrison at Campo de Mayo. This pleased the Patriotic League, because General Dellepiane had opposed its activities. But it displeased the British because Uriburu was suspected of having been pro-German during the war. The British would not have welcomed the prospect of a military revolt if it meant that Uriburu would become president. Tower recorded his appointment with manifest disappointment. (Cf. Despatch No. 114, 29 April 1919, F.O. 371–3504.)

[41] *Review of the River Plate*, 1 August 1919. When Alvarez de Toledo went to London in July he made speeches announcing the country's gratitude to foreign capital and declaring that agitation was being quelled by the use of the Law of Social Defence. (Cf. ibid. 18 July 1919.)

Patriotic League, accompanied by the most representative sections of the city: society, politics, banking, clergy, commerce, etc ... They were two groups separated materially and morally by so great a distance that it could be said ... that Government and People had marched by entirely separately ... Sr Irigoyen led a funeral march ... Dr Carlés marched to the sound of the national anthem. As Sr Irigoyen went by, there was an occasional muted handclap; at the step of Dr Carlés there was a continuous ovation.[42]

This was accompanied by an intensification of the attacks on the government by different opposition political leaders. On 24 June, to mention but one example, the leader of the Progressive Democrat Party, Lisandro de la Torre, published in *La Prensa* a comprehensive indictment of Yrigoyen's personal career. He was attacked as an unscrupulous intriguer who, among other things, had schemed Leandro N. Alem into suicide in 1896. Sir Reginald Tower declared in a despatch to London:

If things continue as at present, and the President's adherents secede from him in continued numbers; if Congress maintain their attitude of refusing to pass measures submitted by the Government; and if public opinion is directed still more openly against the President's policy, I can see no alternative to revolution save by the disappearance of President Irigoyen.[43]

It was at this moment that a vital change occurred in the whole character of the Radical government, which was to have a fundamental bearing on the course of events over the next eleven years. First there was a concerted struggle to rescue Yrigoyen's personal reputation. It led to a sustained attempt, the first on any important scale since 1916, to exploit the populist elements of his leadership, and to project him as the embodiment of the patriotic mystique. The precise nature of the symbolic imagery employed for this purpose was highly significant. It was a covert

[42] *La Mañana*, 26 May 1919. Although these commentaries were biassed, the same point was made by other observers sufficiently frequently to merit its inclusion.

[43] Despatch No. 161, 22 June 1919, F.O. 371–3504. Some further hint of Yrigoyen's standing with the conservative elite groups at this point may be gleaned from the following remarks made by Sir Reginald Tower: 'In my hearing the other day, an Argentine lady was saying that she felt called to emulate the deed of Charlotte Corday, but added that the President unfortunately did not have a bath' (ibid.). The military factions which had been supporting a *coup d'état* in January were still also very active. In the same despatch Tower remarked that although he thought a revolution unlikely, there were widespread rumours of preparations for armed risings and even Yrigoyen's assassination. As in January the main focus of such rumours was the navy.

attempt by the government to win back some of the support it had lost to the Patriotic League. The more critically weak the government's position became, the more strident did its attempts to conserve its popular support in this fashion become.[44] Secondly, Yrigoyen began at this point to use his control over administrative patronage on a massive and systematic scale to cultivate political allegiances. As a result politics largely ceased to be a matter of 'policies', applied towards specific groups. Now the party machine organisation and 'personalism' became the cornerstones of the government's strategy.

The principal explanation for the growth of 'personalism' is thus to be found in the strikes of 1919. It was only because the government was willing to make these adaptations, and to surrender on central issues, that it gradually managed to surmount the political crisis.[45] By the end of the year the only real contact which survived between the government and the unions was with the F.O.M. The maritime workers were protected by a special arrangement which allowed the government to supervise the port area. Outside this limited venue it was unable to intervene. This did not mean that the goals of class harmony and political linkages between Radicalism and the workers were completely abandoned. But the means whereby the goal was sought began, like everything else, to undergo modifications. There was now, for example, a much greater emphasis on social legislation. In a message to Congress in 1919 at the height of the political crisis, Yrigoyen declared:

[44] Referring to the presidential procession on 25 May, *La Epoca* declared, (and the translation is necessarily extremely free): 'We are vibrating like a quivering sword at the sky-blue and white expression of emotion, which on the 24th and 25th symbolised the heart of the Argentines, letting forth a deafening hosanna of triumph and redemption; a mixture of prayer and thunder, echoing and solemn, to the great patrician, in whose manly form, the flag becomes spirit and to whose body the Motherland makes love... The multitude was paying reverence to the great statesman... and was saying to him breast to breast, heart to heart, that he deserved well of his country. It was their president, their great president, severe as a star standing beyond the thousand small components of this universe... As he passed the multitude found identification with its own self ... [it] granted him an apotheosis, an apotheosis tributed to its own live symbol, to the personification of its own flag – its president' (*La Epoca* 26 May 1919).

[45] The Government also managed at this point to regain the support of the party elite by using its control over patronage and candidatures. In November 1919, the conservatives in Congress tried to impeach Yrigoyen, but the party elite, fearful of losing control over the executive after the death of Vice-President Luna, were the first to support him. Viz. Diario de Sesiones, *Cámara de Diputados*, Vol. 6, 1919, pp. 152–74.

It may be possible to deal with immediate problems by means of *ad hoc* measures, but any final solution requires a directive principle of government, conceived in terms of a plan of organised legislation. This will impose the rule of justice over opposing interests to achieve a state of harmony, guaranteeing the stability and efficiency of capital and the profitability of the exercise of labour.[46]

However, government proposals for a system of compulsory arbitration of strikes and collective bargaining won no more support in 1919 than in the past. Again the great stumbling block was the predominance of *laissez-faire* attitudes among both conservatives and Radicals. As soon as the strikes died away the proposals were forgotten.[47]

Afterwards the government continued to be extremely sensitive to discontent in military quarters. In July 1919 the minister of war made an indecisive attempt to break the links between the army and the Patriotic League by forbidding the membership of military personnel on active service. But when the army objected, the government quickly climbed down.[48] By the beginning of 1920 the strained relations between the government and the army were generally recognised by outside observers. *La Vanguardia* commented: 'A government which, while in opposition systematically cultivated conspiracy and revolt, now recognises that the same barbarous procedures may well be applied against itself. It is thus desperately trying to appease those who can give it more than something of a small headache.'[49]

[46] Etchepareborda, *Pueblo y gobierno*, Vol. 2, p. 161. Plans for legislation had been gaining ground in the mind of the government since 1917. See Delia Kamia, *Entre Yrigoyen e Ingenieros* (Weridiòn, Buenos Aires, 1957). But the strike interventions were obviously the preferred method of dealing with the problem.

[47] For a facsimile of the proposals see *Review of the River Plate*, 23 May 1919. Besides the Congress, the proposals were also opposed by the unions. Chapter IV, Article 37, Clause 3 of legislation issued in June referring to the formation of trade unions declared: 'To be a member of a union: (1) For the foreigners – to present a valid certificate of morality issued by the appropriate consulate, by the National Labour Department or by a corresponding agency in the provinces' (quoted in *La Vanguardia*, 10 June, 1919).

[48] *Review of the River Plate*, 25 July 1919.

[49] *La Vanguardia*, 26 January 1920. By this time the Radicals themselves had fully recognised the potential political threat represented by the army. In November 1919, Carlés's proposal for pay increases for the army came under discussion in the Chamber of Deputies. It was opposed by several members of the Radical Party, though their objections were immediately disowned by *La Epoca*. (Cf. 15 November 1919.) A little earlier when the commanders of military garrisons in the provinces announced that they would act alone if there were further major strike outbreaks, this was attacked by a pro-Radical newspaper as 'military insubordination' (*La República*,

The role of the Church

One final feature of 1919 was the involvement of the Roman Catholic Church in the strike question. In September, prompted by the ecclesiastical hierarchy, a Great National Collect was organised, to further, it was said, 'the great task of the social liberation of the worker', and his redemption from the 'revolutionary leader'. The aim was 'to help the worker who does not want to belong to a Resistance Society, whether Socialist, Anarchist, or Revolutionary Syndicalist, giving him the means to escape its despotism'.[50] For the leaders of the Collect the solution of 'the social question' lay in education: 'Nearly all the conflicts between workers and employers would be easily solved if the worker was endowed with a good educational background which would prevent him from falling into the hands of the professionals of revolt ... Ideas rule the movements of the masses; agitation grows from the doctrines which are disseminated. The anti-social sects are the products of their leaders'.[51]

This was the same reasoning which had led in the past to the creation of the catholic unions, the Círculos de Obreros. It had parallels in the efforts made by the Patriotic League to influence the educational system and to found client unions. The mark of these ventures, besides their obsession with the apocalyptic 'agitators', was that they saw the problem simply as a matter of 'education', and again as in the past refused to acknowledge the economic base to the strikes. Underneath, however, this was recognised by some of the Collect's more realistic leaders. In their press manifestos they punctuated their more pious aspirations by crude and shabby appeals to class self-interest: 'Give unto me. What else would you

Footnote 49 (continued)

15 August 1919). There was also some resistance to Carle's attempt to meddle with the State educational system. Radical Party members resigned on the grounds that the League was usurping government prerogatives. (Cf. *La Vanguardia*, 16 July 1919.) By early 1920 *La Vanguardia* was also commenting on signs of competition between the Radicals and opposition parties for military support: 'We ought to add that in this anachronistic effort to flatter the officers in the army and the navy, the conservative party rivals the Radicals. They do not feel any great enthusiasm for the electoral law and hope that one day they may be able to count on the support of grateful officers and a rising of some battalion or other to regain control over the government' (ibid. 26 January 1920). These were prophetic words and invalidate the views of many commentators who have regarded the politicisation of the armed forces as belonging to the period of the 1920s.

50 Press manifesto, 22 September 1919.

51 ibid.

do if you found yourselves encircled by a pack of hungry animals than to throw them pieces of meat?...The barbarians are already at the gates of Rome.'[52] Within a week of its inception in September, 1919 the Collect had gathered over 10 million pesos. Over half a million was contributed by the Mihanovich shipping company.[53] A second stage in December raised the same amount in almost the same time.[54]

[52] Ibid.

[53] *La Epoca*, 27 September 1919.

[54] Ibid. 12 December 1919. This enthusiasm was not matched by constructive notions of how to use the money. A series of abortive semi-measures were attempted, but finally in February 1921 it was decided to return the money to its original donors. (Cf. *La Vanguardia*, 15 February 1921.)

CHAPTER 9

Postscript to the first presidency, 1920–2

The Great Collect was a final sign of the resurgence of the conservative elite groups in 1919. By the middle of the year they had established an iron grip over the Radical government. During the government's last two and a half years there were few of the dramatic events of the past, and generally it was spared the recurrent tortuous decisions which had been the source of so much danger to it before. In its relations with foreign capital the government continued to be extremely careful, and only adopted a critical line when it was absolutely sure of local support[1]. There were a large number of petty disputes with the railway and tramway companies over fares and tariffs, but these did not lead to any basic conflicts. In several cases the railway companies won concessions they had been struggling to achieve for years. Among them was the clarification of the question of their liabilities to municipal rates for lighting and cleaning services. A measure exempting them from these was finally passed by Congress in August 1919.

In these years the Radical government became largely what the conservatives had planned it to be in 1912 – a static pliant instrument, whose only positive attribute lay in its ability to win a certain degree of popular acceptability. In 1920 and 1921 the government largely concentrated on restoring its electoral position with the middle class groups in the federal capital by its use of patronage, and in the provinces outside by means of federal interventions. After 1919 the provinces which had so

[1] This did not prevent individual Radicals making occasional attacks on the British, which were the source of some unease. During the Mitre Law debates in the Chamber of Deputies in 1919, Rogelio Araya declared: 'We, in political terms, are a nation, and therefore independent: but economically we are a colony of England. We are exploited and treated as a colony... We are treated like a country of negroes, although since we are white we are at least done the justice of having explained to us why we should be despoiled, so that we can be happy about it.' (Quoted in *Review of the River Plate*, 15 August 1919.) However, what British observers rarely noted was that Araya was one of the leaders of the dissident Radicals, who at this point were still endeavouring to steal Yrigoyen's thunder whenever they could.

far escaped being taken over by the Radicals fell under their control in quick succession.

In 1920 Yrigoyen began to enjoy the period of his greatest personal dominance in Argentine politics. But it was dominance without real power, since final authority lay in the hands of the conservative coalition, which was dominated by big business and the army. The government was constantly having to look over its shoulder and calculate exactly where it stood with the Patriotic League. It was also still continually having to strive to present itself as the incarnation of patriotism in order to forestall the League's influence: 'Radicalism is synonomous with patriotism ... Only Radicalism can be identified with the desires and aspirations of the fatherland. For this reason the national anthem is sung in its assemblies and its demonstrations are preceded by the national flag.'[2]

With the end of the strikes in the federal capital the government gained a breathing space to recover from the events of 1919. The leading groups in the Labour Association became fully occupied in profiteering from the post-war boom, while the Patriotic League shifted its attentions to the rural areas, discharging its energies in pursuit of largely imaginary Anarchist activities among the agricultural tenants and harvest labourers.[3] Meanwhile the attentions of the army became increasingly focussed on the Patagonian region. Here in 1920, after the collapse of the overseas wool market, there was a rising of pastoral labourers. When the army intervened, the result was the most notorious repressive military campaign in Argentine history. It lasted for over two years.

This episode stands as the greatest moral indictment of all against

[2] *La Epoca*, 8 February 1920.

[3] Comments on the League's activities in 1920 appear in *La Vanguardia*, 29 August 1920, 19 September 1920, 18 October 1920. At the beginning of 1920 the F.O.R.A. also shifted its attentions towards the provinces. On 10 January 1920, *La Organización Obrera* declared: 'This year the Federal Council considers it necessary to attend to the petitions which have come from the unions in the interior ... In consequence the F.O.R.A.'s delegates will travel the whole territory of the country.' There was one minor crisis in the federal capital in 1920. When the F.O.R.A. del Quinto Congreso made an abortive general strike attempt in March, the government overreacted by putting the army on alert. There were also widespread rumours that the Anarchists had established contacts in the police force in Buenos Aires. *Review of the River Plate* reported on 19 March that about eighty members of the force were dismissed on the grounds that they had attended Anarchist lectures. The figure is probably an exaggeration, or the police were made the scapegoats of pressure from the Patriotic League. It was also no coincidence that elections were imminent.

the Radical government. In effect the government carelessly gave the army a free rein to act as it wished and ruthlessly exterminate the strikers, taking advantage of the fact that the remoteness of the region and poor communications prevented the full story becoming known in Buenos Aires until much later. The government had no electoral commitments in the south, because the area was made up of national territories without voting rights and congressional representation. In view of the events of 1919, it seems fair to conclude that the mainly Chilean labourers in Chubut and Santa Cruz became the victims of the government's efforts to mend its fences in military circles. It became a means of buying a certain freedom for manoeuvre in the federal capital.[4]

There remain, however, two other points of interest during this period, which are useful in providing further final perspectives on Yrigoyen's first government. The first was the attempt to develop alternative means of winning working class support with measures aiming to reduce the cost of living. This was to reverse the policy of the past. Instead of assisting the workers to win higher wages, the aim was to reduce prices. On the other hand, it brought the government into potential conflict with new groups. In the past it had been confronted by business leaders; now it was courting opposition from the producer interests. The manner in which it attempted to resolve this problem froms an interesting commentary on its attempt to define its position in terms of consumer and producer groups and its commitments to different regional groups among the producers themselves.

The second main feature of this period is the eventual fate of the relationship between the government and the unions. This throws further light on the mechanics of business opposition to the government in terms of a crucial new variable, the economic cycle. Also it illustrates the effects of changing objective economic conditions upon certain key political structures, the most important being the unions and the Radical Party's grass roots committee organisation.

The cost of living issue in 1920

Until 1920 the government's interest in the cost of living issue was fitful and dominated by its concern to avoid alienating the producer groups in key areas like the province of Buenos Aires. This reflected the struc-

[4] For a recent account of the Patagonian episode see Osvaldo Bayer, *Los vengadores de la Patagonia trágica* (Galerna, Buenos Aires, 1972).

ture of the electorate, and the need to mediate effectively between urban and rural interests. Thus, whenever during the war period there were sudden sharp increases in the prices of basic consumer items, *La Epoca*, in order to resist Socialist Party pressure that the government should intervene, would either try to attribute them to uncontrollable world conditions, or blame unidentified 'speculators'.

An example of the type of action which was sometimes taken came in April 1918. To combat a sudden shortage of wood fuel, the government introduced reduced freight charges on the State railways, whose lines ran towards the forests of the north. Later, requisition contracts for wood were awarded, but to commercial interests connected with the minister of finance, Salaberry. They used the contracts for profiteering purposes and studiously avoided any attempt to bring down the price of wood.[5] On various occasions between 1917 and 1919 the government waived the duties on imported sugar, but only when prices had reached very high levels and imports were unlikely to have any tangible effect on the profiteering activities of local producers.[6] If anything, before 1920, the Radical government was more sensitive towards the producer groups than the conservative administrations had been before 1916. The following remarks by *La Nación* in August 1919 form an adequate comment on the government's general performance in this field up till that time:

> The present government has repeatedly missed the mark in the steps it has taken to relieve the cost of living problem ... It has failed to understand the problems, no doubt because it has looked at them with a view to making demagogic gestures. It is no coincidence that it has always displayed the greatest interest during election periods.[7]

The same was true of the municipal council in Buenos Aires, which traditionally had some role in providing cheap foodstuffs to the urban consumers. In November 1919, Yrigoyen appointed a new intendant for the city, José Luis Cantilo. His arrival coincided with the start of the campaign for the municipal elections, which this time the Radicals were determined to win to offset the defeat they had suffered in November 1918. With great persistence and maximum publicity, Cantilo began to visit different parts of the city and to announce a series of dramatic

[5] *La Vanguardia*, 17 April 1918; *La Nación*, 25 June 1918.

[6] For example, in June 1917 and in August 1918.

[7] *La Nación*, 16 August 1919.

measures for the improvement of public amenities.[8] At the same time he began to throw emphasis on the cost of living problem. He announced plans for the creation of consumer cooperatives with municipal subsidies, municipal control over the food distribution markets, and a system of fixed prices to curb speculative manoeuvres in meat supplies.[9]

But, as soon as the elections were over, the campaign was swiftly dismantled and nothing at all was finally done. Cantilo became a typical Radical city boss, controlling the jobs in the municipal administration and occasionally organising dramatic but meaningless campaigns against hypothetical speculators and food adulterators.

Cantilo's campaign of humbug and hot air was a typical manifestation of the government's increasing willingness to seek to buttress its popularity by a mixture of demogogy and the manipulation of jobs in the administration. However, these more devious techniques did bring more successful election results. By 1920 the conservatives in the federal capital had abandoned their previous support for Lisandro de la Torre's Progressive Democrat Party, and had organised their own movement, the National Concentration. In the 1920 elections this managed to poll 25,000 votes, or 20% of the total. However, the Radicals won the election because they managed to capture an important proportion of the Socialist vote from the year before. The Radicals won 68,000 votes, or 37%, and the Socialists 55,000 votes, or 33%. For the Radicals this was a considerable improvement on 1919.

In the middle of 1920 the spiralling impetus of the post-war boom, and the buoyant demand for Argentine food products in Europe, resulted in higher food prices than at any time before. The effect of the boom was especially marked on the two main staples of popular consumption, wheat and meat. In May 1920, the price of wheat reached 28 pesos per 100 kilos, three and a half times its average level of 1913, and four times its level of May 1916. Between June and November 1920, it fluctuated between 30 and 32 pesos. Meat also rose rapidly, though not to the same extent. In the middle of 1920 it was being quoted at 32 centavos per pound, about double its average price during the war.[10]

Encouraged by Cantilo's successful exploitation of the cost of living issue during the municipal election, early in June 1920 the government responded to the crisis by sending a proposal to Congress introducing

8 *La Epoca*, November 1919, *passim*.

9 *La Vanguardia*, 13 December 1919.

10 Tornquist (May–October 1920).

supplementary duties on wheat exports. The proceeds were to be employed by the State to purchase wheat for local consumption at reduced prices. The main feature of this measure, coming at the time it did, was that it was designed to avoid injuring the producers. It was known that by that time of the year the cereal harvest had been purchased by the exporters, and it was they who were intended to be liable to the duty.[11] In Congress the measure was also pictured as a means to help the working class: 'It cannot be that a worker earning four or five pesos a day should be spending 70 or 80 cents on a kilo of bread. We cannot allow a society of robbers to appear in the Argentine Republic... We ought to pass legislation to give labour its due share, because if not, we are creating a republic of beggars.[12]

The advantage of the measure was that it also appealed to the middle class groups. It was support for their interests, more than for the workers, which allowed it to pass quickly through Congress. But even armed with this, the government found it extremely difficult to affect local prices to any significant extent. The main problem was that most of the wheat was held by the agents of different European governments, who proved extremely unwilling to release the government from the contracts it had previously negotiated with them. Finally in August, when exports were running at such a high rate that they began to threaten re-seeding requirements for the next harvest, the government finally prohibited further exports. But even then it was only able to acquire small quantities of the wheat. A final problem was the millers, who were unwilling to deal with the government's wheat at reduced rates when they were working at full capacity to complete their private orders. In the event, it was not until the following January that bread prices began to fall as the new harvest became available.[13] In this area the government's campaign was a complete failure.

The government also made an attempt to deal with sugar prices at around the same time. Sugar, like wheat, became caught up in the export boom in the middle of 1920.[14] Here the government acted much more positively. Instead of merely attempting to buy sugar, as it had done with wheat, it demanded authorisation from Congress to expropriate 200,000 tons, which it alleged were being held by speculators.

[11] *Diario de Sesiones*, Cámara de Diputados, Vol. 1, 1920, p. 425.
[12] Ibid. p. 428 (Juan J. Frugoni).
[13] Tornquist (1920, 1921).
[14] Ibid. (summary for 1920).

The proposal was also justified in much stronger terms than had been the case with wheat:

The moment has arrived for energetic measures which will finish once and for all with what I do not hesitate to describe as the exploitation of the sweat of the workers, making their living conditions even more precarious. It is perfectly clear that this sharp rise in price is not due . . . to any shortage of sugar, to any rise in the cost of production, nor even to recent climatic occurrences. It is exclusively due to the evil-doings of uncurbed speculators, who want to multiply their riches at the expense of producers and consumers alike.[15]

The measure quickly passed the Chamber of Deputies where by this time there was a large Radical majority. But in the Senate it was strongly opposed by the representatives of the sugar provinces in the north-west, who alleged that it threatened the interests of the producers. It was necessary, they said, to allow the industry high profits in order to boost investment, and to establish the industry on a self-sustaining basis. Unless this support was given the result would be chronic unemployment and mass depopulation of the area:

sugar is the only industry which the north has, and the owners of the sugar mills say they will close down if this law is put into effect. This means that the only way of earning a living in these provinces will disappear . . . The same would happen there as is said to be the case in La Rioja, where 48% of the conscripts have been rejected because of tuberculosis.[16]

This was to embellish the situation of the sugar-workers somewhat, since their standards of living were already not far, if at all, above those of the workers in the poverty-stricken province of La Rioja. Nevertheless the critics of the government's measure did make one valid and important point. They asked why had it been chosen to take action on sugar in such a drastic fashion, while other foodstuffs, such as meat, had been ignored:

And the other industries? Have they nothing to do with the cost of living problem? Meat, for example, has gone up over the last few days to 34 or 35 cents a pound. In terms of the animal on the hoof this is an increase of 200% since 1916. And has not bread gone up more than meat? But the powerful eastern industries are privileged and the executive is not planning to do anything to them, only to the poorest and neediest industries . . . It makes no difference that the economies of five provinces depend on them.[17]

[15] *Diario de Sesiones*, Cámara de Diputados, Vol. 3, 1920, p. 882.

[16] Ibid. Senadores, Vol. 1, 1920, p. 716 (Benito Villanueva).

[17] Ibid. p. 751 (Villanueva).

Apart from its exaggerated view of the penury of the sugar producers, the observation was a fair one. Bread and meat made up something like 60% of food expenditure within the working class, and sugar only about 3%. Had the government's attempt to control sugar prices been successful, it would have been unlikely to have had more than a 1% effect on the cost of living.

The inescapable fact was that sugar was both symbol and scapegoat of the government's attempt to appear to be doing something for the urban consumers, but at the same time to avoid any action which might be construed as an attack on the major producer groups. Among these the sugar barons did not count, for reasons that they themselves were partly aware of:

> What is inexplicable is the antagonism against the sugar industry which the Radical Party has shown ever since it won power. It has been changed from a protected industry to one which is oppressed by the public authorities . . . And this hostility has not only made itself felt against sugar, but against all the industries of the Interior. Exports have been banned of sugar, caper spurge, castor oil, beans, alcohol, all the articles produced in the interior, and especially in the north . . . These measures were designed to cheapen consumption articles, but at the same time exports have been encouraged of the basic necessities of popular consumption, such as wheat and meat, the products of the more populous coastal regions. Why? Can it be by accident or because the inhabitants of the coastal regions are many, and few those of the interior?[18]

This was largely the answer. The only possible area where the Radicals could act without running important political risks was in region of the interior. Although the measure failed because of the Senate's opposition, it was symptomatic of the general trend under the Radical government, which served to enhance the political and economic subordination of the interior.

The only success the government had with the cost of living issue in 1920 was the support it gave for rent control in the federal capital. This was provoked by the desire, it was said, to help 'the middle classes, those who lived on fixed incomes, the workers and the humble.'[19] The Congress eventually accepted a number of temporary measures which imposed a rent freeze, placed restraints on evictions and allowed the import of building materials free of duty.[20]

[18] Ibid. pp. 789–90 (Carlos Zabala).
[19] Ibid. Cámara de Diputados, Vol. 1, 1920, p. 77.
[20] *Review of the River Plate*, 6 August 1920.

This success against the urban landlords, many of whom were foreigners and found it difficult to organise themselves into an effective political lobby, cannot disguise the general failure of the campaign against rising prices in 1920. The government made no attempt to deal with the meat situation, and its efforts to control wheat prices were a complete failure. It was only prepared to act against producer interests in the case of sugar, and this gesture, even had it not failed as it did, was largely meaningless. On balance it revealed at this point a greater sensitivity towards the producer interests in the province of Buenos Aires than it did towards the consumers in the city.

The crisis of May–June, 1921

After 1919 the only real contact with the unions the government had managed to salvage from the wreck of its labour policy was with the Federación Obrera Marítima. In 1920, during the export boom, the F.O.M. was still in a very strong position. It was able to control the selection of the crews of the coastal shipping vessels in the Riachuelo, and could paralyse overseas operations through its control over the lighter and tug workers. It was also able to impose boycotts at will, and in December 1919 the *Review of the River Plate* was complaining about the 'chronic indiscipline' in the port zone.[21] Finally the union enjoyed the protection of the Customs Authority in the port under the arrangement which had been agreed at the end of the lockout in 1919.

There was always extreme friction between the F.O.M. and its old enemy, the Mihanovich Shipping Company, over the questions of boycotts and crew selection. When in January 1920 the union placed a total boycott on the company, it replied by laying up its vessels.[22] This stoppage endured for some thirteen months, when finally a compromise agreement was reached. In spite of every effort it made, the company was unable to win any support either from the transatlantic shippers or from the foreign capital lobby in general. They were all too committed to maintaining the level of shipments during the boom. As in the past, the F.O.M. had the tacit support of the government. A new British minister, Sir Ronald Macleay, described the government's overall position with the workers towards the end of 1920 in the following terms: 'benevolent neutrality ... tempered by insinuations against the coastal shipping

[21] *Review of the River Plate*, 19 December 1919.

[22] Ibid. 30 January 1920.

companies, together with holding out promises for the improvement of conditions for the poorer and working classes and for cheapening the cost of living.[23]

The overall situation, however, underwent a sudden and dramatic change when the boom was overtaken by slump conditions at the beginning of 1921, following the adoption of deflationary measures in Europe. In May 1920, the f.o.b. price of Argentine wheat was 27.60 pesos per 100 kilos. Seven months later it had declined to 17.65 pesos, and it dropped still more afterwards. Similarly the price of meat slipped from an average of 32 cents a pound in 1920 to 22 cents in 1921. The volume of gross exports declined at an even greater rate. In 1920 over 5 million tons of wheat were exported; in 1921 less than 2 million tons. Similarly meat exports declined over the same period from 618,000 tons to 502,000 tons.[24]

While the boom was still continuing in 1920, the complex state of affairs in the port zone had begun to affect the dockers. In previous years they had not played much part in the disputes. However, in 1920, two rival unions emerged among the dockers, one Syndicalist and linked with the F.O.M., and the other Anarchist and linked with one of the few remaining Anarchist groups of any influence, the port carters. When the boom changed to depression the conflict between the two unions intensified, each faction attempting to establish control to prevent its own members being laid off. In May 1921, the contest resulted in the victory of the Anarchists, who then attempted to press home their advantage by organising boycotts against firms employing non-unionised labour.[25]

At this point, and with the clear aim of forcing down wages among the docking personnel in the port, the National Labour Association reentered the scene. Plans were set afoot to challenge the unions by replacing the unionised dockers with unemployed immigrants from Rosario. On 9 May the government replied to this by closing the whole port.[26] This was designed to protect the men from the Labour Association's assault. Meeting a delegation from the F.O.M. on 15 May, the Chief of Police Elpidio González was reported to have said:

[23] Despatch No. 354, 20 October 1920, F.O. 371–4408.

[24] Di Tella and Zymelman, pp. 331–5. According to government figures, between 1920 and 1921 the volume of maize exported declined by 37%, wheat by 66% and frozen beef by 34%.

[25] *El Diario*, 12 May 1921.

[26] *Review of the River Plate*, 13 May 1921.

he had the best intentions towards them ... on the basis of the exclusion of those who were working for the Patriotic League and the National Labour Association. Their intervention suited neither himself nor the president, because if this were to happen it would not solve the problem but aggravate it. He also made it clear that the government supported the idea of bringing the dockers and the carters under its own supervision to prevent the infiltration of elements outside those which were authentically labour.[27]

When this plan became known, the international shippers, supported as in the past by the Labour Association, revived their old threat of an international shipping boycott:

If unfortunately we find ourselves convinced that the authority of the government is to be withheld from those who, in accordance with the institutions and the laws of the country, cooperate in its aggrandisement, we will be necessarily forced to think that the time has arrived to consider advising the companies we represent to cease sending their ships to Argentine ports, while they do not obtain protection and the normal means to continue their operations.[28]

In the past the boycott proposal had always foundered against the heavy demand for Argentine food products in Europe. But, with the depression, this was no longer the case. In 1921, in contrast to the situation in 1918 and 1919, the boycott could be made effective. It soon became apparent that the government also recognised this. On 23 May a decree was issued – which was technically invalid because it did not bear Yrigoyen's counter-signature – announcing the reopening of the port. It was also acknowledged that the Customs Authority would accept both union and 'free' labour. The next day there were serious clashes between different groups of dockers as the Anarchists, Syndicalists and the Labour Association's recruits fought for supremacy.[29]

This outbreak of violence was accompanied by others which led immediately to a state of acute political crisis similar to that in 1919. In response to events in the port, a group of taxi-drivers issued a manifesto attacking the Patriotic League, which had announced its support for the Labour Association. This was followed by an armed assault on their union rooms by members of the League. Union officials who were found there were subjected to various indignities, and forced at gunpoint

[27] Federación Obrera Marítima, *Actas*, 15 May 1921.
[28] Quoted by *La Nación*, 19 May 1921 (Centro de Navegación Transatlántica to minister of finance).
[29] *Review of the River Plate*, 27 May 1921.

to swear allegiance to the Flag.[30] When this led to a strike among the taxi-drivers, it was reported that almost 16,000 private cars had been offered as temporary taxis until the strike was broken. There was also a sudden tremendous build-up in public support for the League among the elite and middle class groups:

> The temporary taxi-drivers who were serving the public yesterday bear the surnames of the most distinguished families of high society. Their appearance on the streets was greeted with bursts of applause from all sides... As on previous days there was great activity in the secretariat of the central council of the Patriotic League. It continues to receive requests for affiliation from thousands of citizens of every social rank, who wish to express their protest against the taxi-drivers' manifesto, that crime against national dignity.[31]

A final ominous note was sounded when it became known that the minister of war was receiving frequent visits from General Uriburu.[32]

It was exactly the same situation as in 1919. The strike issue brought about a state of acute class polarisation, which because of the Patriotic League and the army, immediately developed into a major political crisis. The government was faced by the same dilemma as it had been two years before. As a means to prevent action by the Patriotic League and thus protect its position, it replied by taking the same measures it had taken early in May 1919. A court order was issued ordering the police to arrest the 'agitators'. This was done within a short time. When the taxi-drivers' strike occurred, Cantilo, the municipal intendant, withdrew driving licences from those whom the League alleged were the leaders of the taxi-drivers' union.[33]

Once again, the attempt to appease the League was also accompanied by conciliatory moves in other directions. *La Epoca*, as in 1919, began to attack the Labour Association and to allege that the government was protecting the 'freedom of labour' against the employers' attempt to destroy it.[34] Similarly the government tried to distract attention away from the police by sending social reform legislation to Congress. In 1919 it was Compulsory Conciliation and Arbitration; in 1921 it was a General Labour Code.[35] Finally it tried to lay the blame for the crisis on its old scapegoats, the immigrant communities. This was apparent in an

[30] Ibid.
[31] *La Fronda*, 24 May 1921.
[32] Ibid, 5 June 1921.
[33] *Review of the River Plate*, 10 June 1921.
[34] *La Epoca*, 1 June 1921.
[35] *Diario de Sesiones*, Cámara de Diputados, Vol. 1, 1921, p. 343.

insinuatory decree which appeared on 9 June, introducing more stringent conditions for the landing of immigrants. It was made obligatory to present certificates of good conduct from countries of origin.[36]

There was one central difference with the events of 1919. This time the Syndicalists did not escape. When on 30 May the F.O.R.A. met to discuss action, its deliberations were interrupted by the police, led in person by Elpidio González. The delegates were arrested, and many of them put in detention camps on the island of Martín García in the Plate estuary.[37] A rump group, which had somehow managed to escape from the police, replied by declaring a general strike.

This was the first time the Syndicalists had taken this step. But in the depression conditions of 1921 it proved completely abortive. Among the important unions, only the F.O.M. joined the strike, and then only momentarily when the police, too, moved against it.[38] As soon as the general strike ended and the activities of the Patriotic League ceased, the government attempted to make amends. The police hunt was called off, and as early as 5 June the F.O.M. was permitted to reopen its premises.[39] This was followed shortly afterwards by the release of the detained members of the F.O.R.A. But the damage had now been done. It was quite impossible to maintain any longer the pretence that the government still continued to protect the unions:

> And we reach the end of the day. Sr Irigoyen contemplates his work and senses that public opinion is showing signs of having lost patience, that commerce and industry are warning us that we are running the risk of having no more ships in the port, that the army is murmuring. And Sr Irigoyen gets frightened. He does an about-turn, and tries in a week to put out the fire caused by his five-year betrayal of the nation's highest interests.[40]

In 1921 the government found it impossible any longer to avoid taking action against the mainstream of the union movement. Before its actions had been limited to peripheral groups and scapegoats. One angle to the situation was recognised by Sir Ronald Macleay:

> It seems more than probable that the President must have come to realise from certain signs of dissatisfaction among his adherents that unless he modified

[36] *La Nación*, 10 June 1921.

[37] Ibid. 3 June 1921. One of them, Bartolomé Senra Pacheco, contracted pneumonia and died soon afterwards.

[38] *La Organización Obrera*, 4 June 1921.

[39] Ibid. 18 June 1921.

[40] *La Fronda*, 5 June 1921.

his policy he stood to lose the certain support of the moderate Radical vote not only in the Capital but throughout the country, in return for the problematical adhesion of the unions.[41]

The Government's ability in the past to select scapegoats to bear the brunt of its police measures reflected the fact that in 1919 the Patriotic League, too, had mainly concentrated on similar peripheral groups – the Jews, the Anarchists and the 'Maximalists'. By 1921, however, the League had become more markedly and explicitly anti-union. It is difficult to document the precise manner in which this transformation occurred, but the most probable explanation for it lies in the effects of the depression upon the objectives of the employer groups. In 1919 many of the employers had also been more concerned with the Red scare than with the wage issue. However, in 1921, with the depression, the question of their wage costs had become their foremost preoccupation. The fact that it also in effect became the Patriotic League's provides a clear indication of the extent to which the employers could manipulate, from behind the scenes, a movement which was apparently based upon groups – such as the army, – not directly involved in the struggle between labour and capital.

The decline of the unions

The importance of the post-war depression in bringing about these changes is evident from the perspective of the unions. Long before the general strike took place the effects of the depression on the unions were becoming clearly marked. During 1921 the F.O.R.A. changed its name to the Unión Sindical Argentina, or the U.S.A. In 1920 the F.O.R.A.'s monthly average of subscription paying members was almost 70,000. A year later, as a result of the depression, the U.S.A.'s was no more than a third of this, and in subsequent years the decline continued.[42]

The process of disintegration became marked as soon as the depression began. As soon as the thirteen-month-long Mihanovich lockout ended, the F.O.M. was besieged with requests for sympathy boycotts from unions already feeling the strain of mounting lay-offs. In April 1921, *La Unión del Marino* reported: 'the Federal Council has under study more than thirty requests for boycotts to be levied. To accede to all these will be to declare the general strike of the union.'[43]

[41] Despatch No. 127, 8 June 1921, F.O. 371–5517.

[42] *Revista de Ciencias Económicas*, No. 29 (1927), p. 973.

[43] *La Unión del Marino*, April 1921.

Finally, lay-offs began to affect the F.O.M. as well. In a very short time the great internal unity it had managed to maintain since 1916 was completely shattered. The result, as among the dockers, was a spate of internal disputes, which were nominally ideological or tactical in nature, but which in reality were a reflection of the effects of the depression: 'It is sad what is happening among us. The secret of our past victories has now disappeared – unity... The moral authority of our organisation is losing ground... Isolated conflicts are occurring and there are demands all round for the union's intervention.'[44]

In 1921 the Syndicalist movement, which had played so central a part in the events of the past five years, was thus moving into decline. A further sign of this came when the Socialist Party recommenced its campaign to take over the unions.[45] *La Vanguardia* accused the leaders of the F.O.R.A. of active collusion with Yrigoyen in his attempt to undermine the electoral position of the Socialist Party among the working class. It instanced the fact that the union leaders had been quickly released after the general strike. Also it denounced the arrangements in the port area over the past two years, alleging that corrupt deals had been made between the leaders of the F.O.M. and members of the government.

If the Syndicalists had on occasion lent themselves to some rather discreditable manoeuvres by the government, the events of 1921 finally went to show that the alliance had never reached the institutionalised level the Socialists alleged. What had attracted the Syndicalists was not the opportunity to make corrupt deals, but to exploit whatever support they could get from the government to consolidate their own position. Within the framework of this strategy they had remained pragmatic and unattached, committed to the objectives of mass unionisation and economic betterment. Although it had been apparent for a long time that the government itself wished for a closer relationship to develop, there was still a strong undercurrent in Syndicalism which rejected as a matter of principle any formal ties either with the State or with the political parties:

> Since the working class set itself apart from every party or sect to organise itself as a class and fight capitalism directly, there have been the detractors trying to deny the virtue of the union as an entity, and thus attempting to lead the workers away from their true sphere of action ... But the truth is that while the working class has followed one or another political leader, or been a part

[44] Ibid. May 1921.
[45] *La Vanguardia*, 8 June 1921, *passim*.

of party A or B, while it has become entwined with this or that doctrine, its situation has not improved in the slightest and everything has been reduced to more or less vain promises, whose achievement has always had to await a better opportunity ...[46]

June 1921 was the final fatal blow to Yrigoyen's attempt to use the unions to achieve the objectives he had set himself in 1916. For the last twenty months or so before he left office in October 1922, he was compelled to rely on petty gestures and occasional acts of charity, which *La Epoca* would then make as much of as it could for propaganda purposes. The following petition from a group of railway workers in the province of Buenos Aires became typical of the tone of this final period:

The poor railway worker, whose welfare depends upon the noble souls of the men who rule the destinies of the nation, and who has no greater power than the strength of numbers or the hope that the depths of his miserable condition should move the hearts of those who seek to serve the common good ... recognises the magnanimity of the only president who has taken the people under his protection, lest they suffer too greatly the consequences of their miserable condition.[47]

There was one other feature which deserves to be mentioned at this point because it set the stage for the main form of contact which emerged between the Radical Party and the working class over the next eight years up till 1930. As a result of the depression, the membership of unions in Buenos Aires declined to less than 5% of the total male workforce. Also, neither the different Socialist groups, the Anarchists, nor a small Communist faction which made its appearance in the early 1920s, were able to take over the dominant position which the Syndicalists had enjoyed until 1921. The union movement thus returned to a similar state as in the years between 1910 and 1915. It was extremely small, and its unity continued to be impaired by internal doctrinal disputes. As

[46] *La Unión del Marino*, December 1921.

[47] Quoted in *La Vanguardia*, 15 February 1922. (Petition to Yrigoyen from railway workers in Henderson, province of Buenos Aires.) *La Epoca's* reports were made in a similar tone. On 17 December 1921, *La Epoca* declared, referring to a meeting between Yrigoyen and union leaders: 'The men who govern the country at present are prepared to go to the point of suffering hunger and thirst so that nothing should be lacking for the working classes ... With deep emotion the workers listened to the president and, having expressed their gratitude to him they withdrew, convinced that the present government will always observe an attitude based on concepts of social justice towards the working classes.'

a result the unions lost the position they had enjoyed during the war as the most powerful focus for working class loyalties. Loyalties which had previously been dominated by class institutions now became floating and relatively unattached. During the post-war depression inflation, which before had focussed attention on the wage question, and which had served to charge the growth of the unions, now disappeared.

The advent of conditions of social fragmentation eliminated the barriers which had been apparent during the war to the expansion of the Radical Party's committee-based 'machine' among the working class. Previously the dominance of the wage question and the presence of the unions had prevented them from doing this. Now the swift onset of unemployment made the prospect of the petty favours and charity ventures, which the committee structure represented, more appealing. From this time forward the committees began to be successful in recruiting working class support. During the presidential election campaign in 1922, a new type of Radical Party committee began to flourish. This took the form of specialised local units specifically tailored to attract working class support. An example was one committee in the Boca, which began to acquire some of the characteristics previously belonging to the F.O.M.:

> The sub-committee 'La Marina' is aiming to unite all the sailors and ancillary groups ... so that their needs can be listened to ... and action taken to transmit or obtain from congressional representatives, and then from the national government, every improvement and regulation which may be necessary to allow them to improve their standards of living and enjoy the right to live modestly but decently.[48]

By 1922 then, there were signs that the project of class integration was being pursued with different techniques from those which prevailed between 1917 and 1921. From henceforth the delicately structured Radical Party committee organisation replaced what had previously been done by Yrigoyen through his personal contacts with the unions. It also became the basic foundation of the political supremacy the Radical Party continued to enjoy throughout the 1920s.

[48] *La Epoca*, 26 March 1922.

CHAPTER 10

The Alvear interlude, 1922–8

The war and post-war period of rapid inflation, which was the most important conditioning factor on politics during Yrigoyen's presidency, ended with the post-war depression in 1921. The economic background to the next six-year presidential term was depression followed by a prolonged phase of recovery which lasted until 1929. Although there was a recession in 1925, foreign trade and exports averaged out over the period as a whole above the levels they had attained immediately before the war. During the 1920s agricultural production did not expand as rapidly as during the pre-war period. There was little land left to bring into production, and there was no major investment programme to increase productivity by any great amount. In part such investment was discouraged by signs of changing patterns of world demand for agricultural products. Before 1914 the great boom had occurred mainly with cereals. In the affluent 1920s a shift developed towards meat. This meant the gradual replacement of cereal production by cattle farming, and a correspondingly greater prevalence of extensive farming. Although it went largely unperceived at the time, the 1920s was a period of incipient stagnation in the export economy. This began to encourage efforts at economic diversification.

As before 1914, Argentina's imports were generally higher than her exports, and the deficit was covered by new injections of foreign capital. Of this, however, a growing proportion began to come from the United States. Between 1923 and 1927 total foreign investment in Argentina grew from 3,200 million gold pesos to 3,600 million, and American investment rose from 200 million gold pesos in 1923 to 505 million in 1927.[1] A number of important American companies established themselves in Buenos Aires for the first time, orientating their activities towards the power and consumer durables fields.[2]

[1] Phelps, p. 108. For further comments on trade and investment in the 1920s see Fodor and O'Connell; Díaz Alejandro, pp. 16–21.

[2] Among them were Chrysler, General Motors, RCA Victor, and Colgate Palmolive. Others – like Standard Oil – which had begun their activities before the war, became steadily more important.

The presence of the Americans was also linked to the growth of Argentine industry. Taking a base of 100 for 1950, industrial production between 1922 and 1926 rose from 27.9 to 36.6.[3] A result of this was an increase in imports of capital goods. Between 1923 and 1926 these rose by around 30%.[4] Again the Americans played a leading part. Comparing the period between 1921 and 1930 with 1914 to 1920, American exports to Argentina doubled.[5]

The period therefore coincided with the beginning of an important shift in Argentina's international position. British dominance was still apparent enough at the quantitative level of gross investment and trade. But it was failing to expand in the most rapid growth-areas of the economy, the chief of which were oil, capital goods and consumer durables. The great symptom of a steadily apparent Anglo–American rivalry in Argentina was the growing competition between imported American automobiles and the British railways. The overall result of such changes was the further erosion of the simple nineteenth-century bilateral relationship between Argentina and Great Britain. Argentina still continued to sell her primary staples in Britain, but she was tending to direct her import purchases towards the United States.

By the end of the 1920s this had begun to generate divisions among the landed groups over the question of international trade.[6] There could be no objection in principle to the Americans taking advantage of a growing consumer market in Argentina, so long as the balance of payments remained sound, and overseas export markets remained secure. But the British became increasingly restive over their trade deficit with Argentina and began to demand more privileged access for British goods. This gradually triggered fears in Argentina that the British would retaliate by curtailing their imports of Argentine meat. The problem was that if this happened there was no alternative export market in the United States.

[3] Di Tella and Zymelman, p. 366. For a recent study which gives great emphasis to the growth of industry in the 1920s see Javier Villanueva, 'El origen de la industrialización argentina', *Desarrollo Económico*, Vol. 12, No. 47 (October–December 1972).

[4] Di Tella and Zymelman, p. 307. See also Eduardo Jorge, pp. 43–106.

[5] Phelps, p. 190.

[6] Peter H. Smith, 'Los radicales argentinos' and *Carne y política en la Argentina* (Paidós, Buenos Aires, 1969); see also Roger Gravil, 'Anglo–U.S. trade rivalry in Argentina and the D'Abernon Mission of 1929', in David Rock (ed.), *Argentina in the Twentieth Century* (Duckworth, London, 1975); Pedro Skupch, 'Las consecuencias de la competencia del automotor sobre la hegemonía britanica en la Argentina 1919–33'.

Nevertheless the issue did not become critical until towards the end of the decade. In the meantime Argentina was able to profit from a new export boom and her urban sectors enjoyed new levels of consumer prosperity. In spite of industrial growth, the primary sector continued to be the most powerful governing factor on social development. This meant the apparent revival of pre-war conditions, more foreign investment, more immigration, more urbanisation, and the further consolidation of the pre-war urban social structure.

Politics in the 1920s was still largely dominated by the relations between the landed elite and the urban middle class groups. After 1922 the working class question ceased to be important. Between the trough of the post-war depression in 1922 and the beginning of the main export boom in 1926 real wages rose by around 10%.[7] There were no serious fluctuations in the cost of living as had happened during the war. The result was a move away from the pressure-group politics of Yrigoyen's period, dominated by the unions on the one side, and the business groups on the other.

The unions, with some exceptions, remained weak and divided. The F.O.R.A.'s successor, the U.S.A., continued to decline. In 1923 its monthly average membership was only 26,000, compared with the 100,000 the F.O.R.A. had claimed in 1920. By 1926 this had declined to 15,000, and by April 1927 to a mere 10,400. In four years, by 1927, the U.S.A. had also lost the affiliation of 117 separate unions.[8]

Of the individual unions the most important was the successor to the F.O.F., the Unión Ferroviaria, which was founded in 1922. By 1926 the U.F. claimed support from some 70,000 railwaymen.[9] There were few strikes of any importance, and the new government made no effort to revive the unions' influence. A sign of changing times came with the

[7] Adolfo Dorfman, *La evolución industrial argentina* (Losada, Buenos Aires, 1942), p. 241. Quoted in Di Tella and Zymelman, p. 369. According to Díaz Alejandro, taking a base of 100 for 1914, average wages were 78 in the period 1915–19, 113 in the period 1920–4, and 140 in the period 1925–9. This is a considerable advance on the pre-war figures, and it probably helped in the continuing decline of Anarchism during the 1920s. (*Essays*, p. 41.)

[8] J. Rodríguez Tarditti, 'Sindicatos y afiliados', pp. 973–6.

[9] Palacios, p. 244. The Unión Ferroviaria and La Fraternidad did lend their influence to the creation in 1926 of a new general federation, the Confederación Obrera Argentina. By April 1927, as a result of the support of the railway unions, the Confederation claimed 85,000 members. However, it had little general influence.

appointment of the new minister of marine, who controlled the port area where Yrigoyen had intervened most frequently. This was none other than Rear-Admiral Domecq García, who had led the defence committees during the Semana Trágica.

The presidential succession of 1922

The presidential elections in 1922 were won by the Radicals without much difficulty. The conservative National Concentration failed, like its predecessors, to overcome regional conflicts sufficiently or to capture popular support. In many of the more troublesome and fractious provinces, where the opposition parties were in control or the Radicals were divided, Yrigoyen was able to prepare the way for the elections by the use of federal interventions. The only provinces he failed to win was where there were strong anti-Radical populist parties. This was the case with some of the interior provinces, particularly Mendoza and San Juan. Against this, however, the Radicals carried all the developed coastal provinces, plus the extremely backward ones where there was little tradition of independent voting. The total Radical vote in 1922 was 420,000, about 48% of the total throughout the country.

As his successor in 1922, Yrigoyen chose Marcelo T. de Alvear, who before had been Argentine minister in Paris. Alvear belonged to the patrician group which had founded the Radical Party in the early 1890s. His choice evidently reflected Yrigoyen's desire to maintain the support of the major elite groups, which had been threatened during the strikes and through the growth of the Patriotic League. Because of his long absence the new president had little personal influence in the party and had no apparent contacts with its former dissident groups. Yrigoyen felt confident that Alvear would have to rely on his support, and that he could be controlled from behind the scenes. To assist this, Yrigoyen arranged for the vice-presidency to be held by his own former chief of police, Elpidio González, who was now his most trusted and favoured political associate.

Alvear was thus a symbol of retrenchment and reconsolidation, and he represented something of a sop to the aristocratic groups which had been so troublesome during the period of the strikes. He himself was a believer in the style of programme Sáenz Peña had envisaged in 1912 – an end to the squalor of rigged elections in favour of a new era of 'organic' democracy. Like Sáenz Peña, Alvear sought the means to promote an effective alliance between aristocracy and the people, while seeming to reject the more adventurous and progressive sides of Yrigoyen's policies.[10]

However, from the outset the new government was plagued with severe problems. They stemmed directly from its difficulties in steering a balance between the party's middle class and elite-based groups. By 1922 there were signs that the divisions between them, which had been foreshadowed in the factional battles in 1918 and 1919, had gone too far.

As a condition for their cooperation with Alvear, the aristocratic groups demanded a return to what they pictured as constitutional legality. There were to be no more federal interventions in the provinces by simple executive decree. If federal intervention was deemed necessary, only Congress had the faculties to authorise it. A second condition was that government expenditure was also to be closely controlled by Congress. There was to be an end to Yrigoyen's practice, which had developed since 1919, of sanctioning expenditure by decree or by more surreptitious methods like ministerial resolutions.

The significance of these two conditions did not simply lie in questions of constitutional procedures and proprieties. By 1922 federal interventions and rising State spending had become the main pillars of the patronage system through which Yrigoyen's system of party control operated. Congressional control implied a severe restriction on patronage and thus added up to a direct threat against the professional and bureaucratic middle class groups upon which the Radical Party had come to depend. When it became evident that Alvear was himself wedded to this programme, it was not long before there was talk of the appearance of two new factions in the party, the *alvearistas* and the *yrigoyenistas*. The former were made up mainly of Yrigoyen's old opponents in the party elite, and the latter of his middle class supporters in the committees.

Immediately the new government took over, the middle class groups began to complain about Alvear's cabinet nominations.[11] The new minister of the interior, known for his opposition both to federal interventions and to Yrigoyen's spending policies, was José Nicolas Matienzo. The new minister of finance, Rafael Herrera Vegas, had a similar reputation. Only one of Yrigoyen's personal followers obtained a seat in the cabinet. This was Eufrasio Loza, the minister of public works. From the start relations between him and the rest of the members of the govern-

[10] The best study of Alvear is Manuel Goldstraj, *Años y errores. Un cuarto de siglo de política argentina* (Sophos, Buenos Aires, 1957).

[11] *La Vanguardia*, 25 October 1922.

ment were extremely tense. Loza was committed to increasing the level of public spending in order to widen the availability of political patronage. The other members of the cabinet, especially Herrera Vegas, were strongly opposed to this. As early as December 1922, the *Review of the River Plate* declared: 'There appears to have been some discrepancy of opinion between the minister of finance and his colleague of public works with regard to the assignment of the funds he considered necessary for the construction of new public works in 1923.'[12]

In 1922 the more conservative members of the Alvear administration supported cuts in State spending because in their view it put dangerous strains on the government's ability to service its debts. From 1916 total government spending rose from around 375 million paper pesos to a figure not far short of 600 million in 1922. The biggest rise, accounting for more than two-thirds of the total, occurred after 1919, when Yrigoyen embarked on his effort to win back popular support after the strikes. The complication was that with the wartime interruptions in imports, government revenues, which were mainly levied on imported goods, had also fallen off significantly. During the war the average budget deficit was about 150 million paper pesos, about double the pre-war level. After the war in 1919 and 1920, imports and tariff revenues, did for a time pick up, but not enough to cope with the rapid expansion of government spending at this point. The matter became a serious problem during the post-war depression from 1921 onwards. With the decline in economic activity and employment, pressure on the government from the middle class groups for an increase in spending intensified. A Radical Party official commented in 1922:

> There has developed among our fellow party members a contagious desire to take on positions in the national, provincial, and municipal administrations. The cost of living, the restriction of credit, the paralysis of certain industries and the decline in employment opportunities in others – the general crisis in a word – have left without work or with poorly paid work a great number of people.[13]

This was a clear illustration of the importance the patronage system had begun to acquire by 1922. Yrigoyen, with his eye on the presidential elections, was compelled to increase spending to even greater heights and expand the bureaucracy during the depression. Figures of between 10,000 and 20,000 were freely mentioned as the number of additional

[12] *Review of the River Plate*, 8 December 1922.

[13] Unión Cívica Radical, Circunscripción 11a (Balvanera Norte), *Rendición de Cuentas* (Buenos Aires, 1922), pp. 9–10.

positions he created in the national government, and in the federal capital alone, in 1921 and 1922.[14] To cover its rapidly increasing deficit the government was forced to resort to a large number of short-term loans from local and overseas banks.[15]

The result was the creation of a large and very expensive floating debt. In 1913 the floating debt, excluding the debts of semi-autonomous departments like the State Railways, stood at 94 million paper pesos. By the end of 1922 it had grown to almost 900 million, and to well over 1,000 million including the semi-autonomous State departments. When the issue was brought under discussion in Congress in 1923, it was pointed out that the annual cost of servicing the debt amounted to 126 million paper pesos, or about 30% of total State spending each year.[16] The overall position is summarised in Table 9. This shows, first, the close correspondence between imports and government revenues, secondly the large increase in public spending which occurred after 1919, and finally the increase in the floating debt.

TABLE 8 *National Government Finances, 1913–23 (figures in millions of paper pesos).*

	Imports	Revenues	Expenditures	Floating debt
1913	1,130	350	403	94
1914	730	250	419	256
1915	690	230	400	422
1916	830	233	375	515
1917	860	228	390	627
1918	1,140	298	421	711
1919	1,490	368	428	795
1920	2,120	481	503	682
1921	1,700	495	559	745
1922	1,570	461	614	893
1923	1,970	549	632	875

Source: A. E. Bunge, *Una nueva Argentina* (Buenos Aires, 1940), p. 188; Tornquist, quarterly reports; Peters, pp. 73–4.

[14] *Diario de Sesiones*, Cámara de Diputados, Vol. 1, 1923, pp. 117, *passim* (Rodolfo Moreno).

[15] Harold E. Peters, *The Foreign Debt of the Argentine Republic* (Baltimore, The Johns Hopkins Press, 1934), pp. 50–100.

[16] Rodolfo Moreno in *Diario de Sesiones*, Diputados, Vol. 1, p. 117.

Herrera Vegas, Matienzo and Alvear himself were all determined to make an attempt to reduce the floating debt. In his message opening Congress in May 1923, Alvear declared:

It is one of the decided intentions of my government to include all the expenditures of the nation in the annual budget laws. It is not possible to have sound finances with budgets that do not balance. Expenditure authorised by special laws or by government decrees ought to be avoided ... The public debt of the nation is augmenting year by year with deficits deriving from expenditures of an unproductive nature.[17]

During the course of the debates Herrera Vegas said, referring to himself:

The minister knows that at this time the financial capacity of the republic does not permit the payment of 1,000 million of floating debt and 604 million of budget expenditure. It would mean national ruin. Is it desirable to continue with this debt, which undermines the finances and retards the progress of the country? No it is not possible.[18]

At first in 1922 the new government seemed likely to purge the entire administration as a means of forcing economies. There was a flurry of dismissals and indictments for corruption, led by Matienzo. But soon after this, around February 1923, the government began to be more careful. Rather than cut spending immediately and isolate itself from its main source of popular support in the party, it adopted the alternative course of seeking to increase its revenues. At the end of 1923 it took steps to do this when reforms were passed by Congress increasing the customs valuations of imported goods by 60%.

This measure merits further explanation. An increase in the tariff valuations implied the introduction of new protectionist policies, which apparently stood at variance with the landed interests' traditional preferences for Free Trade and the principle of comparative advantage. It was also a measure which could be construed as favouring the Americans at the expense of the British, because of its implications for local industrial production and the growing dominance of the Americans in the capital goods field. However, what the measure aimed for was a further limited degree of domestic industrialisation. The need for it had emerged when serious balance of payments problems had developed during the post-war depression. Each year between 1920 and 1923

[17] *Review of the River Plate*, 11 May 1923.

[18] Ibid. 25 May 1923.

there were deficits in the balance of payments of between 50 and 200 million gold pesos.[19] The deficits reflected the accelerated decline in exports during the depression, but the much slower decline in imports in the absence of deflationary policies by the State.[20] Further local industrialisation was regarded as a means to overcome this problem. It was mainly designed to apply to sectors like food processing, where raw materials and industrial plant like the frigorificos were immediately accessible. Herrera Vegas, in supporting this policy in Congress, announced himself unwilling to go beyond this framework, in case of retaliation abroad against Argentina's agricultural exports.[21]

Even so, the Alvear Government's tariff policy was mainly motivated by immediate revenue considerations, and beyond it by the problem of safeguarding the unity of the Radical Party. Referring to the tariff valuations in his message proposing the changes in 1923, the president described them as a 'flagrant injustice' and responsible for 'an unsatisfactory decline in national revenues'.[22] By 1923 the tariff valuations were eighteen years old and bore little relation to the prices of imported goods, or to prices in general.[23]

19 Phelps, Table 1, p. 238.

20 This was another reason for justifying cuts in public spending. High State spending had the effect of increasing purchasing power, and maintaining the demand for imported goods in excess of what it would have been had the government's deficits not existed. (Cf. Ibid. p. 58.)

21 *Diario de Sesiones* Diputados, Vol. 1, 1923, p. 451. This is partly an anticipation of similar policies in the 1930s. See Murmis and Portantiero, pp. 3–55.

22 *Diario de Sesiones*, Diputados, Vol. 5, 1922, p. 32.

23 Cf. Solberg, 'Tariffs and politics'. Jorge (pp. 62–5) provides a table of the relationship between the prices of imports and the tariff valuations, and also of government revenues from tariffs. The Alvear measure increased the tariff rate to about the level of 1915. This was still less than the rate in 1906 when the original valuations were introduced. It is important to note also why Yrigoyen had not taken this step. During the period of inflation before 1921, any increase in the tariff valuations would have increased the cost of living at a time when there were already serious strikes and murmurs of discontent among the middle class groups. Generally Yrigoyen had preferred to raise new sources of revenue by transferring the burden of taxation onto the export sectors. This was the case with the abortive income tax measure of 1918 and the emergency tax on exports. These were examples of the government's efforts to restore the pre-war balance in the distribution of income and they parallel its measures in the strikes. However, in July, 1920 Congress did increase the tariff valuations by 20%. This throws further light on the government's campaign to reduce the cost of living in 1920. It exposed further the insincerity of this campaign, and the fact that it was designed to outmanoeuvre Socialist complaints

There was one other aspect of the government's attempts at financial retrenchment in 1923 which impinged upon the position of the working class during Alvear's presidency. In 1923 Congress authorised the government to seek means of consolidating the floating debt. The initial plan was for half the debt to be funded by means of 3% Treasury bonds, a further fifth by means of an internal loan at 6%, and the rest by means of an external loan. Although the government finally managed to consolidate a small part of the debt, its attempts to secure an external loan failed. At the end of the year it therefore adopted a new plan. It proposed a pensions scheme for the working class, which was to be applied to the industrial workers, the mercantile and banking employees, the port workers and the workers in the printing industry. The idea was to use the funds to consolidate the floating debt.[24]

The government found it impossible to disguise the fact that the measure was a forced loan. Efforts to implement it led to the only serious demonstration of political action by the workers during Alvear's presidency. As it was about to be introduced in May 1924, there were a number of abortive strikes similar to those in 1921. Among the unions which took action was the F.O.M. Domecq García replied, however, by ordering the port police to protect free labour against the union. From henceforth until 1928, the coastal and international shippers ruled unchallenged, backed by the ministry of marine.[25]

The pensions scheme was finally abandoned in 1925, principally because it was opposed by the employers, including the groups formerly active in the National Labour Association.[26] Besides revealing the position of the government on the working class question, it was another illustration of its attempts to solve its revenue problems without having to take steps to trim public expenditure, and thus reduce its sources of patronage.[27]

Footnote 23 (continued)

of discrimination against the urban sectors. The emergency tax on exports was still being levied during the post-war depression when Alvear took over the presidency. Pressure among the exporting groups for its removal was another of the reasons for the tariff reforms.

24 *Review of the River Plate*, November 1923, *passim*.

25 Ibid. 9 May 1924.

26 Ibid. 31 July 1925.

27 The government did also attempt to introduce or increase other taxes, though none of these were accepted by Congress. Among the changes it proposed were a tax on moveable property, the raising of the rates paid on landed property (the *contribución*

The party division of 1924

Despite these attempts at compromise, and although the Alvear Government eventually failed to hold back spending, relations between the government and the party deteriorated rapidly. The critical period was in 1923 as uncertainty built up over how far the government would finally go in its attempts to enforce economies. As early as January 1923, Alvear was beseiged with complaints from the parish committee bosses in Buenos Aires that he was failing to buttress their position with an adequate store of patronage.[28] By February 1923, a public rift had developed between the president and Elpidio González.[29] For the rest of the year there was an open feud between Loza, the one *yrigoyenista* in the cabinet, who demanded an ambitious public works policy, and the rest who were committed to financial orthodoxy. On the other hand Alvear's efforts at compromise rapidly alienated him from the conservative members of the cabinet. First Herrera Vegas resigned.[30] Soon afterwards Matienzo also resigned, complaining about the pressure from the *yrigoyenistas* to force him into organising a further spate of illegal federal interventions.[31] But these resignations did little to curb the rising opposition of the *yrigoyenistas*. Eventually Alvear himself came under attack from *La Epoca*, and the party committees began to split between those who supported the president and those who clung to their allegiance to Yrigoyen.

By the end of 1923 the government had lost control over the bulk of the committees and the majority of the Radicals in Congress. At this point *La Vanguardia* declared:

> There is no government. This is because at the moment there are two different governments, one led from Calle Brasil [Yrigoyen's home], whose only aptitude is for preventing anyone else doing anything, and the other, which wants to do something but lacks the needle and thread to do it. There is no government because there is no government party.[32]

Footnote 27 (continued)

territorial) and a tax on the increments in land values. (Cf. Tornquist, October 1923–January 1924). However these were only minor items, and the government did not press them with any great energy. In a memorandum to the government from the Stock Exchange (Bolsa de Comercio), the taxes were described as 'forced expropriation' and 'spoliation'. (Cf. *Review of the River Plate*, 27 July, 1923.)

28 Cf. *La Vanguardia*, 31 January 1923.

29 Ibid. 25 February 1923.

30 Ibid. 4 October 1923.

31 Ibid. 24 November 1923.

32 Ibid. 25 November 1923.

The final break in 1924 followed upon Alvear's attempt to consolidate his position by establishing closer links with the anti-*yrigoyenista* party elite, which had challenged Yrigoyen for control over the party in 1918 and 1919. After Matienzo's resignation, he appointed as minister of the interior Vicente C. Gallo, who was a close political associate of Leopoldo Melo. The difference between Gallo and Matienzo was that Gallo had less inhibitions about using the budget to create a patronage empire. He was also prepared to use federal interventions by decree to establish a new 'personalist' system of control over the provinces. *La Epoca*, whose editors were well experienced in such matters, described Gallo's activities in the following apocryphal terms:

> The same scene can be witnessed daily in the ministry of the interior. The corridors outside the minister's office are full of masses of claimants for administrative jobs. They await the arrival of the minister ... some 100, 200, 300 individuals ... The minister tries to receive them all personally, to shake them by the hand. If they are employees they inform him of their salaries, of their needs and of their desires for self-improvement. If they are not employed and wish to be, he promises to satisfy their wishes ...[33]

In view of the extreme opposition to Gallo among the *yrigoyenistas*, it proved impossible to hold the party together. In the internal party elections in 1924, in many parts of the country two rival lists of office-holders competed against one another. Finally Gallo announced the formation of a new party. It became known as the Unión Cívica Radical Antipersonalista.[34] The term *antipersonalismo* meant opposition to the patronage techniques used by Yrigoyen. But it was a misleading description, since Gallo showed himself as committed as Yrigoyen to the established methods of winning popular support.

Gallo's problem, however, was the same as that of the *yrigoyenistas* in 1923. He had to persuade Alvear and the rest of the cabinet to accept an inflationary budget and allow for the reestablishment of a patronage system. In August and September 1924, there were again protracted wrangles between different ministers over the budget for the following year.[35]

There emerged from this another uneasy compromise where total spending was allowed to rise marginally, but not at the rate Gallo required. Nor did he meet with any more success in persuading Alvear to use federal intervention to clear out the *yrigoyenistas* in the provinces.

[33] *La Epoca*, 1 March 1924.

[34] Cf. *La Nación*, 20 September 1924.

[35] *La Vanguardia*, 29 August, 4 September 1924.

After a great deal of hesitation Alvear rejected this course in the hope that his forbearance might achieve the party's reunification.[36] Eventually, in July 1925, Gallo too was forced to resign, his aim of usurping control over the party from Yrigoyen having completely failed.[37]

The emergence of Antipersonalism was the final result of the party rivalries which had been apparent even before 1916. The Antipersonalist leaders, Gallo and Leopoldo Melo, were each members of the dissident Blue Group whose presence is to be seen intermittently during Yrigoyen's first government.[38] Antipersonalism failed in 1924 and 1925 largely because Gallo was unable to win over the conservative elements of the Radical Party in the cabinet to support his methods of rooting out Yrigoyen's influence.

Nor did the new party manage to acquire any substantial national influence afterwards. Its lack of access to State patronage deprived it of the means of developing a committee system with mass support and capturing control in the provinces. Its only stronghold was the province of Santa Fe. When in 1928 the Antipersonalists announced their candidates – Melo and Gallo – for the presidential elections, they did so in Santa Fe. Only here did they enjoy a majority popular backing.[39]

This suggests once more the relationship between the dissident groups of the Radical Party and the traditional interregional rivalries between the province of Santa Fe and Buenos Aires. It was also a further factor preventing Alvear from exerting his power in support of the new party. He himself was closely associated by family links with the province of Buenos Aires. It seems unlikely that he would have welcomed any significant transfer of influence in the direction of Santa Fe. Antipersonalism

[36] Ibid. 22 March 1925.

[37] *La Nación*, 28 July 1925.

[38] After the collapse of the Blue Group's challenge in 1919, the most irreconcilable of Yrigoyen's opponents had immediately split from the government and founded their own party. This was the Unión Cívica Radical Principista, and it managed to present candidates in the presidential election of 1922, although it won only a tiny proportion of the vote. Yrigoyen's chief opponent during this period was Joaquín Castellanos, the governor of Salta from 1919 until he was deposed by federal intervention. At the end of 1920 he was reported attempting to organise a League of Governors, in Roca's old style, composed of Yrigoyen's opponents. In July 1921, he gained the support of Benjamín Villafañe, Radical deputy for the province of Jujuy and one of the most vitriolic of Yrigoyen's opponents. The *principistas* also won some support at this point from the latter Antipersonalists in the National Senate: Senators Gallo, Melo, Larlus, Soto and Torino.

[39] *La Epoca*, 11 September 1927.

therefore eventually ended up, like its conservative predecessors such as the Progressive Democrat Party, as a mainly regional association with little permanent influence outside its core area.[40]

The central role in the failure of Antipersonalism was thus played by Alvear himself.[41] He was never able to surmount the initial contradictions of his position. He wished to rule through the party and have the support of the popular committees, but his orthodoxy on financial matters prevented him ever acquiring the means to do so. His failure as president indicated one of the basic realities of Argentine politics: it was possible to establish or maintain the alliance between the patrician groups and the urban middle classes only by adopting a flexible stance on State spending and by manipulating the expansion of the bureaucracy for partisan purposes. In a situation like the post-war depression where the elite began to oppose an increase in government expenditure, the alliance was extremely difficult to hold together. Thus the roots of the consensus between the landed groups and the urban middle classes, which Radicalism had achieved before 1916, were being rapidly undermined. What developed from these conflicts largely determined the course of Argentine politics in the 1920s.

After Gallo had resigned, Alvear attempted to form his third cabinet in three years. This time he aimed for a more neutral position through the appointment of José Tamborini as minister of the interior. The step was initially supported by the *yrigoyenistas* to prevent the Antipersonalists from regaining their influence. But as soon as they had strengthened their position in Congress in the elections of 1926, the *yrigoyenistas* once more abandoned the government. Alvear was given an ultimatum to appoint *yrigoyenistas* to key posts in the bureaucracy, to dismiss Yrigoyen's opponents in the cabinet, and finally to turn out the opposition Progressive Democrats in Córdoba by federal intervention.[42]

40 The Antipersonalists also failed to attract the support of the Buenos Aires dissidents, such as José Camilo Crotto, governor of the province of Buenos Aires between 1918 and 1922, Carlos Becú, Yrigoyen's first minister of foreign affairs in 1916, and Rogelio Araya, the leader of the Radical opposition in Congress against Yrigoyen up to 1919. In the 1920s they all largely disappeared from the scene.

41 Thus Radicalism was divided during the 1920s not into two groups but into three, *yrigoyenismo*, *antipersonalismo* and *alvearismo*. The first was a pro-spending party on behalf of the urban sectors of Buenos Aires, and the second a similar group but more orientated towards Santa Fe. *Alvearismo* was an anti-spending party in favour of the export interests of Buenos Aires.

42 *La Vanguardia*, 6 May 1925.

The renewed break between government and Party became apparent when the *yrigoyenistas* in the National Chamber of Deputies refused to pass the 1926 budget.[43]

In 1927 and 1928 Alvear attempted to intimidate the *yrigoyenistas* into supporting him once more by making moves towards the Anti-personalists. But his eventual unwillingness to take concrete steps to support them in the presidential elections in 1928 became apparent in a speech he made at the beginning of the election campaign:

> The Melo–Gallo ticket satisfies my sense of patriotism and my position as a member of the party. In it are two men with wide experience . . . They are Radicals from the party's first days with an unchallengeable background. If the fact of being president does not prevent me from feeling, thinking and speaking in this way, it does, however, prevent me from going any further. This is all I can say.[44]

This left the way open again for Yrigoyen.

The revival of Yrigoyen

In spite of his advancing years, between 1922 and 1928 Yrigoyen maintained his position and his popularity through his tight control over the party committees, and by holding out the prospect of a return to the patronage bonanza of 1922. Party propaganda was largely based on insinuations of this sort, together with attempts to reestablish Yrigoyen's popular charismatic appeal.[45] The campaign enjoyed tremendous success.

[43] Ibid. 28 March 1926.

[44] *La Vanguardia*, 19 May 1927.

[45] As before, the use of charismatic techniques was employed as a device to reduce divisions in the party. As time passed, however, its style and content had changed. In 1919 and 1920 the Radicals had been attempting to outmanoeuvre the appeal of the Patriotic League by presenting Yrigoyen himself as the symbol of patriotism. In the 1920s there was more definite emphasis on Yrigoyen's position as the incarnation of the popular will. An example is the following extract from a hagiographic work published in 1928. Referring to Yrigoyen, it was said: 'The great man is he who by his special nature feels the vibrations of the soul of society and gives them form by means of his own intimate intuitions. The common man knows nothing; the people can only vaguely feel what lies behind its stirrings. But in the great man this sense of longing becomes clear. He represents the force of society. It is made flesh and blood in him and becomes part of him. He makes it human and making it so, he can act on it' (Alberto M. Etkin, *Bosquejo de una historia y doctrina de la U.C.R.*, El Ateneo, Buenos Aires, 1928, p. 194). There was a multitude of publications of this kind in the 1920s.

After the party split in 1924, *yrigoyenismo* began once more immediately to expand on the basis of the local committees. As early as 1925 its internal elections in the city of Buenos Aires were commanding a massive turnout of over 40,000. By 1928 this had grown to 60,000.

As in the period before 1916, Yrigoyen made a sustained attempt to identify with the interests of the dependent middle class groups. From 1925 speeches by the *yrigoyenistas* in Congress were dominated by demands for higher wages for State employees, for an expansion of their social benefits, and above all for increased public spending.[46] The charity activities of the committees once again began to flourish. As in the past they organised medical and legal centres and provided funds for every variant of local activity. An example of the type of appeal the *yrigoyenistas* were aiming for is the following:

> The speaker then referred to the charity activities of our millionaires, who prefer to donate hospitals to the French than to put them here where they are needed. He emphasised how the rich in North America make their donations. They give sufficient not only for the construction of a university or a hospital but they also provide sufficient money for their maintenance. By contrast what our rich people do is simply provide for construction and forget the other necessary things. Which all goes to show, he said, that they are more concerned with their mention in the society pages of the newspapers than with doing anything really useful... On the contrary this festival shows that the U.C.R. is not only concerned with simple propaganda, but its main aim is also to help the poor.[47]

There was also another sustained effort to win working class support in readiness for the presidential elections. In street propaganda in Buenos Aires as much as possible was made of Yrigoyen's relations with the unions before 1922. In 1927, for example, *La Epoca* began a campaign for the revival of the F.O.M. with hints of future privileges it would enjoy on Yrigoyen's reelection.[48]

The more common practice, however, which reflected both the weakness of the unions and Yrigoyen's inability to pursue any alternative course while out of office, was the organisation of specialised party committees in a guild fashion among different groups of workers. They were usually led by administrative or white-collar personnel, and they continued the techniques which had first emerged before the presidential

[46] Cf. *La Epoca*, 27 October 1926.

[47] Ibid. 22 September 1927.

[48] *La Epoca*, 20 August 1927.

elections of 1922. The group most affected was the railway workers. Between 1926 and 1928 committees of railwaymen sprang up in considerable numbers in different parts of the country. They were encouraged by propaganda which romanticised Yrigoyen's personal role during the railway strikes in 1917 and 1918. On occasion this led to suggestions of friction with the unions, especially with the Unión Ferroviaria, which had less of a collaborationist instinct than its predecessor the F.O.F.:

> [the workers] ought to meditate over what are the real interests of the railwaymen. [The unions] ... are divided into so many factions ... and they will never direct their attentions to the individual railway worker or employee...All the railway welfare benefits were sanctioned under the auspices of the most honourable and just government of modern times. For the continuation of these important advances...it is necessary that a good man in every sense of the word should become president of the republic; energetic and just on every occasion; an intelligent, simple working man, with a clear and profound vision of affairs... And we, all the railway workers, ought to organise a common front so that united together we may unfurl our banner with that of Dr Hipólito Yrigoyen...[49]

Yrigoyen also won endorsement from smaller groups, like the tramway workers and the taxi-drivers both in Buenos Aires and Rosario. The success of the committee structure among the working class in the mid-1920s again illustrated the extent to which class loyalties had declined since the war with the end of inflation and the return of prosperity. The unions, as class-based institutions which had served as a barrier to the expansion of Radicalism among the working class in the past, were now giving way to multi-class associations. These reflected the growth of a more open society and the widening of opportunities for social mobility in comparison with the war period.

This important change also coincided with the growing weakness of the Socialist Party in the latter half of the 1920s. In 1923 and 1924 the Socialists had shown signs of revival following the Radical split, and had managed to win a number of important elections in the federal capital. But with the recovery of the *yrigoyenistas* in 1926, they split once more, for the fifth time in twenty years. One group continued to support the legalistic reformist approach favoured by Juan B. Justo. The other group became known as the Independent Socialist Party.

The background to this split is to be traced to the fact that by this

[49] Quoted in *La Vanguardia*, 30 July 1927.

time several of the Socialist Party's leaders had begun to acquire semi-establishment positions, for example, as the lawyers of foreign companies. Their increasing identification with the conservative elite gradually led them to a more flexible and opportunistic position, which conflicted with the rigid opposition to 'creole politics' of the traditionalists in the party.[50] An aspect of this were growing quarrels in the party about the type of party organisation it should adopt. Unlike the parent party, the Independent Socialists began to seek closer links with the urban middle class groups by developing a party machine structure similar to that used by the Radicals, and based primarily on the distribution of personal benefits. But it was not until after 1928 that they began seriously to make their presence felt.

The nationalisation of oil

The emergence of the Independent Socialist Party coincided with important changes in the *yrigoyenista* movement. In spite of the often extreme opportunistic and demagogic tone they adopted after 1925, the *yrigoyenistas* became increasingly concerned to justify their commitment to increasing State spending on something more positive and constructive than mere graft. The initial directions in which they were moving became apparent as early as 1924. Pablo Torello, formerly Yrigoyen's minister of public works, began to support the expansion of the industrial sector and a less *laissez-faire* attitude than in the past towards the country's natural resources. He counselled:

> a completely defensive policy of the country's great economic interests, beginning by protecting the production of all the raw materials in the country which could be used for industrialisation...We are the greatest consumers in South America of imported European foodstuffs, which we could produce at a quality equal to or perhaps better than that of the articles we receive from abroad.[51]

What provoked this gradual move away from traditional Free Trade principles by the *yrigoyenistas* in the 1920s was a semi-conscious recognition of the true nature of the 'dependency' phenomenon among the middle class groups. They began implicitly to accept that it was objectively impossible to go on increasing State spending and expanding the bureaucracy indefinitely. Some solution had to be found for the basic problem of the growth of unproductive tertiary sectors.

[50] For details of the split see Walter, pp. 18–20; also Coca, *El contubernio*.

[51] Quoted in *La Vanguardia*, 29 March 1924.

Their position in 1924 was to some extent reminiscent of that adopted by the Alvear Government in justifying its increase in the tariff valuations in 1923. At this point the *yrigoyenistas* had in general opposed the measure because of its anticipated effect on the urban cost of living. As their links with the middle class groups further expanded after the party split in 1924, however, they were gradually forced to override these objectives. When, for example, in early 1927 the *yrigoyenistas* in Congress proposed the introduction of a new minimum wage on behalf of two key groups, the railway workers and State employees, they demanded that this should be financed by increasing import duties, regardless of the effect on the consumers.[52]

This presaged a major change in the character of Argentine Radicalism in the mid-1920s, and the beginnings of a shift away from its traditional consumer-based Free Trade ideology in the direction of economic nationalism. Nevertheless this commitment never became final or complete. Rather than ever developing into a demand for total structural changes in the economy, the new nationalism tended to coexist with the old style of liberalism, which the Radical Party had previously supported. What it meant was a new emphasis on limited industrial development to benefit the dependent groups among the middle classes, and a greater preparedness to move beyond the strict mould of the primary exporting economy, though without threatening it directly.

The transition crystallised in the strong support which developed among the *yrigoyenistas* for the nationalisation of the country's oil resources, and the establishment of a State monopoly for its refinement and distribution. The emphasis on State control was partly for economic reasons, because only the State was capable of organising and financing an enterprise of this scale. But it also mirrored a number of basic social and political conditions. The introduction of a State monopoly meant that the bureaucracy and the groups directly or indirectly involved in it could be funnelled into a new range of activities. They would remain dependent on the State, but the State would have an additional range of activities at its disposal to respond to them.

The clarity with which this programme was developed and enunciated forms a striking contrast with the amorphousness and lack of definition of Radical doctrines before 1922. For the first time the *yrigoyenistas* had something practical and concrete to campaign on beyond their previous abstract appeal to 'democracy' and the 'defence of the constitution'. Their

[52] Ibid. 23 January 1927.

position on the oil question also contrasted with that the Radicals had taken up before 1922. During Yrigoyen's administration the Radicals, as with so many similar problems, were divided among themselves. Some of them supported the development of the country's oil resources by foreign capital. Others urged the formation of a semi-State corporation supported by domestic private investment. Still more wanted a form of partnership between the State and foreign investment, where the State would take charge of exploration and then organise the granting of private concessions. The government itself had inclined towards the last of these options. In Yrigoyen's messages to Congress there had been no mention of nationalisation or a State monopoly.[53]

A further expression of the change was a growing anti-Americanism among the *yrigoyenistas*. By the mid-1920s Standard Oil had begun to establish an important base for its operations in the country. In 1926 *La Epoca* commenced a prolonged campaign against the granting of drilling rights to the company by the provincial authorities in Salta and Jujuy.[54] From henceforth it became commonplace to attack 'the American oil-trusts'. During a major debate on the subject in Congress in September 1927, such comments as the following were frequently made by the *yrigoyenistas*:

> ...the danger is well known for countries with large oil resources when they also have inside the country the powerful tentacles of a great company. I have no need to name it. All the members know that I am referring to the powerful trust from the North. This has brought all the Latin American republics not only extreme economic and financial difficulties, but also irreparable injuries to their sovereignty and international independence.[55]

Another *yrigoyenista* deputy declared:

> Let us rescue our second great source of wealth. We should not let happen to this what happened with our public lands. Let us save what is the country's life-blood. A single motor in the whole immense territory of the country cannot run without this new spirit, which is also the spirit to lead us industrially, socially and economically to the new Argentina we dream of.[56]

State control over oil thus became so popular a slogan among the

[53] Marcos Kaplan, 'Política del petroleo en la primera presidencia de Hipólito Yrigoyen (1916–1922)', *Desarrollo Econónico*, Vol. 12, No. 45 (April–June 1972), pp. 3–24.

[54] *La Epoca*, 20–23 October 1926.

[55] Oil debates of 1927. Quoted in Etchepareborda, *Pueblo y gobierno*, Vol. 12, p. 57.

[56] Ibid. p. 107.

yrigoyenistas for a number of reasons. It offered a long-term solution to the increasingly critical problem of the dependent middle class groups in the cities, which were the core of Yrigoyen's popular backing. It was a means to justify a return to the high-spending policies of the past. It promised to open up a new range of managerial positions for the middle classes, while avoiding the waste of public funds which the creation of a parasitical bureaucracy would entail. Equally it represented an opportunity to siphon the process of domestic economic growth into completely new fields, and thus provide a new range of occupations for entrepreneurs and workers in the industrial sector. Finally it was conceived as paving the way for a major process of industrial development. This implied a means of escape from the different problems which developed during moments of economic depression and the contraction of export markets.

What made the programme politically feasible was that the oil companies were still in a relatively weak position in terms of their capacity for economic and political leverage. In the past, Yrigoyen's inclinations towards economic nationalism, and the more positive use of State power, had always been limited by the close interrelationship between the domestic sectors and foreign capital. With oil it was different. It was very difficult for the oil companies to mobilise local pressure groups and popular support in the same way as the railway companies had done during the strikes in 1917 and 1918. A strike on the railways led immediately to a threat against the major domestic exporting groups. As events in 1917 had shown, the government had been unable to withstand pressure against it where the exporting interests were involved. By contrast the political bargaining power of the oil companies in the 1920s was small. The support they had was not in the metropolitan area among the major elite groups, but more in the peripheral and politically weaker provinces of the far north, where the oil fields were located.

The *yrigoyenistas* were fully conscious of all these angles to the problem. They had learned important lessons from their experience during the strike period between 1917 and 1919, and were determined to prevent Standard Oil from acquiring the same political influence as the British railway companies. One of their deputies declared in 1927:

> We are aware that capital is among the most feared social and political factors. The economic or financial strength of the firm transforms itself by degrees into political strength and in this way it gradually takes control of a country. It controls weak governments, it extends its tentacles over the administration and

begins to undermine the country's sovereignty, playing a decisive role in the elections and taking over the last bulwark of democracy, the Congress.[57]

Finally the oil campaign also revealed the *yrigoyenistas* in their old guise of protecting the pampas landed interests. The anti-trust movement in 1927 was directed exclusively against the Americans and against Standard Oil. There was little criticism of the British, who had also become active in this field. The advantage this had was that it could be pictured to the exporting interests as promising a return to the old simple bilateral relationship with the British on which they had thrived until 1914. To eliminate the Americans from the power field could be presented as an additional means of protecting the country's traditional export markets; what the British would perhaps lose in coal exports, they would gain in exports of technical equipment for the oil industry. This, it was hoped, would curtail their unease at their mounting trade deficit with Argentina, and thus serve to bolster the traditional primary export structure.[58]

In this fashion the *yrigoyenistas* had discovered by 1927 an ideal popular slogan. They had found a way of advocating change, and with it their old goal of class harmony, without implying any sacrifices by the established primary export interests. If the workers, for example, won higher wages, concessions would come increasingly from within the internal economy. They would avoid raising the old bogy of 'foreign confidence'. It was now possible to straddle a dual position of economic nationalism on one front and traditional liberal internationalism on the other, thus allowing for the reestablishment of some form of compatibility between the export interests and the urban sectors. Oil was largely set apart from the primary exporting economy, and from the various configurations of power and political influence it had produced.

[57] Ibid, p. 186.

[58] Fodor and O'Connell (p. 38) regard this discrimination against the Americans as simply reflecting Yrigoyen's fear as a matter of principle of 'dollar imperialism'. But support for the British makes more sense in terms of the structure of the *yrigoyenista* populist alliance. To be pro-British at this point meant support for the exporting interests i.e. the electorate in the province of Buenos Aires. During the trade boom of the late 1920s there were obviously more grounds for cooperation with the British than there were during the war when the price of coal was rising so rapidly. However, one can agree with Fodor and O'Connell that Yrigoyen's attitudes towards the British had changed from hostility to support. This occurred, as has been seen, in 1919 under the impact of the strikes.

The effect of this, between 1926 and 1928, was to produce a great bandwagon movement in Yrigoyen's favour. He successfully neutralised the opposition to him among the conservative landed and exporting interests. He had the support of the voting sectors of the middle and working class. In the presidential elections there was no force capable of withstanding him. Alvear still refused to give the Antipersonalists any practical assistance and now presided over what was little more than a caretaker administration. The conservative parties, including the Progressive Democrats, still had only local influence. The Socialists were split. Local parties like *lencinismo* in Mendoza and *cantonismo* in San Juan were powerful in their own provinces, but had no influence outside them. The leaders of the northern provinces were unpopular on account of their support for Standard Oil.

The result was an electoral landslide for Yrigoyen in 1928. He carried every province in the country, including the federal capital, with the exception of San Juan. He won over 57% of the total votes cast, an increase of 10% over the presidential elections in 1922. His total vote in 1928 ran to over 840,000. On 12 October 1928, twelve years to the day after his first government had begun, Yrigoyen reassumed the presidency.

CHAPTER 11

Yrigoyen's second presidency, 1928–30

The presidential elections of 1928 were Yrigoyen's greatest personal triumph. Yet within less than two years, on 6 September 1930 he was ignominiously overthrown by a military *coup d'état*. The crowds in Buenos Aires which had given him such fervent support in 1928, now ransacked his house and, for a time at least, acclaimed the new revolutionary government. The situation which developed in 1930 was thus in some respects similar to that in 1919. The government's popular support suddenly drained away and shifted towards new structures of mass organisation. As in 1919, too, these were led by the army, with the conservative elite in close attendance. Another common feature between the two years was the temporary character of the shift. By 1920 the Radicals had recovered sufficiently from the threat posed by the Patriotic League to win a strong majority in the congressional elections held that year. In 1931 the same occurred when they won the election for governor in the province of Buenos Aires. The difference was that in 1919 Yrigoyen had managed to forestall a *coup d'état*, whereas in 1930 he failed completely.

The composition and policies of the new government

In 1928, as a result of the party split of 1924 and the failure to reach agreement with Alvear, *yrigoyenista* Radicalism pivoted more closely than ever before on the support of the urban middle class groups. There were still a large number of *estancieros* who supported Yrigoyen, most of all in the province of Buenos Aires, but the centre of authority in the party had moved markedly towards the professional middle classes.

The change was apparent in Yrigoyen's cabinet in 1928 and in the social backgrounds of many of the *yrigoyenista* members of Congress. In 1928 two key positions in the cabinet, minister of the interior and minister of foreign affairs, were held by men who had emerged from among the party committees. The minister of the interior was Elpidio González, and the minister of foreign affairs was Horacio B. Oyhanarte.

Both were men of middle class backgrounds, who had controlled the party apparatus in two key provinces, Córdoba and Buenos Aires. Oyhanarte in particular was a symbol of the *nouveau riche* element in Radicalism, which won predominance after 1924.[1]

Among the *yrigoyenistas* in Congress the sons-of-immigrants group was now represented in considerable numbers. Many of them had made their way up from the precinct committees, especially those representing the federal capital. They were mainly professional men with university educations, though most owed their positions simply to their control over the local party machines. This was in marked contrast with the position in 1916, when the overwhelming majority of Radical legislators were landowners.[2]

This found reflection in the actions of the new government in 1928 and 1929. Yrigoyen immediately abandoned the cautious approach he had first adopted in 1916 towards State spending and quickly reestablished his grip over government patronage. In many cases he restored to their positions the appointees he had made before leaving office in 1921 and 1922. There was a ruthless purge of Alvear's officials.[3] On 22 February 1929, for example, *La Vanguardia* reported the dismissal of over 3,000 teachers employed by the national government.

As a means to pay off key party supporters who had helped in the election campaign, the presidents of the local committees in the federal capital were brought into close contact with government ministers and with the heads of administration departments. In a short time a great deal of abuse and corruption developed, as the attempt was made to expand government patronage to its limits. By June 1929, it was reported

[1] For González see Arturo Torres, *Elpidio González. Biografía de una conducta* (Raigal, Buenos Aires, 1951). Oyhanarte was the author of a bombastic biography of Yrigoyen published in 1916, *El hombre*. This had done a great deal to enhance the charismatic content of Yrigoyen's leadership.

[2] Some examples of the new group are Diego Luis Molinari, Héctor Bergalli, David Saccone, Pedro Podestá, Pedro Bidegain, Nicolas Selén, Guillermo Súllivan. Bidegain is one of the few *caudillos de barrio* in Buenos Aires for whom there is biographical information. In 1929, after being accused in Congress of having worked for the oligarchy before 1912, he published a short autobiography (*Mi radicalismo*). This is rather interesting. In 1907 he had worked as a fireman on the Buenos Aires Western Railway. Later he had made two unsuccessful attempts to found a business, and only after that had he joined the Radicals. This is a classic case of the 'dependent' middle class phenomenon.

[3] Cf. *La Epoca*, 29 October 1928; *La Vanguardia*, 1 November 1928.

that jobs were being sold on the open market.[4] This made it evident that the committee bosses were anxious to recoup as quickly as possible the heavy investments they had made in Yrigoyen's success before the elections, and to defray the expenses they had incurred during the lean years under Alvear.

Under Alvear some of the ward bosses in the city and province of Buenos Aires had been involved in Mafia-like gambling rackets. They also had some connections with the notorious white-slave traffic in Buenos Aires which, with the resumption of immigration after the war, became increasingly important in the 1920s. However, accusations of their involvement in these activities became much less after 1928. The point would require further examination and investigation to be proven, but it seems possible that gambling and prostitution became a kind of surrogate activity for the ward bosses under Alvear, which reflected their lack of access to more normal political perquisites.

In 1929 the whole system of 'committee government' which Yrigoyen had first introduced in 1919 reached its apogee. The system was held together by an immediate and rapid increase in State spending. It was made possible by the prevailing prosperity held up by a boom in agricultural exports. As the *Review of the River Plate* remarked in August 1929, 'the Argentine Republic is sitting pretty'.[5] As between 1919 and 1922, control over national finances rapidly slipped away from Congress. Whenever the opposition parties made an attempt to bring the matter under discussion, the *yrigoyenistas* simply broke the congressional quorum.

Yet although this was much more of a middle class administration than those which had preceded it, paralleling the growth of the patronage system were the new government's efforts to consolidate its position among the elite groups and the two pressure groups which had been the source of so much trouble in 1919 – the army and foreign capital.

Between 1922 and 1930 relations between the army and the *yrigoyenistas* were generally more complex than has often been acknowledged. Under Alvear, for example, there was opposition in the army and navy to the conservative programme of restricting State spending on the grounds that there was a pressing need for the replacement of military equipment. This was one reason why Alvear's first minister of public

[4] *La Vanguardia*, 3 June 1929. It was also reported that Yrigoyen's personal physician and his secretary were charging fees for audiences with him.

[5] *Review of the River Plate*, 8 August 1929.

works, the *yrigoyenista* Eufrasio Loza, had maintained his position for so long. During disputes over the budget in 1923 and 1924, Loza's attempts to increase expenditure were supported by General Agustín P. Justo, the minister of war, and Rear Admiral Domecq García, the minister of marine.[6] There was also some support within the army for the *yrigoyenistas*' oil proposals, since the army, for military and strategic purposes, was interested in promoting self-sufficiency in the fuel and power fields.

By 1927, however, there were certain groups in the army led by Justo, and prompted by sectors among the conservative elite, which began to show resentment at Yrigoyen's resurgence. There was talk at this point of preventing his regaining the presidency by a *coup d' état.* But in 1928 the extreme anti-*yrigoyenista* groups had little backing. In spite of widespread dislike for Yrigoyen, there was a considerable reluctance to do anything while he enjoyed such firm mass support. Eventually Justo was compelled to deny in public that he was preparing a coup in favour of the Antipersonalists.[7]

Once he had regained the presidency, Yrigoyen did all he could to minimise this threat. Elpidio González began to intrigue for the removal of the government's military opponents from key positions by juggling with the promotion lists.[8] There was also every attempt to prevent opposition in the army crystallising on the subject of anti-Communism, as it had in 1919. Between December 1928 and January 1929 there was an outbreak of unrest among agricultural tenants and labourers in the province of Santa Fe. As rumours began to grow of Anarchist and Communist conspiracies, the government denounced the strike as the work of 'agitators', and quickly dispatched troops to the scene. It was apparent from *La Epoca*'s commentaries that the government took this step to appease the army. The episode may be seen as a minor parallel to the Patagonia affair of 1921–2. A peripheral labour issue, of little importance at the political centre, was exploited as a means to divert the army's attention, and buttress its confidence in the government.[9]

[6] *La Vanguardia*, 27 September 1923.

[7] Cf. Ibid. 22 February 1928; also Potash, pp. 29–54; Marvin Goldwert, 'The rise of modern militarism in Argentina', *Hispanic American Historical Review*, Vol. 48, No. 2 (May 1968), p. 199, *passim.*

[8] Ibid. *La Vanguardia* on 12 January 1929 cited five cases where the beneficiaries of promotion had been retired since 1923 and were given six years back pay.

[9] Cf. *La Vanguardia*, 5 December 1928; *La Epoca*, 23 January 1929. For a further account of the strike see Carl Solberg, 'Agrarian unrest and agrarian policy in Argentina, 1912–30', *Journal of Inter-American Studies and World Affairs*, Vol. 13 (January 1971), pp. 15–55.

Also the new government did not attempt to revive Yrigoyen's old labour policies in Buenos Aires. Here Yrigoyen had obviously learned his lesson from the events of 1919. Instead of providing open government support for the unions, the aim of maintaining control over the working class vote was again entrusted to the committees.

This can be clearly seen in the case of the maritime workers' union, the F.O.M., with which Yrigoyen had the closest personal contact before 1922. During the greater part of his first administration, relations between the F.O.M. and the Radical committee in the Boca had been very poor. Each had been competing against the other for support in the neighbourhood. After the Semana Trágica, for example, the leaders of the F.O.M. accused the members of the committee of having taken part in the repression. Nicolas Selén, the local committee leader, replied in kind by calling the union a 'soviet'.[10] However, ten years later relations between the two had become very close. Selén, who was now a national deputy, had come to regard the F.O.M. as his chief ally in the neighbourhood. In October 1928, there was a short-lived strike in the port against the coastal shipping companies. Selén immediately took the men's side and accused the coastal shipping companies of having financed the Anti-personalist campaign during the presidential elections.

In 1928 Selén also complained about the 'foreign loyalties' of the shipping companies, and their refusal to consider 'the Argentine working man'.[11] Criticisms in these precise terms had been something of a rarity before 1922. They illustrated the new nationalist elements with which *yrigoyenismo* had become impregnated during Alvear's period. Support like this enabled the F.O.M. to reestablish its old influence in the port zone. Although its old secretary, Francisco García, died in March 1930, the union continued to support the government strongly.[12]

The same was true of the other important group during Yrigoyen's

[10] Cf. *La Organización Obrera*, February, March 1919.

[11] *La Epoca*, 7 October 1928.

[12] A former member of the union at this time, José Otero, whom I interviewed in 1969, pointed out that the union was closed after the *coup d'état* in 1930. When the men sent a delegation to the new minister of the interior, Matías Sánchez Sorondo, he asked them why they had supported Yrigoyen in the past. In Otero's words the men replied, 'When the conservatives practise the same policies, the workers will give them their votes.' This illustrated that the collaborationist instinct among the unions did not entirely die after 1921, and that there were many union leaders prepared to exchange favours and benefits with whatever government came to power. This may prove to be one of the key elements in the background to the rise of Peronism in the 1940s.

first presidency, the railway workers. Here the committee structure, which had emerged during the election campaign, maintained its importance. The most Yrigoyen was prepared to do was to have occasional meetings with La Fraternidad and with the Unión Ferroviaria. He avoided any temptation to become embroiled in any of the minor strikes which occurred, being quite happy to rest on his past record in this respect. The advantage of using a committee system was clear enough. The government escaped the stigma of being identified with the 'agitators'. Also the support of the committees was generally too weak an instrument to force through higher wages. Thus the government was able to avoid having to commit itself to supporting, or acting to support, the type of benefits to the workers that foreign capital was likely to oppose.[13]

Accompanying this was the positive active support given to British interests. Although there were still some disputes over the old questions of freight and passenger rates on the railways and the tramways, generally relations with the British were much better than they had been before. By 1929 it was common for *La Epoca* to praise the British, who frequently reciprocated.

Underpinning the new relationship were the provisions of the D'Abernon Missions of 1929.[14] This was a British trade delegation sent to Argentina to seek means of combating American competition and reducing Britain's trade deficit with Argentina. During the negotiations the Argentine government made a number of important concessions. Arrangements were made for the free import of large amounts of railway material for the State Railways. There were also concessions to the British in the textile field, the most notable being a reduction of duties on silk.[15] A

[13] The American ambassador in Buenos Aires, Robert Woods Bliss, semi-accurately described Yrigoyen in the following terms in 1929: 'He can be compared to an old Tammany Hall politician, favourable to the masses and the laboring classes, but who gives communism a free rein.' (Quoted in Roberto Etchepareborda, 'Breves anotaciones sobre la revolución del 6 de septiembre de 1930,' *Investigaciones y Ensayos*, No. 8 (January–June 1970), p. 57. My re-translation.)

[14] At first, in view of events ten years previously, the British were rather wary of Yrigoyen, but within a short time they began to support him. Referring to the D'Abernon Mission on 6 September 1929, the *Review of the River Plate* declared: 'It is interesting to place on record the fact that the Chief of the Mission, Viscount D'Abernon, has maintained a very close and sympathetic contact with the President of the Republic.'

[15] Gravil. There is also a long unpublished study of the D'Abernon Mission by A. O'Connell, which provides a detailed account of the negotiations; also *Review of the River Plate*, 22 November 1929.

little later another carrot held before the British was for the import of oil refinery equipment.[16]

In 1929 Yrigoyen's position had thus become highly conservative in the areas where, after 1916, it had been most progressive. The government's overall strategy in 1929 was to add to or conserve its mass following so far as it could through patronage, and to neutralise the pressure groups by pursuing other policies broadly in accordance with their interests. The aim was to prevent a situation emerging like that in 1919, and pave the way for the government's chief objective, the oil legislation.

Any immediate hope the government had of securing this in 1929 was frustrated by its weakness in the National Senate. Although in 1928 the *yrigoyenistas* had won a great victory at the polls, they were still in a minority in the Senate. The interior provinces had frequently elected non-*yrigoyenistas* during the Alvear period, and former Radicals in the Senate from Yrigoyen's first administration had, by and large, joined the Antipersonalists. The result was that when the oil legislation reached the Senate in September 1929, by a majority verdict it simply refused to consider it.[17]

The government's most pressing need in 1929 was thus to gain control over the Senate. This meant, as in the past, control over the provinces, and the only way of doing this was to dislodge the opposition parties by federal interventions. From here it would be possible to create client administrations which, in areas where there were senatorial elections pending, would send pliant representatives to the National Senate. In 1928 and 1929 the new government therefore took over by decree the provinces of San Juan, Mendoza, Corrientes and Santa Fe.

This brought about a sudden intensification of the old regional disputes which had reappeared at various junctures during Yrigoyen's first administration. The oil issue, federal interventions and the conflict between the government and the Senate were all part of the wider issue of the relations between Buenos Aires and the rest of the provinces, and episodes in a much longer historical tradition of regional squabbles for control over the country's natural resources. Besides marking the first signs of popular economic nationalism in Argentina, the oil issue was also important in the sense of regional and class struggles for control of the country's natural resources. Either the oil would be used to buttress the position of the interior landowning oligarchy, or for the benefit of

[16] Cf. *La Vanguardia*, 25 January 1930.

[17] *La Epoca*, 28 September 1929.

the dependent middle class groups in the city of Buenos Aires. The interior provinces recognised that unless they could stem the federal interventions, the middle class *yrigoyenistas* in the urban coastal regions would gain control over the Senate and use this to appropriate what they regarded as their private resources.

The matter came to a head in the middle of 1929. In 1928 the provinces of San Juan and Mendoza elected senators from the local anti-*yrigoyenista* parties. From San Juan came the leader of the provincial party, *cantonismo*, Federico Cantoni himself, together with a colleague, Carlos Porto. Carlos Wáshington Lencinas was elected for Mendoza. He was similarly the leader of a family-dominated local populist faction, *lencinismo*.

Cantonismo and *lencinismo* were movements of some importance in the late 1920s. They were both local reincarnations of the type of populist alliance originally embodied by Radicalism itself. They were led by large landowners, who recruited their popular support among tenant smallholders, and among the commercial and artisan middle classes of the towns. Originally both these local parties had been part of the Radical coalition. They had seceded from it around 1918, when Yrigoyen began to use federal intervention, and his control over central government finance, to create local carpet-bagger regimes in the interior, which in turn were exploited for the benefit of the urban consumer groups in Buenos Aires. The local interests most affected by this were the wine-producers of Mendoza and San Juan, and the sugar producers of the northern provinces, Salta, Jujuy and Tucumán. Unlike in Mendoza and San Juan, however, the northern provinces were unable to create local political parties with popular support. What conspired against the emergence of politics here was the lesser importance of the smallholder element in the sugar plantation economy.[18]

[18] Carlos Wáshington Lencinas belonged to the second generation of the ruling family dynasty in Mendoza. This had been founded by his father, José Néstor Lencinas, who died in 1919. For an account of his career see Dardo Olguin, *Lencinas, El caudillo radical. Historia y mito* (Vendimiador, Mendoza, 1961). The sugar issue is largely explained in several works by Benjamín Villafañe. Cantoni's point of view can be found in the debates in 1929. One other interesting angle to this problem is the support for the interior provinces in 1929 by the northern river provinces, Corrientes and Entre Rios. One of the reasons for resentments against Yrigoyen here was on account of his support for the F.O.M. Whenever the coastal shipping trade was brought to a halt by a strike in the port of Buenos Aires, the river provinces were left practically isolated. On occasion this provoked bitter complaints in the National Congress from members for the two provinces. (Cf. Alberto Méndez Casariego, *Diario de Sesiones*, Cámara de Diputados, Vol. 5, 1920.)

What made the populist movements of San Juan and Mendoza important in 1929 was that the *yrigoyenistas* needed to control these two provinces in order to control the National Senate. They therefore determined to prevent Cantoni and the others from taking their seats by impugning the legality of their elections. In July 1929, there was a marathon debate in the National Senate, where the whole matter was formally disputed.[19] Superficially the issue was election procedures, but the real questions were political supremacy in regional and class terms. The ultimate issue was who would control the oil: the urban middle classes of Buenos Aires, or the landed groups of the interior.

Cantoni, who emerged as the main spokesman for the interior, had important allies from among other anti-*yrigoyenista* groups of various kinds. He was supported by most of the local conservative parties in the provinces of the interior, and by the Antipersonalist factions based on Santa Fe and other pampas provinces. In the federal capital itself he had the support of the increasingly influential Independent Socialist Party. Finally he also obtained support from some minority extremist Rightist groups, which had appeared during Alvear's period from the residues of the Patriotic League and similar movements of less importance.[20]

The Cantoni debates led to a growing climate of violence in Buenos Aires in the second half of 1929. Among the *yrigoyenistas* a para-military shock-troop organisation appeared in July known as the Klan Radical. The Klan was an expression of the darker side of Radicalism. It was not the first organisation of this sort. During the struggles with the party dissidents in 1918 and 1919 the press in Buenos Aires had made frequent references to a 'presidential praetorian guard'. This, it alleged, was composed of State employees, recruited from the committees, and petty criminals who had been in receipt of presidential pardons from prison sentences. Under normal circumstances in the past, this task force had merely acted to disrupt the election meetings of the government's opponents, but in moments of stress, such as during the Armistice period, guns were frequently in evidence.

The Klan Radical in 1929 was an offshoot of these earlier movements. It was apparently organised by a group of *yrigoyenista* congressmen with direct contacts with the party committees in the city of Buenos Aires. Among its exploits were attacks on the government's opponents

[19] For the Cantoni debates see *Diario de Sesiones*, Senadores, Vol. 1, 1929.

[20] See Marysa Navarro Gerassi, *Los nacionalistas* (Jorge Alvarez, Buenos Aires, 1969), pp. 37–54.

in the streets outside the Congress building, and in December the assassination of Carlos Wáshington Lencinas.

The Rightist groups replied by founding their own organisation in October, the Republican League (Liga Republicana). Armed skirmishes between the two sides became frequent. The Republican League was an openly authoritarian organisation. On 14 October 1929, it issued a manifesto, which made apparent its opposition to the whole concept and practice of representative government: 'The Republican League proclaims that no accidental plebiscite [i.e. the elections of 1928] confers the right of acting against the nation, and that majorities are only worthy of respect, when they elect well. There is a right above that of the citizens and the parties, which is the right of the republic to be well governed.'[21]

In spite of the growing intensity of this struggle, at this point towards the end of 1929 there was little doubt that the *yrigoyenistas* were winning. In August they finally triumphed in the Senate debates. Cantoni and his supporters were not allowed to take their seats. In the street skirmishes in Buenos Aires the Klan Radical was generally victorious, and seemed likely to remain so.

Notwithstanding the violence and the atmosphere of acute tension this struggle brought, in 1929 there was a notable absence of the specific conditions which had made 1919 such a critical moment for the Radical government. In the army the groups supporting a *coup d'état* were still practically isolated. They had neither elite nor popular support.[22] The elite groups themselves were being played off by means of the D'Abernon Mission and the announcements of new agreements with the British. The extreme Rightist groups thus failed to acquire the influence they had developed in 1919. Unlike the Patriotic League, the Republican League had no popular support. Nor was there, at this point at least, any of the

[21] *La Vanguardia*, 15 October 1929.

[22] Both General Justo and General Uriburu were looking for the opportunity to organise a *coup* in 1929, but were unable to do so because the government still enjoyed considerable popular support. The two main authorities on the subject, Potash and Goldwert, concur in relating the *coup* exclusively to 1930. Potash has written (p. 42); 'As a politico-military operation this *coup* was the product of a prolonged period of exploratory talks, a three-month organising effort, and a high degree of last minute improvisation.' This is also supported by the classic account of the revolution, José María Sarobe, *Memorias sobre la revolución del 6 de septiembre de 1930* (Gure, Buenos Aires, 1957). My own point about this is that Uriburu could not act without Justo, and Justo could not either without the support of the landed groups and evidence of widespread popular opposition to the government. Both these conditions were only met in 1930.

talk in the press of 'two governments', which had apppeared in 1919 as Yrigoyen had gradually found his authority slipping away. Although the *Review of the River Plate* saw some evidence of disappointment among the 'vast army of place-seekers, whose admiration and adulation of the Chief Magistrate is not altogether free of the taint of cupboard love', in 1929 there were no defections *en masse* among Yrigoyen's supporters from the previous year.[23] If at times it seemed that patronage was not stretching as far as they would have wished, its skilful application still held the *yrigoyenistas* together.

The great difference between 1919 and 1929 was thus that the emergence of a serious political crisis did not deprive the government of its middle class support. Nor did it trigger the conservative pressure group interests into a united action against the government. This was clearly apparent in the remarks made by the *Review of the River Plate* in October 1929. The *Review* described events as 'significant of nothing more serious than a superficial political turbulence', and defending Yrigoyen from the charge that he had become a 'dictator', declared:

> On what really transcendent national issue the president has played the part of a dictator is not quite apparent, and measured by the comparison with the role of the heads of certain European and Latin American governments . . . his conduct of the affairs of the nation has led to no revolutionary changes in the institutional or political order of events which strikingly affect the social, economic and juridical order of the national life or the republic's relationship with the rest of the world . . . Whatever foundation there may be in the charges of extralimitation of powers which have been levelled against the president, the fact remains that the practical consequences have not been such as to harm the average citizen or businessman. The social order continues undisturbed, and the economic life of the republic has continued in its normal channel. The executives of important commercial and industrial organisations who have had occasion to confer with the president in matters of trade and transport have gone out of their way to give public expression to their sentiments of admiration for His Excellency's obvious ambition to encourage every kind of enterprise conducive to the economic well-being and prosperity of the republic.[24]

In the last three months of 1929 the government had begun to move with great determination towards its second phase of organising new elections in the provinces it had taken over by decree. At that moment it seemed that it had weathered the storm and would be able to make a fresh start with the oil legislation in the congressional sessions of 1930.

[23] *Review of the River Plate*, 10 October 1929.
[24] Ibid.

Depression and revolution

At this precise moment, on the heels of the Wall Street Crash in October 1929, the Great Depression began to make its effects apparent in Argentina. It had been presaged by a growing deficit in the country's balance of payments during 1929. This reflected the drop in agricultural prices on the world market over the year and the slowing down of exports. It also reflected a situation where American funds, which had upheld the balance of payments for the past several years, had gradually moved back to the United States itself in response to speculative opportunities. The fall-off in Argentina's exports was thus accompanied by a drying-up of the investment funds flowing into the country.

The first really critical moment came towards the end of the year, when a combination of adverse climatic conditions and a gloomy outlook among the farming community caused the harvest to fail. The first discernible effect of this was on the urban labour market linked with the external commercial sector. As late as the middle of November 1929, *La Epoca* was happily reporting that the leaders of the railway unions were paying token visits to Yrigoyen with information on the progress of their wage negotiations with the companies.[25] Within a month these negotiations had ceased completely. Instead the railway unions began to besiege members of the government with complaints of lay-offs and rising unemployment.

The advent of depression had an immediate effect on the government. Its previous self-confident approach was soon overtaken by growing hints of desperation. In what became a typically vain attempt to give the impression that it was doing something to protect the railwaymen, in December the government introduced an annual seven-day holiday with full pay on the State lines. It hoped, unavailingly, that the private companies would follow suit, and that it would get the credit.[26]

As in 1921, depression conditions also had an immediate effect on the dockers' unions in the port. Within a short time in 1930, when harvest shipments ought to have been at their height, factional squabbles were reported among the dockers for control over rapidly diminishing employment opportunities available in the port.[27] Another reflection of the impact of the crisis came when José Luis Cantilo, who in 1928

[25] *La Epoca*, 25 November 1929.

[26] Ibid. 19 December 1929. Petty gestures of this sort became a recurrent feature of 1930.

[27] *La Vanguardia*, 14 April 1930.

had been reappointed municipal intendant in Buenos Aires, began to organise supplies of cheap food and consumer goods.[28] These measures were similar to those in 1920 when attempts had been made to offset the rise in the cost of living.

Cantilo's activities in the municipal administration were a measure of the fact that the depression led not only to rising unemployment but also, in a very short time, to perceptibly rising prices. This combination of effects stemmed principally from the major step taken by the government in response to the crisis. In December 1929 it closed the Currency Conversion Board (Caja de Conversión). This meant the abandonment of peso convertibility, which had been in operation since the height of the export boom in 1927. The measure was designed to stem the outflow of gold which resulted from an adverse balance of payments while the Gold Standard was being maintained. It also allowed the Argentine peso to float on the international currency exchanges. Throughout 1930 the peso depreciated, declining on average by about 20% in terms of the dollar and the major European currencies over the year as a whole. This was one of the main sources of the inflationary trend apparent in 1930. Although the prices of agricultural goods generally fell in accordance with the contraction of the overseas market, the prices of imports were forced upwards by the rapid depreciation of the peso.

The sudden wave of inflation was also related to the closure of the Conversion Board in another important way. The system of currency convertibility in Argentina had been devised as a monetary and credit regulator. It related the balance of payments directly to internal credit conditions. Whenever an adverse balance of payments led to an outflow of gold, the volume of paper currency in circulation was designed to contract by a corresponding amount. By reducing bank reserves this would apply an automatic brake to credit and force up interest rates. Thus as soon as the gold stock declined, an automatic deflationary process would be set in motion until the balance of payments reached equilibrium.[29]

[28] Ibid. 26 January 1930; *La Epoca*, 4 July 1930. As in 1920, Cantilo's measures had little substance to them and failed to offer any solution to a situation of rising prices and rising unemployment.

[29] The workings of the Gold Standard in Argentina have been described at length in Phelps, Peters and Ford. The basic aim of deflation was to restore the balance of payments by restricting local demand for imports. If the Gold Standard were abandoned, in theory the same object would be achieved by the depreciation of the peso. This would increase the price of imports and gradually price them out of the market.

On the other hand the government's step, the abandonment of convertibility, meant the detachment of internal monetary and credit conditions from the international sector and the balance of payments. When it ended the convertibility of the peso in December 1929, one of the government's chief aims was to avoid drastic deflation and to maintain, so far as possible, economic activity and credit conditions at their pre-depression levels.

This attempt to cushion the effects of the depression was largely a failure. The collapse of the export sector triggered mounting unemployment. Secondly, by helping to maintain the level of demand, the ending of convertibility simply resulted in the acceleration of inflationary pressures. The effect of this was merely to throw the balance of payments further into disequilibrium. In the financial year 1929/30 exports declined by almost 40% in value, from 1,000 million gold pesos in 1928/9 to only 600 million the year after. There was, too, a marked decline in imports, from 1,135 million in 1928/9 to 735 million in 1929/30. But the decline in imports was insufficient to prevent a net addition to the balance of payments deficit in 1929/30 of 276 million gold pesos.[30]

In all this, however, one of the most critical aspects was that the decline in imports, again allied to local inflation, undercut the government's financial position. Government revenues underwent a swift decline as a result of the decline in customs returns from imports. But spending continued to increase for some time. In comparison with 1929, in 1930 revenues declined by about 9%, but spending increased by the same amount.[31] This reflected the government's desperate efforts to maintain its flow of patronage, and thus hold together its popular support. However, the results of the failure to cut spending were marked increases in the deficit on the government's ordinary revenues, and in consequence a rapidly rising floating debt. In 1930 there was a budget deficit of 350 million paper pesos, and the floating debt reached the astronomical level of 1,200 million paper pesos.[32]

Although government spending on this scale did help to mitigate the effects of the depression to some extent by maintaining the level of demand, its negative effects were also to be seen clearly in inflation and the deterioration of the balance of payments. Its other major effect was on the landed exporting interests. The failure of the government, and other subsidiary administrations, to cut spending, and their frantic

[30] Phelps, Table 1, p. 238.
[31] Peters, p. 155.
[32] Ibid.

search for internal finance to bridge the revenue gap, meant that interest rates and credit conditions remained extremely tight. By 1930 the value of discounted treasury bills, which the government began to issue on an increasing scale to cope with the decline in its ordinary revenues, amounted to one-third of total bank credit outstanding.[33] This had the effect of depriving the traditional major borrowers – the landed interests, linked with the external market – of access to cheap credit. It came at a moment when they were confronted with the catastrophic collapse of their prices and their markets. This had also happened to some extent during the post-war depression, and it lay at the root of the rising opposition among the landed groups to Yrigoyen's high-spending populist policies. But the crisis in 1930 was much more general and profound than it had been in 1921 and 1922.

The government recognised these dangers. Soon after the closure of the Conversion Board it sought to ease the pressure on domestic credit by attempting to transfer its debts abroad by raising external loans. At the end of 1929 it managed to acquire £5 million from Baring Brothers in London, and the following April $50 million from banks in New York.[34] But this was as much as the government managed to get from abroad. The loans were insufficient to alleviate the pressure on internal funds. They also added the further complication that, as the peso depreciated, the government's transfer of its debts abroad meant a corresponding addition to its net indebtedness. This ultimately simply increased its need for new loans, when the sources of supply were rapidly drying up. Any increase in foreign indebtedness was thus a rather dangerous course to adopt. Consequently, as time passed, the possibility loomed closer that unless the government could take steps to reduce its spending by a drastic amount, it was heading towards a default on the overseas debt.[35] What

[33] Ibid.

[34] *Review of the River Plate*, 11 April 1930. Another indicator of the seriousness of the situation came when the government was forced into borrowing from the blocked remittances of foreign companies in Buenos Aires. During depression periods, when the peso depreciated, remittances were held back in the hope of an improvement in the exchange. (Cf. Phelps, p. 122.)

[35] '... when the floating of public bonds abroad was suspended by the contraction of the international capital markets during the depression phase of the economic cycle, the payment of the debt services fell totally on current state revenues. This generally happened when revenues were falling as a result of the decline in the country's overseas commerce ... Under these circumstances the servicing of the external public debt came to absorb exorbitant proportions of current state revenues. There were obviously two ways out of this situation: vigorous cuts in public spending and investment ... or the suspension of debt payments.' (Ferrer, pp. 127–8.)

this would mean in terms of the landed interests is clear enough. From the point of view of their market and investment relationships, such a step could only be contemplated as the ultimate disaster.

Besides becoming increasingly restive over the government's financial policies, the commercial and export interests in Buenos Aires began to complain about the government's failure to check the depreciation of the peso. It was alleged that foreign purchases were being held back for speculative reasons in the hope of further depreciation, and a corresponding cheapening of Argentine products. After the attempt to stabilise the exchange position by means of the loan from New York had failed, there were demands for the reopening of the Conversion Board and the resumption of gold shipments overseas.

In swift succession the groups which had supported the government in 1929 now turned rapidly against it. For example, on 27 June, the *Review of the River Plate* declared in a discussion on the exchange and convertibility question:

> The theory that a fall in the value of the Argentine dollar would, by limiting imports and fomenting exports, offset to a certain extent the unfavourable balance of trade, is daily being proved a falsity... And the pity of it is that all the time Argentina has had, in her heavy gold stocks, a weapon strong enough and flexible enough to minimise the trouble.[36]

There is in these financial and economic issues one of the major keys to the revolution of 1930. In 1930, as opposed to the final year of prosperity in 1929, *yrigoyenismo* had become a major threat to the landed and commercial interests. The government failed to act on the exchange question, it became a major competitor for credit, and it was thought to be increasing the burden of the country's external indebtedness to breaking point. These conditions united the main institutions among the landed and exporting interests against it. In a joint memorandum on the 25th of August, 1930, the Sociedad Rural, the Unión Industrial and the Bolsa de Cereales demanded firm steps to reduce public spending, and to end the depreciation of the peso by reopening the Conversion Board. From here it was only a short step to a military *coup d'état*. Once the disaffected groups in the army had the support of the major economic interest groups, they were able to act.[37]

[36] For further commentaries on the exchange problem see *Review of the River Plate*, 14 February, 18 April, 20 June, 29 August 1930.

[37] I have made no effort here to make a complete analysis of the *coup* from the point of view of the elite groups. The *coup* involves three central groups. These are the army, the landed interests and foreign capital. In the army there was the division between the 'corporatists' led by General Uriburu and the 'liberals' led by General

The collapse of middle class support

At the same time their opportunities of doing so were assisted by another vital factor, the effect of the depression on the urban middle class groups. This destroyed Yrigoyen's popular support completely. In 1929 the government's position in Buenos Aires largely depended on its ability to maintain its popular support by the use of the bureaucracy and political patronage. Its whole system of control depended upon a continuing ability to spend. However, early in 1930, alive to the growing threat from the landed interests, and in a desperate attempt to reduce the floating debt, it gradually began to slow down its spending. At the beginning at least, it was not so much that spending actually declined, indeed it continued to increase, but the rate of increase was insufficient to uphold the patronage structure.

The government was unable to expand its protective umbrella over the middle class groups fast enough to keep pace with the sudden expansion of demand for it which developed in parallel with the depression and rising unemployment. As a result the whole structure through which it maintained its popular support became undermined. The key aspect of this was the sudden erosion of the links between the government and party committees brought about by the depression. As the party itself was thrown completely out of gear, the way was left open for the opposition parties to make a concerted effort to attack and usurp the government's popular support.

The first signs of this came early in 1930 when the *yrigoyenistas* in Congress and in the key organs of the party began to complain that the salaries of administrative personnel were not being paid punctually, and that vacancies were not being filled at a rate fast enough to cope with increasing pressure within the party for relief from the

Footnote 37 (continued)

Justo. The latter's main links (as his presidency revealed), were with the elite cattle fatteners, the *invernadores*. Since this group was directly dependent upon the U.S. owned frigorificos, it has been suggested that this may explain the pro-American oil policy of both Justo's and Uriburu's governments. I would suspect, however, that this policy was also adopted with a view to winning political support in the interior, among the groups which had supported Standard Oil in the 1920s. On the other hand, to judge from the *Review of the River Plate*, the British were not entirely happy with the *coup*, because it threatened to deprive them of the D'Abernon agreement. In comparison with 1919, foreign capital appears to have had a much lesser role as a prime mover in generating opposition to the government. This reflects the different character of the two crises.

depression.[38] Later in the year the government ceased attempting to maintain even its past level of expenditure, and began instead to reduce it. This was followed by attempts to lay off members of the administration. Immediately *yrigoyenista* members of Congress began to table motions calling for legislative guarantees to ensure that their own clientele would not be dismissed from their positions.[39]

By the time of the congressional elections in March 1930, the *yrigoyenistas* were already completely demoralised. The *Review of the River Plate* commented:

> The principal feature of the electoral campaign has been the divergencies between the representatives of the official party, (adherents of President Irigoyen), all over the country, and, judging from present appearances, in very few provinces is a united front being shown to the opposition. In the Federal Capital, the Irigoyenists are undoubtedly very strong, although their prestige has been weakened recently by the departure from the proverbial Irigoyenist policy contained in the phrase 'Del Gobierno a casa'. Both in the Capital and in the province of Buenos Aires the outgoing Deputies have been renominated almost en bloc, which has caused much dissatisfaction among the electorate, many of the leading men in the local 'Comites' having been paid for their loyalty of many years by promises of a National Deputyship ... which promises have proved to be the pie-crust variety, the result being that their numerous adherents are very annoyed about it and in most of the districts two distinct factions in the party have arisen, described respectively as the 'Re-electionists' and the 'Anti-reelectionists', and there is quite a lot of talk of the latter showing their spleen by voting in blank.[40]

Although divisions like this had often occurred in the past, as different factions struggled for preferential access to the sources of patronage, the *yrigoyenistas* had always managed to resolve their differences sufficiently to organise an efficient campaign. There was generally room for the spoils of office and the flow of patronage to be distributed in an equitable fashion, or at least a sufficient number of plausible promises could be made to create a united front. But in 1930 the *yrigoyenistas* prepared for the election weakly and half-heartedly. In the federal capital the party committees failed to mobilise with anything like their customary energy. Throughout the campaign there were unseemly squabbles among and against the ward bosses. Factions within the committees

[38] Cf. *La Vanguardia*, 27 March 1930, *passim*.
[39] Ibid. 1 August 1930.
[40] *Review of the River Plate*, 28 February 1930.

accused them of making 'prearranged deals' over the candidatures, and there were charges that the committees had become 'feudal territories under the monopoly of a single group or person'.[41] All this reflected the increased demands placed on the ward boss committee structure as a result of crippling depression conditions and the despairing efforts being made to hold on to contacts in the government. But as the depression deepened, incomes were eroded by inflation, and unemployment grew, the number of disaffected groups within the party multiplied.

The result of the election in the federal capital was a crushing defeat for the *yrigoyenistas* at the hands of the Independent Socialists. Comparing the election results of 1930 with those of 1928, in the federal capital the vote for the *yrigoyenistas* declined from 152,000 to 83,000. In 1928 their nearest rivals in the capital were the Antipersonalists, who won 60,000 votes. In 1930, however, the Independent Socialists polled 109,000. The *yrigoyenistas* also lost their working class support. The old Socialist Party did very well in working class zones of the city. Here their vote increased from 14,000 in 1928 to 36,000 in 1930, while that of the *yrigoyenistas* declined from 51,000 to 29,000.[42] In the province of Buenos Aires the story was much the same. In 1928 Yrigoyen polled 217,000 votes and in 1930 only 171,000. The Conservative Party of Buenos Aires increased its vote from 73,000 to 154,000. Similar oscillations were also apparent in Córdoba and Santa Fe.

However, the interesting thing about this was that the decline in the *yrigoyenista* vote was much less in the interior provinces, where there were fewer links with the major export sector and where, consequently, the effects of the depression were less marked. In Mendoza, for example, where the great political battle had been fought with the *lencinistas* in 1929, the decline in the *yrigoyenista* vote was from 27,000 in 1928 to 24,000 in 1930. In Salta it was from 20,000 to 17,000 and in Santiago del Estero from 27,000 to 23,000. Overall, the greater distance away from the federal capital, the less was the swing away from the *yrigoyenistas* in 1930. Some of this may be accounted for by corrupt electioneering in the more remote and backward areas. Even so these very marked regional differences suggest clearly that the *yrigoyenistas* lost support in 1930 more as a result of the impact of the depression than because of the political struggles of 1929.

[41] *La Vanguardia*, 16 March 1930.

[42] The figures relating to the working class vote were pointed out to me by Dr Ezequiel Gallo. They are confirmed by my own calculations shown in Appendix 4.

This election turned the tables completely on events in 1929. As soon as the results became known, there were further outbursts of dissatisfaction among the middle level and rank and file *yrigoyenistas*. For the first time in his political career Yrigoyen himself became a target for attack among the middle class groups in the committees. He was accused of having 'failed to help' the party during the election, of favouring 'alien elements', and surrounding himself with a 'new group'. Again this reflected the importance of the patronage link in the government's popular support.[43]

For the first time, also, Yrigoyen's party supporters began to express disquiet at the state of his health. It became customary to attribute the party's misfortunes to his failure to control disputes in the cabinet. However, the situation here was the same as that in the party at large. Different members of the cabinet, González, Oyhanarte and the vice-president, Enrique Martínez, who before had controlled their own expanding subsidiary patronage empires, were now, as a means to protect their own positions, forced into competition with each other for shares in an increasingly restricted State budget.[44] Similar situations were apparent elsewhere in the provinces. In May 1930, the outgoing governor of the province of Buenos Aires, Valentín Vergara, was also attacked by rank and file members of his own party for his parsimony in the distribution of public offices.[45]

This point requires some emphasis, since many accounts of the revolution of 1930 have instanced Yrigoyen's alleged senility as the main reason for the collapse of the government's popular support. It is a view not borne out by the balance of the evidence. During the critical period of 1930, Yrigoyen appeared in public probably more frequently than at any time in his past career. A notable occasion was on 9 July when, breaking with his past habits completely, he conducted a state banquet in Government House for over 400 senior military officers. Later he sent personally a long telegram of congratulations to the army for its efforts during the ninth of July parades.[46] This illustrated his awareness of the dangerous spread of disaffection in military circles.

The difficulty with an interpretation which adopts Yrigoyen himself as the central pivot in events, is that it tends to transform him from

[43] *La Epoca*, 24 May 1930.
[44] This is described in full in Ethchepareborda, 'Breves anotaciones'.
[45] *La Vanguardia*, 4 May 1930.
[46] Ibid. 4 August 1930.

'the wise old leader' of 1928 into the 'senile old man' of 1930 with remarkable rapidity and with little concrete evidence. Nor does it provide any real insight into the collapse of party morale in 1930. Factors like corruption and internal cabinet disputes were as much a feature of earlier years as they were of 1930. On the other hand the depression clearly suggests why 'senility', 'corruption' and the collapse of party morale suddenly became important when they did.

What therefore happened in 1930 was that the depression very quickly destroyed the *yrigoyenista* party. It exposed the delicate extremes of its reliance on State patronage. Once this disappeared, the great bandwagon movement of the export boom period between 1926 and 1929 largely disintegrated. There was no way of reviving it in the midst of an economic crisis of these proportions. In a short time the depression also destroyed Yrigoyen's personal prestige and the image cultivated of him throughout the 1920s as a providential Messiah. Suddenly, in the perceptions of the population at large, he was transformed from a position of hallowed veneration into one of decrepit senility.

During the winter months of 1930 the process of political disintegration accelerated. The government's financial difficulties increased, prices continued to rise and, once the harvest shipments had been completed, unemployment increased at an even steeper rate. As the crisis deepened, the government responded with a strident propaganda campaign to conserve what support it could. Demonstrations of public employees were organised, and attempts were made to expand the Klan Radical into a shock-troop force against the opposition parties. Just before the military *coup* occurred, the government tried to win over prominent conservatives by appointing them to key posts. The day before the *coup*, for example, former President Figueroa Alcorta was appointed head of the Supreme Court.[47]

Perhaps the most interesting example of these efforts by the government to protect itself from attack in 1930 came when its old contacts with the unions were suddenly revived in August. In *La Epoca* a series of manifestos were published, most of them from the railway unions, supporting the elected government. This was an attempt to frighten the opposition groups by raising the old spectre of 1919 of an alliance between the government and the workers. But in 1930 the unions were even less in a position to revolt either in favour of the govern-

[47] *La Epoca*, 5 September 1930.

ment, or for any other reason, than they had been eleven years before. When the *coup* came there was little or no reaction among the working class.[48] Neither the unions nor the workers supported the government sufficiently to rise up in its defence. Nor, with the crippling effects of the depression making its mark on them, had they the means of doing so.

In the critical weeks before the *coup* on 6 September it was again repeatedly evident how important the depression had been in crystallising opposition against the government. Bands of students began to organise violent demonstrations in the streets of Buenos Aires. As a group vitally interested in the opportunities offered by the expansion of State patronage, they had been in the past among the government's principal supporters. The opposition parties also made as much as they could from the depression. An example is the following extract from the preamble to a manifesto issued on 15 August by the Rightist parties and by the Independent Socialists:

> [Considering] that public revenues are being dissipated at the president's caprice and the electoral conveniences of the governing party, at the very moment when these revenues are declining and the tax-payer is undergoing other tribulations as a result of the worsening of the economic situation.
>
> ... that while the country is experiencing increasing difficulties in selling its products abroad, the executive, with inexplicable negligence, has abandoned any pretence of an agricultural policy.
>
> ... that in addition to the institutional crisis there is a grave economic crisis, the result of the depreciation of our money and a complete lack of any positive action by the government.[49]

[48] Diego Abad de Santillán, 'El movimiento obrero argentino ante el golpe de estado del 6 de septiembre de 1930', *Revista de Historia. La crisis de 1930* (Buenos Aires, 1958), pp. 123–31.

[49] 'Manifiesto de la derechas y de los socialistas independientes' (August 1930). Quoted in Sarobe, p. 272. Some years after the *coup d'état* Yrigoyen's vice-president, Enrique Martínez, declared: 'The economic crisis was the great factor which made the revolution possible... Those who instance purely political causes or matters of personal standing ought to be reminded of the country's situation [in 1930]. The value of our money had been eroded by depreciation, the cereals had been left in the soil, misery was knocking at the door of every household. History teaches us that poverty among the people is the worst enemy of the stability of governments' (Quoted in Etchepareborda, 'Breves anotaciones', p. 82.) I would also agree broadly with the following statement by Ricardo M. Ortiz: 'The revolution of September 1930 adapted Argentina to the world crisis, whose effects had begun to be more

The military *coup* of 1930 thus involved two major processes, the alienation of the conservative exporting interests and the power groups among them like the army, and the government's sudden loss of popular support. The evidence seems clear enough that the great factor underlying them both was the economic depression. What 'conservatism' had come to demand in 1930 was a position of political flexibility and direct control over the State to protect its economic interests. During periods of export boom and economic expansion the elite groups could delegate their political power to a coalition movement embracing sections of the urban population like Radicalism. Under depression conditions, by contrast – as to some extent the post-war period between 1921 and 1924 had already shown – the objective supports of the alliance immediately dwindled. A zero-sum situation appeared where one group or the other was forced into making economic sacrifices.

The differences between the post-war depression and the events of 1930 obviously lay in the degree of severity of the two crises. In 1930 the government, having cultivated expectations to such a high degree, found it impossible to devise a means of distributing the sacrifices made necessary by economic contraction. Its attempts to do so merely led to the rapid growth of opposition on every side. Thus, like Alvear before him, Yrigoyen forfeited his control over the urban party organisation, which was the main buttress for his popular support. The situation which had momentarily appeared in 1919 repeated itself, but in a much more emphatic form, and the conservatives and the urban middle classes were able to unite for long enough to overthrow the government.

In this paradoxical fashion the era of party political alliances between the elite and the urban middle classes, which had first begun with the foundation of the Unión Cívica in 1890, came to an abrupt halt. In spite of their support for the *coup d'état* in 1930, in the 1930s the middle classes quickly found themselves divested of access to the fruits of power they had enjoyed under Yrigoyen. For this reason they turned so quickly against General Uriburu's military government. After September 1930, State spending was rapidly and ruthlessly cut to release the pressure on domestic credit, and to prevent the country

Footnote 49 (continued)

marked during the last weeks of 1929. The revolution was not a movement directed against a ruler; it was the consequence of a crisis of structures.' (Ricardo M. Ortiz, 'Aspectos económicos de la crisis de 1930', *Revista de Historia. La crisis de 1930* p. 41.)

defaulting on its external debt. This primarily affected the dependent middle class groups. Later a currency exchange control system was introduced which penalised the urban consumer groups by raising the prices of imported goods. At the same time every possible effort was made to shore up the position of the landed groups. In later years their markets were negotiated for them, they were given liberal credits and encouraged to reduce their costs by forcing down agricultural wages. Radicalism – for many different reasons – failed to recover from the blow inflicted on it in 1930. From henceforth it became, and remained, apart from a few fleeting moments many years afterwards, a party in opposition.

CHAPTER 12

Perspectives

The revolution of 1930 revealed that if Argentina's politics had acquired certain hybrid qualities during the previous forty years, the supremacy of the landed and commercial elite of the pampas had not diminished in any substantial way. The coup swept away the impression that because of the introduction of representative government and the rise of *yrigoyenismo*, power had passed from the elite into new hands. It restored a close and identifiable relationship between economic power and formal control over the State.

Yet this is only partly the story, and it fails to reflect the central transition which had occurred during the previous forty years. In 1890 there was only one relevant political constituency, the elite itself. During the political struggles of that year segments of the elite in the Unión Cívica may be glimpsed fruitlessly attempting to prod the urban middle classes into political activism in their support. But when the crisis of the 1890s passed, stability was restored by a number of factional covenants exclusively within the elite. In 1919 by contrast, and particularly in 1930, the situation had radically changed. The elite was compelled to weigh the position of the urban middle class very carefully, and seek its support before being able to act against Yrigoyen. Had, for example, Generals Justo and Uriburu attempted to prevent Yrigoyen's reelection in 1928, they could well have been faced with a popular counter-revolution. The central importance of this period is therefore that it marked the emergence of a much wider and more complex system of politics than there had been before.

Although between 1890 and 1930 the elite remained unquestionably the dominant power factor in Argentine society, it ceased to act in a political vacuum. The transition to a plural system of politics was apparent as early as 1901 when Pellegrini was hounded from the government by popular pressure. From this time forward the elite was compelled to search for a consensual framework and for political allies if it wished to be sure of its own position, and be capable of protecting and forwarding its essential interests.

The politicisation of new groups led to the adoption of the Sáenz Peña Law in 1912. This major reform was conceived as opening the way for a coalition between the elite and the native middle class groups to restore political stability and in some part to strengthen the elite's hand in its dealings with the immigrant working class. The legislation excluded the immigrants from voting, and made no effort to liberalise and encourage naturalisation, for fear that this would allow for the growth of 'extreme' parties outside the net of conservative control. As a result less than half the potential male electorate was enfranchised. The system was constructed in such a way as to keep the workers subordinate, or at most to offer mere escape valves to hasten the decline of Anarchism. The railway strike of 1912 showed clearly where Sáenz Peña stood on the question of wages. The reform was mainly notable, therefore, for the concessions it gave to the middle classes rather than as a real attempt to get to grips with the working class problem.

It is worth noting that the changes brought about during this period were never fully reversed afterwards. Although the military coup of 1930 marked a conservative restoration, Argentine politics retained afterwards many of its new pluralist features. The coup destroyed *yrigoyenismo*, its coteries of middle class politicians and the specific relationship which had emerged between the elite and the middle class groups during the latter 1920s. But it never achieved a return to the nineteenth century. It is more accurate to say that it succeeded in pushing back the middle classes into the subordinate role Sáenz Peña's generation had intended them to play by eliminating the pivotal role they had established for themselves in the electoral system. In many ways the 1930s marked a backward adjustment in the political structure rather than a complete break with what had gone before. The 'Patriotic Fraud' of the Justo period between 1932 and 1938, when the conservatives rigged elections to uphold their grasp of the presidency, was essentially a more sordid embellishment to the system of limited and controlled participation introduced by Sáenz Peña. In some ways Justo can be seen as the practician of the 'organic' party aspired for by Pellegrini and Sáenz Peña. Both schemes implied the political integration of groups beyond the elite, but in a subordinate and restricted fashion in order to shield government decisions from any excessive penetration by outside groups. Both Sáenz Peña and Justo shared the objective of maintaining in some guise or other the political leadership of the conservative elite, while winning for it a certain degree of popular legitimacy.

The difference between Sáenz Peña and Justo was that in 1912 the elite groups could contemplate delegating control over the State to their political opponents, whereas in the 1930s they were compelled to exclude them by whatever device lay at hand. There were two main conditions which explain this. The first was that in 1912 Radicalism was opposed to the conservative elite only in a very superficial sense. Behind the competitive struggle for office, there was a great similarity of background between elite and Radical leaders and a common commitment to the further development of the established economic structure. The second condition was that during periods of economic expansion the interests of the elite groups and the urban middle classes were compatible enough for a feasible political alliance to be developed between them, and the middle classes admitted into a degree of power-sharing. Neither of these conditions obtained in the 1930s. After the changes of the mid-1920s, Radicalism tended to register and reflect elite interests less than before. Secondly, the depression of 1930 made it impossible to reconcile elite and middle class interests in the same way as before. Thus, under Justo in the 1930s, it was no longer possible to pursue Sáenz Peña's system of delegating the elite's interests to the custody of a class alliance like Radicalism.

Turning in more detail to the history of Radicalism itself, the traditional notion that the party was from the start an organ of middle class interests is clearly mistaken. Before 1924 it was largely controlled by a highly flexible managing elite of landowners. Initially in the 1890s Radicalism revived what in nineteenth-century terms was the familiar pattern of attempting to relocate power and direct control over the State in the hands of a different sub-sector of the conservative elite. Its emergence marked part of the reaction, precipitated by the depression of 1890, to the manner in which government perquisites and subsidies became on occasion the prerogatives of dominant cliques. Many of the abortive Radical rebellions before 1912 were a final flickering of the tradition of civil war through which disputes of this type within the elite were resolved in the nineteenth century.

The strength of Radicalism after 1905 derived from its ability to mobilise popular support by tailoring its appeal to a wide variety of groups in different areas. If in the course of their search for such support the Radicals failed to attract the support of one group, they would turn to its opponents. This was a reason for the veil of metaphor in which they couched their appeal. Until the late 1920s their heterogeneous base of support prevented them even from developing a party programme. A metaphysical ideology and a heavy reliance on Yrigoyen's personal popularity were employed by the Radicals as reconciliatory devices to create artificial bonds among their supporters.

Thus by 1916 Radicalism had evolved into a mass party. Soon after this the transition began in the party which eventually won a dominant role for the middle class groups against the party's original landowner leaders. The crux of the matter lay in the problem of winning elections. The continual battle for electoral majorities led to the rapid elevation of the party's local committees and their middle class leaders. The more the role of the committees expanded, the less important the party's older leaders became, and the more the conservative elite came to distrust the government. Particularly in the city of Buenos Aires, attempts by the Radicals to win the firm support of different urban sectors began to collide with the interests of the elite.

The first major area of conflict during Yrigoyen's first presidency stemmed from the administration's dealings with the working class. The government's aim was to win the working class vote and undermine the Socialist Party by changing the bargaining position of the unions during strikes. The strategy enjoyed some success during the maritime strikes of 1916 and 1917, but it failed when applied against the railway companies in 1917 and 1918. As the strikes began to threaten the interests of the exporting interests and the foreign companies, foreign and domestic business groups united to challenge the government's policy. From this emerged the National Labour Association of 1918 and the Patriotic League of 1919, and under pressure from these two associations the government was forced to abandon its policies.

It is also worth noting in parenthesis that the search for precedents for Perón's relationship with the urban working class in the 1940s has generally omitted to mention the role of the Radical government during the First World War. Both Yrigoyen and Perón sought to develop control over the working class by winning the support of the unions. The main difference between them lies in the scale of benefits each could offer. In most cases Yrigoyen was able to give no more than moral support, and consequently his relationship with the Syndicalists never became formal or institutionalised. Perón did not face an alliance like the Patriotic League with military and popular support. Since by the 1940s the old Free Trade structure had largely disintegrated, the cause of the workers could be argued to non-working class groups as offering a widening of the domestic market to help the programme of industrialisation.

Yrigoyen's involvement with the trade unions and with strikes was an illustration of the rapidly growing political importance of the working class during the early twentieth century. The history of the trade unions between 1890 and 1930 can be broken down into a number of different periods, which correspond in general to conditions in the labour market and the cycles in the export sector. Up to around 1900, coinciding with the depression phase of the 1890s, the unions were extremely weak. Between 1900 and 1910 they were strengthened by the rapid growth of the primary sector. By 1910 they were again showing signs of weakening, as increasing numbers of immigrants saturated the urban labour market. They were further weakened by the readvent of depression between 1913 and 1917. The next recovery phase was between 1917 and 1921. Here a combination of rising exports, recovery in the level of domestic production, rising employment and the redistribution of income away from the wage-earners through inflation, allowed them to attain their greatest importance before the 1940s. The post-war depression in 1921 again brought a sudden collapse. In the late 1920s there were signs of another resurgence led by the railway unions, but this was once more cut short by the Great Depression.

This period of working class history has often been regarded as homogeneous, when a single 'Anarcho–Syndicalist' movement remained dominant. However, there was a great deal of difference between Anarchism and Syndicalism. Anarchism was largely a response to frustrated mobility aspirations among European immigrants and relatively low degrees of differentiation within the urban working class. The rise of Syndicalism coincided with the emergence of larger units of production, higher levels of skill, wage differentials, and with the appearance of native-born workers, whose response to their class position was generally less radical than that of the immigrants. Syndicalism, with its emphasis on wage issues, acquired importance during a period of heavy inflation, which affected some of the previously more privileged groups. Finally, the emergence of a more open society in the 1920s when wages again began to rise, resulted in the unions yielding to some extent to cross-class assocations, such as the *yrigoyenista* railwaymen's committees.

During the war the Syndicalists undoubtedly thrived under Yrigoyen's protection. The successful port strikes of 1916 and 1917 made the F.O.M. the effective leader of the trade-union movement. Equally the sudden retraction of government support from the Syndicalists in 1921, added to the effects of the post-war depression, swiftly led to the collapse of the F.O.R.A. The wartime strikes illustrated that the Syndicalists cared a great deal about the port and railway workers, but much less about other groups such as the municipal refuse-collectors, the meat-packers and the metallurgical workers. The effects of this were dramatically illustrated during the Semana Trágica, when large segments of the working class mobilised spontaneously in a general strike. In part spontaneous mobilisation and violent action were the consequence of low levels of unionisation. The strikes were fought very differently in mid-1919 when the Syndicalists had established a wider and firmer base of support. The wider significance of the Semana Trágica was its illustration of the different levels of ideological coherence between the workers and the groups mobilised in the Patriotic League. The general strike of 1919 was more a series of disarticulated riots than a working class rebellion. The Patriot Movement by contrast, while it acted out of a false and exaggerated view of the causes of working class unrest, was a more fully organised and united action.

The sequence of events during the war also revealed that another central agent in Argentine politics before 1930 was foreign capital. Although their position came under challenge from the Americans soon afterwards, during the war period the British repeatedly showed how powerful an interest group they were in Argentina. If their relationship with the elite was not always altogether smooth – as the wartime disputes over railway freight rates, for example, showed – underneath this was a basic common interest between the two. It was illustrated in particular during the railway strikes of 1912 and 1917. In many ways the British, and their agents on the local boards of British companies, were the prime movers in the reaction to Yrigoyen's labour policy. Because of their relationship with the elite, the British were little affected by the change of government in 1916. During the war period, when they lacked the means to use their economic power directly, they were able to achieve most of their objectives by working through the framework of local politics. They capitalised freely on the xenophobia and extreme class prejudice of native Argentine society. They manipulated lobby associations like the Sociedad Rural through bodies like the National Labour Association. Finally the events of May and June 1921 showed that the British could also exert control over movements like the Patriotic League, which had considerable support outside the domestic business sectors.

After its failure with the unions, and in an effort to stem its loss of popular support to competing associations like the Patriotic League, in 1919 the Radical government turned more specifically to its relations with the middle class groups. This presaged the advent of patronage politics and the growing importance of the political 'machines' in the 1920s. From this point onwards the influence of the middle class groups in Radicalism began to increase rapidly, and from henceforth Yrigoyen's own position came to depend on his ability to maintain the support of the dependent middle classes. From this there developed the central issue of politics in the 1920s, the size and distribution of the State budget.

Considering the overall character and objectives of Radicalism, it was not unlike other conservative popular movements in Latin America. The party aimed to perpetuate itself in power in order to provide a stable system through which benefits could be awared to different social groups simultaneously. It was a party whose *raison d'être* revolved around issues of distribution rather than reform or change. In spite of their support for an improvement in the position of the working class, the Radicals were not a party of social reform. Similarly their links with middle class consumer groups prevented them from developing a commitment to industrialisation, at least until the oil issue became important in the late 1920s. Finally, because of their association with landed groups, which never completely disappeared, they were not a party of land reform. Essentially their aim lay in increasing the rate of economic growth and using the political system as a means of distributing a proportion of the economic surplus to create an organic community.

To reemphasise and further elucidate an earlier point, this period as a whole illustrated the type of conditions which allowed for a widening of the institutional structure, and favoured the growth of popular participation, and those which undermined them. The introduction of the Sáenz Peña Law and the growth of Radicalism after 1905 reflected the common adherence of the elite exporting interests and the urban consumers to an economy based on specialisation in primary exports. This common support for the Free Trade structure, which gave local industry only a secondary role, was strengthened during periods of economic growth as the dominant sectors within the middle class obtained access to the economic surplus by penetrating the bureaucracy and the urban professions.

However, while Radicalism generally thrived on growth, it rapidly crumbled and decayed during periods of stagnation or depression. It was no longer possible for the elite to buy off the middle class groups by permitting an increase in State spending. As both the 1921–4 period and 1930 illustrated, during depression periods the deflationary programme of the producer elite conflicted radically with the inflationary interests of the consumer middle class. Such conditions immediately destroyed the previous implicit alliance between them, and led to an open struggle for power.

A further interesting feature of this society was the character of its middle class. The 'dependent' features of the urban middle class first became marked around 1900. Its emergence as a coherent group coincided with the recovery of the primary sector after the depression of the 1890s and with the appearance of a new generation of upwardly mobile descendants of European immigrants. Its characteristics as a class group reflected the peculiar development of the industrial sector, and the relative absence of opportunities for larger entrepreneurs, native-born managers and senior white-collar employees in the private sector. The upper reaches of the urban middle class tended to occupy a parasitical relationship with the elite, and came to acquire some of its rentier characteristics as a result of its dependence on State spending.

The characteristics of the urban social structure underlay many of the qualitative features of politics during the Radical period. Radicalism became markedly biassed in favour of Buenos Aires against other regions as a result of its need to steer a *via media* between rural producer interests and the urban consumers. Where the two conflicted, as in 1920 or in 1929, concessions to the consumer interests were extracted from the politically less significant interior regions. Although Radicalism developed on a fully national basis, and proved itself capable of adapting to local conditions, it perpetuated and further exaggerated the hegemony of Buenos Aires over other regions.

The social structure of urban Argentina also determined the political importance of the State patronage system and the main stylistic features of the Radicals' local organisation, with its emphasis on geographical ties, and its strong bias towards the tertiary sectors. Similar influences were apparent in the type of benefits in which the committees and the ward bosses trafficked to recruit their popular followings. One reason why the Sáenz Peña Law was so frugal in its allocation of the vote was because the conservative elite had little control over urban occupations outside the bureaucracy. Although politics in Buenos Aires came to have a definite flavour of Tammany Hall, the party machines in Argentina never developed to the same comprehensive level as those in the United States in the late nineteenth century. Because the system in Argentina did not generally incorporate private employers, the most the *caudillos de barrio* could deal in was petty local charity and government offices. It was difficult to expand it into a vehicle for the assimilation and political mobilisation of the immigrants. Beyond its use for purposes of open graft, it was only capable of relatively superficial paternalist gestures, the free medical and legal centres and the famous round of *vino y empanadas* on pre-election night. It could not, for example, provide the immigrants with jobs in commerce and industry. The result was that only the dependent middle classes became fully involved in the political system.

This was also of some importance in the failure of the Socialist Party. Besides having the disadvantage of a reputation for sectarianism, after 1916 the Socialists were outmanoeuvred first by the growth of the Syndicalist unions, and then by the Radical machines. They were unable to develop coherently either as a class party or as a class alliance. The only successful Socialist group of the 1920s was the Independent Socialist Party founded in 1927. The Independent Socialists abandoned Juan B. Justo's aim of introducing social democracy along European lines, and instead swung towards the American system of the urban machine, which seemed better adapted to a society where social mobility was at a premium.

Urban politics could only begin to escape the rather narrow State-dominated patronage structure used by the Radicals through the further growth of an industrial sector. Had industry been stronger before the First World War, a more successful attempt could have been made to bring the immigrants into politics. Although the process of industrialisation still remains incomplete in Argentina, the rapid growth of an industrial economy was one of the leading features of the period after 1930. Bureaucratic populism like *yrigoyenismo* was gradually superseded by new political parties seeking power to apply impersonally directed policies favouring specific aggregate interests, rather than an individually directed system of State patronage. Nevertheless the old system has never been fully superseded, and patronage still plays a very important part in Argentine politics and in the persistence of Radicalism itself.

In most respects Argentina's first experiment with popular democracy ended in failure. Most of the problems it had aimed to solve were as apparent in 1930 as they had been twenty or thirty years earlier. Radicalism failed principally to overcome the problem of political instability. Indeed it became its first major victim in the twentieth century. Unlike similar movements elsewhere, it was unable to devise an adequate formula to reconcile the diverse groups it represented or aspired to represent. In many ways its experience recalled what has become a familiar pattern of abortive reformism in Latin American politics. It illustrated the futility of aspiring for change, or attempting to carry it out, without the necessary instruments of power to do so. The contribution made by Radicalism to the development of Argentine society was more in the nature of anticipation and precedent than performance. While it reflected the emergence of a plural social structure, it also portrayed for the first time the difficulties of applying a system of power-sharing in a society markedly biassed towards elitism and entrenched privilege. If it served temporarily to defer conflict, it could not fully overcome it.

APPENDIX 1

The occupational and class structure of the male population of the city of Buenos Aires by nationality, 1914

The third national census of 1914 contains sufficiently detailed data on occupation and nationality to make possible a number of generalisations on the social and class structure of the city's male population in 1914. There are two principal difficulties which ought to be borne in mind in these calculations. The first is that the census is frequently unreliable. For example, in the listed occupations for the province of Buenos Aires, there appear exactly 500,000 persons described as occupationally 'unspecified'. The problem does not occur on this scale in the federal capital, though there are undoubtedly some errors. The second difficulty is that the census provides no indication of the class position of each person within each occupation. This has to be done by a process of elimination, and on occasion by rather crude estimates. The principal difficulty lies in estimating the size of white-collar groups. For the industrial sector, which was on average very low-capitalised, the proportion of white-collar workers has been estimated at 15%. For the more highly capitalised transport sector, it has been estimated at 20%. Both these figures may be rather high.

At a glance the employed male population of Buenos Aires falls into six groups. At the top of the social scale were the *rentier* groups, formed mainly of urban or absentee landlords and their dependants. Next were the professional classes, civil servants, officers of the armed forces, lawyers, doctors, educators, writers and artists. Then followed the industrial and commercial proprietors, and after them the white-collar employees. Finally came the working class, divided into skilled and unskilled sectors. For purposes of simplicity and homogeneity, these six groups can be reduced to four, the *rentier* and professional groups and the different sectors of the working class being each treated as two groups. This leaves the non-working class sectors divided into three: professional men, the white-collar groups and finally the entrepreneurs.

For the federal capital in 1914 the census records a total occupied male population of 626,861. Leaving aside the professional groups, 204,566 of these were identified as employed in 'industry and manual arts', 44,282 in 'transport' and 206,028 in specifically unskilled activities. The last group was classified as *peones*, day-labourers (*jornaleros*) and unskilled manually occupied commercial employees. The sum total of this whole range of activities, which at first sight seems to be the working class, was 454,876, or 72% of the total occupied population. This figure, however, over-represents the working class, since it included the owners of industrial and commercial firms. Of these, 10,275 were recorded. It also included the white-collar workers in both industry and transport, who may be regarded as middle class. For the industrial sector the white-collar group has been calculated on the basis of 15% of 204,566, which is around 30,000, (an accurate figure would be unjustified). The transport-employed white-collar group has been calculated as 20% of 44,282, say 10,000. This gives a figure of 40,000 for the white-collar groups. Deducting the number of proprietors and the estimates made of the white-collar groups from 454,876, this decreases in size by 50,275. The size of the working class was therefore 404,601, or about 64% of the total employed population. The city's remaining employed population, the middle and upper classes, thus amounts to 36% of the total. The calculations can be summarised in tabular form as shown in Table 9.

According to Table 9, the working class represents 64% of the total male employed population, and consequently the non-working class

TABLE 9 *The estimated sizes of the working and non-working classes in the city of Buenos Aires, 1914*

(a) Total employed male population	626,861
(b) General occupational categories outside obviously middle class groups	
'Industries and Manual Arts'	204,566
'Transport'	44,282
Classified unskilled (*peones*, etc.)	206,028
Total	454,876
(c) Non-working class groups within (b)	
Proprietors	10,275
White-collar industrial personnel (i.e. 15% of 204,566)	30,000
White-collar transport personnel (i.e. 20% of 44,282)	10,000
Total	50,275
The total working class thus equals (b) minus (c) = or 64% of the total employed population	404,601

represents 36%. There would seem little doubt therefore that the working class was a majority of the city's population.

At the same time the city was divided among native Argentines and foreign residents. Among the males the latter exceeded the former by 428,871 to 394,463. These differences in nationality were reflected in the distribution of occupations and in the class structure. Of the native born males, 88,491 or 23%, were either rentiers or professional men. When native industrial proprietors and an estimate for white-collar groups are added the figure rises to about 26%. A further significant feature of the native population was that some 50,000 were employed by the state either in education or the administration. The precise figures are set out in Table 10.

The total number of employed immigrants was 428,648. Of these 149,397 were employed in industry. After deductions are made for employers and white-collar staff, the immigrant working class employed in industry may be estimated at 119,124. Applying the same methods of calculation to the transport sector, immigrant workers in this branch totalled 24,918. At the same time the census estimated a total of 167,446 unskilled immigrant workers. Thus the immigrant working class totalled 311,486, or 72% of the total immigrant population. (See Table 11.)

From Table 10 it is apparent that native workers totalled 293,871, a little less than the immigrant workers. The main difference between the two communities lay in the general absence of an immigrant group

TABLE 10 *The occupational structure of the native argentine population in the city of Buenos Aires, 1914*

Total natives employed	394,463
(a) Non-working class groups	
Rentiers, professional men, bureaucrats etc.	88,491
Industrial proprietors	2,024
White-collar industrial employees (i.e. 15% of total natives employed in industry, 55,169)	8,450
White-collar transport employees (i.e. 20% of total natives employed in transport, 13,051)	2,627
Total	101,592 or 26% of total natives employed
(b) Total natives employed in 'Public Administration' and 'Education'	50,770 or 13% of total natives employed

among the rentier and professional groups. Most immigrants, not among the working class, were proprietors of industrial and commercial firms, or white-collar employees.

The same figures may be used to construct the table for the social structure of the city, which appears in Chapter 1.

These tables support some of the observations made in the main text. Within the middle classes there was a clear specialisation of activities according to nationality. They also illustrate the size of the working class vote. Their significance lies in the fact that they can be seen to have shaped Yrigoyen's policies. Remembering it was the natives who voted, it is not surprising that the Radicals should have chosen to favour the tertiary-employed middle classes and the working class.

TABLE 11 *The class structure of the immigrant population in the City of Buenos Aires, 1914*

Total immigrants employed	428,648
(a) Total immigrants employed in industry	149,648
Industrial proprietors	7869
White-collar personnel (i.e. 15% of 149,648)	22,404
Total immigrant workers employed in industry	119,377
(b) Total immigrants employed in transport	31,147
White-collar personnel (in transport sector) (i.e. 20% of 31,147)	6,229
Total immigrant workers employed in transport	24,918
(c) Unskilled workers	167,446
Total immigrant working class: (a) plus (b) plus (c)	311,741 or 72% of employed immigrants

APPENDIX 2

The rise of Radicalism – an historiographical note

Until recently, studies of Radical populism were mainly of a superficial polemical character. There is no shortage of literature,[1] but much of it has only limited uses for historical research. This appendix contains a brief review of some of the more recent analytical works, which hopefully will allow for a clearer definition of some of the issues and controversies, and help stimulate further research and criticism.

A significant first contribution in the 1950s was the work of John J. Johnson.[2] He regarded Radicalism as the vehicle of the Argentine 'middle sectors', whose role he saw essentially as comparable with that of the middle class in Europe and the United States. The questionable assumption of this view is that it raises connotations of the 'bourgeois revolution', characteristic of industrial society. The Argentine urban middle class was not an industrialising bourgeoisie, but more a dependent appendix of the primary exporting economy. Rather than opposing agrarianism, the urban middle class supported it, mainly for reasons of consumption. Thus neither the rise of Radicalism, nor the revolution of 1930 can be interpreted, I would argue, as a struggle between industrial and rural interests. The importance of this point is that it expresses the key difference between the conventional industrial society and the pluralist primary exporting society. Contrasting economic structures have their complement in differing forms of social and political development. In Argentina the political integration of the urban middle class was achieved without any challenge to the agrarian–commercial structure.

Johnson also neglected the empirical fact that Radicalism was made up of a coalition between segments of the landed elite and the urban

[1] See the bibliography issued in 1970 by Librería Antártida in Buenos Aires, Bulletin No. 7. This contains over 800 titles.

[2] John J. Johnson, *Political Change in Latin America – the emergence of the middle sectors* (Stanford, California, 8th edn, 1967), chapter 6. See also Alfredo Galletti, *La realidad argentina en el siglo XX* (Fondo de Cultura Económica, Buenos Aires, 1961), chapter 2.

middle class groups. The notion of a structurally induced opposition between them thus becomes even less plausible. This was first pointed out in a pioneer essay by Ezequiel Gallo and Silvia Sigal.[3] Their main approach was based on the concept of 'modernisation'. The central propositions of their important and stimulating work may be summarised as follows:

(1) Radicalism represented the political component of a process of 'modernisation', developing as a result of the expansion of primary production for export in Argentina after 1870.

(2) Although the party contained certain residues from a 'traditional' past,[4] it reflected a demand for participation in politics among groups of landowners, excluded from the benefits of power under Roca and his successors, in coalition with similarly mobilised groups within the new middle classes. The party was the product of a reaction to the oligarchy's system of reserved political privileges. Its leadership was controlled by landowners, and not, as in the case of many of the major European middle class parties, by an industrialising bourgeoisie.

(3) It was found that a statistically significant proportion of Radical voters in 1916 was concentrated in areas of high European immigration, high urbanisation and high literacy, these variables being adopted as the basic criteria for 'modernisation'. The party's election supporters were thus concentrated among 'modern' groups.

(4) In spite of a certain regional bias towards the developed coastal regions (Buenos Aires, Entre Rios, Santa Fe, Córdoba), the party inaugurated political life at a fully national level, this being another of its 'modern' characteristics. Particularism and parochialism, which had figured strongly in traditional politics, declined.

The importance of Gallo's and Miss Sigal's study lay in what they said about the development of Radicalism rather than in their contribution to modernisation theory. I personally have not found the concept of modernisation a very useful one. It appears to lead to a definition of the party as an agent of political *modernisation* (i.e. its capacity to respond

[3] 'La formación de los partidos políticos contemporáneos – La U.C.R. (1891–1916)', in Torcuato S. Di Tella *et alia*, *Argentina, sociedad de masas* pp. 124–76.

[4] In their treatment of 'modernisation' the authors accepted the position taken by Gabriel Almond in his introduction to Gabriel Almond and James S. Coleman (eds.), *The Politics of the Developing Areas* (Princeton University Press, 1960). This view abandons any notion of a simple progression to any constant or unilateral standard, insisting instead on the need for a dualistic, bipolar approach, which would accept the retention of 'traditional' residues within a modernising situation.

to the demands of a newly emergent middle class for political participation by means of representative government), led by members of the *traditional* elite, and motivated by and invoking both *traditional* and *modern* values and interests (i.e. a metaphysically and ethically based ideology directed towards the secular objectives of power redistribution). This yields a somewhat confusing picture, which reflects the inherent difficulties of applying the Tradition–Modernisation dichotomy, even in its 'dualistic' revised form, to Argentine conditions.[5]

Any full critique of modernisation would go much further than this. Standards of this sort, when applied to Latin America, frequently involve certain questionable suppositions. They tend to neglect the essential feature of Latin American development, which sets the region apart from the industrial West – the type of external economic links within the region upon which social and political superstructures rest.[6] Gallo's and Miss Sigal's approach fail to capture this because on the whole they adopt socio-cultural criteria of modernisation (e.g. education and nationality). It would also seem open to question whether any such dichotomous scheme is valid at all on the pampean region of Argentina. This was a new settlement, frontier society with very little of the traditional community.

Gallo's and Miss Sigal's contribution did, however, make clear that the party subsisted as a coalition of groups, embracing not only the middle classes, but also members of the established landowning class. They also provided a valuable hypothesis for the politicisation of the urban middle classes after 1890. They suggested that control over the State apparatus became a mass issue owing to the interest on the part of the new middle classes in gaining access to government patronage and administrative jobs. The aim of the Radicals was not so much revolu-

[5] Consider the ambiguities of the following statement made by Gallo and Miss Sigal: 'If we have concentrated so much on the analysis of the "Generation of 1880" (i.e. the oligarchy), it is because the Unión Cívica Radical can be seen analytically as a second component – reaction and complement – to this movement. Up to a certain point, Radicalism completes on a political plane [the country's] assimilation to the European model: here it is "modern" where the "1880 elite" was "traditional". On the other hand in the economic sphere – always with the limit being set at 1916 – the silence of the Unión Cívica Radical in the face of key problems of the economic process and its reaction of a "moral indignation" type suggests a traditional affiliation.'

[6] For an introduction to the main lines of criticism see Rodolfo Stavenhagen, 'Seven erroneous theses about Latin America', in Irving Louis Horowitz, Josué de Castro, John Gerassi (eds.), *Latin American Radicalism: a documentary report on left and nationalist movements* (London, Jonathan Cape, 1969), pp. 102–7.

tion, in the sense of the classic European bourgeois revolution, but redistribution in a regional sense among the landowning groups, and in an inter-class sense between the elite and urban middle class groups. While the party reflected conflicts within the landowning groups over the apportionment of the benefits to be gained through links with foreign capital (communications, mortgage conditions etc), it represented, too, the challenge of the urban groups against the monopoly of political control enjoyed traditionally by the conservative elite. This is largely the view adopted in this book.

In more detail, Gallo and Miss Sigal also attempted to show, from regional voting data in the province of Santa Fe in 1912, the extent to which the Radical vote was tied to indices of modernisation, defined by standards of literacy, urbanisation, and immigrant background. They divided the province into three areas, the backward north, the newly developing south, and the older, developed centre. Three political parties took part in the election of 1912: the U.C.R., the Liga del Sur (led by Lisandro de la Torre), and the conservatives. They obtained the following results on the basis of an indexed measurement of modernisation:

Santa Fe Provincial Election 1912

Region	*Modernisation Index*	*U.C.R.*	*L.D.S.*	*C.*
		% of votes in favour		
South	3.348	30.3	43.4	26.3
Centre	6.158	62.0	9.6	28.7
North	7.855	57.0	—	40.4

The authors observed from this that the Radical (U.C.R.) vote was highest where modernisation levels were highest; by the same token the conservative vote was lowest in the same more modern areas, and highest in the least modern regions. However, the difference between the U.C.R. and the Liga del Sur was also, they held, explicable in modernisation terms. The centre was an area of older immigration compared with the south. While in the south there was a large and increasing number of foreigners, the bulk of the centre's population was native sons-of-immigrants. This was reflected in the division between the two parties over the question of the enfranchisement of immigrants, a measure supported by the Liga del Sur and opposed by the U.C.R. Gallo and Miss Sigal concluded from this that affiliation with the U.C.R.

was more generally associated with areas of older, more settled development, (like the centre), while areas of newer development, (like the south), were likely to engender new parties in opposition to it. This situation, they suggested, very likely resulted from regionally based tensions between newer and older immigrant groups. The south was being settled by immigrants at that time, while in the centre the immigrants had arrived, for the main part, some thirty or forty years previously. The centre was enjoying conditions of entrenched privilege, while the south, as a developing region, was out to challenge this. Thus the appearance of two 'modern' parties.

One might suggest further that another of the characteristics of the central region might be forms of disguised unemployment among the middle class groups of the sort I have described. As the sons of the immigrant colonists sought higher status positions and higher incomes, away from the rural smallholdings, they began, in the absence of industrial managerial roles, to look in the direction of the provincial government for jobs and opportunities. This might help to explain how this region became the core area of Radical support. In the south – a developing, 'new' immigration zone – these pressures were possibly less, although it is very significant that one of the principal demands of the Liga del Sur was for the transfer of the provincial capital, (i.e. the major source of government jobs), from the city of Sante Fe (in the central region), to Rosario (in the south).

On the other hand Gallo's and Miss Sigal's study of voting patterns in Santa Fe in 1912 does not justify their assertion of the link between modernisation and the Radical vote. In this election the Radicals gained almost as many votes in the backward north as they did in the developed centre (57% and 62% respectively). This demonstrated their ability to establish a coalition between backward interior areas and areas of high social pluralism (i.e. between traditional landowners and the new middle class groups). For this reason it is almost as justifiable to define the U.C.R. as a party of tradition as it is to define it as one of modernisation.

The underlying assumption behind the Gallo–Sigal approach is that support for the Radicals emerged spontaneously as part of a rational evaluation by the electorate of each of the major parties. This is probably true of card-carrying party affiliates, but it is less certain as far as the electorate itself is concerned. An alternative approach is to see Radicalism as a managing elite able to generate support in different areas, regardless of whether these were strictly modern or not, and whose electoral strength lay in its capacity to adapt to local conditions and to construct its political 'machines'.

Between 1912 and 1916, the Santa Fe Radical Party split. The bulk of the party continued to follow local provincial leaders, while a minority identified itself with the Buenos Aires faction in the party's national committee. In the 1916 elections of two segments competed against each other on separate tickets. The old conservative party disappeared, while the Liga de Sur had by this time become the Progressive Democrat Party. Adopting the same inter-regional disaggregation as Gallo and Miss Sigal, in 1916 each of the parties won the following percentage vote in each region:

Provincial election, 1916

Region	*U.C.R. (dissidents)*	*U.C.R. (Nat. Comm.)*	*P.D.P.*
South	33.8	26.9	39.8
Centre	47.9	33.2	18.8
North	36.3	51.9	11.8

Source: Cantón, *Materiales para el estudio de la sociología política en la Argentina.*

The results of this election confirmed the weakness of the Progressive Democrats outside the southern region. They also confirmed, as Gallo and Miss Sigal affirm, that the strength of the provincial section of the U.C.R. (now the dissident group), lay in the central area. However, the most significant result of all in 1916 is the structure of the National Committee U.C.R. vote. In 1916, the National Committee Radicals captured the whole of the vote which in 1912 had gone to the conservative party. Indeed it can almost be said that the National Committee Radical Party in Santa Fe in 1916 was the direct political heir of the conservative party of 1912. This can be illustrated by comparing the votes of the two parties over the two periods:

Region	*% Conservative vote in 1912*	*% U.C.R. (Nat. Comm.) vote in 1916*
South	26.3	26.9
Centre	28.7	33.2
North	40.4	51.9

Source: Cantón, *Materiales para el estudio de la sociología política.*

On any 'modernisation scale' this would make the national Radical Party far more traditional than it was modern, since it won a higher percentage of votes in the more backward areas of the province. What these results show therefore is not the association between Radicalism, and modernisation, but the tremendous flexibility and versatility which the national party, led by Yrigoyen, was able to develop between 1912 and 1916. Its expansion was largely uncircumscribed by divisions imposed by socio-economic conditions. In the space of four years it had successfully transformed itself from a sectional organisation, based upon the centre, into a multi-sectional, inter-regional coalition. This demonstrates clearly the importance of 'management' factors. It suggests that the pattern of mobilisation was from above, rather than being 'autonomous' from below.

Over the following quadrennium these characteristics increased. By 1920 the party in Santa Fe had been restored to unity. Applying the same regional breakdown, the election results of 1920 appear as follows:

Region	*U.C.R.*	*P.D.P.*
South	50.6	49.4
Centre	74.7	25.3
North	74.3	25.7

Source: Cantón, *Materiales para el estudio de la sociología política.*

Here may be seen the final product of the process of support-diversification that began in 1916. In 1920 the Progressive Democrats increased their vote in the centre, compared with 1916, possibly because of the support of residue groups in the formerly dissident Radical Party opposed to the *rapprochement* with the National Committee. However, by 1920 the Progressive Democrats were in a minority even in their former bastion in the south of the province. Thus the Radicals had successfully bridged regional divisions to establish an operative coalition at the full provincial level.

Another interesting study is that by Milcíades Peña. In a series of penetrating intuitions this work expresses the central elements of the transition from oligarchy to constitutional government in 1912. Peña emphasised that the aim of the Saénz Peña Law was to increase political

[7] Milcíades Peña, *Masas, caudillos y elites. La dependencia argentina de Yrigoyen a Perón* (Ediciones Fichas, Buenos Aires, 1971) Chapter 1, pp. 7–36. This work was written in the 1950s and published posthumously. It is remarkable for its insights and intuitions.

stability by a process of integration as a means of guaranteeing the country's appeal to foreign investors. He also pointed out the importance of State credits and subsidies in defining the political affiliations of the landed interests, and in shaping the rise of Radicalism. Equally, Peña recognised the aggregative character of Radicalism as a class coalition, but one committed narrowly to the defence of the established structure. He also perceived the importance of the Radical government's working class policy in determining the opposition of the conservative elite. Finally Peña also recognised the vital role of the Great Depression in precipitating the downfall of Yrigoyen in 1930. This corresponds with much of my own interpretation.

Further contributions have served to reinforce the weight of opinion against the interpretation that Radicalism represented the advent to power of an industrial bourgeoisie. In his study of immigrants and entrepreneurs in Argentine politics, Oscar Cornblit pointed out the weakness of the industrial entrepreneurs in Argentina as a political lobby.[8] Most of the industrialists were foreigners and thus unconnected with the Radical Party, which was tied closely at the mass level to native-born groups. Cornblit suggests that this prevented communication channels evolving between the industrialists and the government.

Cornblit's thesis hinges upon the foreign background of the bulk of the industrialists, and consequently their lack of access to the political system. While this is true, a number of further points can be added. To some extent the weakness of the industrialists stemmed from the lack of industrial concentration. Most industrial producers operated on the basis of very small units of production; the few large units were controlled by foreign capital linked to the primary export economy. Thus, in the absence of a large managerial middle class sector, aspirant sons of industrial entrepreneurs were likely to be creamed off into the universities and the professions. Consequently industrial activities, until the 1930s, tended to remain in the hands of foreigners. Thus the weakness of the industrial lobby become a reflection of the prevalent patterns of social mobility within the middle classes.

This was further encouraged, in a manner which reflected much the same phenomenon, by the dominance of consumer over producer interests at the mass level in Buenos Aires society. It was very difficult to engender support for measures like additional tariff protection favourable to local industrialists, when this threatened to increase the cost of living.

[8] 'Inmigrantes y empresarios'.

Besides this, protection tended to be opposed by the elite and foreign capital groups out of fear that it would adversely affect foreign trade by inviting retaliation among Argentina's trading partners.

At the political level, although the *yrigoyenistas* began to support a greater measure of tariff protection and import substitution in the 1920s, this was hardly a viable policy during the war and post-war periods. At this time there was already a form of natural protection as a result of falling supplies of imports. Until 1918 the result was that, although industrial production diversified, the quantity of goods produced fell. This suggested a dependence of a considerable segment of the industrialists on imported supplies, and can be instanced as a further reason for their lack of vocal and unanimous support in favour of protection. Falling industrial production during the war also created unemployment and contributed to inflationary pressures. Under these circumstances it comes as no surprise that the Radical government did not favour protectionist policies. It would seem that there were other pressures working against this than the nationality of the domestic enterpreneurs and their lack of communication channels with government.

APPENDIX 3

The first Radical government and the Argentine Rural Society

In an article on the relations between the Radical government and the major domestic beef interests, Peter H. Smith has strongly stressed the elements of continuity between the pre- and post-1916 periods. He concludes:

> These items of information, taken together, strongly suggest that the Radical leaders, recruited from among the upper and middle class groups, identified their interests with those of the cattle aristocracy. It was not a question of their opposing the beef barons in response to the interests of the urban middle classes. They did not promote in any significant way the interests of the consumers in opposition to those of the producers. They did not hold that an over-dependence on the foreign export sector or that crises in the prices (of primary goods) suggested any need for industrialisation in the national interest. They did not take advantage of the depression in the livestock industry (in 1921–4) to attack it, but they leaped to its defence. In sum, the Radicals did not introduce in any way at all a period of urban–rural conflict.[1]

Much of this is upheld in Chapter 1: the Radical Party was a coalition of groups which, for both producer and consumer reasons, upheld the primary exporting economy; the character of the country's development precluded the development of the classic land–industry conflict apparent in many of the industrialised countries.

But this does not mean that Radicalism simply continued what had gone before. Nor does it mean that the period after 1916 was unmarked by political conflict. The question is what sort of conflicts were they? The central thesis of this book is that there was conflict, but that this was bound up with issues of distribution rather than with the economic structure, such as agriculture versus industry. As the events of the 1920s show, the source of the division between the urban middle class and the landed interests lay with the question of the use of the State. The other issue is the relationship between the Radical government and the urban

[1] 'Los radicales argentinos y los intereses ganaderos', p. 824. (The retranslation is mine.)

working class between 1917 and 1921. If the Radical government did in fact continue to uphold the interests of the livestock producers in the same way as its predecessors, what explanation can be given for the formation of the National Labour Association in 1918, and the events of 1919 and 1921? In a wider sense where exactly did the complementarity of interest between the Radical government and institutions like the Sociedad Rural Argentina end, and where did conflict begin?

The answer to this, between 1916 and 1922, lies in the strike question. Each time the Radical government supported strikers in areas associated with foreign capital and with the export sector, there was an immediate negative response on the part of the Rural Society. This happened most notably during the railway strike of October 1917.[2] Attempts by the government to let the strike run its own course led to talk of a business lockout and other counter-measures against the unions. The National Labour Association showed that groups like the Rural Society became extremely disenchanted with the government and decided to take matters into their own hands.

Further light can be thrown on the relationship between the government and the Rural Society by a more detailed analysis of the frigorifico strikes between November 1917 and February 1918. One of Smith's 'items of information' in support of the thesis of 'no hiatus' is that five of the original eight members of Yrigoyen's first cabinet in 1916 were members of the Rural Society.[3] This suggests to him that the Society had a great deal of political influence on government policy. He goes on from this to discuss the frigorifico strikes, and he makes the conclusions of how the government behaved during the strikes the basis for a general commentary on the Radicals' record on the working class problem. The most significant paragraphs are the following:

> [In 1917] the Radicals soon replied to the pressure of the cattlemen. Yrigoyen, often celebrated as an exemplary model of the rising middle class in Argentina, not only listened to the meat-packers and the cattlemen of the Oligarchy: he sent naval ratings in to break the strike! (By a curious coincidence Yrigoyen's Minister of Marine belonged to the Rural Society.) He then withdrew the troops, but only after the F.O.R.A. had threatened a general strike in support of the meat workers. Even so this was a notable decision: although there might have been some 'professional agitators' inciting the men to strike, to bring the navy in was a tremendously hostile act, which only served to intensify the conflict.

[2] See chapter 6, pp. 145–50

[3] Smith p. 806.

The anti-labour position adopted by the Radical administration during the frigorifico strikes is an interesting anticipation of its conduct during the infamous Semana Trágica of February [*sic*] 1919, when the workers, including the frigorifico workers, took part in bloody battles in the streets of Buenos Aires. It has been suggested at times that this horrific experience extinguished Yrigoyen's sympathy for the workers, which might explain the weakness of the position he took subsequently over labour questions; on the contrary his action during the frigorifico strike implied that he had never really been a firm advocate of labour reform. As the representative of the middle class, he had taken the side of the beef barons and the foreign capitalists, not the side of the workers.[4]

The more general statements of the second paragraph (that the frigorifico strikes were an anticipation of the Semana Trágica, that Yrigoyen was not an advocate of reform etc) can only be judged in terms of my own counter-arguments. The other interesting feature is Smith's assertion that the government's decision to break the frigorifico strikes stemmed from pressure from the Rural Society. If this was so it would introduce another parameter in the discussion of the Radical government's labour policies. Previously an anti-labour position had only resulted when the government's other electoral commitments exceeded what it hoped to gain by supporting the strikers. However, in this case, according to Smith's view, it would appear that its calculations were framed by reference to the interests of an established elite pressure group.

The first point of contact between the government and the frigorificos was during the first port strike in December 1916. When the F.O.M. went on strike, the sailors were followed by a number of dockers, among them those handling cargo from the meat-packing plants in Avellaneda. In a memorandum to the government, the frigorificos threatened to suspend shipments if the strike continued. Although in its reply the government refused to respond to this demand, it did surreptitiously send marines to help in the most vital loading tasks.[5] This indicates, in support of Smith's general thesis, a strong sensitivity on the government's part towards this 'mother industry'.

The first frigorifico strike occurred in June 1917 in the city of Zárate, some fifty miles north of the federal capital in the province of Buenos Aires. The city's economy was dominated by two large meat-

[4] Ibid. pp. 808–9.

[5] *La Prensa*, 6 December 1916.

packing plants, the Frigorifico Hall and the Smithfield Argentine companies. A pay claim in the former led to a strike which quickly spread to the latter. Within a short time the whole town was affected in very much the same way as the strike on the Central Argentine Railway spread into Rosario a little later in July and August 1917.[6] Attempts by the local police to contain the movement led to outbreaks of violence. At the beginning of the strike, delegates from the Anarchist F.O.R.A. del Quinto Congreso were sent to Zárate. The idea was to spread the strike beyond the city into the rural hinterland, thus provoking a movement of agricultural tenants and workers.[7] By interfering with the planting of the seed, this would seriously affect harvest yields at the end of the year.

It was with this danger in mind that the authorities reacted to the strike. By this time the province of Buenos Aires was in the hands of the Radicals after the federal intervention of April 1917. According to a circular from the provincial authorities to the police in Zárate, a copy of which the Socialists in Buenos Aires acquired, orders were to 'proceed with the greatest energy, applying the Law of Social Defence without hesitation against the agitators, [because] if they could be eliminated, the farmers would resume their tasks.[8]

For its part *La Epoca* declared: 'At any time . . . an agrarian strike presents serious social and economic problems for the State. But at this time of the year especially, when an increase in the cultivated area is economically so imperative, rural agitation becomes even more disquieting.'[9]

Thus the police were sent to Zárate not to break the strike, but to eliminate the Anarchists. There was no hesitation in branding them as agitators and using traditional repressive measures against them. Obviously there were no hopes of winning their support as had happened with the Syndicalists. Once the Anarchists disappeared from the scene, government officials began to support concessions for the Zárate strikers. The local police chief, probably an appointee of the deposed conservative provincial administration, was dismissed and the companies were prevailed upon to make a number of concessions.[10] This brought the strike to a swift end.

[6] Reports of the strike can be followed in the press from 6 June onwards.
[7] This aim was announced by *La Protesta*, 9 June 1917.
[8] *La Vanguardia*, 14 June 1917.
[9] *La Epoca*, 14 June 1917.
[10] *La Nación*, 15 June 1917.

There was nothing in the strike to suggest that the government was responding to it in any different way from other urban strikes around this time. The strikers were supported by the authorities, whose main concern was simply to prevent it spreading and developing into an embarrassing movement in the rural areas which would threaten agricultural production. There was no sign that either the meat-packing companies or the beef producers themselves had any influence on the pattern of the government's response to the strike.

However, the more important frigorifico strikes, and the ones to which Smith refers, came at the end of 1917 while the government was still struggling to end railway unrest. The frigorifico movements, like many of the strikes at this time, were triggered by the efforts of the Syndicalist and Anarchist federations to unionise new and numerically important groups of workers. The frigorifico workers were extremely difficult to organise. Already in 1915 the difficulties had become apparent when the Syndicalists organised a union in the American-owned Armour and Swift companies in Berisso. The men had used this opportunity to organise a strike which, because of a lack of organisation, had been overtaken by a wave of inconsequential violence. The De la Plaza government had quickly intervened with troops and the strike had collapsed.[11]

The total labour force of the frigorificos in the province of Buenos Aires was in the region of 10,000 men, made up of casual labourers and permanent staff.[12] There was also a large contingent of female and child labour. Many of the men were from the Balkans. These *turcos* were among the poorest of the foreign immigrant communities.[13] Besides their notoriously poor wages, the presence of female workers on the night shifts had engendered conditions of general promiscuity. Serious industrial accidents were frequent, and the companies did little to guard against them. It was with the aim of improving conditions generally

[11] Marotta, Vol. 2, pp. 199–200. The *Third National Census* (Vol. 7, p. 535) counted 3,600 Argentine workers and 6,800 foreigners in the Buenos Aires meat-packing plants. There were also about 300 women and over a thousand children.

[12] *Boletín Mensual del Departamento Nacional del Trabajo* (April 1919), p. 244.

[13] There was frequent mention of *turcos* in the strikes, and the bulk of police detainees were of Ottoman nationality. (Cf. La Nación, 9 December 1917.) Technically these men should not have been employed, since Britain and the United States were at war with the Ottoman Empire.

that the Syndicalists made another attempt to organise a union in Berisso in November 1917.[14]

As soon as this became known, the managers of the two companies dismissed all those suspected of union activities. They organised an espionage system on the plant floor and prepared for a strike by bringing beds and food into the factory for those who continued working. In spite of this, the F.O.R.A. managed to present a list of demands. When these were rejected on 25 November, the strike began.[15]

Although the Syndicalists played an important part in bringing matters to a head, they were unable to maintain the strike under their supervision. The most they did was to prevent Anarchists from the federal capital moving in in their place.[16] The men elected their own union representatives, and they exercised whatever leadership there was over the strike until it ended. The unfortunate result was a repetition of the events of 1915. There was no organised control over the strike, and the men were quickly provoked into acts of violence when the frigorificos attempted to keep production going. That the F.O.R.A. lost control over the strike is important. Because of this it also quickly lost interest in it. Thus the government's decisions about the use of police during the strike were not inhibited by calculations stemming from its relationship with the Syndicalists.

By this time, in view of the railway strikes, it had become standard procedure to send troops to the scene of any important strike, mainly to forestall acts of destruction and sabotage. As a matter of routine at the beginning of the strike, naval conscripts were sent to the frigorificos with orders to guard the installations. For some time they carried out these duties relatively undisturbed until, on the night of 4 December, the strikers attacked the Swift factory *en masse* in the hope of halting production. Incendiary torches and bombs were thrown over the factory walls and there were pitched battles in the streets outside. When several of the naval ratings were injured, their fellows attacked

[14] *La Organización Obrera*, 15 September 1917; *La Vanguardia*, 14 December 1917. For a general account of the strikes by a participant see José Peter, *Crónicas proletarias* (Esfera, Buenos Aires, 1968).

[15] Smith (p. 807) lists the men's demands as the introduction of the 8-hour day, wage increases, overtime pay, travel allowances and recognition of 1 May as a holiday.

[16] *La Vanguardia*, 1 December 1917.

the strikers and killed several of them.[17] At this moment the strike spread to other frigorificos in Avellaneda.

Afterwards the frigorificos in Berisso were turned into armed camps, equipped with searchlights and machine-guns. By 10 December a mass exodus from Berisso was in progress as the police and the naval ratings began to make sorties through different parts of the town.[18] In the meantime both companies in Berisso continued to recruit replacement workers. By the second week in December the strikers were showing signs of exhaustion. Many of them were reported to be leaving the district to seek employment as harvest hands.[19] Those who returned to work finally did so on the basis of the same pay and the same conditions as before the strike.[20]

It seems clear enough that the involvement of the naval ratings in the strike, beyond their guard duties, came as a result of the strikers' attempts to stop production in the plant. What is less clear is why the campaign of retaliation lasted so long as it did, and why the government took no steps to resolve the strike through a compromise agreement. On the outbreak of the strike in Berisso, the managers of the companies involved approached the minister of agriculture, Honorio Pueyrredón, with the request for troop protection.[21] Pueyrredón agreed to this but urged them to take the matter to arbitration. Again this was a question of standard procedure. Since the companies refused this, the task of arranging arbitration was left to the provincial labour department.

There were signs that the authorities in the province at first tried to solve the strike by favouring the men. *La Nación* declared on 3 December: 'There is a unanimous opinion that the behaviour of the authorities openly responds to the aim of winning the sympathy of the workers for electoral reasons.'[22] On 10 December an abortive approach to the strikers from the provincial labour department was reported in the following way: 'The workers decided not to accept the suggestions (of the labour department) because the offer was insufficient and imprecise, but they thanked the labour department, which they considered well disposed towards the interests of the working classes.'[23]

[17] *La Prensa*, *La Nación*, etc, 6 December 1917.

[18] *La Vanguardia*, 10 December 1917.

[19] *La Prensa*, 21 December 1917.

[20] Ibid. 23 December 1917.

[21] *La Nación*, 29 November 1917. Smith is wrong in attributing this decision to the minister of marine, Alvarez de Toledo.

[22] *La Nación*, 3 December 1917.

[23] Ibid. 10 December 1917.

Finally after the affray of 4 December a federal judge from the Supreme Court declared in a message to local criminal judges:

In view of the fact that the administrative authorities, as at least would appear *prima facie*, are not taking efficacious measures to avoid crimes being committed, it is indispensable that these should be suppressed effectively. If these events are repeated I recommend the greatest zeal on your part in carrying out rapid hearings to avoid the strikers enjoying an impunity which is a discredit to the country.[24]

The change from mild support to hostility came after the clash of 4 December. Although the national interventor in Buenos Aires, José Luis Cantilo, officially continued to support arbitration, he dismissed the chief of police in Berisso and sent an extra detachment of mounted police to the scene of the strike. Before this the police were reported to be favouring the strikers; afterwards it was they who were mainly responsible for what observers described as the terrorisation of the local population.

This decision to send more police to Berisso with orders to act against the strikers stemmed directly from a meeting on 5 December between Pueyrredón and the representatives of the frigorifico companies. The latter declared that the strike had been engineered by agitators, that only a minority of the men supported it, and that more armed protection at the plants was needed. Unless this was given, and this was the crucial argument, there would be a general lockout in all the frigorificos in Argentina, and outstanding contracts would be transferred to Uruguay.[25] *La Nación* commented: 'The prospects can be summed up in the following way, each of which is more alarming than the other: dear meat, a bad effect on the livestock industry, the unproductiveness of the capital invested in the frigorificos, and the unemployment of thousands of workers who operate in the industry.'[26]

Pueyrredón told the frigorifico representatives that he would look into the matter. The next day he was approached by Joaquín S. de Anchorena on behalf of the Rural Society. Anchorena was told by Pueyrredón that Cantilo had now agreed to send police cavalry to the scene of the strike.[27] This made it apparent that the decision to do this had been taken before his visit, and that it was not the Rural Society's pressure which led

[24] Ibid. 5 December 1917.
[25] Ibid. 6 December 1917.
[26] Ibid. 7 December 1917.
[27] Ibid.

to it. What had caused it were the threats made by the frigorificos. Two days after this the police had made over one hundred arrests.[28]

In spite of this the Rural Society was not satisfied. On 12 December it held a meeting at which the strike, and the agitators said to be leading it, were condemned because of the effects they were having on beef production. There were demands for still firmer action from the national government. Finally it was decided to send a delegation of protest to see Yrigoyen.[29] However, for almost a week the president refused to receive the delegation. When Anchorena himself finally managed to see Yrigoyen he returned with the news that his mission had completely failed. Yrigoyen had rejected his advice.[30] This reinforces the previous picture.

On 5 December the strike had spread to the frigorificos in Avellaneda. During this strike the Syndicalist F.O.R.A. was more in evidence. While it led strike meetings, local sections of the F.O.F. organised a number of sympathy strikes, and the maritime F.O.M. enforced a boycott on frigorifico loadings.[31] However, in Avellaneda the matter ended as it had done in Berisso. The companies involved, La Blanca and La Negra, rejected arbitration and, once again under the protection of naval ratings, made efforts to recruit replacement labour. On 18 January 1918, *La Prensa* described the situation in Avellaneda as follows: 'The experience Avellaneda is undergoing as a result of the conflict could not be more serious. There are more than four thousand men without work, and the whole city looks like a war zone on account of the number of armed forces there are there and by the way they behave.'[32]

Although overall the authorities appeared to have taken the same line in Avellaneda as in Berisso, there was one important difference between the two strikes. In Avellaneda the F.O.R.A. was directly involved, the Yrigoyen did everything he could to keep the goodwill of the F.O.R.A., as he had done under broadly similar circumstances during the municipal workers' strike in April 1917. In a meeting with the union leaders in the middle of January 1918, he was reported by the Syndicalist newspaper, *La Organización Obrera*, as having declared that 'he had the best intentions towards the men, and he considered it his duty not only to respect the interests of the companies, but also those of the working classes, and therefore he suggested to the interventor, who was present

[28] Ibid. 9 December 1917.
[29] *La Nación*, 13 December 1917.
[30] Ibid. 14, 16, 19, 22 December 1917.
[31] *La Vanguardia*, 10 December 1917.
[32] *La Prensa*, 18 January 1918.

during the audience, that he should order the police to observe impartial conduct.'[33]

The outcome of this was that the naval ratings guarding the frigorificos in Avellaneda were temporarily withdrawn, and the companies were informed that they would no longer be able to use government tugs to escape the F.O.M.'s boycott.[34] This was followed up by Cantilo with another offer for the arbitration of the dispute. However, the companies once more rejected this. Again there was talk of a lockout and the transfer of the meat contracts. Immediately the tugs and the navy were brought back into the strike.[35] Under these circumstances all further resistance finally collapsed at the end of January.

One final hint of the government's position came after the strike when Pueyrredón approached Sir Reginald Tower with a proposal for a meat convention to complement the wheat agreement.[36] While this was being considered, Tower approached the government to complain about the F.O.M.'s boycott against the frigorificos in reprisal for their dismissal of a number of former strikers. At first the government disclaimed responsibility for this, but after a meeting between the minister of marine Federico Alvarez de Toledo, and the leaders of the F.O.M., the boycott was suddenly abandoned. Indeed Tower reported that a delegation from the union had visited the offices of British shipping companies with a message of goodwill.[37]

The significance of this lies first in the close relationship it suggested between different members of the government and the Syndicalist union leaders. This relationship the frigorifico strikes had failed to impair, although they had shown the Radical government in a rather poor light. Secondly, the episode was an example of the petty gestures the government had begun to make at this point in favour of the British to prevent Tower abandoning the wheat agreement in response to the railway strikes of early February 1918. Thirdly, there was the meat convention the government was planning. This it obviously intended to use in the elections, and it was another reason for its deference towards the frigorificos. With the elections imminent, the government was unwilling to risk the frigorificos carrying out their threat to transfer the meat contracts, and needed to win their goodwill if there was to be any chance of concluding a trade agreement on meat. Had the companies

33 *La Organización Obrera*, 19 January 1918.

34 Ibid.

35 *La Prensa*, 18 January 1918.

36 Telegram No. 57, 7 February 1918, F.O. 368–1876.

37 Despatches Nos. 77 and 88, 24 February and 2 March 1918. ibid.

imposed a lockout, stopped production and transferred the meat contracts to Uruguay, the electoral effects would have been disastrous. It would have affected not just the producers and the Rural Society, but other major sectors of the economy, as well as the consumers in Buenos Aires. Already as a result of the strikes the price of meat had shot up alarmingly.[38] Besides, in electoral terms the importance of the frigorifico workers was negligible. The electorate of the province of Buenos Aires was dominated by the rural interests and ancillary occupations depending on them. Most of the frigorifico workers were in any case non-voting foreigners.[39] It was more or less the same story during the railway strikes, when on several occasions both the police and troops in the province of Buenos Aires acted against the strikers. Unlike in the city of Buenos Aires and in Rosario, there was no political advantage to be won in supporting them.[40]

There is little in the frigorifico strikes to support Smith's thesis that the Government acted under the pressure of the Sociedad Rural. Because the Rural Society, and major business groups like it, recognised their inability to influence government policy in their favour, steps were taken to found the National Labour Association.

The significance of the frigorifico strikes is not that they portray an essentially conservative administration, as deferential to the traditional elite groups as its predecessors. Rather than being swayed by this, the Radical government was ruled by electoral considerations, in this case by the impending contest in the province of Buenos Aires. The example of the frigorifico strikes, and government policy towards them, is thus another illustration of the extent of the political consensus between elite and non-elite groups in Argentina during this period, and also of its limitations.

[38] *El Diario* reported on 28 January 1918 that the price of beef in the municipal market in Buenos Aires had gone up by 20 pesos a head during the strike.

[39] This was noted by *El Diario* when it attacked Radical and Socialist Party committees in Berisso for blaming the navy for the events of 4 December: 'What supine disregard for the facts! These groups which are being supported and flattered are for the most part quite without any stake in the country, completely lacking in political principles, and if perhaps any of them have naturalisation papers we believe they will use them for personal profit and nothing else.'

[40] In August 1917, when the strike on the Central Argentine Railway became general, the police in Tigre broke up the strikers' meetings. Also the Radical candidate for governor in Buenos Aires in March 1918, José Camilo Crotto, took a marked anti-strike position during the election campaign. Finally, in April 1918, General Dellepiane, in anticipation of his role during the Semana Trágica, intervened with troops to combat one of the minor railway strikes.

APPENDIX 4

The working class vote for the Radical and Yrigoyenista Parties in selected areas of Buenos Aires, 1912–30

Table 12 summarises the percentage of votes for the Radicals and the *yrigoyenistas* in national congressional elections between 1912 and 1930. The areas selected comprise the south-eastern section of the city where the majority of working class activities and, it may safely be assumed, the working class vote were concentrated. The three areas are Ward 2 (San Cristóbal Sud) in the *barrio* of Nueva Pompeya, Ward 3 (Santa Lucía) Barrancas, and Ward 4 (San Juan Evangelista) the Boca.

TABLE 12 *The Radical vote in working class areas of Buenos Aires, 1912–30 (percentages).*

		Total Radical vote city wide	Ward 2	Ward 3	Ward 4
1912		24.2	32.2	36.6	27.1
1914		32.0	29.4	32.3	30.9
1916	(Presidential elections)	48.1	38.3	44.0	36.2
1918	(After port and railway strikes)	43.2	44.0	49.9	43.3
1920	(After repression phase in 1919)	37.3	33.3	38.9	35.5
1922	(Post-war depression)	37.6	33.5	36.8	35.9
1926		40.6	40.0	43.3	32.5
1928	(Presidential elections)	54.6	50.8	53.9	48.6
1930	(Great Depression)	28.0	25.8	31.2	29.0

Source: Cantón, *Materiales para el estudio de la sociología política*, Vol. 2.

Although these figures can be no more than a crude guide, they do suggest that working class support for the Radicals did rise significantly in 1918 following Yrigoyen's initial intervention in the strikes. Whereas before 1918 the increase of the Radical vote in these three areas had broadly matched the city-wide trend, in 1918 the increase was disproportionate to that in the city as a whole. After 1918, following the abortive strikes of 1919, the Radical working class vote declined almost to its 1914 level and remained there during the post-war depression. There was a further increase in 1928 which exceeded that in 1918. This suggests that the *yrigoyenistas* had more success with the committee system in the 1920s in winning working class support than they did with the government's strike interventions in 1917 and 1918. The figures for 1930 illustrate the dramatic effect of the Great Depression.

Select bibliography

A NOTE ON SOURCES

The bulk of the data for this book was collected in 1968 and 1969 in London and in Buenos Aires. In London the research was conducted in the library of University College, the British Museum and in the Public Record Office; in Buenos Aires in the Biblioteca Nacional, the library of the Congreso Nacional, the Archivo General de la Nación, the Confederación General del Trabajo, the library of the Banco Tornquist, the Instituto Torcuato Di Tella, the Biblioteca Juan B. Justo, La Fraternidad, the Federación Obrera Marítima, and the Centro de Almaceneros de la Capital.

Most of the material used is freely available to the public. Despite considerable efforts it proved impossible to gain access to private papers. Unfortunately, as yet, in Argentina there is little tradition of preserving private manuscripts for historical investigation, and even less of making them available to *bona fide* scholars.

Initial major sources were the *Review of the River Plate* and Foreign Office despatches from Buenos Aires. Although both of these are biassed strongly towards a British point of view, they are useful both as summaries and, particularly the latter, as a means of gaining some knowledge of government procedures. The absence of private papers meant a great reliance on newspapers. To construct a balanced account I was forced into continually checking and cross-checking different newspaper accounts of events. The major Argentine daily newspapers used were as follows: *La Nación* (1912–30), *La Prensa* (1912–30), *La Vanguardia* (1912–30), *La Epoca* (1916–30), *El Radical* (1915–16), *La Mañana* (1916–19), *La Fronda* (1919–22), *La Protesta* (1909–30), *El Diario* (1912–22). I also consulted occasionally the *Buenos Aires Herald* and the *Buenos Aires Standard*.

The following weekly or fortnightly publications were also consulted: *La Organización Obrera*, *La Unión del Marino*, *Boletín Oficial del Centro de Almaceneros*, and the four-monthly E. Tornquist and Co. Ltd publication, *Business Conditions in Argentina 1914–22*. Other periodicals used were the *Revista Argentina de Ciencias Políticas* and the *Revista de Ciencias Económicas*,

Among official publications in Argentina the best sources are the congressional *Diarios de Sesiones* for the Chamber of Deputies and the Senate. I also managed to gain access to files from the ministry of the interior between 1916 and 1919. However, this material is unclassified and difficult to use. On labour matters the best sources are the *Boletín Oficial del Departamento Nacional del Trabajo*, and the *Boletín Mensual del Departamento Nacional del Trabajo.*

On the unions I consulted the files of La Fraternidad (memoranda, resolutions and circulars) and those of the Federación Obrera Marítima. Both are excellent collections and deserve wider study. I also had access, in the Confederación General del Trabajo, to handwritten minutes for the F.O.R.A. during the period of Yrigoyen's first government. These are invaluable for any wider study of the development of the trade union movement in Argentina. However, in 1969 they were in a rather poor state, and will no doubt disappear unless steps are taken to retrieve them.

Occasionally I was also able to conduct interviews with survivors from the period. Among those interviewed were Sr Sebastián Marotta, Dr Manuel Menchaca, Sr Diego Abad de Santillán, Sr Andres Cabona and Sr José Otero. On the whole former union leaders proved more accessible and useful than politicians.

The only useful bibliographies were a booksellers' list published in 1970 by the Librería La Antártida and entitled *El Radicalismo*. This contains over 800 titles from 1891 onwards. Other useful bibliographies are: Carlos Rama, *Die Arbeiterbewegung in Lateinamerika* (Gehlen, W. Germany, 1967); Leandro Gutiérrez, 'Recopilación bibliográfica y fuentes para el estudio de la historia y situación actual de la clase obrera argentina', *Documento de Trabajo* (Instituto Torcuato Di Tella, Buenos Aires, 1969).

The following is a list of the secondary sources appearing in the footnotes. It should not be regarded as a complete bibliography of the subject, but simply as a summary of the most useful works.

Academia Nacional de la Historia, *Historia argentina contemporánea, 1862–1930* (El Ateneo, Buenos Aires, 1965).

Allub, Leopoldo. 'The social origins of dictatorship and democracy in Argentina' (mimeog. Ph.D. dissertation, University of North Carolina, 1973).

Almond, Gabriel, and James S. Coleman, (eds.), *The Politics of the Developing Areas* (Princeton University Press, 1960).

Arraga, Julio. *Reflexiones y observaciones sobre la cuestión social* (Buenos Aires, no date).

Asociación Nacional del Trabajo, *Versión taquigráfica de lo deliberado por la Asamblea General en la Bolsa de Comercio el dia 20 de mayo de 1918* (Buenos Aires, 1918).

Babini, Nicolas. 'La Semana Trágica', *Todo es Historia*, Year 1, No. 5 (September, (1967).

Bayer, Osvaldo. *Los vengadores de la Patagonia trágica* (Galerna, Buenos Aires, 1972).

Beyhaut, Gustavo. Roberto Cortés Conde, Haydée Gorostegui and Susana Torrado. 'Los inmigrantes en el sistema ocupacional argentino', in Torcuato S. Di Tella *et alia, Argentina, sociedad de masas* (Eudeba, Buenos Aires, 1965), pp. 85–123.

Bidegain, Pedro. *Mi radicalismo* (Buenos Aires, 1929).
Bunge, Alejandro E. *Ferrocarriles argentinos* (Buenos Aires, 1918).
Los problemas económicos del presente (Buenos Aires, 1919).
Una nueva Argentina, (Buenos Aires, 1940).
Bunge, Augusto. *La inferioridad económica de los argentinos nativos* (Buenos Aires, 1919).
Burgin, Miron P. *The Economic Aspects of Argentine Federalism, 1820–1850* (Cambridge, Massachusetts, 1946).
Caballero, Ricardo. *Yrigoyen, la conspiración civil y militar del 4 de febrero de 1905* (Raigal, Buenos Aires, 1951).
Cacavelos, Juan M. and Julio Artayeta. *Hipólito Yrigoyen, paladín de la democracia* (Santa Theresita, Buenos Aires, 1939).
Cancela, Arturo. 'Una semana de holgorio', in *Tres relatos porteños* (Anaconda, Buenos Aires, 1933).
Cantón, Darío. *El parlamento argentino en épocas de cambio, 1890, 1916 y 1946* (Instituto Torcuato Di Tella, Buenos Aires, 1966).
Materiales para el estudio de la sociología política en la Argentina (Instituto Torcuato Di Tella, 1968).
Elecciones y partidos políticos en la Argentina. Historia, interpretación y balance: 1910–1966 (Siglo XXI, Buenos Aires, 1973).
Cárcano, Miguel Angel. *Sáenz Peña, la revolución por los comicios* (Buenos Aires, 1963).
Cárcano, Ramón J. *Mis primeros ochenta años* (Pampa y cielo, Buenos Aires, 1965).
Cárdenas, Felipe (Jr). 'Hipólito Yrigoyen, ese enigmático conductor', *Todo es Historia*, Year 1, No. 2 (June 1967).
Carranza, Adolfo S. *Trabajos sociales* (Buenos Aires, 1918).
Carrasco, Angel. *Lo que yo vi desde el '80* (Procmo, Buenos Aires, 1947).
Casablanca, Adolfo. 'La traición a la revolución del '90', *Todo es Historia*, Year 2, No. 17 (September, 1968).
Casaretto, Martín S. *Historia del movimiento obrero argentino* (Buenos Aires, 1947).
Coca, Joaquín. *El contubernio* (Coyoacán, Buenos Aires, 1961).
Cochran, Thomas C. and Rubén Reina. *Espíritu de empresa en la Argentina* (Emece, Buenos Aires, 1965).
Cornblit, Oscar E. 'Inmigrantes y empresarios en la política argentina', *Desarrollo Económico*, Vol. 6, No. 24 (January–March, 1967).
Cornblit, Oscar E., Ezequiel Gallo and Alfredo A. O'Connell, 'La generación del ochenta y su proyecto-antecedentes y consecuencias', in Torcuato S. Di Tella *et alia*, *Argentina, sociedad de masas* (Eudeba, Buenos Aires, 1965), pp. 18–59.
Cortés Conde, Roberto, and Ezequiel Gallo, *La formación de la Argentina moderna* (Paidós, Buenos Aires, 1967).
La república conservadora, Vol. 5 of *Historia Argentina*, edited by Tulio Halperín Donghi (Paidós, Buenos Aires, 1972).
'Problemas del crecimiento industrial (1870–1914)', in Torcuato S. Di

Tella *et alia, Argentina, sociedad de masas* (Eudeba, Buenos Aires, 1965), pp. 59–81.

De la Torre, Lisandro, 'Una página de historia', *La Prensa*, 22 June 1919.

Del Mazo, Gabriel. *El radicalismo. Ensayo sobre su historia y doctrina* (Gure, Buenos Aires, 1957).

Díaz Alejandro, Carlos. 'The Argentine tariff, 1906–1940', *Oxford Economic Papers*, Vol. 19, No. 1 (March 1967).

Essays on the Economic History of the Argentine Republic (Yale University Press, 1970).

Dickman, Enrique. *Recuerdos de un militante socialista* (La Vanguardia, Buenos Aires, 1949).

Di Tella, Guido, and Manuel Zymelman, *Las etapas del desarrollo económico argentino* (Eudeba, Buenos Aires, 1967).

Di Tella, Torcuato S. *et alia. Argentina, sociedad de masas* (Eudeba, Buenos Aires, 1965).

Dorfman, Adolfo. *La evolución industrial argentina* (Losada, Buenos Aires, 1942).

Etchepareborda, Roberto (ed.). *Hipólito Yrigoyen. Pueblo y gobierno* (Raigal, Buenos Aires, 1951).

Yrigoyen y el congreso (Raigal, Buenos Aires, 1956).

La revolución argentina del noventa (Eudeba, Buenos Aires, 1966).

'Breves anotaciones sobre la revolución del 6 de septiembre de 1930', *Investigaciones y Ensayos*, No. 8 (January–June, 1970).

Etkin, Alberto M. *Bosquejo de una historia y doctrina de la U.C.R.* (El Ateneo, Buenos Aires, 1928).

Fernández, Alfredo. *El movimiento obrero en la Argentina* (Plus Ultra, Buenos Aires, 1935).

Ferns, H. S. *Britain and Argentina in the Nineteenth Century* (Oxford University Press, 1960).

Ferrer, Aldo. *La economía argentina. Las etapas de su desarrollo y problemas actuales* (Fondo de Cultura Económica, Buenos Aires, 1963).

Fodor, J. and A. O'Connell, 'Argentina and the Atlantic economy in the first half of the twentieth century' (unpublished mimeograph, 1970).

Ford, A. G. *The Gold Standard, 1880–1914. Britain and Argentina* (Oxford, 1962).

La Fraternidad, *Cincuentenario de la Fraternidad* (Buenos Aires, 1937).

Galletti, Alfredo. *La realidad argentina en el siglo XX* (Fondo de Cultura Económica, Buenos Aires, 1961).

Gallo, Ezequiel (Jr) and Silvia Sigal. 'La formación de los partidos políticos contemporáneos – La U.C.R. (1891–1916), in Torcuato S. Di Tella *et alia, Argentina, sociedad de masas* (Eudeba, Buenos Aires, 1965), pp. 124–76.

'Agrarian expansion and industrial development in Argentina', in Raymond Carr (ed.), *Latin American Affairs* (St. Antony's Papers, No. 22, Oxford, 1970), pp. 45–61.

'Colonos en armas. Las revoluciones radicales en la provincia de Santa Fe, 1893' (forthcoming).

Gálvez, Manuel. *Vida de Hipólito Yrigoyen*, 5th edn (Tor, Buenos Aires, 1959).

Germani, Gino. *Política y sociedad en una época de transición* (Paidós, Buenos Aires, 1966).

'Social stratification and its historical evolution in Argentina', *Sociologia* (Rivista di Studi Sociali dell'Instituto Luigi Sturzo, 1971).

Gilimón, Eduardo G. *Un anarquista en Buenos Aires, (1890–1910)*, La Historia Popular, No. 71 (Centro Editor de América Latina, Buenos Aires, 1971).

Godio, Julio. *La Semana Trágica de enero de 1919* (Gránica, Buenos Aires, 1972).

Goldwert, Marvin. 'The rise of modern militarism in Argentina', *Hispanic American Historical Review*, Vol. 48, No. 2 (May 1968), pp. 189–205.

Goldstraj, Manuel. *Años y errores. Un cuarto de siglo de política argentina* (Sophos, Buenos Aires, 1957).

Gravil, Roger. 'Anglo–U.S. trade rivalry in Argentina and the D'Abernon Mission of 1929', in David Rock (ed.), *Argentina in the Twentieth Century* (Duckworth, London, 1975).

Gutiérrez, Leandro. 'Recopilación bibliográfica y fuentes para el estudio de la historia y situación actual de la clase obrera argentina'. *Documento de Trabajo*, Instituto Torcuata Di Tella, Centro de Investigaciones Sociales (Buenos Aires, 1969).

Halperín Donghi, Tulio. *Historia de la Universidad de Buenos Aires* (Eudeba, Buenos Aires, 1962).

Ibarguren, Carlos. *La historia que he vivido* (Eudeba, Buenos Aires, 1969).

Johnson, John J. *Political Change in Latin America – the emergence of the middle sectors* (Stanford, California, 8th edn, 1967).

Jones, C. A. 'British financial institutions in Argentina, 1860–1914' (mimeograph Ph.D. dissertation, Cambridge, 1973).

Jorge, Eduardo F. *Industria y concentración económica* (Siglo XXI, Buenos Aires, 1971).

Justo, Juan B. *Teoría y práctica de la historia* (Buenos Aires, 1910).

Internacionalismo y patria (La Vanguardia, Buenos Aires, 1933).

Kamia, Delia. *Entre Yrigoyen e Ingenieros* (Meridión, Buenos Aires, 1957).

Kaplan, Marcos. 'Política del petroleo en la priméra presidencia de Hipólito Yrigoyen (1916–1922)', *Desarrollo Económico*, Vol. 12, No. 45 (April–June, 1972).

Laclau, Ernesto. 'Modos de producción, sistemas económicos y población excedente. Aproximación histórica a los casos argentino y chileno', *Revista Latinoamericana de Sociología*, Vol. 5, No. 2 (July 1969), pp. 276–316.

'Relations between agricultural and industrial interests in Argentina, 1870–1914' (unpublished mimeograph, 1972).

Liga Patriótica Argentina, *Primer congreso de trabajadores de la Liga Patriótica Argentina* (Buenos Aires, 1920).

López, Alfonso Amadeo (ed). *Vida, obra y trascendencia de Sebastián Marotta* (Calomino, Buenos Aires, 1971).

Luna, Felix *Yrigoyen* (Desarrollo, Buenos Aires, 1964).

Maglione Jaimes, Pedro. 'Una figura señera', *La Nación*, 12 January 1969.
Marotta, Sebastián. *El movimiento sindical argentino: su genesis y desarrollo* (Lacio, Buenos Aires, 1960).
Martínez, Alberto B. and Maurice Lewandowski. *The Argentine in the Twentieth Century* (T. Fisher and Unwin, London, 1911).
McGann, Thomas F. *Argentina, the United States, and the Inter-American System* (Harvard University Press, Cambridge, Massachusetts, 1957).
Mitre, Jorge A. 'Presidencia de Victorino de la Plaze', Academia Nacional de la Historia, *Historia argentina contemporánea, 1862–1930*, Vol. 1, Section 2 (El Aleneo, Buenos Aires 1965).
Moreno, Rodolfo. *Intervenciones federales en las provincias* (Buenos Aires, 1924).
Murmis, Miguel, and Juan Carlos Portantiero. 'Crecimiento industrial y alianza de clases', *Estudios sobre los orígines el peronismo* (Siglo XXI, Buenos Aires, 1971).
Navarro Gerassi, Marysa. *Los nacionalistas* (Jorge Alvarez, Buenos Aires, 1969).
Oddone, Jacinto. *El gremialismo proletario argentino* (Buenos Aires, 1957).
Olguin, Dardo. *Lencinas, el caudillo radical, Historia y mito* (Vendimiador, Mendoza, 1961).
Ortiz, Ricardo M. *Historia económica de la Argentina*, 1850–1930, 2 vols. (Raigal, Buenos Aires, 1955).
'Aspectos económicos de la crisis de 1930', *Revista de Historia. La crisis de 1930* (Buenos Aires, 1958), pp. 41–62.
Oyhanarte, Horacio B. *El hombre* (Librería Mendesky, Buenos Aires, 1916).
Palacios, Alfredo L. *El nuevo derecho* (Claridad, Buenos Aires, 1934).
Panettieri, José. *Los trabajadores* (Jorge Alvarez, Buenos Aires, 1968).
Passero, Victor Julián. 'Quiera el pueblo votar. Historia de la primera elección bajo la ley Sánez Peña', *Todo es Historia*, Vol. 3, No. 23 (March, 1969).
Peña, Milciades. *Masas, caudillos y elites. La dependencia argentina de Yrigoyen a Perón* (Ediciones Fichas, Buenos Aires, 1971).
Peter, José. *Crónicas proletarias* (Esfera, Buenos Aires, 1968).
Peters, Harold E. *The Foreign Debt of the Argentine Republic* (The Johns Hopkins Press, Baltimore, 1934).
Phelps, Vernon L. *The International Economic Position of Argentina* (University of Pennsylvania, Philadelphia, 1937).
Pinedo, Federico. 'Testimonio', *Revista de Historia. La crisis de 1930* (Buenos Aires, 1958), pp. 113–20.
Posada, Adolfo. *La República Argentina. Impresiones y comentarios* (Madrid, 1912).
Potash, Robert A. *The Army and Politics in Argentina, 1928–1945. Yrigoyen to Perón* (Stanford, California, 1969).
Puiggrós, Rodolfo. *El yrigoyenismo* (Jorge Alvarez, Buenos Aires, 1965).
Rama, Carlos. *Die Arbeiterbewung in Lateinamerika, Chronologie und Bibliographie 1892–1966* (Gehlen, W. Germany, 1967).

Recchini de Lattes, Zulma. 'El proceso de urbanización en la Argentina: distribución, crecimiento, y algunas características de la población urbana', *Desarrollo Económico*, Vol. 12, No. 48 (January–March 1973), pp. 867–86.

República Argentina, *Third National Census 1914* (Buenos Aires, 1914–1917).

Resumen estadístico del movimiento migratorio en la República Argentina 1857–1924 (Ministry of Agriculture, Buenos Aires, 1925).

Rock, David. 'Lucha civil en la Argentina. La Semana Trágica de enero de 1919', *Desarrollo Económico*, Vol. 11, No. 42 (March 1972), pp. 165–215.

'La Semana Trágica y los usos de la historia', *Desarrollo Económico*, Vol. 12, No. 45 (June 1972), pp. 185–92.

'Machine politics in Buenos Aires and the Argentine Radical Party, 1912–1920', *Journal of Latin American Studies*, Vol. 4, Part 2 (November 1972), pp. 233–56.

Rock, David (ed.). *Argentina in the Twentieth Century* (Duckworth, London, 1975).

Rodríguez, Carlos J. *Yrigoyen – su revolución política y social* (Buenos Aires, 1943).

Rodríguez Tarditti, J. 'Sindicatos y afiliados', *Revista de Ciencias Económicas*, No. 29 (1927), pp. 973–6.

Roig, Arturo Andrés. *Los krausistas argentinos* (Cajica, Puebla, Mexico, 1969).

Romariz, José, R. *La Semana Trágica. Relato de los hechos sangrientos del año 1919* (Hemisferio, Buenos Aires, 1952).

Romero, Luis Alberto *et alia*. *El radicalismo* (Carlos Pérez, Buenos Aires, 1969).

Ruiz, Enrique C. 'El obrero en la democracia argentina', *La Epoca*, 30 September 1920, *passim.*

Sáenz Peña, Roque. *Discursos del Dr Roque Sáenz Peña al asumir la presidencia de la Nación* (Buenos Aires, 1910).

de Santillán, Diego Abad. 'El movimiento obrero argentino ante el golpe de estado del 6 de septiembre de 1930', *Revista de Historia. La crisis de 1930* (Buenos Aires, 1958), pp. 123–31.

F.O.R.A. Ideología y trayectoria (Proyección, Buenos Aires, 1971).

Sarobe, José María. *Memorias sobre la revolución del 6 de septiembre de 1930* (Gure, Buenos Aires, 1957).

Scobie, James R. *Revolution on the Pampas. A social history of Argentine wheat, 1860–1910* (Austin, Texas, 1964).

'Buenos Aires as a commercial-bureaucratic city, 1880–1910: characteristics of a city's orientation', *American Historical Review*, Vol. 77, No. 4 (October 1972), pp. 1034–75.

Skupch, Pedro. 'Las consecuencias de la competencia del automotor sobre la hegemonía económica británica en la Argentina, 1919–33' (Instituto de Investigaciones Económicas, Facultad de Ciencias Económicas, Universidad de Buenos Aires, 1970).

'El deterioro y fin de la hegemonía británica sobre la economía argentina, 1914–1947', in Marta Panaia, Ricardo Lesser, Pedro Skupch, *Estudios sobre los orígines del peronismo*, Vol. 2 (Siglo XXI, Buenos Aires, 1973).

Smith, Peter H. 'Los radicales argentinos y la defensa de los intereses ganaderos', *Desarrollo Económico*, Vol. 7, No. 25 (April–June 1967), pp. 795–829.
Carne y política en la Argentina (Paidós, Buenos Aires, 1969).
Solberg, Carl. *Immigration and Nationalism in Argentina and Chile, 1890–1914* (University of Texas, 1970).
'Agrarian unrest and agrarian policy in Argentina, 1912–1930', *Journal of Interamerican Studies and World Affairs*, Vol. 13 (January 1971), pp. 15–55.
'Tariffs and politics in Argentina, 1916–1930', *Hispanic American Historical Review*, Vol. 53, No. 2 (May 1973), pp. 260–84.
Spalding, Hobart. *La clase trabajadora argentina (Documentos para su historia, 1890–1916)* (Galerna, Buenos Aires, 1970).
Stavenhagen, Rodolfo. 'Seven erroneous theses about Latin America', in Irving Louis Horowitz, Josué de Castro, John Gerassi (eds.), *Latin American Radicalism: a documentary report on left and nationalist movements* (London, Jonathan Cape, 1969), pp. 102–7.
Tornquist, E. and Co. Ltd, *Business Conditions in Argentina, 1914–22* (Buenos Aires, quarterly).
Torre, Juan Carlos, 'La primera victoria electoral socialista', *Todo es Historia*, No. 76 (1973), pp. 42–51.
Torres, Arturo. *Elpidio González. Biografía de una conducta* (Raigal, Buenos Aires, 1951).
Tulchin, Joseph S. *et alia*, 'La reforma universitaria – Córdoba, 1918', *Criterio*, Nos. 1599 and 1600 (9 June, 23 June 1970).
'The Argentine economy during the First World War', *Review of the River Plate* (19 June, 30 June, 10 July 1970).
'Agricultural credit and politics in Argentina, 1910–1930', *Research Previews*, Vol. 20, No. 1 (Institute for Research in Social Science, The University of North Carolina, Chapel Hill, April 1973).
Unión Cívica Radical, Circunscriptión 11a (Balvanera Norte), *Rendición de cuentas* (Buenos Aires, 1922).
Villanueva, Javier. 'El origen de la industrialización argentina', *Desarrollo Económico*, Vol. 12, No. 47 (October–December 1972).
Walter, Richard J. 'Political party fragmentation in Argentina: schisms within the Socialist Party, 1915–1930' (unpublished mimeograph, Washington University, 1972).
Wilmart, R. 'El partido radical. Su ubicación', *Revista Argentina de Ciencias Políticas*, Vol. 10 (1915), pp. 367–76.

INDEX

Index

For EU product safety concerns, contact us at Calle de José Abascal, 56–1°, 28003 Madrid, Spain or eugpsr@cambridge.org.

www.ingramcontent.com/pod-product-compliance
Ingram Content Group UK Ltd.
Pitfield, Milton Keynes, MK11 3LW, UK
UKHW010350140625
459647UK00010B/963

* 9 7 8 0 5 2 1 1 0 2 3 2 2 *